ARCHAEOLOGY AFTER
STRUCTURALISM

ARCHAEOLOGY AFTER STRUCTURALISM

Post-structuralism and the Practice of Archaeology

Edited and introduced by
Ian Bapty and Tim Yates

London

First published 1990
by Routledge
11 New Fetter Lane, London EC4P 4EE
29 West 35th Street, New York NY 10001

Collection © 1990 Routledge; individual contributions
© 1990 the respective contributors

Set in 10/12pt Times, Linotron 202
Disc conversion by Columns, Reading
Printed in England by T.J. Press (Padstow), Cornwall

All rights reserved. No part of this book may be
reprinted or reproduced or utilized in any form or
by any electronic, mechanical, or other means, now
known or hereafter invented, including photocopying
and recording, or in any information storage or
retrieval system, without permission in writing from
the publishers.

British Library Cataloguing in Publication Data
Archaeology after structuralism: post-structuralism and the
practice
of archaeology
1. Archaeology. Theories
I. Bapty, Ian II. Yates, Tim
930.101
Library of Congress Cataloging in Publication Data
Archaeology after structuralism – post-structuralism and the
practice
of archaeology / edited by Ian Bapty & Tim Yates.
p.   cm.
Includes bibliographical references.
Contents: Introduction: Archaeology and post-structuralism
/ Ian Bapty and Tim Yates — The joker is wild, the text
untameable / Gareth Burr — Undermining archaeology /
Willy Maley — Discourse and domination / Shaun
Waterman — The experience and identity of 'woman' / Ruth
Bagnal — On modernity and archaeological discourse /
Christopher Tilley — Archaeology through the looking-
glass / Tim Yates — Archaeology, authority, and the
determination of a subject / Paul Moran and David Shaun
Hides — This perfect body, this virgin text / Jarl Nordbladh
and Tim Yates — Nietzsche, Derrida, and Foucault / Ian
Bapty — The post-modernist threat to the past / Kevin
Walsh. Conclusion: Reading the signs / Michael Shanks.
1. Archaeology—Philosophy. 2. Structuralism. I.
Bapty, Ian.
II. Yates, Tim.
CC72.A68   1990
930.1'01—dc20   90-8175
ISBN 0–415–04500–2

For my parents I.B.
For my parents and for Debbie T.Y.

CONTENTS

List of contributors ix
Preface xi
Introduction: Archaeology and Post-Structuralism 1
Ian Bapty and Tim Yates

Part I: Interdisciplinary Readings

1 The Joker is Wild, the Text Untameable: the Analytics of Homo Analogicus (Anthropology, Post-Structuralism and Post-Modernism) 35
Gareth Burr

2 Undermining Archaeology: From Reconstruction to Deconstruction 61
Willy Maley

3 Discourse and Domination: Michel Foucault and the Problem of Ideology 79
Shaun Waterman

4 The Experience and Identity of 'Woman': Feminism after Structuralism 103
Ruth Bagnal

Part 2: Archaeological Perspectives

5 On Modernity and Archaeological Discourse 127
Christopher Tilley

6 Archaeology through the Looking-Glass 153
Tim Yates

7 Writing, Authority and the Determination of a Subject 205
Paul Moran and David Shaun Hides

CONTENTS

8   This Perfect Body, This Virgin Text: Between Sex and Gender in Archaeology   222
Jarl Nordbladh and Tim Yates

9   Nietzsche, Derrida and Foucault: Re-excavating the Meaning of Archaeology   240
Ian Bapty

10   The Post-Modern Threat to the Past   278
Kevin Walsh

Conclusion: 294
Reading the Signs: Responses to *Archaeology after Structuralism*
Michael Shanks

Index   311

CONTRIBUTORS

Ruth Bagnal	Girton College and Dept. of French, University of Cambridge, England.
Ian Bapty	Emmanuel College and Dept. of Archaeology, University of Cambridge, England.
Gareth Burr	Dept. of Anthropology, University College, London, England.
David Shaun Hides	Dept. of Archaeology, University of Leicester, England.
Willy Maley	Programme in Literary Linguistics, University of Strathclyde, Scotland.
Paul Moran	Dept. of English, University of Leicester, England.
Jarl Nordbladh	Institutionen for Arkeologi, Göteborgs Universitet, Sweden.
Michael Shanks	Peterhouse and Dept. of Archaeology, University of Cambridge, England.
Christopher Tilley	Dept. of Archaeology, St. David's University College of Wales, Lampeter, Wales.
Kevin Walsh	Dept. of Archaeology, University of Leicester, England.
Shaun Waterman	King's College and Dept. of Social and Political Science, University of Cambridge, England.
Tim Yates	King's College and Dept. of Archaeology, University of Cambridge, England.

PREFACE

This volume finds its inspiration in a conference held in Cambridge over three days, 29 June to 1 July, 1988, under the title Discipline–Discourse–Power: The Cambridge Seminar on Post-Structuralism and Archaeology. Despite the specificity of the name, it was a much more wide ranging and comprehensive event, bringing together archaeologists and those working in related disciplines to talk on a variety of themes within structuralism, post-structuralism, Marxism and feminism. Participants came mainly from Britain, but a significant number made the journey from northern and western Europe, and from North America.

The discussions at the conference proved, fairly clearly, that an introduction to post-structuralism is needed to inform archaeology on a broader scale of its claims for attention. This book is not, therefore, so much a record of the conference as a volume inspired by the discussions and one attempting to follow the original thematics while filling in the lacunae that emerged over the three days of presentation and debate. We kept initially to a fairly rigid definition of post-structuralism, selecting for inclusion those papers which most directly addressed its problematics, and would serve most usefully as an introduction to its complex ideas, but in the process of compilation, a wider range of critical thought has been represented. Two of the papers (Bagnal and Burr) were not presented at the conference but were commissioned subsequently. As much as possible, we have allowed the authors freedom to develop their responses as they desired, and the contributions to the book offer a rich and fairly varied reaction to its problematics, and reflect the spirit of the conference.

The book has been structured so that archaeologists and non-archaeologists write alongside each other. Each paper is accompanied by a short editorial introduction, justified by the range of ideas represented, in order to place them in relation to current debates within (post-processual) archaeology. We are aware that this organisation gives us, as editors, a great deal of control over the way in which the papers are interpreted, but the conclusion by Michael Shanks is designed to give the volume the reflexivity and dynamism it would otherwise lack.

PREFACE

We would like to thank the following for their help and support: our co-organisers of the conference, Frederick Baker and J. D. Hill; the chairpersons, John Barrett, Ian Hodder and Chris Tilley; Julian Thomas, Grant Chambers, Peter Dews and Willy Maley for encouragement and interest; the Department of Biological Anthropology and the University Centre, University of Cambridge, for the use of conference and other facilities; our colleges, Emmanuel and King's, for generous financial support without which the conference could not have gone ahead on such a grand scale; and, particularly, Andrew Wheatcroft at Routledge, whose unceasing support, enthusiasm and patience has enabled the contributions collected here to reach a wider audience.

Introduction:

Archaeology and Post-Structuralism

Ian Bapty and Tim Yates

I

If it recedes one day, leaving behind its works and signs on the shores of our civilisation, the structuralist invasion might become a question for the historian of ideas, or perhaps even an object. But the historian would be deceived if he came to this pass: by the very act of considering the structuralist invasion as an object he would forget its meaning and forget that what is at stake, first of all, is an adventure of vision, a conversion of the way of putting questions to any object posed before us, to historical objects – his own – in particular.

(Derrida 1978, 3)

Nearly a decade has passed since the symbolic and structural archaeology conference announced a coherent challenge to to the existing paradigmatic and epistemological structure of archaeology. These ten years have been momentous ones for the discipline. Not only has its practice been transformed with the introduction of new conceptual frameworks (such as the notion of the archaeological record – material culture – as text) but also whole issues, questions and debates that were previously unthinkable have become relatively commonplace – debates about the social implications and embeddedness of scientific and academic study, about the politics of archaeological production, about the context of archaeology and the social sciences in late capitalist society, about the construction of gender relations in the past, and so on. The framework provided by the New Archaeology had provided little, if any, space for consideration of these issues, and although the last three to four years have seen a general mellowing of the initial opposition to structuralism mobilised by the positivists (as elements of structuralist theory are diluted and wash over the international scene), for many processualists it is not only still possible to distance archaeology from these issues, from the present, from society, from contemporary systems of representation, but absolutely vital that we continue to do so (see, for example, Schiffer 1988, discussed by Tilley in Chapter 5).

The strength of the reaction against the innovative and experimental work emanating from Cambridge in the late 1970s and early 1980s is nowhere more clearly demonstrated than in the confrontational and belligerent style adopted by processualists like Binford. It is, of course, to be explained by the very real threat that Hodder and his students offered to the foundations of the new orthodoxy, but also, one suspects, by the fact that it transformed processualism into that orthodoxy. There had been structuralists before of course – Leroi-Gourhan in France or Jarl Nordbladh in Sweden – but neither had any widespread effect even within their own institutional systems, and on an international scale they worked largely in isolation. In the late 1970s, however, these diverse theoretical interests coalesced into a major force which has fulfilled Edmund Leach's much quoted prophecy about the future fortunes of the discipline. Almost overnight, the bright young things of the New Archaeology – these Binfords, these Renfrews, these Schiffers – were transformed from the avant-garde into the old guard, a metamorphosis from which their self image has yet to recover. The New Archaeology was, suddenly, the not so new, and further found itself criticised for not even being particularly new in the first place. And, for the last decade, it is this formation which has been on the defensive while the initiative has been taken up by a new 'new' heresy. Despite the opposition, a structuralist based archaeology has, then, taken root and established itself – at its most widespread in the United States, but at its most intense in Europe, especially in Britain and Scandinavia.

The strengths of the 'movement', which, in the typology of supposed archaeological paradigms, has since become known by the generic term 'post-processualism', is shown most clearly in a number of volumes that have emerged in the Cambridge *New Directions* series. The symbolic and structural conference volume (Hodder 1982) communicates clearly the sense of excitement and experimentation, and the papers it contains remain the clearest and most coherent statement of the structuralist challenge. Since then the initial unity – always perhaps largely illusory – has given way to increasingly divergent postures as the various participants have followed their interests along widely different courses. Some have sought to engage with Marxism and Critical Theory more closely (Miller and Tilley 1984; Miller 1987; Shanks and Tilley 1987a; 1987b), while others, most notably Ian Hodder, have kept Marxism more at a distance, and have forged links with a hermeneutic tradition associated with British liberal historians such as Collingwood, or the theories of agency developed by Anthony Giddens and Pierre Bourdieu. Associated with this latter development has been the emergence of a gender archaeology, the strategic aims of which at present seem rather

INTRODUCTION

limited, but which is perhaps set to have a more general influence on archaeology as a whole.

It is thus possible to say, ten years on, that post-processualism is here to stay even if, at the same time, the identity and coherence of the movement is becoming increasingly unclear. This book is about working through and beyond the traditions in which post-processual archaeology has immersed itself and of forging, on the basis of the groundwork it has taken a decade to complete, new directions for archaeology – new questions, new ways of conceiving both what it is archaeologists do and why they do it, new ways of reading and writing the past. In attempting this advance, the contributors to this volume have looked towards those critics who are generally seen to belong to that movement in philosophy and literature which is known as 'post-structuralism' – although the applicability of this label is open to doubt and seems to fly in the face of the wide diversity and often contradictory aims of the writers in question.

In a sense, of course, archaeology is already post-structuralist – it has absorbed a version of contemporary theory that, in the work of Giddens and Bourdieu, could be described as leading beyond some of the positions articulated by Lévi-Strauss. And, indeed, one of the problems we faced when compiling this volume was that of deciding who and what should be put into this category, a problem especially pressing given that many of the ideas discussed below will not be familiar in an archaeological context. Anyone reading the papers we have selected will be struck by the variety of ideas represented – the stock and standard names are there to be found, Roland Barthes, Gilles Deleuze, Jacques Derrida, Michel Foucault, Julia Kristeva, Jacques Lacan, but alongside them are not only a number of less well-known figures (who are none the less important for being that), but also a number of unusual or unexpected names that seem to carry off whatever meaning this categorisation of 'post-structuralism' may have had in time and space. Thus there are extensive references to Freud, Marcuse and Nietzsche, to Marxists like Louis Althusser and Pierre Macherey, to anthropologists like Gregory Bateson, to novelists like Jorge Luis Borges, Angela Carter or Franz Kafka. All this emphasises not simply the problematics of categorisation, but more importantly that none of the contributors to this book would countenance the ideas with which they are concerned as the universal solution to all the problems that face the construction of the much mooted critically and socially 'aware' archaeology. Post-structuralism is not available on prescription, as the cure to the carefully diagnosed complicities of existing frameworks. Following Derrida or Foucault brings its own problems, and highlights the fundamentally *permeable* and *porous* nature of post-structuralism, which at no point forms a complete or enclosed body of thought. The necessity is always to articulate these ideas within their existing traditions in order to address any particular problem

– the problem of the subject and its socio-cultural identity, as discussed by Bagnal and Nordbladh and Yates below, which produces a chain of references that runs through structuralism and post-structuralism into feminism and psychoanalysis. The papers articulate with structuralism and with radical traditions within structural anthropology (Burr), with Marxism (Tilley; Walsh; Waterman), with Foucauldian analytics (Burr; Bapty), or with Nietzsche (Bapty). A host of possibilities is opened up by these ideas. For Moran and Hides (chapter 7) the question has become that of detaching an understanding of the issues raised by Hegel and Derrida from their institutionalised discursive contexts, fraught as they are with problems of privilege and closure/inaccessibility, in order to experiment with new styles of writing and means of expression which do not return to reliance on the (relatively) esoteric. They countenance a note of caution. Whether or not they are successful in attempting to develop a subversive and reflexively self-conscious style is not as important as the fact that these questions are raised and discussed, and that the writing of the past, its forms and features, becomes the subject for debate. Walsh (chapter 10) similarly raises questions for post-structuralism in relation to the development, during the 1980s, of the commercial, commodified past, and is sceptical about the validity of the work of Baudrillard for mounting a critical debate around this subject. And this is an area in which our vigilance and critical faculties will need to be particularly sharp.

II

The notion of difference that Saussure brought to the study of linguistics, and which forms the basis of structuralism as a movement by its insistence on the referentiality of signs, was bound to have wide ranging effects upon archaeology once the effects of structural anthropology filtered down through the disciplinary and institutional frameworks (frameworks, the only function of which is to limit the horizon, control the range of questions and research, retard mutual influence and so, ultimately, protect each discipline from its neighbours). Saussure, as we know, divided the sign into two elements, the signifier and the signified as the sensible and the intelligible. Thus the signifier 'LEMMING' is connected to a signified – a mental image that is represented (supposedly) by the signifier, and with which it is possible to signify this particular group and order of letters. But, according to Saussure, there was nothing that necessitated this precise combination of letters having this signified, no reason why this creature should have been called this name. The image could have been represented by any number of alternative combinations – donkey, filing cabinet, Munich, Professor of Archaeology – any would have done, and in this sense the signifier is arbitrary. It is only convention that

INTRODUCTION

establishes this connection between the signifier and the signified. The only criterion that the signifier need fulfil is that it be different from the other signifiers of the system, and it was in this insistence that Saussure departed from the body of traditional linguistics which had eschewed such an approach in favour of the assumption – or at any rate isolation – of linguistic forms which can then be compared to other forms and their development over time studied. Saussure insisted on the priority of the synchronic over the diachronic, and thus went against the grain of orthodox practice. Because the signifier was articulated differentially, it could only be understood as it was related and referent to all the other signifiers at any one moment in time. The sign only made sense if it was studied against the background of a system.

In language, therefore, Saussure was able to assert that the value of the signifier is purely negative and differential. In writing, it is possible to write the letter *d* in countless different ways and in many different forms, but all that is necessary for it to signify is that it be different from the other letters of the system – that the letter *d* is distinguishable from the letter *c* or the letter *b* and so on. Thus, Saussure wrote, in language there are only differences *without positive terms*. Attention to the system of language forces us to look closely at the underlying structural rules that govern the generation and correct combination of signs. Thus any particular speech or writing act – *parole* – is seen to be conditioned by a system of grammar – *langue* – comprising regulations that are never, of course, present all at once, but exist only as they are activated by *parole*. A certain reciprocity therefore exists between *langue* and *parole*, which are always articulated in a relation of mutual dependency.

This brief – and inevitably reductive – account of Saussure's linguistics is to set out the basis around which the main strand of structuralism, as a means of analysing cultural phenomena, has grown up, and it is also, therefore, necessary to begin to understand what difference the 'post' of post-structuralism makes. The search for underlying rules between phenomena – the 'high' structuralism of Lévi-Strauss' cross-cultural based anthropology for example – can be understood through Saussure's basic insight, and Lévi-Strauss' emphasis on the synchronic is quite clear. In order to examine a structure it must be totalised, it must be stopped dead. This, of course was not a problem when dealing with the relatively static time frame of the unproblematic 'present' conventionally enclosing ethnographic studies, where areas of analysis were the apparent stability of the kinship system, or the anti-historical time of the myth. But it did mean that history became something bracketed off, returned to only subsequently as an afterthought, an annoying loose end. The problem was *how* to return to this later. And it can be said that post-structuralism attempts this return, this reopening of time and history, by rethinking the diachronic within the synchronic. And this move, crucial as it is, is achieved by rethinking the whole basis of Saussurian difference and the system of thought that holds it in place.

Thus 'post'-structuralism is, in fact, heavily dependent upon structuralism, and it is not so much a move beyond as a move *through* its logic. Derrida, whose texts are most closely associated with this shift, puts the point succinctly, and offers us a convenient description of the emergence of this movement and its defining force in the 1960s, especially around 1968:

> At that time structuralism was dominant. 'Deconstruction' seemed to be going in the same direction since the word signified a certain attention to structures (which themselves are neither simply ideas, nor forms, nor syntheses, nor systems). To deconstruct was also a structuralist gesture or in any case one that announced a certain need for a structuralist problematic. But it was also an anti-structuralist gesture, and its fortune rests in part on this ambiguity. Structures were to be undone, decomposed, desedimented.
> (Derrida 1988, 2)

Properly this description should apply only to Derrida's own work, involving a very detailed analysis and critique of Saussure's original insights. Of course, Lacan's seminars had been examining the linguistic analogy for unconsciousness since the 1940s and 1950s, developing a body of thought that was to have a seminal impact on the debates of the 1960s, particularly following the publication, in 1966, of a collection of Lacan's papers titled *Ecrits*. But nonetheless, it is with Derrida that any introduction attempting to frame post-structuralism finds, if not its actual beginning, at least its most convenient one.

Structures, which structuralism had been labouring to construct, define and understand, were to be undone, decomposed, desedimented. The laborious constructs of the intellectual movement, and many others besides, were to be taken apart, were to be *deconstructed*. Saussure, Derrida maintained, had consistently resisted the most important insight of his work. Firstly by retaining the concept of the sign ('a two sided unity') which left open 'the possibility of thinking a *concept signified in and of itself*, a concept simply present to thought, independent of a relationship to a system of signifiers' (Derrida 1981a, 19) – leaving open a journey back to a sign conceived an outside of difference. And secondly by privileging speech over writing, which collapses the sign wholly into meaning and consciousness, such that in speech 'the signifier seems to ease itself in, to become transparent . . . the exteriority of the signifier seems reduced' (Derrida 1981a, 22). What Derrida does is to insist, as Lacan had also done, that between the signifier and the signified is driven a bar resisting unification and signification, a bar forced through the middle of the sign by difference. For Derrida, the course to this position

INTRODUCTION

is charted through the metaphysical opposition of speech to writing, for writing had always been debased on the grounds that it represents a fall from the presence of meaning, because ambiguity cannot be cleared up by reflection and discussion. Writing had been charged with only representing speech, which is conceived to signify via a direct connection between signifier and signified. But, of course, the signifier in speech is *the same as* the signifier in writing – there is nothing to distinguish the two, and therefore what characterises writing must also be regarded as characterising speech. 'Writing', in Derrida's work, comes to name not empirical writing, but the system of difference that articulates the signifier. Articulated in the same way, speech is already writing, and is, therefore, already *in* difference, and the pure self-presence that had been thought to underlie the phonetic sign is torn open at the seams.

What are crucial here are the implications of difference for the nature of the sign. In an interview with Julia Kristeva, Derrida describes the point succinctly and clearly:

> The play of difference supposes, in effect, syntheses and referrals which forbid, at any moment or in any sense, that a single element be *present* in and of itself, referring only to itself. Whether in the order of spoken or written discourse, no element can function as a sign without referring to another element which is itself not simply present. This interweaving results in each 'element' – phoneme or grapheme – being constituted on the basis of the trace within it of the other elements of the chain or system.... Nothing, neither among the elements nor within the system, is anywhere ever simply present or absent. There are only, everywhere, differences of differences and traces of traces.
>
> (Derrida 1981a, 26)

The sign, articulated by difference, is not present, let alone 'present to itself', it is not a fixed and stable entity, it is inherently unstable, constantly open and constantly changing. The 'presence' of the signifier is deferred onto another signifier which is in turn not fixed but itself caught up in a relation of difference – and so in a long chain of signifiers and differences. The name Derrida gives to this movement and force – *différance* – attempts to capture its two senses by the substitution of an *a* for the second *e* in the French, signifying both to differ and defer, both the passive and the active. Nothing can be outside of these chains and movements, for they would be no more than new marks, at once differed and deferred from other marks. Presence and absence are therefore no longer available as alternatives – they are divided from themselves by the trace within them of difference, because within this system elements differ *from themselves*, cutting off the possibility of anything ever being present to itself: 'We will watch it [presence] infinitely announce itself and endlessly vanish through concealed doorways that shine like mirrors and open onto the labyrinth' (Derrida 1981b, 128).

Set to work within structure, the effects of difference are seen fairly quickly. Every limit that seemed apparently to govern and to guarantee the identity of structure is overrun. Thus, for instance, philosophy, which Derrida describes under the blanket term metaphysics, has attempted to found itself upon positions of pure presence – speech in Plato's *Phaedrus*, the living present in Husserl's *Investigations* and *Cartesian Meditations*, absent being in Heidegger and so on. But *différance* passes through these conceptual frameworks, and offers us a point of entry from which the whole structure can be taken apart. Thus, for example, the distinction made by Kant between *ergon* (primary, essence) and *parergon* (secondary, addition) is taken apart by Derrida (1987). The structure of the *parergon* – the frame of a painting – is always absolutely essential to the *ergon*, and without it, it cannot exist. The *parergon* is shown to be, in fact, more essential than the *ergon*. Like the structure of the *supplement*, which Derrida takes from Rousseau's *Confessions*, it has an undecidable sense which positions it outside of presence/absence and in *différance*. Where the *supplement* means (in French) both addition and replacement, so also 'parerga have a thickness, a surface which separates them not only . . . from the integral inside, from the body of the *ergon*, but also from the outside, from the wall on which the painting is hung . . . from the whole field of historical, economical, political inscription . . .' (Derrida 1987, 60–1). The structure of 'parergonality' both joins and divides the difference between essence and accident, primary and secondary, outside and inside, intrinsic and extrinsic.

Deconstruction differs from a simple critique. It is not, Derrida insists, a method, or even a critical activity. 'It is not an analysis in particular, because the dismantling of structure is not a regression towards a *simple element*, towards an *indissoluble origin*. These values, like that of analysis, are also philosophemes subject to deconstruction' (Derrida 1988, 3). 'The movements of *différance* cannot be controlled or introduced by the critic, they can only be followed or brought out – it is *not* the function of a subject, a critical genre. It is more a property of texts, of structuring, of bringing out "a relation of the work to itself" ' (Derrida 1984, 124).

And yet the question is raised – and Derrida does not address it – of how meanings are actually produced, of how texts and the system of which they are a part avoid being constantly torn open and deconstructed. If Derrida has not addressed the issue of ideology, then Roland Barthes has. In his study of modern bourgeois myth *Mythologies* (Barthes 1973), Barthes drew the distinction between a first order of language, which contains the ordinary or manifest content, what he calls *denotation*, and a second order *connotation*, contained within the first, which would be the

INTRODUCTION

ideological. An ideological discourse operates at the second level but through the first – myth would be the latent plane of connotation beneath the manifest plane of denotation, And Barthes' essays in *Mythologies* are, of course, the classic putting to work of an ideological analysis in these terms.

But, as Foucault at least nominally rejected the problematics that ideology involved (see Waterman, chapter 3), so Barthes was also led to reject this distinction between the levels of meaning production and signification. In his later work, in the late 1960s and the 1970s, ideology is no longer seen as a secondary text that takes over a primary and original text, since the separation between denotation and connotation is no longer possible. In *S/Z* (Barthes 1974), in which Barthes rejects not only his earlier interpretive frames but also the notion of a latent structure, he writes:

> ... denotation is not the first sense, but pretends to be; under this illusion, it is ultimately only the *last* of connotation (that which seems at once to found and close the reading), the superior myth by which the text pretends to return to the nature of language, the language of nature.
> (Barthes 1974, 9)

The level of denotation is, therefore, the point at which connotation seeks to naturalise and so hide itself. It is present and active from the very beginning, from the first moment of meaning. In place of a structuralism founded on the distinction between surfaces and depths, *S/Z* mediates a very different conceptualisation of the text:

> The text, in its mass, is comparable to a sky, at once flat and smooth, deep, without edges and without landmarks; like the soothsayer drawing on it with the tip of his staff an imaginary rectangle wherein to consult, according to certain principles, the flight of birds, the commentator traces through the text certain zones of reading, in order to observe therein the migration of meanings, the outcropping of codes, the passage of citations.
> (Barthes 1974, 14)

The text, to the Barthes writing after the middle of the 1960s, is without an origin, and the reader is freed from the tyranny of the Author: 'To give the text an Author is to impose a limit on that text, to furnish it with a final signified, to close the writing. ... When the author has been found, the text is "explained" – victory to the critic' (Barthes 1977a, 147).

The dethroning of the Author opened up the text to multiple readings – 'by refusing to assign a "secret", an ultimate meaning, to the text (and to the world as text)' – the emphasis of criticism is shifted and set free of these limits – 'a text's unity lies not in its origin but in its destination ...

the birth of the reader must be at the cost of the death of the author' (1977a, 148). And it is here that a distinction is made between the 'readerly' (lisible) text, which encourages the reader to take part in the production of meaning only as a passive consumer, and the 'writerly' (scriptable) text, in which the reader is forced to adopt a more active role and to 'write' or 'complete' the text as s/he reads. The utopian vision would be, for Barthes, that of 'a mobile, plural reader, who nimbly inserts and removes the quotation marks, who begins to write *with me*' (Barthes 1977b, 161).

III

If the origin of the text is to be problematised, then it is in order to release
the potential of the text to mean. According to Frank Lentricchia (1983, 173), the point of Derrida's working of and through the concept of *différance* is not to destroy all grounds and remove from the critic the responsibility of examining the contexts of the production, but to pose new questions for an historical labour. The point is to open texts up to *différance*. Derrida himself puts the point fairly succinctly on a number of occasions, and insists that breaking the two sided unity of the Saussurian sign does not destroy the question of production and the attachment of signifier to signified: 'For us the rupture of the "natural attachment" puts in question the idea of naturalness rather than that of attachment' (Derrida 1976, 46).

The strategic conceptual role of *différance* is to force into the light all those processes that appeared to guard against the radicalism of history – questions of closure, convention, system, ideology and power become of enormous importance. 'Where are the borders of a text? How do they come about?' (Derrida 1979, 85).

Thus deconstruction does not practise a radical 'death of the author' despite the problematisation of the origin (the *arche* of archaeology for instance) through notions like the trace. Within *différance*, history has to attempt to comprehend 'the becoming space of time and the becoming time of space' (Derrida 1973, 136), the movement captured in the silent *a* of *différance* – of differing as both a spatialisation and a temporalisation. But it is also important to understand the extent to which Derrida's readings of philosophy and literature make use of fairly orthodox concepts of time and place. Thus, for example, behind his well known criticisms of Foucault's *Madness and Civilization* offered in an article entitled 'Cogito and the History of Madness' (Derrida 1978, 31–63) are assumptions which Derrida does not question – assumptions about Descartes, his *Meditations*, his period and genre. The point is to isolate those aspects of the text which have permitted it to be used and read

INTRODUCTION

historically in a particular way, the *supplement* for instance:

> It is certainly a production, because I do not simply duplicate what Rousseau thought of this relationship. The concept of the supplement is a sort of blind spot in Rousseau's text, the not-seen that opens and limits visibility. But the production if it attempts to make the not-seen accessible to sight, does not leave the text . . . it is contained in the transformation of the language it designates. . . . We know that these exchanges can only take place by way of the language and the text, in the infrastructural sense that we may give to that word, and what we call production is necessarily a text, the system of writing and reading which we know is ordered around its own blind spot.
>
> (Derrida 1976, 163–4)

Deconstruction is therefore a force of immanent critique – though doubtless Derrida would find that description far from unproblematic. It works within formations that already exist – the tradition of western metaphysics which, because it extends, in Terry Eagleton's words, all the way from Plato to Nato, it is fairly easy to accept as already determined. Thus, for instance, while the techniques and processes of a deconstructive reading may be 'well attuned to the exposure of hidden contradictions within ideology, "a revelation of its hidden aporias" ' (Butler 1984, 114), it remains problematic to the extent that Derrida is unable to account for how meanings actually *do* take place. Such an account would, of course, involve him in a departure from the 'internal' and 'immanent' nature of his work, where concepts are drawn from the interior of a text – *différance* from Saussure, *supplement* from Rousseau, *pharmakon* from Plato, *hymen* from Mallarmé, and so on, and are turned against the text – and account for a position outside of that particular production, outside of the text in question. And it would involve him in specifying the particular conditions of writing in terms open to closer definition than those of 'trans-historical' metaphysics, which, because of its ubiquity, seems even to stand outside of history. The kind of articulation of deconstruction attempted by, for instance, Michael Ryan (1982) with Marxism, or the more guarded and selective response offered by Frederic Jameson (1983) or Terry Eagleton may be taken as indicating that *différance* in itself is insufficient for fulfilling all the purposes for which we would wish to use it. As Dews (1987, 37ff.) points out, Derrida is not concerned with challenging or transforming structures so much as with laying them bare, revealing their veiled functions and hidden activity. But to a great extent, Derrida himself appears to be aware of these problems, and since the later part of the last decade he has become increasingly emphatic about the political implications of deconstruction. Some of his more recent material is important in offering a guide as to reading towards history as text and the 'social text', and is discussed by Maley below, who finds that Derrida's potential contribution to an archaeology may, in one sense, be greater than that of Michel Foucault, whose value to the discipline and its development of critique has in some ways appeared more immediate than that of deconstruction.

Whether Foucault's 'histories' are really histories in the orthodox sense is a question about which much ink could be spilt – he certainly uses apparently 'historical' data in his analyses, where Derrida's work appears to be a more fundamentally 'textual' practice. Indeed Foucault has charged deconstruction with this limitation, and accused Derrida of 'a pedagogy that teaches the pupil that there is nothing outside of the text' (Foucault 1979a, 27) despite the fact that his own discussions of the place of the author (Foucault 1977a), or of the all-embracing extension of language and materiality (Foucault 1977b), might seem to align him with just such a position. To a certain extent, this web of ambiguity which Foucault weaves – the ambiguity equally inherent in the paradox of both Foucault's 'archaeology' as an analysis of the past supposedly beyond 'history', and of his 'genealogy' as an analysis of the past where 'history' is rehabilitated only through the new paradox of situating it within a post-structuralist frame – is precisely the method of his iconoclastic project, precisely invoking a consistent irony which internally maintains the trace of his externally fraught relationship to thinkers such as Derrida or Barthes. The scheme of his 'historical' analysis is, then, almost deliberately to draw implicitly the criticism of other contemporary critics with whose work his own might seem theoretically and epistemologically aligned, as much as it is to distance explicitly the orthodox tenets of empiricist history, or the accepted framework of the history of ideas. It is out of the always latent instability of this rhetorical network that he builds, like Nietzsche, a history substantial and 'real', and yet one conceived more as the missing myth of the modern age, than as the reconstruction of an abstract, reified, 'true' past feigning to point away from the conditions of its own production.

It was the 'archaeological' method Foucault elaborated through his works of the 1960s where this rebellion against the traditional framework of history was most immediately and ambitiously manifest. For Foucault, all the apparent innovation of twentieth-century historiography – such as, for example, Collingwoodian idealism or the *Annales* school's concern to construct a many-stranded history evading and exploding the limited domain of the 'event' – had not been sufficient to escape the immediate legacy of late nineteenth-century positivism, and the more insidious and underlying acceptance of 'history' as a particular density known and understood; it was how to frame the understanding of what happened within history, not history itself which was the problem for the western historiographic tradition. According to Foucault, the answer could only

INTRODUCTION

be to go beyond this maligned space occupied by the signifier 'history' altogether. Thus, 'Archaeology' rejected 'history' as implicitly associated with the study of the pre-ordained, unproblematic, order of a teleological, horizontal progress, powered by the necessity of some immanent, silently unfolding rationality, and focused instead on what Foucault refers to as the 'constant verticality' behind that facade. Archaeology was to be juxtaposed to the 'history of ideas or science', while aiming 'to uncover the regularity of a discursive practice, the basis upon which theory and knowledge become possible' (Foucault 1977c, 44).

Foucault's archaeology, then, sought to recover the irrationality of past discursive practices to the side of reason, revealing in the same movement the irrationality of the conventional historical reason which rejected these practices as the debased beginnings of itself. In the same way that archaeology is conventionally understood to be the study of past material culture, of artefacts, so for Foucault 'archaeology' is the study of the past, not in terms of outcomes and events with their origin in the machinations and ideas of the individual subject, but in the study of the contingencies and conjunctures running through the material, object world of discourse, where the subject is formed only as one more effect, one more provisional construct of a particular set of prevailing discursive relationships. The outcome of the 'history' of madness offered in *Madness and Civilization* (Foucault 1967) is not so much to see the rise of humanitarian concern for the insane as the final emergence and triumph of some naturally embedded reason or truth, as it is rather to see madness in the late eighteenth/early nineteenth century now allocated and regimented through a different economy of discourse where madness had become, in the emergence of the post-Enlightenment world view, a condition lurking within reason, a new danger which must be submitted to a very different technology of control and, ultimately, repression.

The status of archaeology as a kind of anti-history was always problematic however, founded on a contradiction increasingly evident as Foucault extended his archaeological studies to medicine, linguistics, economics and the natural sciences (Foucault 1974; 1975). The paradox was, that as a new totalising system of knowledge, claiming to outflank history entirely, archaeology found itself resting on precisely the same foundations, the same claim to 'truth', as that of orthodox history. The historical *a priori* of the *episteme* around which the archaeological analysis of the past was organised must ultimately swallow Foucault as well, rendering him and his work as one further symptom of the pattern of development he had set out to dissemble and reconstitute.

Foucault's response to this dilemma was to dispense with the archaeological framework and much of the carefully described and elaborated analytical schemes of classification which went with it, and to adopt instead the paraphernalia of a revised Nietzschean genealogy. In this guise, the aim is no longer to displace history altogether. Rather, within 'history' it is to enable a different kind of analysis based on an emphasis on what in a sense becomes, for Foucault, a new transcendental signified, an emphasis on *power* – albeit a constantly self-effacing 'transcendental signified' occupying a space in Foucault's thought corresponding to that where Derrida had opened *différance*. To understand Foucault's departure here, it is important to see the full significance of a relationship to Nietzsche which some have been inclined to see more as a superficial, than a real, shift from the premises of archaeology; that involves comprehending what it is that the genealogical Foucault means by power as something more than mere obedience to the almost obligatory referents of the 'left' thinker. Thus what is not implied, even despite the nominal appearance and subject matter of a work like *Discipline and Punish* (Foucault 1977c) is power as fundamentally a force of appropriation and repression, that power, for example, which in an orthodox Marxist position controls the dislocation of forces and relations of production in the class structure of capitalist society. Indeed, for Foucault such a characterisation of power is exactly one of the means by which the recent disciplinary ordering of society has been facilitated, is one of the traces on which modernity rests (see Foucault's difficult relationship to Marxism (Smart 1983)). Even when turned to reveal the social asymmetries of society, the repressive model of power still constitutes power as a closed density, as a limited phenomenon associated with certain kinds of structure rather than others, in a way that conceptually restricts rather than enables the possibility to examine and resist the interplay of discourse and institution, that underestimates from the start the multi-dimensional channels through which the network of what Foucault calls 'Juridico-Discursive' forces operate. The repressive view of power, even when connected to a critical intent, is based therefore on the same metaphysics of limit and identity, of a power/non-power relationship which is one more extension of the hegemony of the Cartesian presence/absence duality. It is within a Nietzschean concept of power as expansive and creating, as a fundamental force of life (that is, a basically *active* force – see Bapty, chapter 9) not only before, but even *as* it takes the form of restriction, tyranny and repression, where Foucault paradoxically finds the means to break the apparent indivisibility of the Cartesian union. In a way analogous to deconstruction, Foucault's conceptualisation of power thus involves not simply asserting it as an active over a passive agency, of something all pervasive as opposed to something constrained, but rather of rewriting entirely the word 'power' into a meaning that sits outside such polarity of reference, that is all inclusive exactly in the sense that it evades determination by an exclusive/inclusive bracket.

However, this is not to say that Foucault is reproducing a post-structuralism directly compatible with that of Derrida, and this is where the debt to Nietzsche is more than simply one of terminology. Foucault's interest in a concept of power, however rhetorically shaped, is to use that concept to reveal a certain truth, to grasp a new basis for the understanding of discourse, and indeed, exactly to make meaning of concepts such as history. From the start, Foucault's genealogical project, his analysis of power/knowledge relations, is fundamentally reconstructive rather than (in a Derridean or conventional sense) deconstructive, it points away from the search for originary unity, but away too from even the suggestion of a retreat instead into nihilism. So, following Nietzsche, Foucault does not condemn history either as mode of repressive power, or as a presence inevitably flawed in the all-embracing conspiracy of western metaphysics, rather he seeks to transform the ground on which history operates and equally to dispose of the idea that history can ever be escaped (as archaeology had boldly claimed). Power is not just everywhere, it is everywhere as in the first instance a process of begetting and becoming, as the drive towards Nietzsche's basic 'will to freedom'. While none of this is to deny the harsh reality of power as repression, it is to suggest that the way to truly undermine the locus of that power is to investigate how such repression is seen perversely to *serve* life. The 'analytics of power' Foucault proposes should not 'concentrate the study of the punitive mechanisms on their "repressive" effects alone ... but situate them in the whole series of their possible positive effects, even if these seem marginal at first' (Foucault 1977c, 23). Moreover, with the realisation of power as a procreative force is the justification to dissolve reliance on the logic of metaphysical polarity; this is facilitated in the movement set in motion as power covertly identifies itself as the silent origin of Foucault's analysis through the very rhetorical object of that analysis to identify power elsewhere. And it is in this sense that Foucault now seeks to produce through the medium of history, not instead of it, a genealogy.

Reference to Nietzsche helps to clarify this fundamental point. As for Nietzsche, the final legitimation of what he called the 'eternal return' marked by the becoming of the 'superman' was to be found at the juncture where the value of truth itself was questioned, where, in Nietzsche's terms, the 'will to power' was at last divorced from the 'will to nihilism', so for Foucault it is here that a critical use of the subjective is to be found – evading the pitfalls of an anarchistic nihilism on the one hand, and the attractions of the misguided will to truth on the other. It is here that genealogy is lodged, suspended in the tension between the Nietzschean concept of power, and a continued concern with the old archaeological problems of knowledge and the constitution of the subject. Out of this tension Foucault draws the rhetorical figures around which his works of the 1970s are based, such as, for example, the distinction between the 'bio-power' power of the body and that power exerted over the body elaborated in *Discipline and Punish* (Foucault 1977c); within genealogy such a polarity is a space of continual self-displacement and opening, not the claim to reveal a new presence, a new knowledge, as it might have been in archaeology.

Yet that said, from a Derridean perspective, it might seem that genealogy is still open to equivalent criticisms to those offered for archaeology. Genealogy may well share with deconstruction 'the rejection of the metahistorical deployment of ideal significations and indefinite teleologies' while opposing 'itself to the search for origins' (Foucault 1984, 77). Yet in the same breath it is also 'gray, meticulous, and patiently documentary' aiming to 'isolate the different scenes where they [events and discourses] engaged in different roles' only by a process of analysis that 'requires patience and a knowledge of details, and . . . depends on a vast accumulation of source material' (Foucault 1984, 76–7). Talk of meticulous documentary, patiently observed detail, the capacity to isolate scenes and structures in the past, might all seem explicitly to reintroduce the spectres of identity and the origin, indeed re-announce the claim of a metaphysical truth, even as all that is denied. One might indeed be inclined to argue that genealogy is flawed by a greater contradiction than archaeology had been; at least the latter had been consistent within its own limits, where genealogy, certainly from the perspective of other post-structuralisms, must seem internally inconsistent from the very beginning.

To go beyond this apparent *impasse* it is necessary again to trace the link with Nietzsche, this time in the more oblique sense of seeing the embeddedness of Foucault's, like Nietzsche's project, in the actual process of reading; genealogy is constituted in the active moment of understanding and following an analysis, not merely through such judgement as might be gained on the basis of those relatively few (but to the commentator attractive) programmatic and polemical outlines of his work Foucault gives. So the very process of commentary in a resumé such as this, that process, to paraphrase Foucault, of saying for the first time what has already been said, and tirelessly repeating what was never said, almost has the unavoidable effect of casting Foucault in a mistaken light, of making solid in his work what was never meant to be solid. That vast accumulation of detail which forms the 'cyclopean monument' of genealogy is not so much to privilege the natural identity of the particular interpretation, to locate meaning in the scholarly recovery, cross-referencing, and study of detail as an end for itself, as it is exactly to create a maze of dislocation and repetition in which meaning as truth is dispersed and lost and meaning as genealogy is found in the becoming moment of interpreting that mass. Genealogy combats the ploys of metaphysics exactly in the excess with which it seems to pander to them.

INTRODUCTION

Foucault's genealogical texts are to be read more at the level of a sequence of Nietzschean aphorisms, than they are even a stylised or parodic version of an orthodox piece of historical writing. In so far, then, as this discussion of Foucault has not been based around more detailed exegesis of works such as *Discipline and Punish* (Foucault 1977c) or *The History of Sexuality* (Foucault 1979b; 1986; 1988) that is because the understanding of those books can only be fundamentally misrepresented in brief summaries of the explicit arguments they nominally present; it is in the process of reading now perceived as rather a creative writing, working through recognition of the inability to close a final metaphysical meaning – that is, in a sense, of the reader participating in a discourse of confession, such as that which for Foucault has been central to the development of western concepts of sexuality, but where admission of guilt is now seen as productive rather than repressive – where Foucault's genealogical meaning is opened, where the meaning of *The History of Sexuality* is to be found. Foucault is forever trying to avoid the ploys of 'simple' meaning, of direct sense; rather he wishes to find himself 'Surrounded by words, taken up and carried beyond any possible beginning' (Foucault cited in Sheridan 1980, 121) – and, indeed, any possible end.

Foucault's genealogical project in many ways complements and intertwines with that strand of cultural criticism represented by Gilles Deleuze and Félix Guattari's two-volume work *Capitalism and Schizophrenia*, which remains one of the most mysterious and important texts of post-structuralism. The first volume of the project, which was published in France in 1972, *Anti-Oedipus* (1984), very rapidly stirred up a controversy. A frontal assault on the Oedipus complex, the values of the family, and the recovery of the ego, it ravages and pierces the repressive framework of Freudian and post-Freudian theory. The central problem is that of desire, which has been defined, since Plato, as 'a void in a subject that has been filled by the acquisition of an object' (Bogue 1989, 89), and codified by Lacan within whose conceptual architecture Guattari, as a practising psychoanalyst, had worked until the late 1960s. For Deleuze and Guattari, however, desire is something positive and productive, not negative; it is production, and the body of a self is not a lack of being 'filled' by subjectification, but a machine cut up by the various machines of 'desiring-production'. Desire, belonging to the unconscious (in which there is no such thing as negation) is the potentially subversive and disruptive force against which society and history are played out (see Nordbladh and Yates, chapter 8), and which the Oedipus complex, with which psychoanalysis is in complicity, attempts to force into territories and self-limiting circuits:

> Psychoanalysis, at the most concrete level of therapy, reinforces this apparent movement with its combined forces. Pychoanalysis in itself

ensures this conversion of the unconscious. In what it calls the pre-Oedipal, it sees a stage that must be surmounted in the direction of an evolutive integration (toward the repressive position under the reign of the complete object), or organised in the direction of a structural integration (toward the position of a despotic signifier under the reign of the phallus). The aptitude to conflict of which Freud spoke, the qualitative opposition between homosexuality and heterosexuality, is in fact a consequence of Oedipus: far from being an obstacle encountered from without, it is a product of oedipalisation, and a counter effect of the treatment that reinforces it.

(Deleuze and Guattari 1984, 74)

Against the tyranny of analysis and of the ego, Deleuze and Guattari propose a 'schizoanalysis', designed to liberate desire from the unconscious, to subvert the current structures and precipitate change, 'promoting visions of revolutionary psychological formation and new earths to inhabit' (Leitch 1981, 213). Published eight years after the French edition of *Anti-Oedipus*, *A Thousand Plateaus* (1988) takes the critique developed in volume one further, and in a different direction. Psychoanalysis recedes from view, and the text is written around fifteen 'plateaus', dealing with different periods of time, the plateau referring to the work of Gregory Bateson (1972) who claimed to have discovered a 'non schizomogenic structuring' of society in Bali, where instead of the rising crescendo and climactic structure of occidental culture and sexuality, a pitch of intensity is reached and maintained, not dissipated. Each of the fifteen plateaus is dated and named, but there is no plateau organising them in a series, no line of evolution or teleology. Randomly organised, the component essays of *Mille Plateaus* disrupt all the orthodox emphases of history, and form points of open focus in a landscape without any boundaries. What 'unites' everything is a rejection of the limitations of ego and of the law of castration (the Oedipal codes) which reunite history in retrospect from that point, and an emphasis upon the Nietzschean concept of a becoming which holds everything in flux. Against this, as described in plateau 5, society attempts to hold itself in place by regimes of signs, and they emphasise that language is not designed to communicate information but to categorise, impose order and thereby control. Words form themselves into the *mots d'ordre* which are these regimes and which have two sides, the content level, such as the prison system in Foucault's *Discipline and Punish* (Foucault 1977c), and an expression level, the acts which bring about transformations of bodies, such as judgements, verdicts and classifications (Bogue 1989, 138). The *mots d'ordre* is the way by which desiring production is kept under control socially and historically.

Difficult as it is, it is likely to be the form of writing used by Deleuze and Guattari, writing so many strands of post-structuralist, structuralist, psychoanalytic and Marxist thought, that will prove decisive in finally transforming the way in which we write and practise history:

> It criticises structuralism, particularly the Lacanian variety. It openly deplores all hermeneutics. It aims to liberate the flow-breaks of desire. It is Barthesian. To let the libidinal schiz-flows breach all borders and barriers. It is Derridean. To unleash molecular forces so as to undo all molecular formations. It is Foucauldian. To set revolution growing.
>
> (Leitch 1983, 220)

But it raises the question of the subject, without a consideration of which it is impossible to understand the potential impact of post-structuralism upon archaeology.

IV

Derrida writes:

> Now if we once again refer to the semiological difference, what was it that Saussure in particular reminded us of? That language [which consists only of differences] is not a function of the speaking subject. This implies that the subject (self-identical or even conscious of self-identity, self-conscious) is inscribed in language, that he is a 'function' of the language. He becomes a *speaking* subject only by conforming his speech ... to the system of linguistic prescriptions taken as the system of differences.
>
> (Derrida 1973, 145–6)

At the heart of the post-structuralist position (and there is probably a degree of conformity on this point which allows us to speak, provisionally, in the singular) is the attack upon the notion of the subject as the origin of meaning, as situated at the origin and in some sense partially outside the chain of signifiers it seeks to articulate. For metaphysics, which is the main target of Derrida's critique, the subject was an essence that in some sense is external to the meaning of its self-representation – thus Descartes' *cogito* escapes self-doubt only at the point of its own perception of itself, its self-knowledge, and it is around this certainty that the various chains of signification can be hung and so determined. In, for instance, the phenomenological rethinking executed by Edmund Husserl, two types of language can be identified, an essential language of expression, comprising the signs of thought, and a secondary language of indication, composed of signs charged with responsibility for indicating to an outside point a discourse which has already taken place on the inside. Two forms are therefore identified – presentation (expression) and representation (indication) which Husserl arranges hierarchically and axiologically. Derrida's reading (1973) undoes this priority and so collapses all meaning into a structure of indication, characterised by ambiguities and fissures of sense.

The consequence of this argument is that it is no longer possible to consider the subject–object duality as an essential polarity, for both must be understood in relation to the system of signifiers in which they are articulated. Thus Derrida argues that the proper (i.e. personal, unique, individual) name is still part of a system of writing, and therefore of classification, because the activity that divides the proper from the objects that surround it is itself a categorisation, one that separates the human/individual from the material/object. By virtue of being a sign inscribed within a system of signs, the subject can no longer be treated as as an effect of a system of written prescriptions: '. . . the proper name was never possible except through its functioning within a system of classification and therefore within a system of differences . . .' (Derrida 1976, 109).

> Subjectivity – like objectivity – is an effect of *différance*, an effect inscribed in a system of *différance* . . . it confirms that the subject, and first of all the conscious and speaking subject, depends upon the system of presence, that the subject is not present, nor above all present to itself before *différance*, that the subject is constituted only in being divided from itself, in becoming space, in temporising, in deferral.
>
> (Derrida 1981a, 28–9)

In contrast to the Cartesian formulation, and to those like Edmund Husserl who try to construct a system of meaning around the subject as self-presence, post-structuralism asserts that the subject cannot be self-present, and that its identity is a social and cultural production. The subject becomes through the movement of a signifying chain, and it is within this chain, which articulates the space/time of the subject, that the familiar metaphysical notions of intentionality, consciousness, and meaning are defined. Rather than being the essence of existence (rather than 'being' therefore), the sign that announces subjective identity/ontology is itself already a common name, a classification, 'sufficiently equivocal to hold . . . the non proper as well as the proper' (Derrida 1984, 64). So the signature, about which Derrida has written a great deal, has to be *iterable* – repeatable – and therefore has to fill the same requirements as any graphic mark.

What would be at issue here, then, would be precisely the role attributed to the subject in the interpretive space of the text. What Derrida reminds us is that the subject is only to be read in the form of a text, that it is not located on the exterior of a text but is articulated on its inside. Thus it becomes possible to oppose the idealism manifested in the

INTRODUCTION

work of the Yale school inspired by deconstruction by applying more generally the notion of the text, such that analysis becomes the aim of examining how texts interpolate readers into their body. If everything is a text, then the production of meaning must be seen as a form of intertextuality – i.e. the way in which text works another text to produce a new text. The ontology of the author as a point of origin is undone – though this need not involve a total erasure of the author as a radical Barthesian 'death of the author'.

The subject is to be seen not as constitutive of ideologies – as someone who manipulates or is manipulated by ideology – but as ideologically constituted. This is clearly one of the informing ideas behind Foucault's project, and explicitly so when it emerges in 'genealogical' form, and the question becomes how such 'fundamental' categories as sexual identity are formulated out of the object relations of discourse and power as apparently natural, and scientifically analysable entities. At a rather different level, an application of this notion is also to be found in Lacan's theories by which the subject 'becomes' through its entry into '*la symbolique*', the symbolic, a generic term for all the processes of signification, including language but also other forms of discourse.

The subject becomes, for Lacan, by a process of splitting and identification (the 'mirror' and 'castration' phases). When I take on the mode of representation, and learn to refer to myself as 'I', I take on a completed pre-existent system of relationships (differences), in which space has been allocated to me. Like the image reflected in a mirror, it is an idealisation presented back to me, a specular identification, and therefore there is, within the sign 'I', a split between me as the subject of the sentence and the 'I' that is not represented in the sentence at all. The subjective – I, formed as I acquire language – is situated with respect to chains of signifiers, such that not every 'I' is equal – the point of entry into the symbolic and cultural system is therefore already mediated, according to culturally significant variables of sex, class, colour, race, etc., which can be understood as the attachments made to the subject as supplementary significations. Becoming a subject is therefore bound up in a process by which I become 'me', white, male, middle class etc. The subject 'is' not, cannot 'be'. It is a text to be read as a text. The symbolic order is that which gives to the subject its identity as a subject, allowing it both to signify and to become signifiable, for the signifier is first that which represents the subject for another signifier, not for another subject.

The subject, then, comes into being through its entry into the symbolic system, and this establishes the concept of the subject as onto-judicial rather than simply ontological. Man, Foucault insisted, 'is an invention of recent date', and that once its position within the modern period and discourse are removed, it will vanish 'like a face drawn in the sand at the edge of the sea' (Foucault 1974, 387). The alliance of notions of human essence and integrity can be linked directly to the emergence of social-judicial psychology, which allows legal systems to assault for crimes the body of an individual conceived as the origin of the crime. In a sense, the criminal/victim thus becomes a necessary exercise to protect society from its own complicity and guilt.

There is, however, no need to assume that the discourses into which we are 'subjected' are homogeneous and coherent, and if we take the issue of women's position and identity within contemporary western societies, it is quite clear that the discourses that are responsible for the construction of the subject are multiple, incomplete and contradictory. Catherine Belsey puts the point succinctly: women

> participate both in the liberal humanist discourse of freedom, self-determination and rationality and at the same time in the specifically feminine discourse offered by society of submission, relative inadequacy and irrational intuition. The attempt to locate a simple and coherent subject position within these contradictory discourses, in consequence to find a non-contradictory pattern of behaviour, can create intolerable pressures.
>
> (Belsey 1980, 65–6)

It is here that we can begin to see more clearly the ambiguity inherent in structuration, since the stability of subjective identity/positionality depends precisely upon the ability of systems/subjects to keep the contradictory nature of their own constitution from coming to fruition – to keep in place the unacknowledged conditions of action and to keep from attention the unintended consequences of action.

The desire to found a non-contradictory mode of self-expression could, of course, be a cause and focus for the feminist movement (and Belsey maintains it is precisely because the contradictory discourses of women's position could not be stabilised that a feminist discourse has appeared). It is to be doubted to what extent a Lacanian position can be used without serious modifications. Coward and Ellis (1977) are optimistic, and their fusion of Marxism with structural/Lacanian psychoanalysis is productive. 'Marxism cannot conceive of a subject who remains outside the structure, manipulating it or acting as a mere support, if it did so it would cease to be a revolutionary philosophy' (Coward and Ellis 1977, 61). Ideology becomes, typically, 'a machine of representation, a practice to produce a specific articulation, that is, producing certain meanings and necessitating certain subjects as their supports' (Coward and Ellis 1977, 67). But the point must also be that the Lacanian position is insufficient, since it recognises only the post-subjective identity, and therefore represents the subject and the process of subjectification as inevitable and irrevocable. Lacan's situating and decentring of the subject differs from that of Derrida to the extent that Lacan's definition of the pre-subjective as 'lack'

INTRODUCTION

is far closer to Heidegger's erased 'being', to a negative ontology, than is recognised by Coward and Ellis. Ultimately, Lacan's discourse must determine the subject as a species of being-present. If 'there is something missing in the Marxist [i.e. Althusserian] analysis of the subject' (Coward and Ellis 1977, 82) then this can only partially be solved by turning to *Ecrits* and *La Seminaire*.

In fact, Lacan's formulation of the subject remains essentially phallocentric or phallogocentric. For Lacan, what determines the subject and assigns to it full identity and subjectivity (as opposed to the partial and specular identity of the mirror phase) is the identity of the phallic signifier where exchange (along a chain of signifiers) is no longer possible. Thus in the Oedipal or castration complex, the subject finds its identity by forcing its desires into the framework delimited by Oedipal triangularity (mama-papa-me) and submitting to the rule of the phallus as the name-of-the-father (for it is the father who prohibits masturbation/incest and enforces the socio-cultural frames of the sexual desires). Feminists have been justified in objecting to the language that is used by Lacan, and Culler (1983a) is correct to point out that merely denying that the 'phallic-signifier' refers to a penis does not amount to a vindication of Lacan's choice of concepts. What is perhaps more interesting, however, is the way in which women have begun to rework the psychoanalytic formulas of Lacanian psychoanalysis, and have been led to align themselves with the unconscious, the pre-subjective, or what Julia Kristeva calls the 'semiotic' or 'pre-thetic', all of which amount to a rejection of the 'phallocentric' conditions of identity.

It is inappropriate and moreover counterproductive to attempt to find a 'real' woman, a proper signifying space, since these are specular identifications mediated through the cultural constitution of a superego or ego-ideal, the conventionalised model of self through which the subject perceives its own identity. To talk of a 'woman' in the sense of a definitive identity is to force political and social conceptualisations to play the rules of the game, and thus to continue to conform to societies' norms and systems of reproduction. Thus for Hélène Cixous 'you can't talk about *a* female sexuality, uniform, homogeneous, classifiable into codes, any more than you can talk about one unconscious resembling another' (Cixous 1980, 246).

Women's unity, therefore, renounces the conditions of identity and becomes the infinite, the inexhaustible, the dissolution of all forms of identity and the rejection of all classifications. To define a woman is to censure her – 'Female sexuality has always been theorised within masculine parameters' (Irigaray 1980, 99). If it is the rule of the father as the law and ontology of the phallic signifier which, for Lacan, guarantees the symbolic order through the triangularity of the Oedipus complex, then women mark their resistance and difference from this position, their distance from this order, by asserting the plurality of their sex. Where for Freud and Lacan women's sex is not a sex – not the site of the presence of a vagina, but the site of the absence of a penis – Irigaray asserts women's plurality. The woman cannot be threatened with castration for touching her genitals, because she touches herself constantly and cannot be forbidden from doing so, 'for her sex is composed of two lips which embrace continually. Thus within herself she is already two – but not divisible into ones – who stimulate each other' (Irigaray 1980, 100).

Women evade and subvert the laws of castration, escaping the polarity between active and passive sexuality which Freud saw as the precursor of puberty and the only reality of sexual difference among children. The woman would begin as the passive side of the polarity which would later become that of the feminine. '*She is neither one or two*. She cannot, strictly speaking, be determined either as one person or two. She renders any definition inadequate' (Irigaray 1980, 101). A woman 'has sex organs everywhere', and the geography of her sexuality evades the (male) law of genitality established via the Oedipus complex. The woman's world becomes, therefore, in contrast to phallic finitude, 'a sort of experience in expansion for which no limits could ever be fixed and which, for all that, would not be incoherency' (Irigaray 1980, 104).

This argument could be shown to realise woman's identity in what Derrida has elaborated as the rule of the *hymen* in opposition to that of the phallus. Where the phallus is singular, determining, seminating, and so guaranteeing the symbolic order, *hymen* divides. In the French it has two meanings, both the vaginal membrane and marriage – at one and the same time, therefore, both virginity and consummation, purity and impurity, inside and outside, self and other. *Hymen* creates differences, keeps them apart (differentiates them) while at the same time joining them, preventing them from separating.

The debate over how to found around this notion a political strategy, and what the implication of women's plurality is, has been vigorous, and some of the criticisms levelled at, for example, Cixous are justified. By embracing women's identity as the irrational, Cixous is led into accepting an essentially masculine position. Julia Kristeva's work, which attempts to steer a middle path the two forms of feminism that have coexisted uncomfortably in France since 1968, offers the clearest statement of what is at stake:

> The belief that 'one is a woman' is almost as absurd and obscurantist as the belief that 'one is a man'. I say 'almost' because there are still many goals which woman can achieve: freedom of abortion and contraception, day care centres for children, equality on the job, etc. Therefore we must use 'we are women' as an advertisement or slogan for our demands. On a deeper level, however, a woman

cannot 'be': it is something that does not even belong in the order of *being* . . . In 'woman' I see something that cannot be represented, something that is not said, something above and beyond women and ideologies.

(Kristeva 1980, 137)

What is at stake, indeed, in the issue of identity is the question of strategy. Nordbladh and Yates (chapter 8) note that within archaeology and anthropology a division is made between biological sex and cultural gender, where the former is assumed as a natural, given division, and the latter as a secondary realm of cultural construction. They point out that biologically the two poles of gender are not as clear cut as has often been assumed, and that other combinations of chromozones are possible than the simple male (XY), female (XX) opposition. Semantically, they examine the notion that sexuality can be forced into this framework, and again find that a naturalised ground of sexual identity cannot be located – culture is implicated as far back as one can go, therefore nature and culture form a continuum, breaks in which are the acts of power and ideology. Their argument endorses Deleuze and Guattari's assertion that man 'does not live nature as nature, but as a process of production. There is no such thing as either man or nature now, only a process that produces the one with the other and couples the machines together' (Deleuze and Guattari 1984, 2).

V

Post-structuralist thought is marked by diversity, indeed it intrinsically produces diversity as it opens the radical potential of the structuralist emphasis on difference. To summarise the aims of post-structuralism, to attempt to pull that diversity into some systematic set of concepts, must, in a sense, run contrary to post-structuralism's very departure. Perhaps then, to maintain the post-structuralist insight, we should not so much conclude at this point, as merely set out certain fluid themes around which the shift towards a post-structuralist archaeology might be conceptualised; for the rest, the text of this book must be left to write itself.

Archaeology after Structuralism

Identity

Post-structuralism is a discourse on identity where structuralism was a discourse 'about' or with identities. In this development structures are to be torn apart and destroyed, not simply recovered and reconstituted.

Thus post-structuralism is a discourse on form as well as content – everything is in difference, which drives a knife through presence. One mark of this process is the destruction of the space occupied by the idea of context. As identity is founded in non-identity, so context can no longer be neatly defined within parameters engendering themselves from the outside as a concrete exemplification of what they govern on the inside. The question eternally becomes: What parameters tell us how to apply the parameters, and to what context do these meta-rules themselves belong?

This assault on identity and the attendant notion of context – and the domination by those terms of the conventional possibility of an archaeology – is variously taken up in this volume. The problem of context is directly articulated by Yates (chapter 6), Moran and Hides (chapter 7) and Bapty (chapter 9), as it develops into a necessary critique of contextual archaeology, and more generally by Maley (chapter 2) in relation to his Derridean critique of Foucault. More specifically, the authors adopt a variety of rhetorical postures to outstrip the inevitable claims of context in the post-structuralist positions/archaeologies they propose. Burr (chapter 1), Yates (chapter 6) and Tilley (chapter 5) all argue for the use of the apparently insane, irrational, abnormal and irreverent as a means to this departure. Bapty (chapter 9) appeals to a Nietzschean process of 'overcoming', Moran and Hides (chapter 7) to the particularity of personal experience and knowledge set against the dominant presence of the author, and accepted rhetorical convention.

A further elaboration of this theme is in relation to the key question of the special kind of context associated with the western concept of subjectivity. As post-structuralism dispels the myth of natural identity, so it dispels the self-constituted subject prescribed by the Cartesian *cogito*, the subject as a founding presence, a basic unity of being, outside language, outside materiality. The papers in this volume identify this issue as a basic site on which to activate a post-structuralist critique. For Yates (chapter 6) the unity of the subject is to be replaced by the Freudian/Lacanian notion of the unconscious: as a structured set of signifiers, subjectivity is an effect, a function of the displacements between the symbols and imaginary orders operating, for example, in the rock art of Bronze Age Scandinavia. Nordbladh and Yates (chapter 8) similarly question the indivisibility of the subject which has preserved the cultural production of the male/female distinction, and suggest that a feminist archaeology should more radically seek to dissolve that duality. Bagnal (chapter 4) outlines the feminist movement in post-structuralism as it has been articulated through the work of Cixous, Kristeva, Irigarary in relation to this problem.

INTRODUCTION

Writing

Post-structuralism involves a basic emphasis on writing, and on reading as itself a process of writing, that is as one more extension of, in Derrida's terminology, the play of *différance*, one more supplement to what was always already written. According to the rule of the supplement, writing adds as it completes, and through this process there must always be an excess, a remainder beyond any apparent statement of presence.

The post-structuralist theory of writing leads, in this volume, both to an explicit consideration of how strategies of writing the past, or of writing about cultural phenomena more generally, should be undertaken, and more implicitly to an examination of how the idea of writing as difference and supplementarity can open to new meaning the density of 'history' which archaeology occupies. There is, then, a general emphasis on reading/writing (archaeological) texts as literature in a deconstructive framework, from Burr's (chapter 1) invocation of the genre of 'magical realism', to Yates' (chapter 6) use of Kafka and psychoanalysis, and Maley's (chapter 2) more 'orthodox' Derridean stance. Alternatively, for Tilley (chapter 5) and to a certain extent Waterman (chapter 3) and Bapty (chapter 9), reading/writing is to be pursued in relation to a more Foucauldian theory of discourse, and the explicit attempt to write through, and therefore to identify, the play of power relations.

The more implicit analyses of the effects of the post-structuralist general theory of writing as difference are seen as wider issues, such as the notion of 'history', and the apparent absoluteness of the past/present relationship are questioned. Walsh (chapter 10), in his discussion of post-modernism and the public presentation of the past, points to the danger of a reified present, of a history conceived as a single unproblematic identity before the post-structuralist space, before, in a sense, writing. Tilley (chapter 5) in his 'history' of Anglo-American archaeology, begins to explore more directly what happens when the excess of the present which, through the action of the supplement, must always be in the past (in this case the recent past of archaeology) is acknowledged, and Yates (chapter 6) considers the radical potential of this movement in terms of an analysis of the distant past openly posited around Freudian psychoanalysis. In these ways, history, if never an absolute contingency, can now begin to be written *as* writing, that is as a realm where the contingent must rhetorically emphasise itself, and be used to break down the falsity of such divisions as past and present.

Materiality/Textuality

Materiality is conventionally invoked by western metaphysics as a limiting principle – the principle of externality. Thus, for example, in contextual archaeology, the 'material' model of material culture demarcates its limits as a purely discursive entity; the material is the 'other' of the 'discursive'. In post-structuralism, however, the invocation of the material is revealed in its paradoxical nature, a paradox continually disturbing the unity of identity and context. Material culture is a text which must be read, but now that reading is action – it is, as we have seen, always already writing. Archaeology, as the study of material culture is, in a sense, now moved to centre stage, since there can be no culture that is not material culture, which is not an effect of textuality.

The ramifications of this point, overlapping with the expansion of writing and the rupture of context, are fundamental to this book, and its intent to announce an archaeology no longer accepting its own disciplinary regulation within a limited field of study. This point is made in a number of different ways by Tilley (chapter 5), Yates (chapter 6) and Bapty (chapter 9), and implied by the freedom with which the signifier 'archaeology' runs through the nominally 'non'-archaeological texts of, for example, Maley (chapter 2) and Moran and Hides (chapter 7). At one level, and paradoxically, the post-structuralist emphasis on textuality/ materiality ironically confers through the play of non-identity the 'identity' archaeology has always craved; it is the possibility of this paradox this volume aims to explore.

VI

Yet, of course, it would be wrong to give the impression that the papers in this book slavishly subscribe to post-structuralism without stopping to question it, or see an 'easy' emergence of a post-structuralist archaeology. On the contrary there are many notes of caution. For Maley (chapter 2) the ultimate validity of Foucault's archaeological/genealogical project is to be closely questioned, and similarly Waterman (chapter 3) is critical of post-structuralism's – and more particularly Foucault's – rejection of ideology analysis, as it seems also to reject the basis for a valid political practice. Walsh (chapter 10) espouses related doubts in his consideration of post-modernism, post-structuralism and the heritage industry, emphasising the difficulty of combating the recent appropriation of the past in the heritage boom by anything less than an equally absolute response. He endorses Foucault's statement that there are lines of force, not sense, and like Waterman (chapter 3), calls for an articulation with Marxism as ultimately a more fruitful strategy.

Ultimately, of course, this book is about questions, not answers. New questions, not the old dressed up to look a little more rigorous/scientific/ logical, minor tinkerings and adjustments being the usual means by which archaeologists – some post-processualists included – have used radical ideas to (paraphrasing Lentricchia) increase the noise without noticeably increasing the speed or performance. We hope that this book goes deeper. Phil Kohl has written that archaeology is nothing today if not acutely self-conscious. In this book, we have disagreed: it is often little more than acutely louder. A break, an epistemological shift, is required, and it is towards this that we have worked here. To paraphrase Barthes: the birth of a critical practice can only be achieved at the cost of the death of an archaeology.

NOTE ON FURTHER READING

It is not, of course, possible to give a comprehensive bibliography of all the interesting or relevant material – the literature both 'primary' and 'secondary' (a classically deconstructable distinction!) is enormous, although a large amount deals very specifically with the implications for literary theory, etc. Perhaps the most accessible general surveys are those of Culler (1983a), Leitch (1983) and Norris (1982), which deal with the main range of post-structuralist authors, though perhaps biased towards Derrida, and not always as critical as they might be. The five essays in Sturrock (1979) are more balanced and provide a good introduction to the main critics. There are volumes on Derrida, Barthes, and Foucault in the Fontana Modern Masters Series (Norris 1988; Culler 1983b; Merquior 1985), though the latter is rather unsympathetic toward its subject. Other volumes on Foucault are numerous, the best being those by Dreyfus and Rabinow (1982) and Sheridan (1980). Note should also be made of a forthcoming volume which contains essays on Barthes, Derrida and Foucault discussed in an archaeological framework (Tilley in press). On Lacan, see the survey by Coward and Ellis (1977), which owes more, perhaps, to Laplanche and Leclaire's (1972) account than to Lacan's own, but that is not necessarily limiting. MacCannel's volume (1986) is interesting, but lacks direction, while Frosh (1977) places Lacan in a wider psychoanalytic perspective. The only volume to deal with feminist post-structuralism – the work of Cixous, Irigaray and Kristeva – is by Moi (1985), who sets their work in a wider perspective than just that of post-structuralism. Deleuze and Guattari are covered in a recent volume by Bogue (1989) much of which, regrettably, remains opaque, and is heavily biased against Guattari; it contains, however, a useful bibliography for locating other commentators. Some of the figures whose impact outside France has been less marked, particularly Lyotard, are discussed by Dews (1987), who compares post-structuralism with the Critical Theory tradition.

Other useful surveys, of varying depth, spread and sympathies, and differing in the extent to which they articulate post-structuralism with other traditions, are worthy of mention: Jameson (1972; 1983) offers some stimulating discussion, particularly on the place of Marxism within post-structuralism, on which see also Ryan (1982) which should be read bearing in mind the comments made by Eagleton (1986). Lentricchia (1983) discusses the impact of the French avant-garde on American literary criticism, and surveys the American Yale 'school' of deconstruction (de Man, Miller) in a manner more critical than that of Leitch (1983) who covers the same material.

REFERENCES

Barthes, R. (1973) *Mythologies*. St Albans: Granada.
Barthes, R. (1974) *S/Z*, trans R. Miller, New York: Hill & Wang.
Barthes, R. (1977a) *Image-Music-Text*, trans. S. Heath, London: Fontana.
Barthes, R. (1977b) *Roland Barthes*, trans. R. Howard, New York: Hill & Wang.
Bateson, G. (1972) *Steps to an Ecology of Mind*, London: Intertext.
Belsey, C. (1980) *Critical Practice*, London: Methuen.
Bogue, R. (1989) *Deleuze and Guattari*, London: Routledge & Kegan Paul.
Butler, C. (1984) *Interpretation, Deconstruction and Ideology*, Oxford: Oxford University Press.
Cixous, H. (1980) 'The laugh of the Medusa', trans. P. Cohen and K. Cohen, in E. Marks and I. de Courtivron (eds) *New French Feminisms: An Anthology*, Amherst: University of Massachusetts Press.
Clifford, J. (1988) *The Predicament of Culture: Twentieth-century Ethnography, Literature and Art*, London: Harvard University Press.
Coward, R. and Ellis, J. (1977) *Language and Materialism*, London: Routledge & Kegan Paul.
Culler, J. (1983a) *On Deconstruction*, London: Routledge & Kegan Paul.
Culler, J. (1983b) *Roland Barthes*, London: Fontana.
Deleuze, G. and Guattari, F. (1984) *Anti-Oedipus: Capitalism, and Schizophrenia*, London: Athlone.
Deleuze, G. and Guattari, F. (1988) *A Thousand Plateaus: Capitalism and Schizophrenia*, London: Athlone.
Derrida, J. (1973) *Speech and Phenomena*, trans. D. B. Allison, Evanston: North-Western University Press.
Derrida, J. (1976) *Of Grammatology*, trans. G. C. Spivak, Baltimore: Johns Hopkins University Press.
Derrida, J. (1978) *Writing and Difference*, trans. A. Bass, London: Routledge & Kegan Paul.
Derrida, J. (1979) 'Living on: border lines', in H. Bloom *et al.*, *Deconstruction and Criticism*, New York: Seabury.
Derrida, J. (1981a) *Positions*, trans. A. Bass, London: Athlone.
Derrida, J. (1981b) *Dissemination*, trans. B. Johnson, London: Athlone.
Derrida, J. (1984) *Signesponge*, trans. R. Rand, New York: Columbia University Press.
Derrida, J. (1987) *The Truth in Painting*, trans. G. Bennington and I. Macleod, Chicago: Chicago University Press.
Derrida, J. (1988) 'Letter to a Japanese friend', in D. Wood and R. Bernasconi (eds) *Derrida and Différance*, Evanston: North-Western University Press.
Dews, P. (1987) *Logics of Disintegration: Post-Structuralism and the Claims of Critical Theory*, London: Verso.
Dreyfus, H. L. and Rabinow, P. (1982) *Michel Foucault: Beyond Structuralism and Hermeneutics*, Brighton: Harvester.

INTRODUCTION

Eagleton, T. (1986) *Against the Grain*, London: Verso.
Foucault, M. (1967) *Madness and Civilization: A History of Insanity in the Age of Reason*, trans. R. Howard, New York: Vintage.
Foucault, M. (1972) *The Archaeology of Knowledge*, trans. A. Sheridan, London: Tavistock.
Foucault, M. (1974) *The Order of Things: An Archaeology of the Human Sciences*, trans. A. Sheridan, London: Tavistock.
Foucault, M. (1975) *The Birth of the Clinic: An Archaeology of Medical Perception*, trans. A. M. Sheridan Smith, New York: Vintage.
Foucault, M. (1977a) 'What is an author?', in M. Foucault, *Language, Counter-Memory and Practice: Selected Essays and Interviews*, trans. D. F. Bouchard and S. Simon, Oxford: Blackwell.
Foucault, M. (1977b) 'Language to infinity', in M. Foucault, *Language, Counter-Memory, Practice: Selected Essays and Interviews*, trans. D. F. Bouchard and F. Simon, Oxford: Blackwell.
Foucault, M. (1977c) *Discipline and Punish: The Birth of the Prison*, trans. A. Sheridan, London: Allen Lane.
Foucault, M. (1979a) 'My body, this paper, this fire', trans. G. Bennington, *The Oxford Literary Review* 4(1): 4–29.
Foucault, M. (1979b) *The History of Sexuality, Volume 1: An Introduction*, trans. R. Hurley, London: Allen Lane.
Foucault, M. (1984) 'Nietzsche, genealogy, history', in P. Rabinow (ed.) *The Foucault Reader*, London: Peregrine.
Foucault, M. (1986) *The History of Sexuality, Volume 2: The Use of Pleasure*, trans. R. Hurley, London: Viking.
Foucault, M. (1988) *The History of Sexuality, Volume 3: The Care of the Self*, trans. R. Hurley, London: Allen Lane.
Frosh, S. (1987) *The Politics of Psychoanalysis*, London: Macmillan.
Hodder, I. (ed.) (1982) *Symbolic and Structural Archaeology*, Cambridge: Cambridge University Press.
Hodder, I. (1986) *Reading The Past: Current Approaches to Interpretation in Archaeology*, Cambridge: Cambridge University Press.
Irigaray, L. (1980) 'This sex which is not one', trans. C. Reeder, in E. Marks and I. de Courtivron (eds) *New French Feminisms: An Anthology*, Amherst: University of Massachusetts Press.
Jameson, F. (1972) *The Prison House of Language*, Princeton: Princeton University Press.
Jameson, F. (1983) *The Political Unconscious: Narrative as a Socially Symbolic Art*, London: Methuen.
Kristeva, J. (1980) 'Woman can never be defined', trans. M. A. August, in E. Marks and I. de Courtivron (eds) *New French Feminisms: An Anthology*, Amherst: University of Massachusetts Press.
Laplanche, J. and Leclaire, M. (1972) 'The unconscious: a psychoanalytical study', *Yale French Studies* 48, 118–75.
Leitch, V. B. (1981) *Deconstructive Criticism: An Advanced Introduction*, London: Hutchinson.
Lentricchia, F. (1983) *After The New Criticism*, London: Methuen.
MacCannel, J. F. (1986) *Figuring Lacan: Criticism and the Cultural Unconscious*, London: Croom Helm.
Merquior, J. G. (1985) *Foucault*, London: Fontana.
Miller, D. (1987) *Material Culture and Mass Consumption*, Oxford: Blackwell.
Miller, D. and Tilley, C. (eds) (1984) *Ideology, Power and Prehistory*, Cambridge: Cambridge University Press.

Moi, T. (1985) *Sexual/Textual Politics: Feminist Literary Theory*, London: Methuen.
Norris, C. (1982) *Deconstruction: Theory and Practice*, London: Methuen.
Norris, C. (1988) *Derrida*, London: Fontana.
Ryan, M. (1982) *Marxism and Deconstruction: A Critical Articulation*, London: Macmillan.
Schiffer, M. (1988) 'The structure of archaeological theory', *American Antiquity* 53: 461–85.
Shanks, M. and Tilley, C. (1987a) *Re-constructing Archaeology*, Cambridge: Cambridge University Press.
Shanks, M. and Tilley, C. (1987b) *Social Theory and Archaeology*, Cambridge: Polity.
Sheridan, A. (1980) *Michel Foucault: The Will to Power*, London: Tavistock.
Smart, B. (1983) *Foucault, Marxism and Critique*, London: Routledge & Kegan Paul.
Sturrock, J. (1979) *Structuralism and Since*, Oxford: Oxford University Press.
Tilley, C. (ed.) (in press) *Reading Material Culture*, Oxford: Blackwell.

Part One
INTERDISCIPLINARY READINGS

CHAPTER 1

Archaeology has certainly since the 1960s, but in other ways for much longer, had a close relationship with social anthropology. This connection, has, of course, been maintained within post-processualism which, taking its initial lead from structural anthropology, has continued to be influenced by the work of social anthropologists, most recently and notably the theoretical essays of Pierre Bourdieu. An account of the implications of post-structuralism/post-modernity for a neighbouring discipline, is, therefore, an appropriate way in which to open this volume.

The questions raised are of direct and not merely marginal relevance. As recent explorations into hermeneutics have emphasised, archaeology shares with anthropology the interpretive problem of both understanding another culture/frame of cultural reference, and of the relationship of descriptive or observational language and of writing to the world it sets out to describe and understand. The questions raised by Burr – about the death of the author, the structures of rationality and writing and their relationships to an individualism and Cartesianism which bears upon the very concept and nature of 'man' – are of central importance within archaeology. For those to whom hermeneutics offers a strategy of protection from difference the post-structuralist challenge sounds out clearly – cultures do not even 'know themselves', and a practice must embrace all that it has previously excluded and exiled if it is to see itself a little more clearly. In particular, the politics of knowledge and science and their place within the post-modern world are issues that we cannot afford to ignore, and we have much to learn from the recent experience and current debates within anthropology, from the new directions, conceptualisations, forms and ways of writing with which post-modern ethnography is currently experimenting.

1

The Joker is Wild, the Text Untameable: the Analytics of Homo Analogicus (Anthropology, Post-Structuralism and Post-Modernism)

Gareth Burr

'Would you tell me, please, which way I ought to go from here?'
'That depends a great deal on where you want to get to,' said the Cat.
'I don't much care where –' said Alice.
'Then it doesn't matter which way you go,' said the Cat.
'– so long as I get somewhere,' Alice added as an explanation.
'Oh you're sure to do that,' said the Cat, 'if only you walk long enough.'
Alice felt that this could not be denied, so she tried another question. 'What sort of people live about here?'
'In that direction,' the Cat said, waving its right paw round, 'lives a Hatter;[1] and in that direction,' waving the other paw, 'lives a March Hare.[2] Visit either you like, they're both mad.'
'But I don't want to go among mad people,'[3] Alice remarked.
'Oh you can't help that,' said the Cat: 'we're all mad here. I'm mad. You're mad.'[4]
(Lewis Carroll, *Alice's Adventures in Wonderland*)

This paper will attempt a radical challenge to the epistemological premises of theoretical anthropology by asserting, following the recent discourse theorists, the mediated, negotiated and metaphorical nature of language, thought and action. My thesis will be that fantasy and reality are dimensions on the same continuum and that this has profound implications for understanding the paradoxical nature of writing, speaking and the human condition. This involves an argument about the possibility of developing an analytics, a style and a strategy which effaces traditional oppositions such as description and explanation, inductive and deductive, truth and method, theory and practice, essence and appearance, fact and fiction. The insufficiency of these static oppositions can be exposed through discussion of contemporary theoretical positions of hermeneutic and post-structuralist writers who reduce not to dualisms but to process and realise the universe in a continual state of becoming. Recent positions emphasising the aesthetic nature of society are also engaged in exposing the gravity and seriousness of internal dualistic opposition and domination of one relation over another and the social procedures of exclusion and internal constraint on expression and communication. This paper will clarify some positions whose concerns are with cultural representation, authorial subjectivity, textual creation, aesthetic expression, and whether they are sufficient, intellectually, with regard to lived experience and social fragmentations. It will also assess the post-structuralist declaration of 'the death of the author,' a trend in literary criticism applicable to all writers and more importantly to all readers, which has had notable influence among anthropologists engaged in writing post-modern ethnographies. I want to explore some possible parallels between literary genres and approaches emphasising the magical reality of the material cultural world, which writers today (literary, philosophical and anthropological) have tried to convey, where the reality of fantasy takes on new dimensions, and where we discover the sinister reality of an unacknowledged metaphor we regularly use. Finally, the paper will discuss what really is at stake in our discourse which, according to Foucault, takes us into a major theoretical overhaul and a radical social and political critique.

By way of an introduction and in order that we know the tradition within which post-structuralist and post-modern theorists are writing and, to an extent, reacting to, and also to explore the contingencies of our discourse more generally, I want very briefly to identify some important moments in the development of western philosophical discourses, which have influenced our convictions considerably. Recent critiques of post-modernism are theoretically and empirically misguided not only because there is no single post-modernist theory but also more importantly because post-modernism is absolutely a sequential consequence of modernism. In a sense there is nothing new in what is being said. It is drawing out the implications of what has been said in diverse ways, both radical and reactionary. This is a necessary corrective, as there is no monolith, and that cliché which appears so often – the erection of straw men – demonstrates the point.

Descartes, in formulating his paradigm-shifting dictum *cogito ergo sum*, ironically, and without himself or anyone else knowing it, was inverting the whole medieval theological viewpoint. Descartes, the first 'existentialist', doubted everything except that *he was doubting*. Thus he had absolute proof of his existence. He proclaimed that the thinking subject *is the only certitude*. In doubting everything he must be doubting God. This inverted the view of medieval Scholasticism that God was an absolute and that the human world of Choice, Will and Action were irrational, unworthy and questionable, unless guided by Divine Will. Descartes, a devout believer trying to prove the existence of God, was in fact proclaiming the death of God. Enlightenment philosophers soon brought the rediscovered rationality to a dead end. Absolute Reason led to Hume's scepticism and Berkeley's contention that there is no real world. Their analytic empiricism reigned until Kant postulated the cognitive synthetic a priori in his *Critique of Pure Reason*. Naive empiricism was rejected and a basis laid for the social understanding of knowledge. Hegel and Feuerbach inverted contemporary theological discussions in which God was seen to be objectifying himself in Jesus Christ and in humanity, by considering humanity to be objectifying itself in God. And for Hegel objectification is a three-faceted process, externalisation, separation and sublation; thesis, antithesis, synthesis. Marx grounded the Hegelian schema of an external triadic constituting contradictory dialectics in historical and material contingency, called praxis. He claimed the process whereby property was freed to achieve its purely economic form is the same process whereby individuals (appear to) seem progressively detached from their community; he realised the historical contingency of all process. Individualism is a grounded historical experience. It is within the social relations of capitalism and a specific ideology that individuals appear as autonomous, free and self-contracting subjects. It is the ideological means serving specific capitalist ends, once a European problem, now a world problem. So we cannot postulate the theoretical starting point of isolated and rational individuals on which society is to be built. This is the philosophical insight of Hegel and Marx. They related everything to process, to the simple fact that the universe is in a continual state of becoming. Heraclitus said 'You can never step into the same river twice'; a post-modern realisation might add that you cannot step into the same river once.

Twentieth century thought is still overwhelmingly dominated by nineteenth century thinkers. Revolutionary activity at the end of the eighteenth century and throughout the nineteenth caused and was caused by revolutionary thought. The old aristocracy was challenged and the middle class had to secure their triumph by suppressing any potential counter-revolution by the proletariat. Modernism, and the avant-garde artistic and cultural movement, developed through a tension between the established 'high' culture and the popular 'mass' culture. The emergence of a bourgeois modernism guaranteed the possibility of a successful capitalist consumerism. The cultural movement of modernism constituted the self in every respect in accordance with the most important determination of capitalist production – capitalist consumption. This signals the necessity for a radical change of emphasis in analysis: the consumption of modernity is the post-modern predicament.

A discussion of three important moments in the developing perception of ethnography as a process of signification, subjectification and intersubjectivity will help us to isolate some central features of present theoretical predicaments. Three anthropological contributions – involving (1) an awareness of aesthetic innovation and experimentation, (2) an exposure of power/knowledge dimensions, and (3) a realisation of an inevitable authorial subjectivity – seem to contain, when put together, the core of the post-modern message. So, far from being a completely new phenomenon, post-modernism is an eclectic and connective trend derivative of much of what came before.

Firstly, Gregory Bateson's *Naven* (1953) challenged the constraints of accepted forms of ethnographic description. His was an experimental ethnography which was contemporary with the expressed parallels between the experimentation of French ethnography and the artistic fashion of surrealism. The point is that innovation in ethnography is experimentation in writing, presentation and expression of ethnographic material. Secondly, Edward Said's *Orientalism* (1979) states the 'no escape' injunction that whether sympathetic or not ethnographers are representatives of colonial regimes, and so as a consequence there is always an asymmetry between the describer and the described. The aesthetic revolution, taking *language* seriously if nothing else, is exposed as manipulating education for creativity, leading to an indulgence in abstruse solipsims – textual, conceptual and intellectual. It can be soured when seen as a decadent west romanticising at the expense of the rest. Thirdly, Derek Freeman's publication of *Margaret Mead and Samoa* (1983) was not only challenging Mead's Samoan ethnography, but was also, by implication, challenging those who accepted Mead as an eminent anthropologist. The possibility of scientific objectivity in ethnographic reporting is undermined when two ethnographers, in good faith and without misunderstanding, arrive at mutually incompatible representations of an ethnographic 'reality'. Thus it becomes a question of an inevitable authorial subjectivity and of the creative way we construct the objects of which we speak. These three concerns, intricately connected as they are, constitute the structure of this paper.

I. POST-STRUCTURALISM, POST-MODERNISM AND TEXTUALITY

The hermeneutic tradition strives to undermine our confidence in the commonsense interpretative approaches to our own as well as others' presentations – in speech and texts – of lived experience, where no one has access to the 'original' text of reality. It is a subversive enterprise, pointing to the self-contradiction and incompleteness of ostensibly integrated and authoritative texts, be they of cultures, of history or of the self. So in opposition to a single truth, hermeneutics posits the 'narrative truth'. Interrelated meanings are drawn out, translated and examined in order to disclose the mutually translatable and untranslatable dimensions of both cultures. It is a method promising to do justice to 'the mental and material operations of living' (Rebel 1988), an approach which decentres us and brings us back to ourselves; the paradoxical movement towards understanding without going beyond the given, always leads back to the here and now (Ricoeur 1979, 63–99).

The potential chaos which the project threatens is averted by the ordering and systematisation of Clifford Geertz' method. His formulations give an overall thrust that seems antithetic to the original intention of hermeneutic writers. Ethnographers who emerged out of the same school have been at pains to distance themselves from Geertz. Serious displays of obvious 'Geertz bashing' indicates this (Clifford 1983, 132–3; Rabinow 1985, 242–3; Crapanzano 1986, 72–4). Geertz' writing needs consideration here to elucidate some related arguments. His persuasion is that both our and the other's 'experience' of historical process is embedded in 'mutually alien and equally dignified conceptual and expressive languages'. The alterity which cultural relativism stresses results in a finished sense of 'internal cultural hegemony' (Rebel 1988). This points away from the question of an historically experiencing self, with all the conflicts and uncertainties that it involves, which the advanced anthropological deconstructionist schools embrace. With the notion of the undecidability of the signifier, post-modern approaches see cultures as partly ineffable, even to their own participants, and everyone is a potentially deconstructive reader, especially those who are victims of a double bind, capable through experience of locating 'the sleight of hand at the limit of the text', where they are on the threshold of meaning and on the threshold of sense.

Ethnographers who are interested in reading their own experience during research hope to confront these matters which have been taken largely for granted. Encounters with the ethnographers' questions brings about a self-consciousness in the other, and an awareness of the limits of their texts (Rabinow 1977, 151–3). Post-modern ethnography can attempt to overturn the relation of dominance of 'text' over 'discourse' by exactly privileging dialogue (discourse) over monologue (text). As opposed to the ideology of the transcendent observer it emphasises the emergent, participatory and co-operative nature of understanding; thus the necessity of making a polyphonic text. This signals a movement towards the recognition of the sonorous and perspectival relativity involved in the participatory and engaged reality of ethnographic fieldwork (Tyler 1986, 126–9). Before discussing this in greater detail, it is appropriate to examine the contemporary French theorists, who have been most influential in these developments.

It is clear enough that the main input into these debates is from post-structuralist literary criticism. The inauguration of the crisis in signification came with Bakhtin and Medvedev with their critique (1928) of the Russian Formalists. Their argument was that the words of a given text, far from achieving literary stability, generate more and different words in the mind of the reader. The joker is wild. The text is in a semantic space uncontrolled by the author. These arguments have been restated by the contemporary French successors of structuralism, with statements such as Barthes' that 'the birth of the reader must be at the cost of the death of the author' (1977, 148). Old doctrines of functionalism and materialism became outmoded when structuralist and intellectualist strategies were instigated at the level of conceptuality, textuality and formalisation. Deconstruction is post-structuralism and relies on a close relationship with structuralism for its effect. Structuralism, far from being refuted has rather been released to realise further possibilities. It can modify its form and encompass its own critique. If structuralism is to be dismantled, then so too has the whole system of western thought since Plato, and contemporary French philosophers are aware that these stakes are high.

A paradox is structurally inevitable once oppositions and dualisms operate in a system of reasoning (such as sensibility and intelligibility; conscious and unconscious; mind and body; contingency and necessity; signifier and signified). There is a transcendental dualistic illusion that we are subjected to in analysis. An analytics of a post-structuralist type proceeds by continually effacing fixed relations, blurring traditional distinctions with a graphic logic (Derrida's *écriture*) to follow the movement of dualisms. If they are movable, then maybe they are removable. Whichever way it goes it rapidly develops into a paradox. A good example is the classic Platonic postulation that the whole of life could be a dream, thus there is no ground for anyone to say that they are definitely awake (Plato, Descartes and, in a modified form, Berkeley, all made this point). However, that we may be 'only dreaming' has meaning only if it is distinguished from 'being awake', and the possibility of this distinction is negated with the assertion that *all* life is a dream. It is a paradox of structural oppositions, and more than that it is a paradox of the very language with which we formulate the problem. Language is not neutral. It never is, and this is the point, the point which cuts both ways.

The opposition of sanity to madness and serious to fictional discourse needs assessment in the same light. Derrida elaborates the idea that all writing and all language is fundamentally metaphorical, that the literal is the figurative. Thus the crisis of the signifier mentioned above. However, the metaphorical, like dreaming and reality, is in an oppositional transference with the literal, only having meaning with relation to it. So in deconstructing the literal, the metaphorical is also deconstructed. So it is an either/or, or neither/both. A chiasmic reversal. A paradox. We can see necessity with contingency and the determination of free will. Even

Pangloss in Voltaire's *Candide* could see that they were organically and inextricably linked. When asked by an officer of the inquisition, 'Then don't you believe in Free Will, sir?' Pangloss replied, 'Your Excellency must excuse me . . . Free Will is consistent with Absolute Necessity, for it was ordained that we should be free. For the Will that is determined . . .' (Voltaire 1947, 35).

Therefore, we should not read Derrida, Barthes, Post-modernists, magical realists or anyone *literally*. Nor metaphorically in the traditional sense. They are elucidating a new way to understand reading and writing. It is the movement of signification, from signifier to signfier, and its effects – a mirage; it is not a coherent philosophy, nor can it be when the language, and the subject, is not even assumed as understood.

It is very difficult to separate, exactly, recent hermeneutic approaches from post-structuralist and post-modernist ones as they are inextricably linked. James Clifford, in *The Predicament of Culture*, is in the tradition of all three. He discusses the tradition of the Parisian avant-garde and surrealist movement in art and ethnography (the pre-structuralist heritage), emphasising its importance, especially for the development of post-structuralism. Foucault and Barthes are dead but still very influential. Baudrillard is more representative of the post-modern lift-off, actually applying in descriptive analysis what the writing culture school are doing in anthropology. So the terms post-modern and post-structuralist are not directly interchangeable. Post-modern ethnography ploughs through in the wake of the crisis in representational signification, gaining at the expense of positivist approaches. Political discourse in its totalising frame, and scientific discourse in its atomistic frame, differ from post-modern ethnographic discourse which is totalising and detotalising, realising a new way towards a non-traditional transcendence. Baudrillard, in a post-modern sociological discourse, tries to instigate a realisation of the value of the simulacrum, of society not as surreal but as hyperreal. The trends have common themes; disenchanted views where stable orders are seen as 'constructed, artificial and indeed often ideologically repressive' (Clifford 1988, 118). Baudrillard, in his latest book (1987) extrapolates a hologram of our society as an ultramodern quantum reality, where the fatal implosion of the Cartesian subject is dramatically portrayed.

Continental literary criticism, in the methodology of Derrida, does not recognise the separation of serious philosophy from frivolous literature. All language, and thus all philosophy, is fundamentally and inescapably metaphorical. Barthes' declaration of the death of the author is indicative of the point that communication is never complete, there are only readers who can only ever interpret, where misunderstanding and miscommunication invades too much for it not to be taken seriously into account. The meaning of a text is the sum of its misreadings. This signals the end of individualism, of ego and monad autonomy, and the beginning of decentred and deconstructed subjects, lining in a post-society of discursive heterogeneity without a centre and without a norm. These post-structuralist concepts influence post-modern sociology. Baudrillard reappropriates Plato's concept of the simulacrum, an identical representation for which there is no original, to describe the culture of ultracapitalism, where any original idea of what is going on has long been forgotten. The past as a referent is bracketed off and then effaced, and we are left only with texts. Exchange value (money) is an encompassing ideology and the memory of use value has disappeared into oblivion. Intertextuality, where one aesthetic in historical sequence influences another (for example a book, a film, another film, another book and maybe a painting), is built in for the aesthetic effect and its history replaces 'real' history (whatever that may be).

This is the paradox of inversion, where 'not only are Picasso and Joyce no longer ugly; they now strike us, on the whole, as rather "realistic"; and this is the result of canonisation and an academic institutionalisation of the modern movement generally' (Jameson 1984, 56). Descartes' *cogito ergo sum* has a paradoxical double aspect, firstly with the modernist art movements that worshipped the author/artist as God – the creator; and secondly with post-modern movements that reactivated Nietzschean proclamations of the death of God/author,[5] where the subject and the sign are decentred. We cannot escape ambiguity of interpretation, especially not the highly rationalist formulations of Descartes, which make possible both the birth and the death of the individual subject. The death of the author/subject/man is a natural and inevitable consequence of its birth.[6] Roland Barthes projects his insights so that they struggle universally, with quasi-anthropological credibility, as in his empire of signs he cites the far east:

> in the ideal Japanese house, devoid or nearly so devoid of furniture, there is no place which in any way designates property; no seat, no bed, no table provides a point from which the body may constitute itself as subject (or master) of space. The very concept of centre is rejected (burning frustration for western man everywhere provided with his armchair and his bed, the owner of domestic position.
> (Barthes 1979, 13–14)

The decentred sign and the decentred subject is precisely Jacques Lacan's thesis. He identifies schizophrenia as a breakdown of the signifying chain, of its temporal organisation and meaning, where a signifier is no longer capable of relating to other signifiers, but exists in dramatic isolation. Its vividness and overwhelming power emerges because the signifier gains a material and a literal intensity. Discontinuity, heterogeneity and fragmentation become the overriding feelings. The assumed nature of any relationship is questioned, for example the relationship between signifiers and the relationship between people. Nothing is taken for granted. Young infants live this immediacy, but have to submit themselves to the mediating symbolic order of language. Thus in the Oedipus complex the child moves from an immediate relationship with its mother to a mediated one where a symbolic law intervenes, actualised by the figure of the father, prohibiting union with her. The symbolic substitution, inherent in language, is a precondition for subjectivity and singularity. Through appropriating their forename and the grammatical concept of 'I' the child realises itself as a subject. Thus an originally obscure and incommunicable 'reality' is replaced by a mediated and constructed consciousness – a 'fantasy' in any positivist sense, but a reality in another. We constitute ourselves when we look in the mirror as a child. We are an imaginary entity, a specular identity, right from the beginning. In the development of our consciousness, we learn about ourselves through a spectral image, the mirror image. Mirroring is a constituting reality.

The death of the author and the birth of the reader is another example of the whole shift of emphasis in analysis. From production to consumption, from cause to effect, from depth to surface, in order that all those original priorities are reversed if not altogether effaced. The project is not superficial; the notion of superficiality is deconstructed, as are all the related dichotomies such as latent and manifest, authenticity and inauthenticity, essence and appearance. Intertextuality, of one aesthetic (text) in its relation to another, displaces the criticism of it as being depthless. The earlier surrealist technique of parody is replaced by the post-modern pastiche, which is imitation and mimicry but without any of the former's ulterior motives towards satirical effect. Pastiche is 'black irony' and 'blank parody', where laughter is conspicuously absent (Jameson 1984, 65).

The joker or the court fool, in Shakespeare's plays, constituted the dual and ambiguous aspect of combining folly with wisdom: jesting could at times be so close to the truth as to be deadly serious, so devoid was it of any laughter function. King Lear's court fool is unambiguously the wise man, as he is in 'Ran', a Japanese Buddhist mythological rendition, and we are not laughing at such a fool. In the Tarot the fool appears twice: at the beginning, and at the end, where the figure stays the same but the meaning has changed. The joker is wild.

In the Essay 'The Schizophrenic in Language: Surface and Depth' (1979) Gilles Deleuze discusses Lewis Carroll in relation to Antonin Artaud. His thesis is the profound difference between apparent similarities. Whereas Carroll works out the intertextuality of surface meaning, the depthlessness of language, for Artaud there is only depth. Artaud writes of Carroll from an asylum:

> I do not like surface poems or languages which smell of happy leisure moments and intellectual triumphs . . . When one digs into the shit of the individual being and his language, the poem must necessarily smell bad; 'Jabberwocky' is a poem that its author has taken special pains to keep outside the uterine being of suffering into which all great poets have dipped, and from delivering themselves into the world, they smell bad . . . It is the work of a man who ate well, and you can smell it in his writing.
>
> (Artaud 1970, 184)

Artaud's contempt for Carroll is very relevant to the post-modern debate on language, thought, action and experience. His condition is that of experiencing the materiality of the signifier in all its vividness. The word hits hard and he takes it in the gut. The 'uterine being of suffering' is this breakdown in the signifying chain that Lacan speaks of, where each signifier stands on its own, isolated and with a rough edge. The fundamental difference between these conflicting dimensions could be described by the phrase 'you are what you eat' as opposed to 'who you eat with', in its most metaphorical and literal senses. Both representing the positions of one or the other. The infant goes through the pre-linguistic state of oral mania, stuffing anything into its mouth. Thus the eating/speaking dichotomy. Eating is a bodily operation, it is corporeal, it is an action and a passion, which a young infant is engrossed in, with a primordial connectedness with everything around it. It emerges out of this through the appropriation of speech and articulation of grammatical forms which more importantly constitute its subjectivity. Eating is depth and speaking is the movement of surface signifiers; an operation of incorporeal events. The child soon learns its identity by 'who it eats with'. Symbolic substitution and mediation, through the acquisition of language, decentres a previously primordial reality. It is on the surface that the entire logic of meaning is held. To articulate their difference is to venture on to the threshold of meaning, and on to the threshold of sense.

Alice's adventures are discoveries of surfaces: once through the sinking and burrowing, Alice's movements become lateral, animals of depth are replaced by playing card characters without thickness. Depth is the reverse side of the surface. The sequel, *Through the Looking-Glass*, extends the surface reality further. Events are a surface and temporal sequence of intertextuality, a signifier relating to another and a signified becoming another signifier in an endless succession. Events are radically different from things, but in the mirror, corporeal bodies are rendered as flat and depthless and they become incorporeal events. Depth is realised on the surface in the same way as we are aware of three-dimensional space in the two-dimensional image on the surface of the mirror. Alice, as the ultimate in a fantastic and escapist dream, provides us with a remarkable parallel with Lacan's thesis that as a child we constitute ourselves through a mirror stage.

Understanding the duality of bodies and objects/expression and meaning is extremely important. Artaud and the schizophrenic's expressions never rise to the surface but stay with the body, the depth, the smell, the shit, the violence and the fornication. 'All writing is pig-shit', Artaud says. Carrollean language, by contrast, plays on the esoteric and hermetic meaning of expression. The two dimensions are like two surfaces of a mirror where what is on one does not resemble what is on the other. Carroll's is the language of incorporeal meaning. Alice has left the depths of her mother's body without having yet developed her own. She breaks through to the surface of the pool of her own tears, a surface which is flat: exactly her predicament, where dangers 'snatch laterally'. The displacements between the language of madness, the language of childhood, and the poetry of both, are as monumentally different as they are superficially similar.

With the genre of magical realism (Gabriel García Márquez, Carlos Fuentes, Jorge Luis Borges, Angela Carter), structures of reality are explored by juggling with time and fact and history and space and reality. They are asserting: 'the freedom that lies behind the mask, within dissimulation, the freedom to juggle with being and, indeed, with the language which is vital to our being, which lies at the heart of burlesque' (Carter 1985, 103).

So the boundaries between fact and fiction are effaced. In reading what are we asked to believe? Is it true that 'seeing is believing'? Are we being asked to suspend disbelief? There is a parallel in anthropology, with the magic of material culture forms, where fantasy and reality are intertwined. There is a dualism which emerges as a paradox because the definitions we start with are dissolved in the process. Our fantasies are externalised – decorating the house; 'art' creation . . . writing! Objectifications of subjectivity. In fact the whole fabricated human world, buildings, cars, roads, cities – all are expressions of the human fantasy consciousness, which we reappropriate and internalise in a process of alienation and objectification realised by Hegel and Marx and rendered further with fuller implications by Danny Miller (1987, 19–49). It is this objective 'real' world we refer to when we dismiss our dreams and fantasies. The word 'real' takes on a new meaning, and we realise the enormity of our own creativity.

Angela Carter's 'Fevvers' has the confidence to believe that she can transform the man she loves:

> so that he too, will put his poor shoulder to the wheel and help to give the world a little turn into a new era that begins tomorrow. And once the world has turned on its axle so that the new day can

dawn, then, ah, then! all the women will have wings, the same as I.
(Carter 1985, 285)

The political dimension is a reality, its significations as potent as Franz Fanon's. *Nights at the Circus*, where Fevvers appears, is set during 'the hinge of the nineteenth century', in:

> those last, bewildering days before history, that is, history as we know it, that is, white history, that is, European history, that is, Yanqui history – in the final little breathing space before history as such extended its tentacles to grasp the entire globe.
> (Carter 1985, 265)

The politicisation of knowledge is familiar in a post-Foucauldian world, where we know that power components are integral in the dialectics of being and knowing, in speaking and in writing. These are the unacknowledged conditions of our rationality, its hidden agenda, leading to unintended and undesirable consequences – power/knowledge, reason, agency and violence – my aim is finding a strategy and a style which can successfully unravel the logic of their complicity.

II. POST-MODERNISM AND ETHNOGRAPHY

Frederic Jameson asks whether the post-modern syntagm will be able to take in a culture increasingly dominated by space and spatial logic: 'It is empirically arguable today that our daily life, our psychic and cultural languages are today dominated by categories of space rather than by categories of time' (Jameson 1984, 64).

Knowledge in the west is based on a metaphor which largely passes unnoticed. This is the image of knowledge as a landscape. Discourse – writing and speaking – can hardly escape it as its imagery is so strong and deep rooted. It subconsciously deceives us into thinking that knowledge, as we appropriate it, is unquestionably objective, mapping one to one with the world. Even more than that, that *it is* the world. This is the potency of the metaphor. Anne Salmond illustrates this in her article 'Theoretical Landscapes' (1982). We journey through intellectual *territory* to reach a destination. Understanding is seeing and knowledge is clear sight. Facts are natural objects and knowledge is their possession. Intellectual activity is work and knowledge is its product. The landscape imagery gives us the impression of a theoretical observer who is detached and scientifically surveying an objective world. The contrast is that 'in Maori thinking truth is always contingent upon situational factors, knowledge claims are tied to power, the environment has a right to reply and one is vulnerable to its rebuttals' (Salmond 1982, 85). Sinister political and militaristic allusions are always implicit in academic arguments, with associated metaphors like: *authority*, *disciplines*, *realms*, *rules and revolutions*; *boundaries*, *domains*, *borders*, *frontiers and barriers*; (getting more sinister), *gaining and losing ground*, *defence*, *attack*, *retreat*, *counter-attack*, *stalemate*, *surrender and truce*. So it is pretty clear that *knowledge is a territory* and *argument is war*. Lakoff and Johnson (1980) argue that it leads to intellectual imperialism.

Root metaphors lie at the heart of our language and our thought. *Ethos*, *eidos* and *pathos* are inescapable categories which have sedimented into our very being, constituting us and our discourse simultaneously. They have a reality in the separations of aesthetics, science and politics. Our root metaphors are scientific realities, we realise that saying, seeing and doing correspond respectively with words, things and deeds, which has an equivalence with the division in the cerebral cortex of areas of association, sense and motor, which are: 'metaphors of present, past and future . . . and of time, space and movement as categories of intuition, and of subject, object and verb as grammatical categories of understanding . . .' (Tyler 1986, 175).

The metaphors of words, things and deeds constitutes the most essential aspects of Melanesian societies. The whole project of Melanesian anthropology was a development out of the insights of Marcel Mauss, who realised not only that society is constituted in and through exchange, but showed the extent to which persons are implicated in things and vice versa: 'This bond created by things is in fact a bond between persons, since the thing itself is a person or pertains to persons . . . to give something is to give a part of oneself' (Mauss 1954, 10).

With an emphasis on the consideration of time and the temporal process and sequencing of gift exchange, we can substitute a notion of the rule with the notion of strategy, which is to 'reintroduce time, with its rhythm, orientation and irreversibility' (Bourdieu 1977, 9).

There are countless ethnographic examples that illustrate the theoretical opposition of fantasy and reality, and the domination of one over the other needs a radical overhaul. If these theoretical oppositions and dominations continue, so will external relations of separation, exclusion and domination. Nancy Munn (1978), though not as explicitly as Salmond, provides us with an insight into the power dimensions of Walbiri and Pitjantjatjara knowledge. Though this was not the central thesis of her ethnography, we can read it as a sub-text. There was a marked difference between female and male art in these aboriginal groups. The female's art was unspecific and general, whereas the male's showed knowledge of the ancestors, and its potency came from the procreative powers of the ancestors. It is secret knowledge, hidden from women. Women's art was an inversion of men's, in that it exactly is not allowed to be what men's art is, because to *be* a man is to *know* of the ancestors. This provides ethnographic demonstration that the political component is integral to the dialectics of being and knowing. Her central concern was an almost post-structuralist one which is very relevant to my theme; to portray the conceptual interchangeability of subjects into objects, of persons and things in this society. Objects and landmarks for them are petrifications, externalisations and the metamorphoses of once living ancestors who communicate through dreamtime. We call it fantasy – they call it reality. Thus western notions of the separation of people from things, of humans from animals, of culture from nature and of mind from body, really does reflect the arbitrary nature of our epistemology and the occidental contingency of our configurational universe (on these relations in archaeology, see Yates, chapter 6).

In their attempts to abolish the use of words, the professors at the Academy of Lagado ordered that things were to be substituted for words in social interaction. Gulliver witnesses the project on his third voyage:

> Since words are only names for things, it would be more convenient for all men to carry about them such things as were necessary to express the particular business they are to discourse on . . . I have often beheld two of these sages almost sinking under the weight of their pack, like Pedlars among us, who when they met in the streets, would lay down their loads, open their sacks, and hold conversations for an hour together; then put up their implements, help each other to resume their burdens, and take their leave.
>
> (Swift 1970, 158)

This provides Annette Wiener with valuable insight into the Melanesian process 'from words to objects to magic' (Wiener 1983), from incorporeality to corporeality, as it signals a movement from Carroll's words to Artaud's materiality. In Melanesia, words spoken in magical use must become physical things in order to cause the desired effect. To achieve domination over someone, to violate their space, one must enter into their body through an object which is the vehicle of signification. Words and objects are interchangeable, as are persons and things. These realisations are crucial for the development of a post-modern ethnographic discourse which can hopefully escape the dichotomies and disjunctions of positivistic and atomistic western scientific discourse.

We have to understand post-modernism in an encompassing sense. There is nothing singular and monolithic about it, it is everything from Maggie Thatcher as a high priestess of deconstruction to the radicality of the neo-anarchists. And it is all a corollary to modernism as an incomplete project, reminiscent of the title of Habermas' supposed critique. The critique of post-modernism is not successful (Jameson 1984; Habermas 1985) because it is attacking an empty category which has been constructed, deflecting away from the obvious point that, whether we like it or not, we are all post-modernists now, and from that there is no escape. Whether as right-wing iron reactionaries, signalled in an extreme way by Thatcher deconstructing the high modernist architecture of the education system or the welfare state, or as post-neo-Marxists, it cannot be denied that the world has shifted from modernity to post-modernity.

In *Writing Culture: The Poetics and Politics of Ethnography* (Clifford and Marcus 1986) ethnographic discourse is seen as the necessary corrective to the positivist and totalising discourses of science and politics. Post-modern ethnographic evocation is neither scientific nor totalising in the traditional senses of these terms. As its name *ethno*graphy reminds us, its power is ethical, and its technology is writing. Ethnography will always be an unfinished project. It does not transcend through a metalanguage, it transcends through an evocation which goes beyond separations of signifier and signified, form and content, sensibility and intelligibility.

Scientific discourse mythologises itself in its positivistic rhetoric of authority. The language of communication fails science, and integrated with science's heights of rationality is an overriding political irrationality. There are no neutral scientists doing neutral scientific research without being embedded within an economic and social setting, and within a non-rational encompassing political ideology (see Tilley, Chapter 5). A post-modern ethnography is vital if the positivism and totalising hegemony of the establishment is to be discredited. Operating multi-directionally and through evoking emergent possibilities of past, present and future, ethnography, therapeutically, is concerned with the effects of poetic and ritual performances, and with poetry as a performative break, and with its re-creation in the text. The 'seeing is believing' mentality pervading positivist traditions creates a whole visualist ideology of ocularcentric discourse, antagonistic to the mythical and ethical reaches of a post-modern ethnographic discourse.

Post-modern ethnography is fragmentary. Life is not organised around the totalising categories we imagine – kinship, economy or religion, and experiences do not present themselves to the fieldworker as theoretical microcosms nor as understood totalities (Tyler 1986, 132). The only globally encompassing consciousness in the world today is capitalism which is itself fragmentary. The only totality is fragmentation. There are an infinite number of allegories to choose from. Textual transcendentals and invocations of holism are allegorical and expressive metaphors. The rational, essentialist, positivist and totalising promises are therefore suspect as the ground on which they are based is inevitably tropical.

III. RADICAL POLITICAL CRITIQUE

It is possible to extend and to radicalise these arguments by reference to the work of Michel Foucault. It is important to recognise him as the 'historian of the present' (Foucault in *Telos* 32, summer 1977). With his notion of counter-memory we must not remember the past so much as break it to form a new present. His project is an attempt to assess modern rationality and our cultural predicament. It involves a whole complex of notions, institutions, scientific concepts, judicial-police measures, modalities of knowledge and 'a whole history of the subject of reason' (Foucault in *Telos* 55, spring 1983). 'Discourse' for Foucault is thought as institutional and social practice embedded within an episteme – his word for a paradigm. With no unitary reason and no transcendental subject, he establishes the historical a priori – concerned to show how historically situated our presuppositions are and where fantasy in discourse is a reality in social practice. He moves towards the analytics of power/knowledge relations, cementing it at the level of social practices and within specific discursive and institutional apparatuses. He articulates that which traditional reason excluded: madness, chance, discontinuity and difference.

Foucault's method is threefold, to question our will to truth (his power/knowledge formation), restore to discourse its character as an event (the historical a priori) and reject the sovereignty of the signifier (Foucault 1979a, 66). There is no privileged discourse. No firm foundations for thought. In *This is not a Pipe* (1983) Foucault explores the fundamental gap between language and the world, between signifier and signified, to show that an image (the pipe) cannot at any point connect with the words. Also, words may well obscure as much as they illuminate that which is signified. Though this is a very ethnocentric, if not Francocentric, perspective (consider the Melanesian process), it does give us an insight into his playful, punning and ambiguous humour. He adopts provisional, controversial and highly provocative arguments, discarding the methodological analysis that so many slave over, as methodology, whether structuralist or hermeneutic, does not really concern him.

Though Derrida is deeply implicated in his critique, being 'the most decisive modern representative' of a very traditional system (Foucault 1981, 50) there is yet a strong similarity between Derrida's grammatology and Foucault's power analytics. Both reject the category of totality. Foucault's working of discourse/practice is not part of a totalised theory but operates like a hawk, flying over historical process, and attacking the appropriate topic. Derrida's deconstruction and grammatology is similarly void of any ultimate 'truth' function, and similarly exists in a nomadic homelessness. The most profound difference in their methods is that whereas Foucault is positive in enabling 'the other' to articulate and represent itself, Derrida's strategy operates like a bullet – as purely destructive, functioning to negate and deconstruct 'the other'. (For a detailed comparison of Derrida and Foucault, see Maley in chapter 2 of this volume.)

ARCHAEOLOGY AFTER STRUCTURALISM

After Cartesian rationalism inverted the cosmic order by positioning the human subject as central, it was possible to dispense with the irrational and the mad. Descartes' problem of the rational faculty – knowing the fallibility of sensory perception – was a necessary epistemological exercise, and madness becomes simply an empirical disorder. Foucault identifies this as a very important event, that Cartesian doubt had cast away the danger and the open menace of 'the problematic of madness':

> Madness is placed outside the domain where the subject secures its rights to the truth . . . madness is exiled. If a man can always be mad, Thought, as the sovereign exercise of a subject compelled to perceive the truth, cannot be insane . . . making the familiar Renaissance experience of a rational Unreason impossible.
> (Foucault 1967)

Insanity is thus disqualified from 'serious' discourse. Doubt becomes a point of reference prior to all meaning and reason; a zero point, making a Cartesian philosophical discourse possible.

Foucault enables madness to speak and to be heard. His publication of *I Pierre Rivière, having slaughtered my mother, my sister, and my brother* . . . (1975), a forty-page explanation of his actions by a man who brutally killed his family, written before he was executed; his interest in Antonin Artaud, Nietzsche, Sade and Nerval, constitute his efforts to reactivate madness into the domain from which it had, since Descartes, been excluded. The implications of the earlier discussion on Lewis Carroll and Antonin Artaud demonstrate a revealing double aspect to Foucault's work. The genealogical point is that when viewed from the right angle there is a 'profound visibility to everything'. Depths are not hidden but are intertwined with surfaces. A genealogist unmasks the sham by revealing 'not a timeless essential secret, but the secret that they have no essence or that their essence was fabricated in a piecemeal fashion from alien forms' (Foucault in Rabinow 1985, 78). Foucault recognises the need for voices, especially those considered 'mad', to be heard which have (metaphorically and, who knows, literally) vomited over bourgeois sensibilities and the 'nice' civilised discourse which has excluded them. Thus the double aspect that although Foucault endorses the Carrollean message that the world is not 'a play which masks a truer reality' but that it is as it appears, he does realise the need for another dimension, a dimension which is the most radical of all and which completely evades systematisation to the extent that it may become unintelligible and where it may destroy any values and all values in one foul gesture. This is Foucault's radicalism.

So Foucault reactivates the romantic spiels of a madman as he can be seen to be picking up where Nietzsche left off in *Ecce Homo* (1979), his linking of knowledge and power, his neo-anarchist commentaries on the social order and his romantic, literary, anti-ontological and anti-metaphysical 'genealogies' were directed against the Cartesian heritage of clear and concise formulations. He resisted monolithic systems of interpretation explicating not an analysis but an analytics. Nietzsche denied historical process as it was teleologically understood, traditionally; social history had been and would always be a succession of different forms of domination, without reason; except for the pursuit of a will to power. European reasoning, rationality and science, Nietzsche argued, was just another will to power – only by intellectuals and scientists this time. Will to power was integral to organic life and would never end.

> The faith on which our belief in science rests is still a metaphysical faith . . . The Christian faith, which is also that of Plato, that God is truth and truth divine . . . But what if this equation becomes less and less credible, if the only things that may still be viewed as divine are error, blindness and lies; if [truth] . . . turns out to be our longest lie?
>
> (Nietzsche 1956, 288)

The Foucauldian genealogist undermines ideal significations and original truths. Instead, 'invasions, struggles, plunderings, disguises, ploys' and 'the singularity of events outside of any monotonous finality' are recorded. Subjection, strategies and domination are constantly at work. Foucault's complete reduction to historical a priori marks an important difference to Nietzsche. Whereas Nietzsche identifies morality and social institutions with the tactics of individuals, Foucault identifies strategies without particular strategists. Relations of force work themselves out in a whole 'network of relations, constantly in tension, in activity' (Foucault 1979b, 26). His style sidesteps the theory and method approach providing instead an interpretative analytics of our modern or post-modern situation. Deleuze said that Foucault was a sort of modern map-maker, 'maps made for use not to mirror the terrain':

> It is not to the great model of signs and language that reference should be made but to war and battle. The history which bears and determines us is warlike, not language like. Relations of power not relations of sense . . .
>
> (Foucault 1979a)

Origins are not in question for Foucault. There is no first or single cause or defined essence. We never read 'power is . . .'. He rejects essentialist and reductionist theories, and launches a critique of many established theoretical conceptions of power. Power is not something an individual wields, a judiciary notion, nor is it something that arises from the economic depths and then percolates up through to politics at the 'top' of society, the Marxist notion of base and superstructure. Undefined and without any essence, power runs straight through people. It is everywhere, a force which cannot be pinned down. Conscious also that power is represented catachrestically, Foucault deliberately mixes his metaphors to break the hold of anyone. Power in the Platonic sense is an invention, so he writes of the different 'powers' in different societies at different times.

Discourse does not have any bounded units. It always goes beyond, as all language is figurative. All language is tropic. The discourse of the self is made up of tropes. Language and discourse is never value free. Every action, every statement constitutes a position. It always has an effect in relation to others. With no centre to discourse and no prototype, it is not possible to refer to any final authority. This is Foucault's attack. There is no established signifier, no scripture exists a priori. If there is no script before, society does not (a) exist 'before', or (b) follow a script. Signifiers are attached to already established signifieds, where the signified is the referent. Wittgenstein might persuade us that all there are is signifiers, but this would be wrong because there is always recourse to phenomena.

Nietzsche and Foucault were masters of rhetoric, symbolic of their contempt for Cartesian *clarté*. Foucault exposes the social-scientism of theory and practice as divorced from data, where dry academic and analytic writing preserves for itself an autonomy and sustains the classic function to protect philosophy from its social and historical contingencies. The rational individual as a theoretical starting point is rejected. Madness and reason, as distinct categories, are effaced when he describes the madness of wisdom, the folly of knowledge and science's attempts to impose order and legitimate itself. The rational mind is its ultimate support and, once exposed, claims to truth and knowledge are done away with. The real motives, which are the will to power, to order, to influence and to control, result in a form of textualism (where, in the phrase of Derrida, there is nothing outside of the text), the dialectics of spirit, the hermeneutics of meaning.

The political and philosophical problem for us is not to free the individual from the state but to liberate ourselves from the individualisation institutionalised by the state, and we do this by realising all the different forms and modes of subjectivity.

Foucault brings us to the brink of a radical and overwhelming social and political critique. He warrants comparison to Sartre in many respects, for the unquestionably political doctrine which he explicated. Both disputed the Cartesian concept of the rational subject as the epistemological and ontological ground of reality. Instead Sartre's starting point was experience as the primary reality, where a person is acting in relation to others, not the detached solitary subject implied by the dictum *cogito ergo sum*. When the arbitrary ordering of experience and even the utterly arbitrary nature of the world is realised we know we need some principle of intelligibility. We realise the magnitude of the existentialist predicament through choice and decision, where we realise ourselves as fundamentally free agents, and are thus overwhelmingly burdened with the responsibilities for the consequences of our action. Sartre joined the communists because it was the party of agency; he rejected the Marxist necessity of historical materialism but appropriated the concept of 'praxis' as an existential mode. Though Sartre and Foucault's convictions differed considerably, they shared an ambivalent relationship to traditional Marxism, with the same end result – political radicalism.

CONCLUSION

The social procedures of exclusion and the internal constraint on expression and communication, as the result of insidious relations of dominance, are all part of the hidden agenda in established western discourse. Privileged commentaries and discursive traditions are ordered and control what is and what is not said – the violence of silence. The historical exclusion of children, women and the mad from social discourse is a subtle and insidious form of violence (Foucault 1981). The masters of violence are traditionally seen as the holders of power. This means that other forms of violence, control and domination are easily overlooked. Our ever-changing essentialism of labelling what is violent means that we are always discovering and pointing the finger at external manifestations of power and violence. Isolation of the human violence to animals; to the natural world; or to one another, usually means seeing it everywhere except in the sacred area of reason itself (Laing and Cooper 1974). There is in fact always some small amount of hidden essentialism in our theoretical predilections that denies the ubiquity of violence and power.

Rigid dichotomies drive the category of violence into well-worn ruts of the individual versus society, nature versus culture. The same difficulty is integral to questions of power and agency. Having a dichotomy of ideas and things, we demand empirical validation to give substance to an idea, so power is comprehended as it is instantiated and dramatised through force and violence. Material metaphors and tropes are invoked to represent it and essentialise it. So we are always defining it in terms of something else, that which it isn't. Thus we are back again to the crisis in representation.

Essentialism creates, then, an impossible task for itself. We cannot establish the exact causes and necessary conditions of human action. Clear-cut distinctions of intentional and unintentional, and teleological and probabilistic are epistemological assertions based on the supposition of a knowing, reasoning and conscious mind. This constitutes an enormously important political fact, once only relevant to the west, but now relevant to the whole world because of the very forced universalisation of our arbitrary epistemology – our ethnocentric imaginings of concentricity instead, in fact, of our eccentricity. The political implication is that the agent becomes answerable, and responsible, and is subject to inspection and control. Psychiatrists, teachers and the law, by right, can intervene.

The violence of internal domination of Cartesian reason over emotion, mind over body and Freudian super-ego/ego over id, of animus over anima, legitimates the external and institutional exercise of power and violence, for example of men over women, adults over children, the sane over the mad. This is the cement in the architecture of patriarchy and capitalism. Wilhelm Reich has exposed these dimensions in their most extreme form – as they appeared in Hitler's Germany. Once framed in legalistic and bureaucratic language, the judgemental enquiry into inner states is permitted. It becomes evident that established discourses which essentialise and individualise – so that the rational mind guided by 'a clear and distinct idea' (Descartes, *passim*), and the rational mind as the knowing and controlling agent of action – have got very deep social and political implications for the world.

The doctrine of individualism in the west leads to destruction and violence. 'I'm all right Jack!' is the entirely serious title of the problem. Louis Dumont (1980, 1987) claims that egalitarianism, from individualism, contains an ingrained and unacknowledged racism. Evil and violence are externalised, as we have seen, and conceptually unencompassable. The isolation and systematic exclusion of the anti-social aspects of humanity in the west, the sick, the insane and the criminal, constitutes a violence which is integral to our very epistemological foundations. Established western theoretical axioms have had profoundly regrettable consequences.

Theoretical overhaul leads to positive political action: taking a position. Decision dispels ambivalence. You have to stir the shit and come out smelling of it. Those who do not smell stink of a bourgeois morality, keeping well at a distance. An unacceptable individualism. This is the doctrine of engagement; the politics of action. After Foucault the grounds of the debate become political *not* relative; which means neither 'letting a thousand flowers bloom' nor giving everything an equally valid status. It becomes a question of arguing for and against what you believe in. Middle of the road liberalism is where you get knocked down by the radicals. In an interview recently, Andrei Tarkovsky said with passion: ' "Don't be neutral in your judgements. Not ever." Then he smiled' (Tarkovsky 1989). The war against western bourgeois 'neutrality' has been activated with manifold Nietzschean fervour; we only have to live up to it.

My concluding thesis is an intuitive recognition of the metaphorical and non-rational basis of thought and action. We need a political philosophy of active radicality based upon an assumption of irrationalism, a realisation of the influencing force of myth, and the power of projective impressions over critical judgement. Only an anti-rationalist analytics can reveal why exact scientific reasoning does not deserve any epistemological primacy. This is obvious when we realise that there is no theoretical Archimedean point from which analysis can commence, as all our categories of analysis inescapably partake of the social reality they seek to depict. We assume in our society that we do not have mythological thought, but our myths are, in fact, science and objectivity. With the hegemonic categories of ontology, epistemology and metaphysics destroyed, we can integrate what is known into the structure of knowing and dissolve the categories of subject, object and language so that they become concepts, or even better, senses, understood as constituting one another. We need a recognition that political and power components are integral to the dialectics of being and knowing; a realisation of the politics of truth. Theoretical potency comes from encompassing the contrary and moving on. This is why it is necessary to encompass the full fragmentary consequences of the post-modern syntagm, appropriating the concept of the analogue, as opposed to the homologue, which is *an agreement or correspondence between things otherwise different*. Only *then* can we move on to the story of 'Homo Analogicus'.

NOTES

1. Post-structuralists.
2. Post-modern theorists.
3. A 'normal' person's response.
4. Our inescapable predicament.
5. See the argument in the opening sections of the paper that the 'death of God' can be traced back to Descartes, a Nietzschean dictum applied to 'the author' and also extended to 'the subject'.
6. The death of man is the ultimate consequence of Lévi-Strauss's structuralism: his own insight.

REFERENCES

Bakhtin, M. and Medvedev, P. M. (1928) *The Formal Method in Literary Scholarship*, trans. A. J. Wehrle, Baltimore: Johns Hopkins University Press.
Barthes, R. (1977) *Image-Music-Text*, trans. S. Heath, London: Fontana.
Barthes, R. (1979) *L'Empire des Signs*, trans. Noel Burch as *To the Distant Observer*, London: Scolar Press.
Bateson, G. (1953) *Naven: the Culture of the Iatmul People*, Stanford: Stanford University Press.
Baudrillard, J. (1987) *L'Autre par lui-meme*, Paris: Gallimard.
Bourdieu, P. (1977) *Outline of a Theory of Practice*, Cambridge: Cambridge University Press.

Carroll, L. (1970) *The Annotated Alice*, London: Longman.
Carter, A. (1985) *Nights at the Circus*, London: Picador.
Clifford, J. (1988) *The Predicament of Culture: Twentieth Century Ethnography, Literature and Art*, Cambridge, Mass.: Harvard University Press.
Clifford, J. and Marcus, G. (1986) *Writing Culture: The Poetics and Politics of Ethnography*, London: University of California Press.
Crapanzo, V. (1986) *Waiting: the Whites of South Africa*, London: Paladin.
Deleuze, G. (1979) 'The schizophrenic in language: surface and depth', in J. Harari (ed.) *Textual Strategies*, London: Methuen.
Dumont, L. (1980) *Homo Hierarchicus*, Chicago: Chicago University Press.
Dumont, L. (1987) *Essays on Individualism*, London: Chicago University Press.
Foucault, M. (1967) *Madness and Civilisation*, London: Tavistock.
Foucault, M. (1972) *The Archaeology of Knowledge*, London: Tavistock.
Foucault, M. (1975) *I, Pierre Rivière, Having Slaughtered My Mother, My Sister, My Brother . . .*, New York: Random House.
Foucault, M. (1977) *Language, Counter-Memory, Practice*, New York: Cornell University Press.
Foucault, M. (1979a) 'The order of discourse', in R. Young (ed.) *Untying the Text*, London: Routledge & Kegan Paul.
Foucault, M. (1979b) *Discipline and Punish*, London: Peregrine.
Foucault, M. (1980) *Power/Knowledge*, ed. C. Gordon, New York: Random House.
Foucault, M. (1981) *The History of Sexuality*, London: Penguin.
Foucault, M. (1983) *This Is Not a Pipe*, Berkeley: University of California Press.
Freeman, D. (1983) *Margaret Mead in Samoa*, Cambridge, Mass.: Harvard University Press.
Habermas, J. (1985) 'Modernity, an incomplete project', in H. Foster (ed.) *Postmodern Culture*, London: Pluto.
Jameson, F. (1984) 'Postmodernism or the logic of late capitalism', *New Left Review* 146.
Laing, R. D. and Cooper, D. G. (1971) *Reason and Violence*, London: Tavistock.
Laing, R. D. and Cooper, D. (1974) *Reason and Violence*, London: Tavistock.
Lakoff, G. and Johnson, M. (1980) *Metaphors We Live By*, Chicago: Chicago University Press.
Mauss, M. (1954) *The Gift*, London: Cohen & West.
Miller, D. (1987) *Material Culture and Mass Consumption*, Oxford: Blackwell.
Munn, N. (1978) *Walbiri Iconography*, Ithaca: Cornell University Press.
Munn, N. (1980) 'The transformation of subjects into objects . . .', in R. Berndt (ed.) *Australian Aboriginal Anthropology*, Nedlands: University of Western Australia Press.
Nietzsche, F. (1956) *The Birth of Tragedy and The Genealogy of Morals*, trans. F. Golffing, New York: Doubleday.
Nietzsche, F. (1979) *Ecce Homo*, London: Penguin.
Rabinow, P. (1977) *Reflections on Fieldwork in Morocco*, Berkeley: University of California Press.
Rabinow, P. (1985) *The Foucault Reader*, London: Peregrine.
Rebel, H. (1988) 'Cultural hegemony and class experience', Unpublished.
Ricoeur, P. (1979) *Paul Ricoeur: Hermeneutics and the Human Sciences*, ed. J. Thompson, Cambridge: Cambridge University Press.
Said, E. (1979) *Orientalism*, London: Routledge.
Salmond, A. (1982) 'Theoretical landscapes', in D. Parkin (ed.) *Semantic*

Anthropology, ASA Monographs, London: Academic Press.
Swift, J. (1970) *Gulliver's Travels*, New York: Norton.
Tarkovsky, A. (1989) 'Untameable Tarkovsky', *The Guardian*, 20 April.
Tyler, S. (1986) 'Postmodern ethnography . . .', in J. Clifford and G. Marcus (eds) *Writing Culture*, London: University of California Press.
Voltaire (1947) *Candide*, London: Penguin.
Wiener, A. (1983) 'From words to objects to magic', *Man* 18(4).

CHAPTER 2

Of all the post-structuralists that figure in this volume, it is Michel Foucault who is probably the most familiar, since his work, more particularly 'historical' than that of more 'structuralist' post-structuralists like Derrida and Lacan, has already had at least a passing impact in post-processual archaeology. His appeal is understandable since he is concerned with understanding the processes of change and with exploding the orthodox limits of historicity, where other critics' readings are more temporally and textually located, and so less immediately applicable within a discipline whose rationale has always been the claim to study the long-term dynamics and development of societies.

And yet there is a danger here of juxtaposing critical work without realising the radical potential offered by a fusion of ideas, the danger that deconstruction will not be appreciated by an audience to whom not only Derrida's objects but also the style of his work remain a barrier resisting understanding or appreciation. Deconstruction has more to offer an 'archaeology' (both ours and Foucault's) than is recognised in Foucault's impassioned opposition to its textual precision and rhetorical indulgences. In this paper, Maley examines the integrity of the historical methodology of Foucault and Derrida, and finds the latter to be more meticulous in his questioning of historical objects. Usually, Derrida's critique of *Madness and Civilization* is disarmed to the extent that it can always be objected that Foucault would later abandon the project of 'archaeology' himself. But in fact, for Maley, the same question must be asked of some of the finest pieces of his later work, the 'genealogies' of power, such as *The History of Sexuality*.

The point is less, perhaps, that one should prefer one critic or body of thought/method over another, than that we should attempt an integration of the two – which is by no means precluded by some essential incompatibility. What is necessary is that deconstruction is seen to take a place in the development of a critical archaeology in which, finely tuned as it is to revealing the margins, points, and lines of force that are of central significance, offers us one of the richest and most promising range of ideas and techniques.

2

Undermining Archaeology: From Reconstruction to Deconstruction

Willy Maley

What does post-structuralism have to offer archaeology? Will it merely provide the subject with a new set of pedagogical practices designed to confer upon it the apparent status of a rigorous science at a time when official education policy discriminates against the non-technical? Or, rather, will the absorption of post-structuralist thought into the mainstream of archaeological inquiry result in a much deeper transformation of the discipline than was ever effected by either Marxism or structuralism?[1] The present discussion around the textuality of history and the historicity of texts has important interdisciplinary implications outside of the established terrain of literature and history. By raising questions of language, truth, objectivity and knowledge, this controversy over the place of history – archaic, integral, monumental – in the reading of literature – traditionally essential, idealistic, original – situates itself at the intersection of the human sciences, providing access to different disciplines, including archaeology.[2]

In this paper it will be suggested that two of the most influential strands in current French critical theory – Foucauldian discourse analysis and Derridean deconstruction – are not easily assimilated into traditional systems of thought as mere ancillary rhetorical strategies. In particular, it will be argued that deconstruction is not just another theoretical support, one more 'find' on the site of intellectual remains to which archaeologists are invariably forced to resort in order to improve upon the discourse of discovery which the institution continues to demand of their profession. Deconstruction, on the contrary, undermines the very foundations of archaeology, and it does so through a sustained critique of history which constantly threatens to disrupt those comfortable notions of origin and identity which sustain traditional representations of the past.

This paper is divided into three parts. The first section will outline briefly the most significant features of the public dispute between Derrida and Foucault over the question of archaeology as history. In his response to Foucault's efforts to write an archaeology of the human sciences, advanced initially in the form of a review of *Madness and Civilization*,

Derrida elaborates his own position, or, to be more precise, positions, on archaeology, history, and the obsessive search for beginnings (Derrida 1978). His reservations concerning the archaeological enterprise *per se* call for serious consideration by all those labouring in the field who desire a more rigid theoretical framework to present their findings than has hitherto been available.

The next segment offers, through a reading of the *History of Sexuality*, a critique of Foucault's historiographical approach which seems to vindicate Derrida's reservations concerning *Madness and Civilization*. By focusing on the fraught issue of paedophilia it is possible to show that Foucault's panoptic view of history is fundamentally flawed, leading itself as it does to a totalising and ultimately repressive urge. The final portion of the essay is devoted to a reconstitution of the recent debate on apartheid between Derrida and two doctoral students from the University of Columbia. Here Derrida is seen to employ a concept of *arche-writing* which, it will be argued, is far less inclined to closure than Foucault's discursive practice. The conclusion suggests ways in which discourse analysis and deconstruction as *ways of reading*, impinge upon the archaeological interpretation of the surviving material evidence of the human past.

ARCHIE'S EULOGY

Whatever one might think of the theoretical positions of Michel Foucault there is no doubt that it is he, and not Jacques Derrida, who has actually done some history rather than just talk about it.
(Eagleton 1988, 110)

In the preface to *Daybreak*, Nietzsche styles himself 'a subterranean . . . one who tunnels and mines and undermines'. He goes on to describe himself, in his capacity as a philologist, as a 'teacher of slow reading' (Nietzsche 1982, 5). The renaissance in Nietzschean thought which has materialised in the main through his adoption by radical French philosophy in the post-war period brings together these two processes. The result is a subversive reading strategy which questions the fundamental tenets of western culture. From the early, innovative writings of Georges Bataille to the most recent provocative rereading undertaken by Gilles Deleuze and beyond, the place of Nietzsche in contemporary thought is assured. The 'beyond' referred to here must surely evoke the names of the two most eminent French thinkers of the post-modern era, Jacques Derrida and Michel Foucault.[3]

The Nietzschean aspect of their thought has caused Derrida and Foucault to be lumped together in Anglo-American surveys of post-structuralism, as though the existence of a common source of inspiration was sufficient proof of a common project or methodology. Yet Nietzsche is only one, albeit the most recurrent, source of continental post-structuralism, and the difference between Derrida and Foucault cannot be reduced to divergent readings of his contradictory and heterogeneous texts. Post-structuralism is not the critical monolith some opponents view it as.[4] One exceptional instance of their differences occurs in Derrida's reading of Foucault's first major work, *Madness and Civilization* (Foucault 1967), published two years after the latter book under the heading 'Cogito and the History of Madness' (Derrida 1978).[5] Derrida's principal objection to Foucault's reconstructive 'archaeology of silence', that is, a history of the exclusion, since Descartes, of the speech of madness from the discourse of reason, was that it reproduced the repressive hypothesis it set out to undermine, an hypothesis which Derrida felt was itself mistaken:

> Is not an archaeology, even of silence, a logic, that is, an organised language, a project, an order, a sentence, a syntax, a work? . . . A history, that is, an archaeology against reason doubtless cannot be written, for, despite all appearances to the contrary, the concept of history has always been a rational one. It is the meaning of 'history' or *archia* that should have been questioned first, perhaps, a writing that exceeds, by questioning them, the values 'origin', 'reason' and 'history' could not be contained within the metaphysical closure of an archaeology.
>
> (Derrida 1978, 35–6)[6]

Thus Derrida indicates that the Foucauldian idea of reconstructing madness as the other of reason calls upon reason for that very act of reconstruction. Instead, Derrida proposes – and he generously acknowledges Foucault's own allusions in this direction – that the history of madness, coincidental as it is with the madness of history, might be used to deconstruct the notion of historicity. This corrective to Foucault's project is commensurate with Derrida's continuing work on the textuality of history.

Foucault's response to Derrida's criticisms was as contemptuous as it was unequivocal. In the concluding paragraph of an uncompromising essay, first printed as an appendix to the English translation of *Madness and Civilization*, in which he repeated his original claim that Descartes excluded madness from his discussion of the Cogito, Foucault savaged Derrida with what one critic has described as inordinate 'virulence' (Spivak 1976, lxi). This closing statement has been quoted in full elsewhere but it nonetheless deserves to be reproduced here as an indication of the profound anxiety felt by Foucault in the face of Derrida's deconstructive strategy:

> Today Derrida is the most decisive representative of the [Classical] system in its final brilliance; the reduction of discursive practice to textual traces; the elision of the events that are produced there in order to retain nothing but marks for a reading; the invention of voices behind texts in order not to have to analyse the modes of implication of the subject in discourse; assigning the spoken and the unspoken in the text to an originary place in order not to have to reinstate the discursive practices in the field of transformations where they are effected.
>
> I do not say that it is a metaphysics, metaphysics itself or its closure, which is hidden in this 'textualisation' of discursive practice. I shall go much further: I shall say that it is a trifling, historically well-determined pedagogy which very visibly reveals itself.
>
> (Harari 1979, 41)[7]

Note here the way in which Foucault opposes 'discursive practice' to 'textual traces', as though the latter were easily assimilated into the former, as though it were simply a matter of 'reduction'. As we shall see, the Derridean concept of the text and its stratagems – trace, supplement, pharmakon – cannot be reduced to language or writing as such. For now it is sufficient to record Foucault's charge against Derrida concerning what he calls 'the elision of events . . . in order to retain nothing but marks for a reading'. It is time to turn our attention to one example of just such an elision on the part of Foucault himself.

FOUCAULT AND THE OVERSIGHTS OF ARCHAEOLOGY

It is not easy to classify the writings of Michel Foucault. He was a polymath who waged war incessantly against every piece of academic orthodoxy which came his way. Whether carefully charting the emergence of an all-too-easily recognisable category of human behaviour such as madness or sexuality, meticulously mapping out the development of specific intellectual fields such as political economy or natural science, or laboriously tracing the genesis and contours of established institutions like the prison and the clinic, Foucault was always displacing the commonplace, overturning assumptions, upsetting conventions.

A celebrated scholar, he was frequently photographed hunched over a desk littered with yellowing manuscripts. His reputation for producing detailed historical analyses from a diverse range of literary materials earned him the respect of writers in a wide variety of disciplines. His almost obsessive eye for detail, his familiarity with a vast array of archival evidence, his breathtakingly intimate knowledge of facts, all served to justify the rather grand title conferred upon him at the Collège de France in Paris in 1970, when he assumed the chair in 'The History of Systems of Thought'. The number of texts devoted to discussions of his work since his untimely death in 1984 is ample testimony of his immense contribution to what might broadly be termed 'cultural studies'. He has been called, among other things, an archaeologist of western culture.

If the foregoing verges on the eulogistic, its intention is to prepare for the criticisms which follow. The focus here will be upon a remarkable passage in Volume One of the *History of Sexuality* (Foucault 1979), one of his most mature works, which seems to me to highlight the dangers inherent in any project as ambitious as that undertaken by Foucault, namely, the tendency to totalise. Having introduced the critique of 'the repressive hypothesis' by way of a discussion of the 'incitement to discourse', singling out the anonymous Victorian autobiography *My Secret Life* as the exemplary text in the genre of confessional sexuality, Foucault proceeds to recount an historical event which unfolded in France at a time roughly contemporary with that book's composition:

> One day in 1867, a farm hand from the village of Lapcourt, who was somewhat simple-minded, employed here then there, depending on the season, living hand-to-mouth from a little charity or in exchange for the worst kind of labour, sleeping in barns and stables, was turned in to the authorities. At the border of a field, he had obtained a few caresses from a little girl, just as he had done before and seen done by the village urchins round about him; for, at the edge of the wood, or in the ditch by the road leading to Saint-Nicolas, they would play the familiar game called 'curdled milk'. So he was pointed out by the girl's parents to the mayor of the village, reported by the mayor to the gendarmes, led by the gendarmes to the judge, who indicted him and turned him over first to a doctor, then to two other experts who not only wrote their report but also had it published. What is the significant thing about this story? The pettiness of it all; the fact that this everyday occurrence in the life of village sexuality, these inconsequential bucolic pleasures, could become, from a certain time, the object not only of collective intolerance but of a judicial action, a medical intervention, a careful clinical examination, and an entire theoretical elaboration. The thing to note is that they went so far as to measure the brainpan, study the facial bone structure, and inspect for possible signs of degenerescence the anatomy of this personage who up to that moment had been an integral part of village life; that they made him talk; that they questioned him concerning his thoughts, inclinations, habits, sensations, and opinions. And then, acquitting him of any crime, they decided finally to make him into a pure object of medicine and knowledge – an object to be shut away till the end of

his life in the hospital at Mareville, but also one to be made known to the world of learning through a detailed analysis. One can be fairly certain that during this same period the Lapcourt schoolmaster was instructing the little villagers to mind their language and not to talk about all these things aloud. But this was undoubtedly one of the conditions enabling the institutions of power to overlay this everyday bit of theatre with their solemn discourse. So it was that our society – and it was doubtless the first in history to take such measures – assembled around these timeless gestures, these barely furtive pleasures between simple-minded adults and alert children, a whole machinery for speechifying, analysing, and investigating.

Between the licentious Englishman, who earnestly recorded for his own purposes the singular episodes of his secret life, and his contemporary, this village half-wit who would give a few pennies to the little girls for the favours the older ones refused him, there was without doubt a profound connection: in any case, from one extreme to the other, sex became something to say, and to say exhaustively in accordance with the deployments that were varied, but all, in their own way compelling. Whether in the form of a subtle confession in confidence or an authoritarian interrogation, sex – be it refined or rustic – had to be put into words. A great polymorphous injunction bound the Englishman and the poor Lorrainese peasant alike. As history would have it, the latter was named Jouy.

(Foucault 1979, 31–2)

Foucault's famous penchant for the minutiae of social intercourse, his passionate feel for facts, and his inordinate ability to tease out of an apparently unproblematic sequence of events or utterances the lineaments of a profound discontinuity, all these aspects of his methodology are clear here. But there is something missing. It will soon become obvious that Foucault reproduces the faults he so eloquently castigates 'the system' for committing. He acts as a Panopticon, casting a Cyclopean eye over only one side of an incredibly complex social narrative. Setting on the familiar theme of the individual versus the bureaucracy, he champions one participant. In so doing, he excludes from analysis matters which may appear at first sight marginal, tangential, incidental to the main thesis, but which, on closer examination, reveal themselves to be absolutely central to the work in hand (Foucault 1977a, 195).[8]

As a reconstruction of the past, this analysis is found wanting in a number of crucial respects. There is room here to draw attention only to the most glaring oversights. My initial point addresses Foucault's representations of Jouy's consciousness, intelligence, or presence of mind. The thing to note is that Foucault casually refers to Jouy in his opening sentence as 'somewhat simple-minded'. He goes on to repeat this charge when he alludes to the 'barely furtive pleasures of simple-minded adults and alert children'. In the concluding paragraph of his analysis he describes the same individual as 'a village half-wit'. All of this sits rather awkwardly beside the eloquent barrage directed against those members of the medical profession brought in by the judge to examine Jouy. We are told 'that they went so far as to measure the brainpan, study the facial bone structure, and inspect for possible signs of degenerescence the anatomy of this personage who up to that moment had been an integral part of village life'. Yet, despite the cultivated tone of indignation, Foucault himself was able to come to the same conclusion as the experts he so articulately denounces. The disturbing equation which Foucault appears to formulate presumes an identity between manual labour and intellectual deficiency, an assumption founded not upon medical examination but, worryingly, upon an unselfconscious social prejudice.

My second point involves the question of labour and political economy. The Jouy of the closing paragraph, 'this person who up to that moment had been an integral part of village life', is a very different person from the Jouy of the opening paragraph. We recall that this earlier Jouy was 'employed here then there, depending on the season, living hand-to-mouth from a little charity in return for the worst sort of labour, sleeping in barns and stables'. What kind of integrity is being talked about here? What authorities would remove from the community a personage who was an integral part of the community? Was not the very fact that Jouy, as a victim of the socio-economic changes then ravaging the French countryside, was no longer an indispensable element in the production process one which encouraged the local authorities in their moves to investigate, interrogate, and, ultimately, incarcerate this 'integral part of village life'? Is there anything 'timeless' or 'eternal' about the preponderance of surplus labour in Bonapartist France? Foucault's version of events is curiously at odds with other comments he has made, after Marx, concerning the preponderance of (relative) surplus labour in nineteenth-century France (Foucault 1977a, 221). Here he is more interested in defending the old order of things than in condemning the new. What gets left out of this account altogether is the way in which the emergence of a whole series of professions and institutions of order coincided with the creation of a mass of unwanted labour. Jouy's withdrawal from society is as much about responses to the perceived threat of social disorder from masterless men as it is about control of (male) sexuality.

My third point concerns one character in Foucault's critical narrative who receives scant attention during the course of his subtle and searching analysis – the little girl with whom Jouy plays the 'familiar game called "curdled milk" '. It is significant that Foucault chooses to retain this euphemistic term for what actually happened between Jouy and the little girl. Perhaps the reader's sympathy for the male victim of Foucault's account – and it is obvious throughout that it is Jouy that we are being asked to identify with, his plight we are meant to deplore – would have modified had other expressions such as 'masturbation', 'interference', or 'paedophilia' been used. Foucault's negative thesis on the Enlightenment – broadly, he argues that new and sophisticated forms of oppression went hand-in-hand with putative liberalisation – has been the subject of adverse reviews from the bourgeois liberal tradition in Anglo-American historiography (Stone 1987, 270–4; 283–94). In my judgement there is much to be said for the scepticism expounded by Foucault, and his pessimistic view of history is borne out by recent work on child abuse in nineteenth-century England, which suggests that state intervention on the part of maltreated children was fuelled almost entirely by fear of delinquent disorder rather than any genuine feelings for the young person at risk.[9] Foucault refuses to extend his critique of the Jouy case to an indictment of official hypocrisy, electing to dismiss the little girl rather than question the motives of her guardians, and in doing so he undercuts the radicalism of his arguments, being as myopically authoritarian as those whom he purports to despise.

The act of interference itself is introduced in a carefully staged manner. Indeed, Jouy is exonerated almost immediately on the grounds that his actions were a dumb imitation of those of 'the village urchins around him'. We learn first that 'he had obtained a few caresses'. Later, we are informed that he did so in exchange for a 'few pennies', and that he was compelled to resort to this activity with 'little girls' due to the fact that these were 'favours the older ones refused him'. In order to emphasise the mental incapacitation of Jouy, Foucault contrasts 'simple-minded adults' with 'alert children'. At least one of them was alert enough to distinguish a childish game with a childish name from abuse by an adult.

What is significant about this story is not the pettiness of it all but rather its significance. The tragedy of agrarian unemployment and its concomitant, rural poverty, is here compounded by the indefensible practice of child abuse. In his efforts to protect Jouy from the bureaucratic authorities he so despises, Foucault is forced to defend the reprehensible actions of one unfortunate individual against the interests of another, largely ignored victim of the events in question. Foucault elides the actual historical conditions which gave rise to Jouy's presence in a community of which he was far from being an integral part. Foucault is guilty in this instance of 'encyclopaedophilia', of a totalitarian, completely one-sided, all-encompassing approach to a cultural problem of exceptional density. In looking over the evidence with such a panoptic eye, he overlooks key aspects of the socio-historical context. In defending Jouy's honour, he puts one individual before another. His passionate critique of the Panopticon devised by Jeremy Bentham for the surveillance of prisoners in early nineteenth-century England is undermined by the fact that this Cyclopean instrument appears to be his own chosen mode of observation in recounting the Jouy case, giving rise in the end to a stultifying cellular perspective.

Foucault is renowned as an eloquent spokesman for the deviant against the dominant, but in his partisan report upon the Jouy incident his propensity for berating the system overcomes any concern for dialectics or dialogism. The politics of Foucauldian discourse analysis are here seen to falter clumsily before questions of class and gender. Foucault's reading of the text on Jouy is clearly weighted in favour of male pleasure and activity as against female passivity, receptivity, complicity, acquiescence, and, as is implied in the allusion to 'alert children', deviousness.

In spotlighting Foucault's chauvinism and a-historicism in this particular passage, I am not simply suggesting an oversight, or blind spot on his part. Rather, I am arguing that the very nature of Foucault's project – archaeological, genealogical, historical – is such that he must inevitably succumb to the chauvinism of universalism and the politics of individualism. This sidelight on Foucauldian discourse theory brings into sharp focus the shortcomings of an approach which is, on the one hand, systematising, and, on the other, reductive. To contend that this one example of misreading throws into doubt the whole critical enterprise of Foucault might seem an extreme position to assume, but it agrees with Foucault's own insistence upon the tangential case as one which reveals features of the central condition. In grappling with Marxism, Foucault urges us to view the labour camps of the Gulag Archipelago not as an aberration, but as an indictment of that system of thought which effectively brought them into being:

> Like all political technologies, the Gulag institution has its history, its transformations and transpositions, its functions and effects. The internment practised in the Classical age forms in all likelihood a part of its archaeology. The Gulag question, on the other hand, involves a political choice. There are those who pose it and those who don't.
>
> (Foucault 1980, 135)

Foucault poses it, and for him doing so means, among other things:

> Refusing to question the Gulag on the basis of the texts of Marx or Lenin or to ask oneself how, through what error, deviation, misunderstanding or distortion of speculation or practice, their theory could have been betrayed to such a degree. On the contrary, it means questioning all those theoretical texts, however old, from the standpoint of the reality of the Gulag.
>
> (Foucault 1980, 135–6)

UNDERMINING ARCHAEOLOGY

Thus the Gulag question seems to undermine Marxist political theory by allegedly exposing its totalitarian tendencies. Marx and Lenin themselves would have approved of Foucault's logic, since they considered colonialism to be the most obvious starting point for a critique of capitalism on the grounds that it was at the so-called periphery of the system of capitalist production that its inherent contradictions were most apparent. The pattern of revolutions in the twentieth century and the accompanying shifts in the balance of global power bears witness to the accuracy of this theory of marginal perturbations unsettling an entire social system.

Foucault, far from undermining Marxist theories of the state and revolution is endorsing them when he calls for the Gulag to be taken as a barometer of the political climate in order to suggest the inclemency of Marxism–Leninism. In a similar fashion, the question of the little girl in what for Foucault is essentially Jouy's story, reveals the extent to which his own system of thought is susceptible to a total eclipse of the other. He focuses upon Jouy as the sole victim of historical circumstances in the episode recorded above – and even on this question of history, Foucault's supposed forte, there are, as I have indicated, glaring omissions – suggesting that the archaeology of knowledge can become an archaeology of ignorance. Foucault's history is gendered, and this fact must place a question mark against those male critics who have so sheepishly adopted his insights without pausing to consider his oversights.

A materialist 'history of bodies' such as Foucault intends in the *History of Sexuality*, is an incomplete project if it concerns itself exclusively with male bodies at the expense of female ones. It is ironic that Foucault's history of sexuality, unlike the history of madness, questions the repressive hypothesis traditionally mooted by radical philosophers, preferring instead to suggest that sexuality is forced to speak its own name rather than being buried in some archaic silence. If in that earlier work Foucault was preoccupied with the representation of repression, he is turning in his later work towards expression as a mode of repression. This new approach has more in common with psychoanalysis than with history, and brings Foucault – and it is precisely here that the irony resides – in line with Derrida, contrary to his previous antipathy.

From the opening of Foucault's 'history', with its retention of the juvenile expression 'curdled milk', to the incredibly bad taste of the joke about Jouy's name at its climax we are at one and the same time subjected to an elegant denunciation of the French municipal authorities in the latter part of the nineteenth century and a male chauvinist vindication of paedophilia.[10] It is when Foucault indulges in the dangerous practice of naming and gaming that he is most vulnerable to criticism. Conversely, the next advocate of close reading, Jacques Derrida, is at his best when taking apart, with the aid of what can appear to the casual observer as mere wordplay, the culturally constructed names and games which govern the social text. It is to Derrida and his special brand of reading that we now turn.

DERRIDA AND THE RACE AGAINST TIME

Foucault is not the only post-structuralist thinker to echo Marx in suggesting that the marginal, fringe case is one which might reasonably offer insights into the structure or system itself. The limits of any system are often best understood with reference to the limits themselves. Derridean deconstruction invariably occupies itself with what in mainstream philosophy or literary theory might be regarded as non-canonical texts and incidental topics. If traditionally tangential matters preoccupy Derrida as much as they do Foucault, it is because 'these always constitute the most certain and most decisive indices wherever essential conditions are to be grasped' (Derrida 1977, 209).[11]

I now want to consider the work of Derrida through a discussion which arose through the publication of a short text which he was asked to produce in support of an exhibition assembled by The Association of Artists of the World Against Apartheid, in Paris in November 1983. The text, entitled 'Racism's Last Word', was first published in the theoretical journal *Critical Inquiry* in 1985, then reproduced the following year as part of a special edition of the same periodical on the subject of race and its representations (Derrida 1986a). This time it was printed alongside a scathing attack on Derrida by two graduate students at Columbia University, Ann McClintock and Rob Nixon, who reproached Derrida for being unduly concerned with the word *apartheid* and ignoring the historical context in which it was applied, or, as they argued, in which it was no longer applied. Their sustained polemic against Derrida, published as 'No Names Apart: The Separation of Word and History in Derrida's "Le Dernier Mot du Racisme" ', deployed an army of facts and footnotes to suggest that Derrida's text, with its call for action against apartheid, was simplistic in the extreme because 'until one embeds the analysis of racial policy in the dense everyday life of South Africa such calls to action will remain of limited strategic worth' (McClintock and Nixon 1986).

Derrida's response, which appeared in the same issue of *Critical Inquiry*, constitutes an extremely lucid statement of deconstructive criticism (Derrida 1986b). Beginning with a reminder of the precise context in which his original missive was composed and presented, a context which rendered it part of a genre other than the critical essay, Derrida proceeds, with delicious irony, to prove himself the better historian by illustrating the way in which his critics deliberately misread him in order to reconstruct his own arguments into a critique. Written in the form of an 'open letter' addressed specifically to his young detractors, Derrida's second text on the subject of apartheid saw him present his arguments in a much more concrete and coherent fashion than was possible in the original document for the exhibition, where constraints of length and language prompted a condensed and synoptic format.

The most significant aspect of this rejoinder was the way in which Derrida felt compelled to mix his customary theoretical abstractions with a smattering of cathartic reproof. For example, his oft-misquoted statement that 'there is nothing beyond the text' (*il n'y a pas de hors-texte*) is quoted against him in the opening paragraph of 'No Names Apart'. This elicits a yelp of protest. The phrase was originally used by Derrida in a chapter on Rousseau's *Of Grammatology* entitled '. . . That Dangerous Supplement . . .', where it serves to undermine the myth of natural presence thrown into doubt within and outside Rousseau's writings. The logic of the supplement is not confined to the boundaries of the book, then, but runs right through the social text (Derrida 1976, 158–9).

The perverse and persistent misreadings of his own formulation, which allow his critics to distort the thoroughly materialist history Derrida himself has been arguing for through text after text, forces him to elaborate upon this statement, providing us in the process with the nearest thing to a manifesto of deconstruction we have:

> *text*, as I have used the word, is not the book. No more than writing or trace, it is not limited to the *paper* which you cover with your graphism. It is precisely for strategic reasons that I found it necessary to recast the concept of text by generalising it almost without limit, in any case without present or perceptible limit, without any limit that *is*. That's why there is nothing 'beyond the text'. That's why the text is always a field of forces: heterogeneous, differential, open, and so on. That's why deconstructive readings and writings are concerned not only with library books, with discourses, with conceptual and semantic contents. They are not simply analyses of discourses such as, for example, the one you propose. They are effective or active interventions, in particular political and institutional interventions that transform contexts without limiting themselves to theoretical or constative utterances even though they must also produce such utterances. That's why I do not go '*beyond*' the text', in this *new* sense of fighting the word text, by fighting and calling for a fight against *apartheid*.
>
> (Derrida 1986b, 366–7)

Derrida's critics would wish him to restrict himself to readings of texts in the narrow sense, to philosophical and literary texts, leaving the political text to 'activists', like themselves. But there is nothing beyond the political text, no sanctuary, no ivory tower from which the social scene can be safely surveyed.

In what is much more more than a compelling rhetorical flourish, Derrida suggests that those who argue for such a distinction or division between academia and politics are deeply implicated in the politics of *apartheid*:

> In short, you are for the division of labour and the disciplined respect of disciplines. Each must stick to his role and stay within the field of his competence, none may transgress the limits of his territory. Oh, you wouldn't go so far as to wish that some sort of *apartheid* remain or become the law of the land in the academy. Besides, you obviously don't like this word. You are among those who don't like this word and do not want it to remain the 'unique apellation'. No, in the homelands of academic culture or of 'political action', you favour instead reserved domains, the separate development of the community in each domain assigned to it. Not me.
> (Derrida 1986b, 368–9)

Thus Derrida in one way endorses Foucault's notion of the apparently incidental as endemic. Just as Foucault argued for the posing of the Gulag question in order to present a critique of Marxism, so Derrida opens the question of apartheid to a deconstructive reading in which the policy of separate development is seen as not simply 'out there', beyond the pale of philosophical enquiry, and, by extension, of criticism. By deconstructing the familiar opposition of inside and outside upon which so much of western thought is dependent, Derrida reveals the limits of an empiricism which, in its obstinate determination to remain objective, succumbs to the racism of universalism.[12]

Derrida's concept of writing, like his concept of the text, is more archaeological in many ways than Foucault's concern with discursive practices, even with those which construct the sexuality, sense and sentences of bodies and minds. The broad notion of *text* as physical graffiti, and of the world as text, rather than vice-versa, is an infinitely more useful one from the point of view of the knowledge of archaeology than the Foucauldian idea of an archaeology of knowledge. The former suggests that the stratified, monumental concrete residues of human culture can be read as closely and critically as any modern social narrative, whereas the latter divests the subject of its historical specificity by endowing it with a panoptic power as the history of histories. My own feeling, and one which I have tried to communicate in this essay, is that archaeology, as a discipline, has more to gain from Derridean deconstruction, which approves its efforts to read the past in the material residues of human culture, than from its appropriation as general term for the discursive history of the human sciences undertaken by Foucault.

CONCLUSION

The Derrida–Foucault confrontation offers a unique glimpse into the workings of post-structuralism. My chief aim in reconstituting this famous controversy is to show that whilst archaeology, a field devoted exactly to *reconstruction* might, with some justification, fear being undermined by *deconstruction*, it could nonetheless become a discipline which undermines, challenging its own assumptions about, and representations of, culture and society. By opening itself now to deconstructive questioning, rather than persisting in its present course of obstinate resistance or piecemeal appropriation, archaeology might avoid the pitfalls of structuralism and enjoy the 'constructive' criticism of this intricate and systematic form of interpretation which has only recently supplanted it. There are no signs yet that deconstruction will inherit the earth, but the stimulating conference which spawned this volume of essays is one indication of the growing influence it exerts in the human sciences. If archaeology is to take its rightful place in a newly emerging configuration of interdisciplinary studies, then it ought to show itself receptive to the undermining activities of the deconstructive turn.

NOTES

1. On structuralism as a method of archaeological explanation see Gellner (1982). The best introduction to post-structuralism is via the volumes of collected essays on the subject which have appeared over the last decade. See especially Harari (1979), Young (1981), Attridge *et al.* (1987). For a recent informative if journalistic account of its British reception see Easthope (1988). A more theoretically elaborate critique is offered by Dews (1987).
2. There is a growing bibliography on this topic. In addition to the collection edited by Attridge *et al.* (1987), see Parker (1981), Culler (1981), and Eagleton (1988).
3. Derrida constantly urges such a close, slow reading against the haste of the nuclear age. See for example Derrida (1984). For the French Nietzschean tradition see Bataille (1945), Deleuze (1983), Foucault (1977b), Derrida (1981a). See also Derrida's remark that 'Nietzsche is, for me, a very important reference' (Derrida 1981b). A new set of perspectives is available in Wood and Krell (1988) – see especially a fascinating article by Schrift (ibid., 131–49).
4. For other interventions in the Foucault–Derrida debate, see Said (1978), Wordsworth (1987). The Foucauldian historiographic method is reappraised by Noujain (1987).
5. Foucault's contention that Descartes deliberately banishes madness from his discussion of consciousness finds a curious echo in Lenin's aside, concerning matter – 'that which is most familiar and immediately given to man, the existence of which no one save the inmate of a lunatic asylum can doubt' (Lenin 1976, 169).
6. See also Derrida's more recent comments upon the rationality of reason in Fabb *et al.* (1987).
7. I have elected to cite the passage from J. Harari's introductory chapter in *Textual Strategies: Perspectives in Post-Structuralist Criticism* (Harari 1979), which

appears to me to offer the most faithful rendition: 'Critical Factions/Critical Fictions', p. 41.
8. As history would have it, the Seeley library in Cambridge is built along the lines of the Panopticon.
9. For a historical overview of the problem see Parton (1985, 21–36), also Segalene (1983, 173–87).
10. In the English edition a superfluous translator's note informs the reader of the phonological resemblance between Jouy and the past participle of *jouir*, the French verb meaning, among other things, to come in the sexual sense.
11. On deconstruction in general see in particular Bloom *et al.* (1979), Culler (1983), Sallis (1987).
12. See Barker (1983, 6–15), Gates (1986, 402–9). '. . . we must attack the racism of egalitarianism and universalism in as many languages as possible' (Gates 1986, 409).

REFERENCES

Attridge, D., Bennington, G. and Young, R. (eds) (1987) *Post-Structuralism and the Question of History*, Cambridge: Cambridge University Press.
Barker, M. (1983) 'Empiricism and racism', *Radical Philosophy* 33: 6–15.
Bataille, G. (1945) *Sur Nietzsche*, Paris: Gallimard.
Bloom, H. *et al.* (1979) *Deconstruction and Criticism*, London: Routledge.
Culler, J. (1981) *The Pursuit of Signs: Semiotics, Literature, Deconstruction*, London: Routledge.
Culler, J. (1983) *On Deconstruction*, London: Routledge.
Culler, J. (1988) 'The call to history', in J. Culler (ed.) *Framing the Sign: Criticism and its Institutions*, Oxford: Blackwell.
Deleuze, G. (1983) *Nietzsche and Philosophy*, trans. H. Tomlinson, London: Athlone.
Derrida, J. (1976) *Of Grammatology*, trans. G. C. Spivak, Baltimore: Johns Hopkins University Press.
Derrida, J. (1977) 'Limited Inc a b c . . .', trans. S. Weber, *Glyph* 2: 162–254.
Derrida, J. (1978) 'Cogito and the history of madness', in J. Derrida, *Writing and Difference*, trans. A. Bass, London: Routledge.
Derrida, J. (1981a) *Spurs: Nietzsche's Styles*, trans. B. Harlow, Chicago: University of Chicago Press.
Derrida, J. (1981b) *Positions*, trans. A. Bass, Chicago: Chicago University Press.
Derrida, J. (1984) *Signeponge = Signsponge*, trans. R. Rond, New York: Columbia University Press.
Derrida, J. (1986a) 'Racism's last word', trans. P. Kamuf, in H. L. Gates (ed.) *'Race', Writing and Difference*, Chicago: Chicago University Press.
Derrida, J. (1986b) 'But beyond . . .' (Open letter to Anne McClintock and Rob Nixon), trans. P. Kamuf, in H. L. Gates (ed.) *'Race', Writing and Difference*, Chicago: Chicago University Press.
Dews, P. (1987) *Logics of Disintegration: Post-Structuralism and the Claims of Critical Theory*, London: Verso.
Eagleton, T. (1988) 'Last post', *Textual Practice* 2(1): 105–11.
Easthope, E. (1988) *British Post-Structuralism Since 1968*, London: Routledge.
Fabb, N., Attridge, D., Durant, A. and MacCabe, C. (eds) (1987) *The Linguistics of Writing: Arguments Between Language and Literature*, Manchester: Manchester University Press.
Foucault, M. (1967) *Madness and Civilization: A History of Insanity in the Age of*

Reason, trans. R. Howard, New York: Vintage/Random House.
Foucault, M. (1977a) *Discipline and Punish: The Birth of The Prison*, trans. A. Sheridan, London: Allen Lane.
Foucault, M. (1977b) *Language, Counter-Memory, and Practice: Selected Essays and Interviews*, trans. D. F. Bouchard and S. Simon, Oxford: Blackwell.
Foucault, M. (1979) *The History of Sexuality, Volume 1: An Introduction*, trans. R. Hurley, London: Allen Lane.
Foucault, M. (1980) 'Power and strategies', in C. Gordon (ed.) *Power/Knowledge: Selected Interviews and Other Writings by Michel Foucault, 1972-77*, Brighton: Harvester.
Gates, H. L. (1986) 'Talkin' that talk', in H. L. Gates (ed.) *'Race', Writing and Difference*, Chicago: Chicago University Press.
Gellner, E. (1982) 'What is structuralism?', in C. Renfrew, M. J. Rowlands and B. A. Segraves (eds) *Theory and Explanation in Archaeology*, London and New York: Academic Press.
Harari, J. (ed.) (1979) *Textual Strategies: Perspectives in Post-Structuralist Criticism*, New York: Cornell University Press.
Lenin, V. I. (1976) *Materialism and Empirio-Criticism*, Peking: Foreign Languages Press.
McClintock, A. and Nixon, R. (1986) 'No names apart: the separation of word and history in Derrida's "Le Dernier Mot du Racisme" ', in H. L. Gates (ed.) *'Race', Writing and Difference*, Chicago: Chicago University Press.
Nietzsche, F. (1982) *Daybreak: Thoughts on the Prejudices of Morality*, trans. R. J. Hollingdale, Cambridge: Cambridge University Press.
Noujain, E. G. (1987) 'History as genealogy: an explanation of Foucault's approach to history', in A. P. Griffiths (ed.) *Contemporary French Philosophy*, Cambridge: Cambridge University Press.
Parker, A. (1981) ' "Taking sides" (On History): Derrida Re-Marx', *Diacritics* 11(3): 57-73.
Parton, N. (1985) 'Children as victims: cruelty and neglect in history', in *The Politics of Child Abuse*, London: Macmillan.
Said, E. (1978) 'The problem of textuality: two exemplary positions', *Critical Inquiry* 4: 673-714.
Sallis, J. (ed.) (1987) *Deconstruction and Philosophy: The Texts of Jacques Derrida*, Chicago: Chicago University Press.
Schrift, A. D. (1988) 'Foucault and Derrida on Nietzsche and the End(s) of "Man" ', in D. Wood and D. F. Krell (eds) *Exceedingly Nietzsche: Aspects of Contemporary Nietzsche Interpretation*, London: Routledge.
Segalene, M. (1983) *Love and Power in the Peasant Family: Rural France in the Nineteenth Century*, trans. S. Matthews, Oxford: Blackwell.
Spivak, G. C. (1976) Translator's Preface, in J. Derrida, *Of Grammatology*, Baltimore: Johns Hopkins University Press.
Stone, L. (1987) *The Past and the Present Revisited*, London: Routledge.
Wood, D. (1987) 'Beyond deconstruction', in A. P. Griffiths (ed.) *Contemporary French Philosophy*, Cambridge: Cambridge University Press.
Wood, D. and Krell, D. F. (eds) (1988) *Exceedingly Nietzsche: Aspects of Contemporary Nietzsche Interpretation*, London: Routledge.
Wordsworth, A. (1987) 'Derrida and Foucault: writing the history of historicity', in D. Attridge, G. Bennington and R. Young (eds) *Post-Structuralism and the Question of History*, Cambridge: Cambridge University Press.
Young, R. (ed.) (1981) *Untying the Text: A Post-Structuralist Reader*, London: Routledge.

CHAPTER 3

Post-processual archaeology has been much concerned with the problem of ideology – both as the concept of ideology can be used to enable interpretations of the relationship of material representation to social structure in the past, and also, at a self-reflexive level, as 'ideology criticism' is used to analyse the position of archaeology itself in the present.

For post-structuralism, this process of ideology analysis is immediately questionable as it seems to represent just one more manifestation of 'logocentrism', one more attempt to totalise, to close the unity of an absolute truth. Yet in so far as most post-structuralist critics do share at least a wider political sympathy with the aims of ideology criticism as a strategic device, and indeed to some extent with the need for 'absolutes' in a realistic programme of political action, the question of ideology also comes to question the ultimate validity of the radical pretences of post-structuralism itself.

In this paper, Waterman explores this tension in relation to the critic in whose work it is perhaps most openly manifest: Michel Foucault. Foucault summarily rejects the classic Marxist conception of ideology and the precepts of the 'Dominant Ideology Thesis', carrying with it as it does the claim of the 'will to truth' and the elevation of a knowledgeable 'aware' observer/analyst over the manipulated ideological subject who is observed. Waterman argues that in this move, Foucault both mischaracterises the ground a mature ideology criticism might occupy, and also fatally disables the integrity of his own project by robbing himself of the means to examine the micro-level operation of power which Foucauldian genealogy nominally sets out to analyse.

3

Discourse and Domination: Michel Foucault and the Problem of Ideology

Shaun Waterman

The concept of ideology occupies a crucial place in many of the theoretical frameworks utilised in intellectual disciplines ranging from sociology to literary criticism. In particular, of course, the concept is important to the intellectual traditions of Marxism and more recently, Critical Theory. In the latter indeed the project of *ideologiekritik* is an essential armature of both the ethical and epistemological aspects of its critical stance: and the concept of ideology is therefore a vital part of the moral and intellectual ground from which Critical Theory's critique is launched.

Some of the reasons why the concept may be important in Marxist theory have come to light as as result of debates over the 'Dominant Ideology Thesis' (Abercrombie *et al.* 1980). One important factor would appear to be the need to explain the continuing unwillingness of the proletariat to constitute itself as a class-for-itself, self-consciously waging the class struggle on the political as well as the economic front. Writing of the 'Dominant Ideology Thesis', Lodziack characterises its ubiquity thus:

> The dominant ideology thesis is not so much a 'thesis' as a self evident truth amongst a majority of the Left . . . [its] popularity . . . can be seen to arise, in the main, from the need to explain the failure of the class struggle to materialise into the revolution predicted by Marx.
>
> (Lodziack 1988, 12)

In more straightforward political Marxist discourse, it is clear that – quite aside from any analytic value which it has – the concept of ideology is important for other reasons, not least as a concept used rhetorically to label and censure opposing political perspectives and analysis. Ralph Samuel, writing of the Manichean character of the class terminology applied by the Communists in the 1940s provides an example of such censure when he writes that 'in the battle of ideas', 'existentialism was bourgeois ideology, historical materialism a proletarian science' (Samuel

1987). While the 'Dominant Ideology Thesis' has been criticised, this has been largely on empirical grounds, the argument being – to put it crudely – that the thesis does not 'fit the facts' (cf. Abercrombie *et al.* 1980; Lodziack 1988). Critiques raising similar questions have appeared on the pages of *New Left Review*, as part of the debate between Stuart Hall (1985) on the one hand, and Bob Jessop *et al.* (1984; 1985) on the other. Barker, on the other hand, has called into question the epistemological and methodological procedures of (neo)Marxist ideology criticism in a more general way (Barker 1987).

However, neither of these approaches interrogates the conceptual foundations of the very notion of ideology as such. Furthermore, though the empirical critiques of the 'Dominant Ideology Thesis' have clear political implications which are spelled out (in some cases with considerable force),[1] Barker does not enlarge on the political consequences of his more conceptually oriented critique. As this paper aims to show, however, different conceptual approaches to the question of ideology do underpin – albeit often implicitly – much broader differences in political strategy and practice.

It is the radical rejection of the concept of ideology in the work of Michel Foucault – and, centrally, its political consequences – which is the subject matter of this paper. This rejection is closely bound up with his critique of Marxist and what Foucault calls 'Para-Marxist' theory. Indeed, he generally makes his dissatisfaction with the concept of ideology the central issue when invited to define or clarify his position in relation to Marxism (e.g. Foucault 1980a, 58). In particular, the three reasons for this rejection which he lists with uncharacteristic clarity in a 1977 interview are analysed here, and their relation to the other themes in his work examined:

> The notion of ideology seems to me to be difficult to make use of for three reasons. The first is that, like it or not, it always stands in virtual opposition to something else which is supposed to count as truth, now I believe that the problem does not lie in drawing the line between that in a discourse which falls under the category of scientificity or truth and that which falls under some other category, but in seeing historically how effects of truth are produced within discourses which in themselves are neither true nor false. The second drawback is that the concept of ideology refers, I think necessarily, to something of the order of the subject. Third, ideology stands in a secondary position relative to something which functions as its infrastructure, as its material, economic determinant, etc. For these reasons I think that this is a notion that cannot be used without circumspection.
>
> (Foucault 1984a, 60)

DETERMINATION AND INTERPRETATION: 'THE ORGANISED SUSPICION OF LANGUAGE . . .'

At first sight, it might appear that Foucault's third objection[2] – which might be termed the problem of determination – does not actually apply to recent (and especially fashionable) writing on ideology. Most contemporary theorists would probably concur with Thompson's admonition to 'acknowledge that ideology is partially constitutive of what in our societies, "is real" . . .' (Thompson 1984, 4).

Indeed, Thompson might be said to be something of a moderate in this regard in comparison with those followers of Althusser, who seem quite prepared to claim that ideology is wholly constitutive of the 'real' in any society (cf. Hirst 1980). Of course, Thompson was not the first to make this observation – Marx himself pointed out that 'when an idea grasps the minds of the masses, it becomes a material force', and there are few Marxists today who would subscribe to the kind of crude economic determinism espoused during the 'Second International' period.

However, Foucault's comments concerning 'infrastructure' or 'determination' appear as more than simply a critique of economic determinism when considered side-by-side with his critique of totalising (or, as he has provocatively called it, 'totalitarian') theory (Foucault 1980b, 80–1). There are two sets of issues here, the analytical and the political. From its analytical aspect, Foucault sees totalitarian theory as representing an unreflexive attempt to wish away the irreducible specificity of discourse, and it should be added, of other categories of historical and social events, practices and institutions which make up the superstructure.[3] In *The Archaeology of Knowledge*, for example, he seems to be suggesting that the attempt to explain events and statements in all their multiplicity and specificity, by reference to some 'other', to some distant origin or *telos*, often amounts to little more than a rhetorical or intellectual sleight of hand:

> . . . according to [this practice in historical/social scientific analysis] all manifest discourse is secretly based on an 'already said'; and . . . this 'already said' is not merely a phrase that has already been spoken, or a text that has already been written, but a 'never said', an incorporeal discourse, a voice as silent as a breath, a writing that is merely the hollow of its own mark. It is supposed, therefore, that everything that is formulated in discourse was already articulated in the semi-silence that precedes it, which continues to run obstinately beneath it, but which it covers and silences. The manifest discourse, therefore, is really *no more than the repressive presence of what it does not say*; and this 'not said' is a hollow that undermines from within all that is said. . . . We must renounce all those themes whose function is to ensure the infinite continuity of discourse and

its secret presence to itself in the interplay of a constantly recurring absence. . . . *Discourse must not be referred to the distant presence the Origin, but treated as and when it occurs.*[4]

(Foucault 1972, 25, emphasis added)

Thus Rabinow writes that Foucault finds ideology criticism unsatisfactory because it persists in seeing discourse 'as [a] reflection, no matter how cleverly mediated, of something supposedly "deeper" and more "real" . . .' (Rabinow 1984, 10). However, by using the concept of reflection (with its strong connotation of Base and Superstructure), Rabinow limits Foucault's critique to Marxist theories of ideology in an indefensible manner. His critique could equally well be applied to theories of ideology which do not incorporate the Base/Superstructure metaphor at all.

For example, Thompson, working towards an analytical description of the way that Critical Theorists use the term, defines ideology as 'meaning in the service of domination' (Thompson 1984, chapter 1). Thus discourse is defined as ideological if it legitimises, dissimulates or reifies relations of power. Discourse is not analysed 'as and when it occurs', but by reference to 'the distant presence of the Origin' – in this case the structures of domination which it 'serves'. Thompson makes this clear in the account of his three-stage methodology for interpreting and criticising ideology: '. . . *reconnecting* discourse to the relations of domination which it serves to sustain; such is the task of interpretation' (Thompson 1984, 138, emphasis added).

From the point of view of *The Archaeology of Knowledge* therefore, Thompson is no less of a Totalitarian theorist in this regard than Plekhanov, his comments concerning the necessity for dialogue with the subjects of ideological discourse notwithstanding (Thompson 1984, 15).

For Foucault, *reconnection* is mere discursive prestidigitation, for it rests on an interpretive practice which he regards with a degree of scorn evidenced by his characterisation of it as 'the organised suspicion of language'. Basically, Foucault argues that, since all discourse is already interpretation, the interpreter of discourse confronts an infinite – and infinitely regressing – task: the interpretation of the interpretation of . . . and so on. It as if the interpreter were standing between two mirrors, facing an endless sequence of diminishing size and clarity: '[T]here is nothing to interpret, for fundamentally, all is already interpretation, each sign is not the thing which offers itself for interpretation, but the interpretation of other signs . . .' (Foucault quoted in Callinicos 1982, 33).

Crucially, it is the discourse itself that must be taken at its face value, respected, as it were. Marxist practitioners of ideology criticism have used the 'Sigh of the Oppressed' principle,[5] in order to avoid the contemptuous attitude towards the subjects of ideology which might otherwise characterise their practice. Hall, for example, has argued that genuine fears – such as of rape or assault – are drawn on by ideological constructions of a 'crime wave' to fuel popular authoritarian attitudes.[6] The fears, needs, etc., of the subjects of ideology are thus recognised as genuine (at some level), albeit given distorted expression.

However, while evincing a certain respect for the *subjects* of ideology, this conception – in Foucauldian terms – continues to treat their discourse itself with contempt, by insisting on its interpretation as the distorted expression of something 'supposedly "deeper" and more "real" . . .'. It is Foucault's insistence that the specificity of discourse must be respected that links his critique of determination and interpretation into a wholehearted rejection of the analytical principles of ideology criticism. The political consequences of this are discussed below.

'TOTALITARIAN' THEORY

From its political aspect, Foucault has suggested that the totalising intellectual aspirations of Marxist theory cannot be separated from the authoritarian characteristics of the Soviet state and the realities of the Gulag (Foucault 1984a, 52–4; cf. Maley, this volume). Smart, a commentator sympathetic to Foucault, has argued that the two are connected by the way in which Marxism's totalising aspirations can lead to 'the production of a form of knowledge which goes hand-in-hand with the development of systems of technical control and bureaucratically organised forms of administration' (Smart 1983, 30).

Smart's problem remains the identification of the characteristics of Marxist theory which make this true, for Foucault is typically difficult to pin down on this point. If Foucault's characterisation of Marxism as Totalitarian is based on its claim as to the ultimately explicable character of the social world,[7] it remains unclear how far his own social analysis can escape from such a stricture. Foucault has repeatedly stated that history has no 'meaning', but that this does not mean that it is incoherent or unintelligible: 'On the contrary, it is intelligible, and should be susceptible to analysis down to the final detail, but this in accordance with the intelligibility of struggles, of strategies and tactics' (Foucault 1984b, 56).

Hoy claims that Foucault's conception of power as 'intentionality without a subject' enables him to explain historical developments (in the sense of providing a 'Grid of Intelligibility' – namely the will to truth) while not positing relations of causality (Hoy 1986, 128). Without dismissing this point as mere sophistry, it is clear that the difference between a 'Grid of Intelligibility' and an a priori set of causal relations may not be as readily discernible as Hoy would wish.

It seems both more reasonable and more sympathetic to Foucault to suggest that the political critique of Totalitarian theory which he offers is centred, not so much on its claim to explain, but rather on the fact that it construes an internal relationship between the explanation which it offers and a project that it proposes. As Marx himself made abundantly clear, the object of his work was to change society, not merely to interpret it. Moreover, owing both to the moral/normative and teleological aspects of Marxism, the project of radical social change is internal to the representation of the society which it presents. It ought, in short, to be impossible to accept Marx's critique of capitalism without being a socialist.

Totalitarian theory may indeed be a veridical discourse – defining an object domain and rules for the formulation of true statements about it[8] – but it is not this which is at the heart of Foucault's political critique of it. From the political, as opposed to the purely analytic, aspect, it is more useful to see Foucault's rejection of ideology as based not on his critique of explanation and interpretation, but rather on his vision of the power network and its technologies. What is politically invidious for him in Totalitarian discourse is the constitution of its object-domain (society) not as a field of intelligibility (of which Foucault himself is probably 'guilty' after all), but rather as a target of intervention, as a field in which there are both 'deviant' subjects – requiring normalisation – and 'normal' subjects (Foucault 1980b, 82–5; Smart 1983, 28).

From Foucault's point of view, this model is common to both social technologies such as psychiatric theory, and certain forms of political practice such as Marxism–Leninism. There can be little doubt that many Marxists generally regard ideological consciousness as 'deviant' in that it fails to correspond to the normative model of Marxist theory. In fact, the 'device' of ideological consciousness is probably an analytical consequence of the ambiguities with which the definition is riddled – it appears impossible to define exactly what ideological consciousness is except by reference to the 'normal' class consciousness with which it fails to correspond.

The questions Foucault seems to be posing, therefore, are these: given that both are interventions to make 'deviant' subjects 'normal', what is the substantive difference between the treatment of those defined as mentally ill, and the forging of class consciousness among those defined as caught up in ideology? Are not practitioners of these types of intervention engaged in the same kind of 'normalisation' which is the ineluctable mark of every region of the power network?[9]

One difference presents itself immediately. Practitioners of social technology, it can be argued, operate within and on behalf of the state, practitioners of political–ideological 'normalisation' do not. This is a complex and difficult question, and it is not possible to examine it satisfactorily here. Suffice it to say that, from Foucault's point of view, the difference is neither so readily apparent, nor so important, as it might first appear.

To begin with, the incorporation of social technologies such as psychiatry or medicine into the state is a relatively recent phenomenon. The historic origins of such practices are to be found in individual philanthropy rather than in Government. Moreover, Foucault has consistently argued that the power network and its technologies do not 'emanate' from the state. On the contrary, the state is intertwined with and rests upon them, and the blurring or calling into question of the taken-for-granted line between 'state' and 'not-state' is one of the foundation stones of Foucault's re-conceptualisation of power (Foucault 1979, 93–4).

One consequence of all this is clear at once: not only is there no coherent political principle to be 'extracted' from Foucault's work, but his actual theoretical stance is incompatible with such a project. This impression is borne out by Foucault in one of his final interviews, where he says:

> I would more or less agree with the idea that in fact what interests me is much more morals than politics or, in any case, politics as an ethics. . . . I mean that *the questions I am trying to ask are not determined by a pre-established political outlook and do not tend toward the realisation of some definite political project*.
> (Foucault 1984c, 375; emphasis added)

This is not to say that Foucault's work is apolitical. Indeed, in the same interview, he makes it clear that there are important political dimensions to his work. However, the formulation of coherent and durable political programmes is inimical to both the spirit and the letter of his work. Moreover, this fact is a direct consequence of Foucault's rejection of the concept of ideology: there can be no programme in a discourse which sets its face against intervention in the social world. It would seem that a Foucauldian politics – if there can be said to be such a thing – could only echo the sentiments of Souvaraine, that disciple of Bakunin's in Zola's *Germinal*, when he replies to Etienne's demand to 'tell me what your programme is': 'Any reasoning about the future is criminal, for it prevents pure destruction and holds up the march of revolution' (Zola 1954, 237).

How much potential this leaves for political action is clearly open to dispute. Dews has stated that Foucault – when he is consistent – lapses into 'extreme spontaneism' (Dews 1984, 90). However, not all commentators are so critical. Paul Gilroy, a social theorist who is sympathetic to at least some aspects of Foucault's work, appears to embrace this rejection of programmes:

> There can be no single or homogeneous strategy for combating racism. . . . I think that the programmatic approach to this question is part of the problem: what we should do depends on who we are and where we find ourselves . . .[10]

Certainly, there *are* problems with the political consequences of using certain notions of ideology. For example, Althusserian conceptions appear to allow no room for the role of experience of proletarian subjects who are 'in ideology', except the reproduction of ideological relations. The only path to consciousness is through a scientific understanding of one's own position. In short familiarity with a series of dense theoretical texts. Exactly what space this leaves for political action on the part of proletarian subjects who are not familiar with *Lire Le Capital* is unclear. Asked what he would say to a woman who was 'a real fan of the Queen', for example, Paul Hirst replied:

> This woman's opinion is a directly political one, which must be answered in political terms. It is useless to say to the woman, 'you are a victim of a certain kind of ideology'. A mode of discourse like that is never convincing – *it reduces the people concerned (who 'believe' what they say) to the status of dupes to be taught lessons. It is both patronising and apolitical.*
>
> (Hirst n.d., 20)

Clearly this is a case where the relationship between theory and ideology is somewhat obscure, for the woman evidently *is* 'a victim of a certain kind of ideology'. Hirst's awareness of the political futility of attempting to explain this to her, however (and the inexplicable inverted commas with which he attempts to deny the political reality of her expressed attitudes), betrays his understanding of the problematic status of any Althusserian political practice.[11] 'Patronising and apolitical' is an excellent characterisation of the political practice, of, for example, many revolutionary socialists: '*Your* beliefs are ideology, *my* beliefs are based on a scientific understanding of the principles of Marxism–Leninism.'

Similarly, Barker accuses the cultural theorists that he criticises of 'operating within a model of enlightenment', that is to say of positing their work on their own rectitude of understanding as against the ignorance or mistakenness of the ideological subjects they 'study' (Barker 1987). There is a certain amount of justice in this accusation, though he ignores the sensitivity with which Hall, for example, documents the ways that subjects of ideology create tolerable worlds for themselves 'inside' its structures.

Hall is at pains to stress that ideological understandings of the world are real 'subjectively' as well as 'objectively'; that is to say that subjects 'use' the understandings of the world which ideology offers to them to make sense of their experience (Hall *et al.* 1978). He has often argued, for example, that the political success of 'Thatcherism' is based on its ability to present understandings of the world which are capable of making sense of the contradictory experiences of the British working class in an era of industrial decline and economic restructuring.

Even such an intelligent application of the 'Sigh of the Oppressed' principle, however, creates certain problems. These originate in the gulf which it immediately creates between the 'theoretician' ('outside', ideology if only by implication) and the political subject ('inside' it).

One way of superseding these problems is suggested by Thompson, who, on the basis of Habermas' theory of communicative action, calls for dialogue with the subjects of ideological discourse to be made a basic principle of ideology criticism:

> [T]hese interpretations [of ideological discourse] . . . have to be justifiable in the eyes of the subjects about whom they are made. Such interpretations thus provide a positional basis for the *self-criticism* of the subjects whose discourse is the object of the interpretation . . .
>
> (Thompson 1984, 15; chapters 8–9)

There are two problems which Thompson's approach raises. Firstly, it is posited on a humanistic understanding of the character of the ideological process and its subjects. Such an understanding is open to dispute, and the issues it raises are dealt with at greater length below.

Secondly, it raises a more immediate political problem. There is implicit in the 'Sigh of the Oppressed' principle the recognition that the subjects of ideology are not entirely or simply 'wrong' in their expressed attitudes. However, the corollary of this is that ideology might actually be said – at a given level – to serve the interests of its subjects: racist white proletarians *do* have their short-term material interests advanced by racist ideology, though their broader, long-term interests are undoubtedly damaged by it.

Given this, dialogue with the subjects of ideology is unlikely to be useful unless conducted under conditions where those long-term interests are, or can be made, immediately apparent and real. So far as Thompson is concerned of course this is not a problem, because he subscribes to the humanistic (and perhaps politically naive) thesis that each of us has an interest in ending the oppression of all of us, *and* that we are each capable of realising this to be the case.

Clearly, pragmatic solutions to these problems have been and continue to be found by those engaged in political practice who operate with a concept of ideology. Dialogue with the subjects of ideological discourse is *the* first principle of any effective political practice, and one does not have to embrace Habermas' humanism to advocate it: 'As for people who are politically backward, Communists should not slight or despise them, but should befriend them, unite with them, convince them, and encourage them to go forward' (Mao 1967, 275).

Foucault's rejection of 'determination' and 'interpretation' – analytic principles which underlie all traditions of ideology criticism – and the critique of interventionist social analysis with which it is bound up appear to render the formulation of coherent programmes for social renovation within the parameters provided by his work at best pragmatic, uncertain and piecemeal, at worst unstable if not impossible.

SUBJECT, REPRESSION, POWER

Secondly, Foucault points to the problem of the subject. This is very manifest in what might be called the hermeneutic tradition of ideology criticism – for example in the work of Ricoeur and Thompson. The key to understanding Foucault's criticism of this tradition is his deep scepticism regarding the almost (and in some cases, openly) humanist nature of the ontological and ethical claims which it makes regarding the human subject.

Ontologically, hermeneutics works with a notion of the constitutive subject.[12] That is to say that idea of the knowing subject is an intrinsic feature of human existence, and that to interpret the social world is therefore to re-interpret a domain which has already been interpreted by the subjects who live in it.

Ethically, there is the claim that these pre-interpretations must be awarded some kind of privileged status in social enquiry. Moreover, there is what Foucault calls 'the inadequate and possibly dangerous' idea (Foucault 1980a, 59) that domination and power distort or disfigure the subject in some way (the Repression Thesis).

For Foucault, these claims are completely untenable. For him, the subject is a construct, and much of his work is actually concerned with the investigation of how power and the technologies which it invests, the knowledge which it constitutes, produce human bodies *as* subjects in the first place:

> We should discover how it is that subjects are gradually, progressively, really and materially constituted through a multiplicity of organisms, forces, energies, materials, desires, thoughts etc. We should try to grasp subjection in its material instance as a constitution of subjects.
>
> (Foucault 1980b, 97)

It is this aspect of Foucault's project that Rabinow emphasises when he characterises it as a 'genealogy of the modern subject' (Rabinow 1984, 7). What Foucault is studying is not the understandings of their world which subjects entertain, but the way that these subjects are themselves produced by power. It thus makes no sense to speak of domination distorting or repressing subjects, since it is this domination, this subjection (to use a play of words of which Foucault was fond) which produces these subjects in the first place.

As Dews points out: 'In modern philosophy, it is a view of the status and capacities of the subject which defines the content of the concepts of domination and freedom' (Dews 1984, 79). Thus it is no surprise to find that these different conceptions of subjectivity underpin divergent ways of thinking about power, and in particular about the way power sustains or reproduces itself.

Thompson is quite explicit – ideology, he says, serves to sustain power by imbuing the social world with meanings which legitimise, dissimulate or reify relations of domination (Thompson 1984, 130–1). By representing power to the subjects dominated by it, ideology helps to explain the persistence of domination. This is necessary because, according to the Repression Thesis, no one could rationally conclude that they ought to be dominated. Put simply, this perspective argues that ideology, by misleading subjects as to the character and/or existence of their domination, prevents them from acting in order to end it. A parallel here can be drawn with certain Marxist uses of the concept.

For example, Stuart Hall *et al.* (1978) have argued that ideological representations of crime in the media obscure the complex social and institutional mechanisms involved in the process of crime and policing, thus mobilising political consent for the transformation of the state in an increasingly authoritarian direction. Others have suggested that commodity fetishism, by concealing the true character of production relations from the productive agents, inhibits the formation of class consciousness (Mepham 1972).

What these conceptions share is a notion of real interest which is anterior to the subject's constitution as a political agent. For Thompson, subjects have a real interest in ending the domination which they are unable to perceive owing to ideological obfuscation. For Hall, on the other hand, subjects are induced by their constructed fear of an ill understood and semi-mythical 'crime wave' to act against their real interests by supporting authoritarian policies. Couzens-Hoy argues, indeed, that such a notion of real interests is a necessary feature of any conception employing the Repression Thesis (Hoy 1986, 124–6). What distinguishes the Marxist tradition from the Critical Theory one are their very different ways of deriving these interests.

For Thompson, and the Critical Theorists more generally, *all* human subjects have an interest in human emancipation, and it is therefore in everyone's interest ultimately to criticise ideology. Hence his contention that *ideologiekritik* must necessarily be grounded in the *self*-criticism of the subjects of ideological discourse, and should provide a basis for that self-criticism (cf. Thompson 1984, chapters 8–9).

For Marxists, on the other hand, human subjects have *class* interests, which are mutually irreconcilable between different classes. Furthermore, these interests are objective in that they derive from the subject's position in the process of production under capitalism, irrespective of whether they act to further them or not. For this reason, certain Marxists have argued that the experience of the subjects, even (or in some cases, especially) proletarian ones, cannot provide a basis for *ideologiekritik*, which is only possible given a properly scientific understanding of the laws of capital – as Althusser does (Althusser and Balibar 1970). The political problems attaching to this analysis have already been identified.

Where Marxists have adopted the less arrogant 'Sigh of the Oppressed' principle, it has become necessary – as was pointed out earlier – to recognise that the political interests of the proletariat are neither entirely straightforward nor completely unitary. The process of production under capitalism also divides the working class, fracturing it across lines of gender, race and generation, and creating conflicts of interest – albeit only in the short term – *within* the class.

It is interesting to note the political and intellectual trajectory of the best practitioner of this tradition of ideology criticism. Although in his early work, Hall appears to subscribe to a fairly conventional Marxist model of political interests, his later work demonstrates a definite turn against the idea that interests can be considered anterior to the constitution of subjects as political agents (cf. Hall 1988).

To what extent this new position (which might be said to endanger the ethical and epistemic basis for Hall's socialist project) is a logical development of the 'Sigh of the Oppressed' principle must be open to debate. It certainly does not seem logical to propose that because a subject may not be immediately aware of their long-term interests or may be acting against them, they therefore do not have any. The key question here, as intimated earlier, is a sensitivity to the circumstances under which subjects can be made aware of their long-term interests, and the manner in which such an interest can best be cultivated.

There might appear to be parallels between the perspectives on the reproduction of power relations outlined above and Foucault's comments that a certain way of speaking about power (what he calls the 'Juridico-discursive' notion) is 'the general form of its [power's] acceptability' in modern society (Foucault 1979, 86). Such impressions are misleading, however, for Foucault has consistently criticised both Critical Theory and Marxism for actually using the 'Juridico-discursive' concept of power. This notion, he argues, sees power as law; as the power to say 'no'; power as limit or constraint; power which is: '. . . no condition to produce . . . incapable of doing anything, except to render that which it dominates incapable of doing anything either, except for what this power allows it to do' (Foucault 1979, 85).

It is this notion that is at work in the humanist Repression Thesis. For Foucault this is an utterly inadequate way of thinking about power. For him, power is productive, far from constraining subjects, power (at the risk of labouring the point) creates them. This, for Foucault, is one of the ways that power reproduces itself, in and through subjects:

> The individual is an effect of power, and at the same time, or precisely to the extent that it is that effect, it is the element of its articulation. The individual that power has constituted is at the same time its vehicle.
>
> (Foucault 1980b, 98)

Our belief, our actions, our characters and personalities, indeed our very souls are an effect of power; they are invested in our bodies by the operation of the techniques and technologies of power; by surveillance, discipline and training amongst others.

MATERIALITY, MEANING AND PRACTICE

At this point, another reason why Foucault does not find the concept of ideology useful emerges. Ideology criticism is almost exclusively concerned with discourse, with meaning – that body of work claiming descent from Althusser and generally known as 'Screen' theory being a good example (Hall 1980; Morely 1980). Foucault, on the other hand (at any rate after the publication of *The Archaeology of Knowledge*) is primarily concerned with the investigation of practices, for example, the four great techniques of discipline: tabulation, manoeuvre, exercise, and tactics.

This clearly involves the study of discourse – Foucault investigates these techniques through the examination of monographs, manuals, etc. which were written about them. However, for Screen Theory, or other semiological approaches to the study of ideology, the analysis of discourse is concerned principally with the ideological *effects* of that discourse and therefore with the interpretation of the meaning which it reveals to, or the subject positions which it articulates for, the reader.

Foucault, on the other hand, has repeatedly stated that discourse is transparent and needs no interpretation (e.g. Foucault 1984a, 57). This is clearly a controversial claim, but we must see it in the light of his own concerns. Foucault reads discourse not in order to ascertain its ideological effects on the reader – the meanings with which it imbues the social world or the subject positions which it articulates – but rather to find out about the practices which it describes, typically in enormous detail (or in *The Order of Things* and *The Archaeology of Knowledge*, to determine the internal rules that govern its enunciation).

DISCOURSE AND DOMINATION

For Foucault it is the technologies of power which these practices serve, rather than the meanings or subject positions articulated in discourse, which constitute the subject:

> [That which] bears and determines us has the form of a war rather than that of a language: relations of power not relations of meaning . . . . 'semiology' is a way of avoiding its violent, bloody and lethal character by reducing it to the calm Platonic form of language and dialogue.
>
> (Foucault 1984a, 56)

Hence the way the category of the subject is deployed is problematic, from Foucault's point of view, even in those theories of ideology which share his anti-humanist insistence on seeing the subject as an historical and social construct. One possible overcoming of this problem is suggested by a return to Althusser. For him, ideology is material in the crude sense that it operates above all through practice, through our actions and daily rituals. He paraphrases Pascal on religion: 'Kneel down, move your lips in prayer, and you shall believe' (Althusser 1971, 40–4). To this extent, 'Screen' theory's Althusserian patrimony is very much in doubt, as are the credentials of many others claiming descent from him whose problematic is exclusively discursive. There are two other important consequences of returning to Althusser in this fashion.

Firstly, the question of ideology is displaced from the problematic of consciousness, and made a matter of *action*. The subject's ideas '. . . are his [*sic*] material actions inserted into material practices governed by material rituals which are themselves defined by the material ideological apparatus . . .' (Althusser 1971, 43). Just as we might advise ourselves to watch what someone *does*, rather than to listen to what they say, so the critique of ideology must concern itself with the documentation of action/practice/ritual/apparatus, from which – as Althusser reminds us – the governing ideology of institutions can be determined. Ideology should be criticised not through the laborious and intellectually questionable process of 'drawing out' the 'preferred reading' of a text, but through the analysis of practice – the imprint of ideology on the material.

Once this is accepted, the door may also be open to a new reading of Foucault's history of the development of the carceral system. His impatience with the interpretive practice at the heart of semiological approaches to the question, and the fact that his analyses of the carceral concern themselves exclusively with practice rather than discourse is thus not necessarily a barrier to the consideration of those analyses as critiques of ideology.

Clearly, such a reading would not meet with the approval of Foucault himself, and the thematic and theoretical shift which it imposes on his work is considerable. Nevertheless, the detailed account of the practices, rituals and institutions that make up the carceral which he presents may give us an excellent opportunity to deduce the ideologies which 'govern' them. Indeed, Foucault appears to present us with an outline of these in his many descriptions of the will to truth – the driving force inflecting the practices of the carceral.

Moreover, within this rereading, the source of the political struggles against the carceral which Foucault documented and took part in is entirely unclear. As has been shown, his rejection of the concept of ideology is bound up with his stridently anti-humanistic rejection of the 'Repression Thesis' and characterisation of modern subjectivity as the product of carceral. Given this, it is hard to see how he can even account for such struggles, let alone find a reason for supporting them.

TRUTH, POWER, AND JUSTIFICATION

Finally, the thorniest question of all must be examined, the problem of Truth, of the epistemic 'other' of ideology. This is the most difficult of Foucault's three objections, not just because it raises many difficult and complex issues, but also because it is here that he comes closest to some fairly intractable problems in his own work. For this reason, it is worth restating in full:

> [L]ike it or not, it [ideology] always stands in virtual opposition to something else which is supposed to count as truth. Now I believe that the problem does not lie in drawing the line between that in a discourse which falls under the category of scientificity or truth and that which falls under some other category, but in seeing historically how effects of truth are produced within discourses which in themselves are neither true nor false.
>
> (Foucault 1984a, 60)

So, Foucault here indicates that he is not concerned to distinguish truth from ideology, but rather to illuminate the prevailing 'Regime of Truth'; to discover what are the rules which (in a given discursive field at a given point in time) determine that certain statements will be True and others not.

Clearly there is more at stake here than a simple divergence of interests, for Foucault is raising a question which fundamentally challenges not only the practice of ideology criticism, but also some themes in his own work. The question is, of course, one of justification: on what basis can the practitioners of ideology criticism characterise the discourse of others as ideological?

Crudely, there are three responses to this challenge which ideology criticism can offer. Firstly, it can lay claim to scientific status, whether in straightforwardly positivistic terms, as, for example in the work of Trew

(1979a and b), or in terms of dialectical theory, such as Colin Sumner (1979) has done. Clearly, such a response is tendentious in the light of the somewhat shaky epistemic foundations of what Foucault was fond of calling 'the dubious sciences'. For those who subscribe to deconstruction, such claims are purely rhetorical.

For Foucault, on the other hand, the truth value of such claims to scientificity is not the point at issue, since he is concerned to illuminate their effects rather than their epistemic status. He characterises these effects in two ways. Firstly, they constitute the discourse within which and for which they are made as a veridical discourse. That is to say a discourse capable of creating a field of knowledge; constituting objects and rules for the formulation of true propositions about them.

More powerfully, such epistemological *hubris* renders a discourse capable of producing certain specific political effects. As Foucault makes clear in a set of questions which he poses to those attempting to establish the scientific status of Marxism, psychoanalysis, or ('even worse') semiology, he regards these effects as overwhelming, if not entirely invidious:

> What types of knowledge do you want to disqualify in the very instant of your demand: 'Is it a science?' Which speaking, discoursing subjects – which subjects of experience and knowledge – do you want to 'diminish' when you say 'I who conduct this discourse am conducting a scientific discourse, and I am a scientist'? Which theoretical–political *avant garde* do you want to enthrone . . .? When I see you straining to establish the scientificity of Marxism, I do not really think that you are establishing once and for all that Marxism has a rational structure and that therefore its propositions are the outcome of verifiable procedures; for me you are doing something altogether different, you are investing Marxist discourses and those who uphold them with the effects of a power which the West since Medieval times has attributed to science and has reserved for those engaged in scientific discourse.
>
> (Foucault 1980b, 85)

There are two points that should be made here. Firstly, claims to scientific validity are by no means the only way that a discourse and its practitioners can establish their authority. What Foucault points to is the special character of the power that attaches to discourse which successfully lays claim to scientific status in contemporary western society. It is the extent to which this power has historically been implicated in the imperialist conquest of three-quarters of the world which gives such resonance to Foucault's denunciation of its effects.

However, it is important to remember that the truth claims of a discourse as well as *silencing* 'subjects of knowledge and experience', will also empower others to speak and act. This is particularly important where the validity claims of a discourse are *not* based on its scientific status, and where, therefore, its authority does not derive from the 'effects of a power which the West since Medieval times has attributed to science'. Foucault himself has suggested that there is an 'underside' to power: '[A] certain Plebeian quality or aspect . . . the measure of plebs is not so much what stands outside relations of power as their limit, their underside, their counterstroke . . .' (Foucault 1980c, 138–42).

Who is silenced when the will of the 'plebs' is voiced?

The second response which practitioners of ideology criticism can make to Foucault's objection is to reject any claims to privileged access to the truth. One can deny – as Paul Hirst (1979) has done – the existence of any epistemic 'other' to ideology, and simply admit that one's own course is ideological. Unfortunately, as Thompson points out, this not only leaves the problem of justification unresolved, it also strips the concept of ideology of its critical potential: without truth, science, or some other 'other', there are no grounds for criticising ideological discourse (Thompson 1984, 90–8). Moreover this response results in a kind of relativism which is intellectually unexciting and politically vacuous (cf. Elliot 1986).

Finally, one can attempt to resolve the problem as Thompson, following Habermas, has attempted to do: by postulating a hypothetical epistemic 'other' for ideology, but not claiming exclusive possession of it (or at least, claiming not to claim exclusive possession of it) in the way that practitioners of 'scientific' ideology criticism do.

For Habermas, the internal logic of communicative action – that is speaking – presupposes the potential for rational agreement between subjects given a set of circumstances in which discourse could be freed from relations of dominance and uncoerced communication can take place. These hypothetical circumstances form what Habermas calls the Ideal Speech Situation. It is in this situation that equal, rational, discoursing subjects could reach consensus about the truth and can thereby generate the epistemic 'other' which ideology criticism needs in order to remain intellectually coherent.

However, in drawing on this concept to sustain the project of ideology criticism, Thompson reasserts his humanistic claims concerning the nature of interpretation, and the internality of the self-reflection of the knowing (or 'responsible') subject to the process (Thompson 1984, 140–5), thereby opening himself again to Foucault's scepticism regarding them.[13]

On the other hand, Thompson's approach is valuable in that it does indeed seem to offer a reasonably accurate description of what it is that the practitioners of ideology criticism do. So long as we are engaged in a process of political development, we must accept that the ground from which we launch our critique may shift; that the epistemic 'other' against which we measure ideology is neither fixed nor monolithic; that, in a word, the truth is not one.

The perceived necessity for a monolithic, static, and intellectually watertight 'Truth' as a precondition of *ideologiekritik*, and the idea that without such a 'Truth' there can be no basis for the criticism of ideology, is the consequence of an intellectual absolutism that is politically sterile. Once again, I would stress that it is not necessary to embrace Thompson's humanism (nor Habermas' elevation of consensus to the first principle of communicative action) in order to accept that his description of the practice of ideology criticism offers a model for a coherent political practice.

In the final analysis, however, given Foucault's constant insistence on the internal connection between the constitution of knowledge and the production and reproduction of power, he clearly regards the claim that Truth reveals power, while Falsity conceals it, as unsustainable. Power produces a 'Regime of Truth', a knowledge which is no less true for being the product and precondition of power than the subject is less a subject for being a historical or social construct.

Clearly, however, the problem of justification is also a problem for Foucault, given that much of his work has the appearance of a detailed, heartfelt, and scathing critique of the development of the carceral system. How can Foucault launch this critique, given his refusal to claim that his own work is epistemologically or ethically privileged above the power/knowledge which forms its object? This is a difficult and complex question and a few brief reflections upon it will have to suffice here.

Firstly, this refusal has to be understood in the context of Foucault's rejection of a metaphysics of progress as the foundation for the analysis of history and society. For Foucault, it is not necessary (or even possible) to evaluate current practice on the basis of either a coming utopia, or a lost golden age – and thus Geertz is wrong in his identification of *Discipline and Punish* as a 'kind of Whig history in reverse' (Geertz cited in Hoy 1986, 143).

The technologies of power utilised in the modern age are no 'better' or 'worse' than those utilised three hundred years ago, they are merely different. At most, they are more thorough, but not necessarily more efficient for all that. Their efficiency can only be measured in relation to the goals which power sets itself. In relation, in other words, to the Will to Power, whose growth has already outstripped its increasing capacities.

Moreover, to protest against the actual forms taken by power relations in our societies, Hoy maintains, it is not necessary to believe that one knows how to rid oneself of them: 'We can certainly regret what is bad for us now without knowing . . . that proposed ways to mend things will not actually produce other injustices' (Hoy 1986, 144). Even the most sympathetic commentators, however, seem forced to admit the existence of a 'tension' between the theoretical and normative aspects of his work (Dreyfus and Rabinow 1986, 114), or to conclude, like Hoy, that Foucault's project 'is probably too limited [in prescriptive terms] to justify the strident polemical tone of his criticism of the carceral society' (Hoy 1986, 143).

More important than the intellectual consistencies which it creates in his *oeuvre*, however, is the political paralysis which it induces. This is clearly visible – to take but one example – in 'On Popular Justice: A Discussion with Maoists' (Gordon 1980). The degree to which Foucault's ideas (at the risk of labouring the point) are incapable of providing the basis for *any* political action is evidenced by the series of evasions in which he takes refuge whenever he is pressed to give a detailed account of the source, character or direction of resistance to power or the social technologies in which it is embodied (Dews 1980, 90).

The reason for this is immediately clear. The authority which derives from truth claims in discourse is an essential armature for the formulation of political programmes. Without some means of distinguishing correct ideas from incorrect ones, calling for political action with any conviction is impossible.

Discarding the concept of ideology and rejecting a metaphysics of progress which postulates the necessity of human emancipation does not mean accepting the inevitability of particular, local or 'micro'-level instantiations of a power network, and indeed it was resistance to these micro-level incursions which formed the object, not only of much of Foucault's writing, but of his political practice.

It does, however, appear to rule out the possibility that there can be any programmatic or strategic basis for these resistances, let alone any guarantee of their success. Foucault is prepared to acknowledge the need for political struggle, even if he is vague about why, but it is a struggle without direction and without hope. To rephrase Gramsci, we must not allot Foucault the posthumous motto: 'Pessimism of the intellect, pessimism of the will'.

ACKNOWLEDGEMENTS

I would like to thank Teresa Brennan, Ben Cashdan and Tim Yates for their invaluable comments on earlier drafts of this paper.

NOTES

1. Lodziack concludes by quoting Gerry Adams, the President of Sinn Fein (Lodziack 1988, 16).
2. To a large degree the division between these three objections is arbitrary – the analytic principles and theoretical presupposition which underlie them are

interconnected. Dealing with each in turn is a slightly artificial way of clarifying the issues involved.

3. Foucault makes this clear in his critique of Rusche and Kirscheimer's book *Punishment and Social Structure* in *Discipline and Punish*.

4. It should be made clear that this quotation is drawn from Foucault's so-called 'middle' or 'archaeological' period, when a number of commentators have identified him as advocating an extreme form of 'discursive determinism'. This categorisation is unsatisfactory: Foucault's insistence on the specificity (*not* the determinant character) of the level of 'things said' in his writings at this time appears more of a methodological foray with a purely heuristic status, rather than the adoption of an ontological stance. It is the emphases and the subject matter of his 'later', 'genealogical' period which are different, rather than the philosophical armature. Indeed the attempt to identify chronologically distinct 'Foucauldian positions' – in the tradition of Grand Theory – at different points in his intellectual biography seems hostile to the spirit of his entire project. On the other hand, it is clear that (as a number of commentators have pointed out) any effort to define a coherent 'Foucauldian system' – again in the Grand Theoretical tradition – is also doomed to failure. Few great writers have been truly consistent, and the approach adopted here is consequently thematic. There are certain concerns which run through Foucault's work, and my primary aim here has been to discuss them, rather than attempt to identify points at which they contradict each other.

5. cf. Marx: 'Religious suffering is at the same time an expression of real suffering and a protest against real suffering. Religion is the sigh of the oppressed creature, the heart of a heartless world, and the soul of soulless circumstance. It is the opium of the people' (Marx 1977).

6. See Hall (n.d.) and also Haug (1986) for a similar argument in respect of commodity fetishism, which masquerades as the 'satisfaction' of the distortedly expressed, but still real, needs of the subject.

7. This claim, of course, is part and parcel of its aspirations to scientific status, an integral part of its 'Totalitarian' character which will be dealt with later at greater length. For this reason, much of the discussion that follows is also relevant to Foucault's third reason for rejecting the concept of ideology – the problem of justification or truth.

8. The expression originates from the French historian of science, Bachelard. For a discussion of its use by Foucault, see Gordon (1980, 240–2).

9. As an account of Foucault's views, this has probably strayed into the realm of exigetical fantasy. On the other hand, Foucault was indeed keen on sketching a relationship between Marxism's theoretical shortcomings and the authoritarian purposes to which psychiatry was turned in the Soviet Union (e.g. Foucault 1984a, 52–4).

10. P. Gilroy, answering questions following the presentation of his Runnymede Memorial lecture: *Some Problems in Anti-Racist Strategies*, 23 July 1987.

11. Nor is he alone in this. One of the more intelligent of the criticisms that John Dunn has levelled at structuralist Marxism runs along similar lines: '[Those who] adopt a social theory (such as that of Professor Althusser) which repudiates such a conception [of human subjects as agents] in its entirety . . . will in fact be left with an external (and implicitly contemptuous) vision of the agency of most human beings, and a vision of themselves and perhaps their more intimate political associates in which this external and contemptuous vision is compulsively suspended, to be replaced by one which could scarcely avoid sentimentality and self-deception' (Dunn 1985, 131).

12. For Thompson, who draws on Giddens here, the subject is both constituted *and* constituting. Nevertheless, Foucault's criticisms regarding the humanistic tendencies of this tradition remain applicable.

13. For a more detailed critique of Habermas' concept of the Ideal Speech Situation, specifically in relation to Foucault, see Hoy (1986) and Dreyfus and Rabinow (1986).

REFERENCES

Abercrombie, N., *et al.* (1980) *The Dominant Ideology Thesis*, London: Allen & Unwin.

Althusser, L. (1971) *Essays on Ideology*, London: New Left Books.

Althusser, L. and Balibar, E. (1970) *Reading Capital*, London: New Left Books.

Barker, M. (1987) 'Mass media studies and the question of ideology', *Radical Philosophy* 46: 27–33.

Callinicos, A. (1982) *Is There a Future for Marxism?*, London: Macmillan.

Dews, P. (1980) 'The eye of power', in C. Gordon (ed.) *Power/Knowledge*, London: Pantheon.

Dews, P. (1984) 'Power and subjectivity in Foucault', *New Left Review* 144: 72–95.

Dreyfus, H. L. and Rabinow, P. (1986) 'What is maturity?', in D. C. Hoy (ed.) *Foucault: A Critical Reader*, Oxford: Blackwell.

Dunn, J. (1985) *Rethinking Modern Political Theory: Essays 1979–83*, Cambridge: Cambridge University Press.

Elliot, G. (1986) 'The odyssey of Paul Hirst', *New Left Review* 159: 81–105.

Foucault, M. (1970) *The Order of Things: An Archaeology of The Human Sciences*, trans. A. Sheridan, London: Tavistock.

Foucault, M. (1972) *The Archaeology of Knowledge*, London: Tavistock.

Foucault, M. (1977) *Discipline and Punish: The Birth of the Prison*, trans. A. Sheridan, London: Allen Lane.

Foucault, M. (1979) *The History of Sexuality, Volume 1: An Introduction*, trans. R. Hurley, London: Allen Lane.

Foucault, M. (1980a) 'Body/power', in C. Gordon (ed.) *Power/Knowledge: Selected Interviews and Other Writings by Michel Foucault, 1972–77*, London: Pantheon.

Foucault, M. (1980b) 'Two lectures', in C. Gordon (ed.) *Power/Knowledge: Selected Interviews and Other Writings by Michel Foucault, 1972–77*, London: Pantheon.

Foucault, M. (1980c) 'Power and strategies', in C. Gordon (ed.) *Power/Knowledge: Selected Interviews and Other Writings by Michel Foucault, 1972–77*, London: Pantheon.

Foucault, M. (1984a) 'Truth and power', in P. Rabinow (ed.) *The Foucault Reader*, London: Peregrine.

Foucault, M. (1984b) 'Truth and method', in P. Rabinow (ed.) *The Foucault Reader*, London: Peregrine.

Foucault, M. (1984c) 'Politics and ethics: an interview', in P. Rabinow (ed.) *The Foucault Reader*, London: Peregrine

Gilroy, P. (1987) *There Ain't No Black in the Union Jack: The Cultural Politics of Race and Nation*, London: Hutchinson.

Gordon, C. (1980) 'Afterword', in C. Gordon (ed.) *Power/Knowledge: Selected Interviews and Other Writings by Michel Foucault, 1972–77*, London: Pantheon.

Hall, S. (1980) 'Recent developments in theories of language and ideology: a

critical note', in S. Hall *et al.* (eds) *Culture, Media, Language*, London: Hutchinson.
Hall, S. (1985) 'Authoritarian populism: a reply', *New Left Review* 151: 115–24.
Hall, S. (1988) *The Hard Road to Renewal: Thatcherism and the Crisis of the Left*, London: Verso.
Hall, S. (n.d.) 'Thatcherism among the theorists', unpublished paper.
Hall, S. *et al.* (1978) *Policing the Crisis: Mugging, the State, and Law and Order*, London: Macmillan.
Haug, W. F. (1986) *Critique of Commodity Aesthetics: Appearance, Sexuality and Advertising in Capitalist Society*, Cambridge: Polity.
Hirst, P. (1979) *On Law and Ideology*, London: Macmillan.
Hirst, P. (n.d.) *Problems and Advances in The Theory of Ideology – A Talk by Paul Hirst: Opening Session of the 1st Communist University of Cambridge*, Cambridge: Cambridge University Communist Party.
Hoy, D. C. (1986) 'Power, repression and progress', in D. C. Hoy (ed.) *Foucault: A Critical Reader*, Oxford: Blackwell.
Jessop, B. *et al.* (1984) 'Authoritarian populism, two nations and Thatcherism', *New Left Review* 147: 32–60.
Jessop, B. *et al.* (1985) 'Thatcherism and the politics of hegemony: a reply to Stuart Hall', *New Left Review* 153: 87–101.
Lodziack, C. (1988) 'Dull compulsion of the economic: the dominant ideology and social reproduction', *Radical Philosophy* 49: 10–17.
Mao Tse-Tung (1967) 'The role of the Chinese Communist Party in the national war', in Lin Pao (ed.) *Quotations From Chairman Mao Tse-Tung*, Peking: Foreign Languages Press.
Marx, K. (1977) 'The Holy Family', in D. McLellan (ed.) *Karl Marx: Selected Works*, Oxford: Oxford University Press.
Mepham, J. (1972) 'The theory of ideology in *Capital*', *Radical Philosophy* 2: 12–20.
Morely, D. (1980) 'Texts, readers, subjects', in S. Hall *et al.* (eds) *Culture, Media, Language*, London: Hutchinson.
Rabinow, P. (ed.) (1984) *The Foucault Reader*, London: Peregrine.
Samuel, R. (1987) 'Class politics: the lost world of British Communism', Part 3, *New Left Review* 165: 52–92.
Smart, B. (1983) *Foucault, Marxism and Critique*, London: Routledge & Kegan Paul.
Sumner, C. (1979) *Reading Ideologies: an Investigation of the Marxist Theory of Ideology and Law*, London: Academic Press.
Thompson, J. (1984) *Studies in the Theory of Ideology*, Cambridge: Polity.
Trew, A. (1979a) 'Theory and ideology at work', in R. Fowler *et al.* (eds) *Language and Control*, London: Routledge & Kegan Paul.
Trew, A. (1979b) 'What the papers say: linguistic variation and ideological difference', in C. Sumner (ed.) *Reading Ideologies: an Investigation into the Marxist Theory of Ideology and Law*, London: Academic Press.
Zola, E. (1954) *Germinal*, London: Penguin.

CHAPTER 4

One of the greatest contributions post-processualism has made to archaeology has been to force the issue of gender into a wider arena where it has received critical attention. But, although archaeology has become very open to this problem of the construction of sexuality, 'feminist' archaeologies have been very narrow in their engagement with feminist literature in other disciplines – a situation that is particularly hard to understand given the interdisciplinary pretensions of the rest of post-processualism, amongst which this book is doubtless to be included.

That there is a 'feminism' 'after' or 'beyond' structuralism is made clear by Bagnal in this chapter. What is at issue here is the very identity of 'woman' on which this practice is to be based, and therefore the very identity of the structures which hold her in place. Each of the three critics discussed here – Cixous, Kristeva, Irigaray – has taken up different strands of post-structuralism, most obviously deconstruction as part of a wider critique of Lacanian psychoanalysis, in order to problematise the concept of 'woman', which would represent a censure being placed upon her and therefore a complicity with the very patriarchal system it is seeking to overturn. In Lacanian terms, the conditions of identity are always *phallic*, the phallic signifier ('not a penis') representing the stability around which the chains of signifiers are arranged.

To these critics, much of what passes as 'gender archaeology' (eschewing the politically charged name of 'feminism') would be indisputably 'bourgeois', indicating an interest in securing for women a place in the existing order and hierarchies of power, rather than an overturning of the patriarchal system itself. While the differences between Cixous, Kristeva and Irigaray are themselves important, a very great deal can be learnt from their work about the philosophical and strategic legitimacy of 'being a woman', and about the wider terms at issue in the struggle for change. Although there is obviously still a place for a politics using woman's identity as a focus for action, it is also to be emphasised in its deconstructive aspect, in the need to take structures apart, a process which produces no 'zero point' or point of presence, in order *then* to assault and subvert the conditions that guarantee their reproduction.

4

The Experience and Identity of 'Woman': Feminism after Structuralism

Ruth Bagnal

In this paper I will be treating the three women writers whose reputation dominates French feminism – Hélène Cixous, Julia Kristeva and Luce Irigaray – in relation to a problem with an undoubtedly feminist bias. It is true that issues associated with feminist practice – the politicisation of women's experience and the attendant debate on the constitution, therein, of a 'feminine' identity – are problems which both inform their works and, to an extent, find their articulation within them. In them, the volatile body of French feminist practice is considered critically, and in part, created. Yet it would be a mistake to assume that all three writers are equally and typically representative of French feminism, or even that they would all state an allegiance to it, despite the contributions their work has made to debates which consider the status of women.

There is no easy assimilation, then, of their work to a French feminist project itself characterised by theoretical and practical difficulties. In the first instance, 'feminist' itself is a contested term in the context of recent French writing. It works as a term of division and recrimination rather than as a designation of a range of 'pro-women's' undertakings; as an accusation of complicity with the established principles of patriarchal definitions of power. A 'feminist' practice may refer to a reformist lobby of activists working for a parity within the social and political establishment, while some women counter this institution with an 'elsewhere', a woman's place outside the bounds of patriarchy and a positing of female specificity.

These self-cancelling extremes and countless intermediate positions are upheld within the range of what can only be called French 'feminisms' at the risk of supporting in this term a coherence of intention, direction and methodological assumption which such a splintering of political energies would erode and undermine. With parity and specificity set up as limits of feminist objectives and objections, the resistance of 'feminism' to its definition in terms of its components, its instantiations, will emerge as a precipitate of its political practice and as the mainstay of its theoretical arsenal.

THE EXPERIENCE AND IDENTITY OF 'WOMAN'

Fundamental to the generation of feminist thought, and a condition which vitally affects its undertakings, is a recognition of the fact that the object of its attention is always already implicated in a system of representations and power relations. A successful feminist critique must articulate the issues of the conditions of production of a discursive femininity and of an engagement with the material conditions of women's existence. The theoretical and practical resistance to this preconstructed condition is suggested by, and developed in, French feminist activity. With the work of Cixous, Kristeva and Irigaray I will show what is difficult in, and indicative of the ways in which the instruments and insights of contemporary intellectual debates are used to explode the restrictions of this condition, and to expose the (false) stability of conventional appeals to the self-evidence of experience and the integrity of identity.

What is at issue here is to see the way these appeals are diffracted in and around the decisive and divisive term of our enquiry: 'woman', a term which separates, initially, the female from the male and, further, the material from the discursive.[1] It is the way in which these divisions have (been) worked, their analytical elaboration and the motives for their conflation which, as they engage Cixous, Kristeva and Irigaray, will form the basis of the following essay.

I shall begin with the work of Hélène Cixous: already polemic, already problematic, her statements will be used to establish the terms on which the other writers will be seen to elaborate. The force of Cixous' argument lies in an appeal to the potential of getting women to write, of getting the feminine into writing. I shall go on to explore the very different interpretations of the feminine in writing which emerge in the works of Julia Kristeva and Luce Irigaray.

Julia Kristeva's criticism of the institution of French feminism opens into a philosophical debate on the nature of the feminine as such. Her sense of the 'feminine' emerges not in the 'naive, romantic' sense of an identity, but as its theoretical underpinning; as its negative but nonetheless creative component. Luce Irigaray's analysis returns to the conditions of this continued association of 'woman' with the negative pole of an established, and masculine, positive one. Experience of the historical and theoretical limitations imposed on 'woman' under this system is both the motive and the method of its critical undoing.

HÉLÈNE CIXOUS: TAKING FLIGHT

Fortunately when someone says 'woman' we still do not know what that means even if we do know what we want to say. . . . I no longer know when I say 'woman' whether I am talking about a person you would call 'a woman'.

(Cixous 1988, 40)

Cixous confronts the non-coincidence of woman-as-she-is-spoken and woman-as-she-is-lived with some ambivalence. There is the assurance of intention: 'we do know what we want to say', and this stands as security against a language resistant to the expression of this intention, and resonant with real opposition: 'we still do not know what that means' (its signifying potential lies beyond our control and understanding). There is a recognition that this form of representation, incommensurate with, and inaccessible to, its object, is the unique and unreliable means of communication available to the 'woman' in question. This state of difficulty is shot through with instability: the world is 'no longer' what it was and is 'still . . . not' what it might one day be. The conditions of textuality imposed on that potential are so binding that the prospects of differentiation between a 'woman' and 'a person you call "a woman" ' collapse into the isomorphism of intentionality and meaning – in French, both *vouloir dire* – and suppress the potential for the speaker to think outside the limits of her speech.

Cixous' campaigning for the feminine in writing is an effort to expand the capacities of writing to accommodate a female speaker and a female subject, a place from which she can see through (the imposture/imposition of) the grid through which she is conventionally seen. As advocate of a specifically feminine textual practice, Cixous must take issue with the supposition this entails of a feminine identity grounded in feminine experience. She upholds the experience of women's bodies as a source and supply of the pluralising principle of woman's liberation. Yet she recognises the implication of the feminine experience in, and inflection under, a dominant conceptual system which by definition stands in opposition to these very women's claims. The feminine experience we know is predicated on patriarchy, its contours mapped out in advance by the system through which such an 'experience' must negotiate a sense of its 'identity'.

The confusion of levels at which to pitch 'experience', and evidence of the political exploitation of this ambiguity, is put forward persuasively as an argument against investment in the feminine, in the opening editorial statement of the *Questions Féministes* review:

> It is dangerous to place the body at the centre of search for female identity . . . the political class of men (defined in the relation of oppression) defines us as a biological class in order to justify by nature its power as oppressor . . . our social class of 'women', a product of the political, has indeed the material contours of our biological category because of the effects of ideology.
> (Marks and de Courtivron 1980, 227–8)

Cixous rejects the implications of this argument, however, and its calls for a strategic bracketing of the somatic. She recognises and resents the threat of exploitation; she knows the assertion of female specificity is discursively bound to the sedimenting of effects and the hardening of a sentiment into a statement:

> By constantly saying 'I am a woman' we are creating a sort of forced truth. And the worst of it is that the more we say it, to avoid being swept along by the current far away from the native shores, the more securely we moor ourselves to avoid being separated, the more we contribute to reinforcing the limitation of the forces, to restricting the native territories and to fortifying the prejudices. We are closed in, we enclose ourselves, we enwoman ourselves. And the worst of it is that what was the sweet and inexplicable and intimate truth, the magic hand on the heart, beneath which we could faint with joy, becomes a phrase.
> (Cixous 1988, 50)

It is therefore paradoxical that Cixous should be speaking out, not only for the coming of women to writing, but for their writing *as women* in a sense determined by their anatomical sex as opposed to that of men. The assertion of anatomical difference is not, however, the only form the 'feminine' takes in the course of Cixous' writing: her use of gender terminology suffers a calculated slippage across a range of applications from the immediately anatomical to culturally posited attributes, and into the inflexions of speech and language itself. Somewhere within this undivided spectrum lies the potential for both repression and invention. It is with these disarming stakes that Cixous argues for a 'feminine' which will have its effect both as an element of textuality and the result of an extra-linguistic force. On the strength of such displacements Cixous sweeps between the referential and the textual with a rhetoric that ultimately stands or falls on the guarantee of its transitivity; and within which is located the basis of her manifesto and the power of her critique.

Cixous' now classic text 'The laugh of the Medusa' (Cixous 1976) projects a feminist aesthetic in the space cleared by a programme of demystification of the dominant cultural text. In this sense, 'woman' is already strategically allotted a range of positions which defy her fixed location in any single place: speaker and addressee, subject of oppression and agent of emancipation, representative of the common condition and yet irreducible to to an abstract concept of the 'feminine'. It is a woman constituted, vitally, in her own terms:

> Woman must write her self: must write about women and bring women to writing, from which they have been driven away as violently as from their bodies – for the same reasons, by the same law, with the same fatal goal. Woman must put herself into the text.
> (Cixous 1976, 875)

Cixous' insistence is this: that women gain access, as women, to textual practice which, like language and like human life, is sexed. Writing is gender-inflected as a condition of its material basis in a gendered human body and/but this condition is suppressed by a male-dominated discursivity.

Somewhere, unrealised and untheorised, the potential exists for a feminine writing. Unrealised, owing to its repression; untheorised by nature of its challenge to precisely that which can be conceptualised or contained within the reflective and recuperative mechanism that orders all, insidiously, around its own designs: 'A woman's instinctual economy cannot be identified by a man or referred to the masculine economy' (Cixous 1986, 82). 'These judges . . . make us answer their stupid summons stupidly, justify the non-justifiable, speak silence, crush the music under the millstone of words, lie by swearing to tell only the truth' (Cixous 1988, 49).

This passage shows a slippage from the hold of mechanistic repetition to insinuate a sense of oppositional resistance to this forced collaboration, this insistence on the same; and yet the woman is condemned within this framework only to resist, reply, reflect on opposition, not articulate her own intentions. A feminine practice, a feminine production, exists only in so far as it exceeds institutionalised norms. The feminine resides in an imperative that is an appeal at once to absolute alterity and to a material impulsion drawn from the bodily experience of gendered subjecthood.

Such a powerful investment in anatomy as a basis for determining 'the feminine' and, further, in defining a relation to writing threatens to feed directly back into the metaphysics Cixous exposes in the opening pages of 'Sorties':

> Where is she? . . .
> Father/mother
> Head/heart
> Intelligible/palpable
> Logos/pathos
> Form . . ./matter . . .
> *Man*
> Woman.
>
> (Cixous 1986, 63)

The question must be asked: how far does it suit a feminist polemic to uphold the anatomical? It seems that Cixous is claiming for the feminine the more direct relation to the body that has always been assigned to her. Yet, given this access to the material ground of linguistic inscription, a further insistence is made on the sexual differentiation of the speaking subject: both for men and for women 'there is an anchoring point somewhere in a far distant reality' (Cixous 1988, 18): 'These are the backgrounds of inscription, of thinking in the text. If I write letting some of my body come through, then this would be different, depending on whether I have experience of a feminine or masculine body' (Cixous 1988, 151).

In this sense, what will be revealed in a woman's language is a woman's body: 'For once she blazes *her* trail in the symbolic she cannot fail to make out of it the chaosmos of the "personal" – in her pronouns, her nouns, her clique of referents' (Cixous 1976, 886).

What are at stake, now, are male *and* female relations to language, as impressed with the stamp of sexual specificity. Even so, the applications are not equal and the feature of this gendered access to expression is the privileged status of the masculine and the subordinate, but irruptive, potential of the feminine. Cixous has implicated the male sex in the constitution of the discourse which it dominates, insisting that this privilege derives from a gender-determined base. Male paradigms are not only politically invested, but anatomically underpinned; and the organisation of a privileged discourse reflects not only the institution of this privilege but also the grounds which determine particular tropes as effective of its very institution:

> What is the other? If it is truly the 'other' there is nothing to say; it cannot be theorised. The 'other' escapes me. It is elsewhere, outside: Absolutely other. It doesn't settle down. But in History, of course, what is called 'other' is an alterity that does settle down . . . It is the other in a hierarchically ordered relationship in which the same is what rules, names, defines and assigns 'its' other.
> (Cixous 1986, 71)

This recuperation of alterity is the mark of an economy which organises around its own anxiety the poles of identity and difference, revealing in this construction its obsession with property, appropriation, one-ness and own-ness: 'a masculine bias: the fear of losing the attribute' (Cixous 1986, 80). Cixous reassigns this strategy its gendered, rather than universal, truth value; which leaves her free to hypothesise in a 'feminine' economy of difference not just a rival one, since here this kind of opposition no longer obtains: 'No longer would the common logic of difference be organised with the opposition that remains dominant. Difference would be a bunch of new differences' (Cixous 1986, 183).

There is a characteristic imprecision in the siting of this difference. It remains unclear whether it issues from a transcription of anatomy; or a drawing of plurality to *figure* femininity. The property of heterogeneity amongst women is assimilated to the property of heterogeneity within the woman herself. In its resistance to the singular – the site of reduction of the potentiality in/of 'woman' – the difficulty lies in the slippage from one plane of experience to another, refusing the temptation of a choice between alternatives. For Cixous, promotion is the idea of a discursive femininity different from bodily (sexed) existence but rooted in the manifest differences of gendered (cultural) experience. Answering with precarious ambivalence a crude biologistic backdrop to establishing the terms of sexual identity, this co-location of registers threatens to collapse into anatomy the properties of symbolic systems; or into language the material conditions of a subjected sex. It is against these untenable conditions of a volatile femininity that Cixous maintains her manifesto of feminine potentiality.

Challenging difference with diversity, and similarity with a series of shifting displacements, Cixous' strategy of unsettlement unfolds not in harmonised theory but by exemplification of the process it recommends: 'She breaks with explanation, interpretation and all the authorities pin-pointing localisation. She forgets. She proceeds by leaps and bounds. She flies/steals' (Cixous 1986, 96).

It is with urgency and exuberance that Cixous sustains her whole critique. Her writings are infused to this degree with stylistic and affective investment, with a disconcerting commixture of registers and items of reference. These many-layered writings defy the commentator to produce anything but a list of generic or thematic labels which look to be distributed into infinity as the works unfold, so disparate is their range. Such a facile rubrication only goes to show the resistance of the writing to this strategy of recuperation and containment: only prolonged exposure to the text can give the sense of the sustained but slippery argument which characterises Cixous' style(s). Cixous confounds conventional principles of classification and interpretation, making a mockery of the urge to assign a writing style to a set of normative generic enclosures; and making a heresy of the attempt to handle the disparate and disarming elements of her writing by bringing to bear on them a unifying interpretation which restricts their reference to a single plane. Such a strategy is shown as reflecting, in the selection of a privileged theme, not only the particular concerns of a given reader, but also the effect of the general reading system which rewrites proximities as property and the manifestation of differences as the repeated instantiation of the same. For Cixous, it is the privilege of the feminine to disrupt this monolithic and male-centred system. Such then is the appeal of Cixous' insurgency in action, creating a space for 'woman' to assert her identity and speak it, distinct(ive)ly:

> If woman has always functioned 'within' man's discourse . . . now it is time to displace this 'within', explode it, overturn it, grab it, make it hers. Take it in, take it to her woman's mouth, bite it with her woman's tongue, make up her own tongue to get inside of it. And

you will see how easily she will well up from this 'within' where she was hidden and dormant to the lips where her foams will overflow.

(Cixous 1986, 95)

JULIA KRISTEVA: WOMEN'S TIME/WOMEN'S PLACE

If this – Cixous – is feminism, Kristeva is hostile to it. Kristeva supplies, in her writing on the topic, the cogent summaries of tendencies within feminism which clarify its divergent perspectives and which reduce it to irresolution between contradictory narratives; and she underlines the paradox of a 'feminist' relation to a dominant social system it opposes, but in which and *by* which it is constructed and contained.

Yet it would be a mistake to take this criticism, and the antagonistic tone in which it can be voiced, as the index of a purely negative contribution to a feminist critique of discourse and society, on Kristeva's part. A significant part of her writing addresses, albeit critically, the crisis of feminine specificity; and these accounts re-emphasise the function and value of continuing to question a feminine identity and a 'woman's' experience in writing.

When dealing with women's issues, Kristeva sets a theoretical distance between the aspects of women's rights, and of women's relation to textual practice.[2] This confirmation of a difference between women's condition or status, and a writing practice, comes as a response to the collection of traps into which feminism may fall as a result of a too-easy contamination of the two. There is a place in Kristeva's theory for a feminine aspect in writing, but only as understood in theoretical terms of the constructions of verbal articulation and personal identity. To some extent Kristeva argues, too, for a special relationship of women to writing, in their 'attempts . . . to break the code, to shatter language, to find a specific discourse closer to the body and emotions, to the unnameable suppressed by the social contract' (Kristeva 1986, 200). This relation draws less, though, on the specific contents of women's experience than on the valorisation of experience itself as a means of understanding, as opposed to theoretical research:

> trying to explore the function and constitution of this contract, starting less from the knowledge accumulated about it (anthropology, psychoanalysis, linguistics) than from the very personal effect experienced when facing it as a subject and a woman.
>
> (Kristeva 1986, 200)

It is, nevertheless, a primarily theoretical perspective which Kristeva's writings express. Under this analytical light the principal terms of our feminist debate are refracted into the theoretically recuperable issues of experience as methodology, identity as a construct and 'woman' as an effect of textuality. This is not to say that Kristeva manages ultimately to resist a return to arbitrary and conventional images of the feminine, nor is it that other analyses fail to stand up to her criticism: arguably they will be enhanced by an understanding of the terms of their constitution offered by a Kristevan critique. Kristeva's hostility to feminism will be shown to be based on a critique of the conditions of resistance to, and self-recognition in, a dominant discursive practice. Her making of this strategy of resistance a woman's privilege, and her recovery of the vital contribution of the feminine to this discursive practice in the conventional space of material and the maternal, are, however, consistent difficulties which must be accounted for. They are, perhaps, slips as indicative of the difficulties in feminism as her difficulties are characteristic of the oblique analytical tactics by which her theory describes its very limitations.

In her essays 'About Chinese women' (Kristeva 1986, 139–594) and 'Women's time' (Kristeva 1986, 188–213) Kristeva sets out both the divergent and disappointing extremes of the tendencies within feminist politics as it has been established. One is to opt for an identification with the political structures currently governing society to the exclusion of women, the other to recognise and reinforce the separate status of women:

> We cannot gain access to the temporal scene, that is, to the political and historical affairs of our society, except by identifying with the values considered to be masculine. . . . Others . . . refuse this role and sullenly hold back, neither speaking nor writing, in a permanent state of expectation.
>
> (Kristeva 1986, 155)

Both are seen to perpetuate the very structures they seek to oppose, and to confine women either to an alienated participation in society – they function there, by necessity, as men (do) – or to an infinite exclusion from social practice. They identify with all that this society disowns and, thus, can do without.

If the stakes of assimilation are unacceptable, the implications of a supposed separatism prove to be a focus for more concerted criticism in Kristeva's work. It is principally against the claim of a political and textual realisation of an independent femininity that Kristeva argues when she speaks with contempt about a 'woman's writing', 'writing the body', as an expression outside the institution of language, 'a cry, a refusal, hysterical symptoms' (Kristeva 1986, 155) is seen as a retreat from any political engagement. As a supposedly successful linguistic expression it fails to establish a claim to syntactic specificity; also, it celebrates its vocabulary as a natural attribute, when this lexis speaks rather of a position, determined by a particular, political relation, established by an act of power. It is, further, a commonplace for the advocates of a 'woman's writing' to renounce all the attributes of rationality in the establishment of its own discursive space. This is a crucial misrecognition of the political motivation, and the political effectiveness, of annexing such a powerful discourse to those who occupy the place of power. Such a rejection of the rational leads in what it takes to be its own logic, but which is really a consolidation of this established power, to an abdication of the very access to self-determination. Toril Moi sums up this attitude in respect of the sexual political relations it involves: 'We must aim for a society in which we have ceased to categorise logic, conceptualisation and rationality as "masculine", not one from which these virtues have been expelled altogether as "unfeminine" ' (Moi 1985, 160).

It is in the face of substantial opposition from kinds of feminism which see in these 'virtues' the contamination of maleness with strength, who see the tools men used to fashioned in men's image, suiting only their purpose and thus less than useless to a woman, that Kristeva finds support from Toril Moi, Simone de Beauvoir, and Catherine Clément.[3] The vital retention of discursive rationality relies on the potential separation of logical categories of thought from the positions they have been used to underwrite – so the women may 'identify with certain values: not with the ideological (these are combated, and rightly so, as reactionary) but rather, with the logical and ontological values of a rationality dominant in the nation-state' (Kristeva 1986, 194). With this selective identification comes a displacement of the untenable extremes of feminist practice: 'Let us refuse these extremes. Let us know that an ostensibly masculine, paternal identification, because it supports symbol and time, is necessary to have a voice in the chapter of politics and history' (Kristeva 1986, 156).

This access to the worlds of politics and history must be understood as a strategic identification; a mobilisation of the techniques used for, and elaborated in, social contact, in order to extend the span of its attention outside itself – 'by listening, by recognising the unspoken in all discourse, however revolutionary, by emphasising at each point whatever remains unsatisfied, repressed, new, eccentric, incomprehensible, that which disturbs the mutual understanding of established powers' (Kristeva 1986, 156) – and on to itself, in order to expose its *'ostensibly* masculine, paternal' privilege and release its potentiating insights into the establishment of powers.

It is the necessity of this dissident complicity that Kristeva continues to stress. A challenge can only really come from *within*. Any formulation of an opposition must recognise the rules of such formulations as applied to itself; and any revolutionary position can only be so designated in respect of the authority it seeks to overthrow. It is only thinkable *in terms of* this given and governing situation: it can (only) be accommodated by the structure it sets out to disrupt.

Dissidence is complicity in this political analysis. Maintaining within this necessary position of complicity a sense of self-determination and of dissidence is not such an inevitability. Seen again in sexual political terms, the implication of acknowledging the imbalance of these power relations is a loss of confidence in the status of independent feminine subjectivity, painfully evoked by Christiane Rochefort:

> You had to refuse the so-called female values, which are not female but a social scheme, and to identify with male values which are not male but an appropriation by men . . . of all human values, mixed up with the anti-values of domination-violence-oppression and the like. In this mixture where is your real identity?
> (Marks and de Courtivron 1980, 185)

In this mixture your real identity can no longer be maintained as a concrete precipitation of lived experience; but, mobilising this mixture, identity can come to be understood less as the continuity, than as the constitution of consciousness, displacing the anxiety of experience on to malleable theoretical grounds.

Kristeva follows a post-Freudian model for the understanding of the constitution of subjectivity. She uses the theories of Freud and Lacan in a critique of what passes for conscious identity, which brings to bear upon the subject the conditions of its material and social existence. These conditions are what grounds and governs the subject's sense of self, and what enables the speaker to assume a subject position in language. Her subject is a subject-in-process: a generative process which assures continuity as a state of continuous change; and a judicial process which assigns meaning, confers the status and limitations of linguistic subject-hood on the agents of its articulation, guarantees the implementation of the law in respect of the subject who is subject *to* it. Kristeva assumes an alienated self, a subject constituted out of an imaginary (specular, and deceptive) projection of unity and identity.[4] The 'transcendental subject' on which a systematic theory of meaning is elaborated is rejected as the false reification of the indices of a more unstable access to language. The illusion of identity is what authenticates the individual, and it is at this illusionistic cost that selfhood can be articulated on the fragmented material substrate of human experience. The common sense of human subjectivity is overwritten by its illusory status. Identity is given to the self as a self's image: the figurative substitute for an absent selfhood; and as a compensation for the intervention of difference. Individuation is a trope of dependence where the contiguity of substance – (figuring) the desire of the mother in psychoanalytical relational terms – is rewritten as the conformity of appearance – answering to the law of the father.

THE EXPERIENCE AND IDENTITY OF 'WOMAN'

Identity is the assumption – and a false assumption – of subjective coherence which mediates the body and the text. This self-image prefigures the split – the *thetic* break, in Kristeva's terms – which establishes subject and object, which 'constitutes an attribution . . . a positing of identity and difference . . . the nucleus of judgement or proposition' (Kristeva 1986, 99). Language is articulated on a split subjectivity, on a split *in* subjectivity. The 'I' by which I represent myself is only a partial realisation of my imagined self, a temporary position taken up by a subject-in-process.

Kristeva takes up the psychoanalytic theory of the unconscious in order to gain access to the state or stage of subjectivity unrealised in this linguistic formation, in the symbolic order, the order of representation. Underpinning the symbolic act as the material condition of its possibility, and the site of psycho-social organisation, is the state of flux Kristeva calls the *chora*. The chora is a part and precondition of an effective signifying process. Not (yet) a position or a positioning function it 'precedes and underlies' positionality (Kristeva 1986, 94). It is a stage or a state of subjectivity derived principally from its disruptive effect on the complacent text of conscious understanding; valorised for its irruptive and revitalising force which brings about creative transformations within the symbolic order. The chora, prefixed as semiotic (that is, pertaining to signification) participates in creative symbolisation and is only separable from it in theoretical terms: 'Theory can "situate" such processes and relations diachronically within the process of the constitution of the subject precisely because they function synchronically within the signifying process of the subject himself' (Kristeva 1986, 96).

The theoretical terms Kristeva mobilises are, though, those of Freudian and post-Freudian analyses of the unconscious and of sexuality. The chora, qualified as maternal, slots into psychoanalytical developmental accounts of gender determination in ways which appear to reduce the feminine to the material grounds and nourishing functions which uphold the abstract relations of paternal filiation. The traces of this assimilation in *Revolution in Poetic Language* (Kristeva 1984) are elaborated in essays which deal both with the theory of textuality and, by extension, with the strategies of feminist activism. From this theoretical position *within* textual practice, what is feminine dislocates itself from the more conventional claims of feminist analysis:

> If the feminine exists it only exists in the order of significance of the signifying process, and it is only in relation to meaning and signification, positioned as their excessive or transgressive order, that it exists, speaks, thinks (itself) and writes (itself) for both sexes.
>
> (Kristeva 1986, 11)

The feminine, then, has no gendered dependence on the sex of the speaking subject, but resides in the relations of textual configurations. For all its designation of radical alterity to the symbolic: as pulsional pressure, as that which 'rends and renews' the text but is not recuperable within it, this 'feminine' must be recognised for what it is as a part of language. Kristeva's 'feminine' is determined within textuality, and not independently constituted outside it, not a separable instance which can secure a woman's place beyond the symbolic order.

Kristeva's feminine is the voice of paradox. Its positive or distinctive realisation is refused in favour of its productive and implosive, unstable potential. As it comes to figure the dissident and disruptive position, it is valorised for its revolutionary force – 'if we call the moment of rupture and negativity which underlies the novelty of any praxis "feminine" ' (Kristeva 1980a, 167) – and it is this theoretically woman's configuration that Kristeva commends to feminist practitioners as a newly valorised alterity –

> A woman cannot 'be' . . . a feminist practice can only be negative, at odds with what already exists so that we may say 'that's not it' and 'that's still not it'. In 'woman', I see something that cannot be represented, something that is not said.
> (Kristeva 1980b, 137)

'Woman' is determined as a relation within the symbolic order; the attributes adduced to her there speak less of her essence or specificity than of her determination within this institution. The ability to fit into this system is to be understood as a property of the representation not a property of the object. Yet if the 'woman' in Kristeva's question is an aspect of textuality, there remains a gendered subject in society in whose interest it is to expose the terms of her definition in this descriptive system. Although the main thrust of her argument supposes a human subjectivity difficult enough to negotiate for both sexes, there is a suggestion that the potential imbrication of theory and experience is a peculiarly female privilege:

> It can now be seen how women, starting with this theoretical apparatus, might try to understand their sexual and symbolic difference in the framework of social, cultural and professional realisation, in order to try, by seeing their position therein, either to fulfil their own experience to a maximum, or – but always starting from this point – to go further and call into question the very apparatus itself.
> (Kristeva 1986, 198)

This productive ambivalence of 'representation *by* language and experience *in* language' (Kristeva 1986, 55) is offered as a political method which turns on the principles of its own philosophical foundations. Luce Irigaray's work offers an example of this feminine specificity which can be measured both against the feminine potential Kristeva signals, and against her insights into its necessary implications in the existing bounds of political practice.

LUCE IRIGARAY: THE PROPERTY OF THE SUBJECT

Irigaray combines insights into the textuality of gender with an observation on the gender of textuality. Where other feminists are more than ready to leave the interpretation of masculine relations to sexuality for men to work out, Irigaray works back over precisely this area in order to draw out the implication of the feminine in masculine representations of sexuality as such. To fix gender within a system of representations is to escape its reduction to anatomically determined principles, but to assume a neutrality in the discourse that sets these terms of sexuality is to overlook the advantage that neutral-cum-universality stands to gain for its speaker. Irigaray resubmits the representation of sexuality to a criticism of its already gendered assumptions. She argues through the self-evidence of male privilege under patriarchy to relocate this institution as the instrument and effect of a unifying intentionality corresponding to a strictly masculine set of ideals: 'The truth the subject takes to be that of the world is still a double of *his* truth, which remains obscure to him' (Irigaray 1981, 14, my translation). 'What poses problems in reality turns out to be justified by a logic that has already ordered reality as such' (Irigaray 1985b, 88).

This strategy is indicative of an oppressive agency which *imposes* a certain condition on its environment in order to secure for itself the confirmation of its own privilege and power. What is established by this is a repressive, hierarchical organisation: 'The teleologically constructive project it takes on is always also a project of diversion, deflection, reduction of the other to the same' (Irigaray 1985b, 74).

Irigaray maintains that such a constructivist teleology is characteristic of the economy of the male imaginary. Its procedure is to establish in advance the contours of a particular identity and to look to the world and to 'woman' to confirm this speculation. It is in this sense that Irigaray commits the concept of identity to an economy which exploits its own definition of the 'feminine'. An authentic femininity responds to a more fluid, and pluralised, location of identifications which exceeds the formulations derived in respect of the male. Identity is the precipitate of the male imaginary and it can only offer an alienated and exploited version of femininity to those who would locate 'woman' within its conceptual limitations. To the extent that this construction imposes its own conditions on femininity it will, though, be seen to expose the anxieties proper to itself.

'Woman' is caught up in a logic of oppression where the subject is invariably masculine, and the complement precisely that which reflects and reinforces this assumption of precedence and priority. 'Femininity' is an identity stamped on female subjectivity by representational systems in which 'she' figures as a subject at the cost of conformity to 'his' established contours; or suffers as an object under the same regime:

> We can assume that any theory of the subject has always been appropriated by the 'masculine'. When she submits to such a theory, woman fails to realise that she is renouncing the specificity of her own relationship to the imaginary. Subjecting herself to objectivisation in discourse – by being 'female'. Re-objectivising her own self whenever she claims to identify herself 'as' a masculine subject.
>
> (Irigaray 1985a, 133)

The experience of being the subject of a certain discourse can be used to gain access to the determining conditions of such a discourse. A strategic identification with this 'object' position will reveal, by the nature of the limitations it imposes, what the stakes of the 'subject' are in such a system. By assuming, knowingly, the position historically assigned to her, 'woman' can enact her oppression in an ironic and interpretive register, can discover the scene of her exploitation without being reduced to it – in so far as it exposes, in itself, the conditions which have constructed her as such: 'She is not I. But I'd like to be "she" for you. Taking a detour, by way of her, perhaps I'll discover at last what "I" could be' (Irigaray 1985b, 17–18).

In the particular form of 'her' oppression, she reflects the premises informing the behaviour of the oppressor; and this relation is most successfully realised, not in the details of 'her' individual actions, but precisely in the reflexive function in which 'she' is reduced. By miming the mimetic function, playing (with) the role of the mirror reflection, Irigaray will be able to read back the the images imposed on the reflective surface as indices of the – male – desire for self-representation:

> I am trying . . . to go back through the masculine imaginary, to interpret the way it has reduced us to silence, to muteness or mimicry, and I am attempting, from that starting point and at the same time, to (re)discover a possible space for the feminine imaginary.
>
> (Irigaray 1985b, 164)

Irigaray's practical challenge is to reopen the discursive figures of philosophy in order to have them give up their feminine dues, to show what distortions have been effected on the feminine in the reassuring construction of a male identity. Systematic frameworks are seen to be articulated, inadmissibly, on a disavowal of the inexorable proximity of things as their relations are redetermined under a consequential, constructivist optic. It is the violence and insistence of these transformations that Irigaray exposes as a fundamental principle of theoretical/speculative procedures.

In an undertaking to re-establish these displaced material relations, a psychoanalytic method will gain access to the unconscious mechanisms of their repression. It is the persistent irony of this same psychoanalytic theory that it is the first to reveal its own participation in the specular economy of hierarchical systems which its methods are used to undermine. The Freudian theory of the psychic construction of gender reads as an exemplum of its own undoing in Irigaray's treatment. Where Kristeva mobilises such a theory as an explanation of inter-subjective relations under patriarchy, Irigaray reads the theory as symptomatic of such a society. For both writers a key stumbling block or 'blind spot' of Freudian analysis is its incapacity to deal successfully with female homosexuality – exclusively feminine relations. Irigaray reads past Kristeva's insight into this problematic to infer the repression of these relations as an index of homosexual, monolithic and masculinist privilege underwriting Freudian theory.

In the extended, opening essay of *Speculum*, Irigaray works through the conditions of production of the feminine in the Freudian discourse on sexuality, to expose its insistence on an economy of 'the same'. Freud's theory of castration anxiety and his attendant speculations on the construction of 'normal' femininity are worked into the texture of Irigaray's essay, which develops as an intricate dialogue between his statements, and her sustained interpretive criticism of their unrecognised assumptions of male bias. Such a perspective forecloses on the possibility of 'difference' understood as the mutual and plural relations which would figure a 'feminine' accountable to this logic of the singular and the same. Difference is sanctioned only as a difference in proportion, a difference in degree, and not a difference in kind; and it is under these conditions that Freud considers 'woman' as a reduced reflection of the determinant features of the male.

Femininity is established only in (inverse) relation to the Oedipal theory of castration. Sexual difference is a tributary of, that is, internally determined by, the projection and representation of the same: 'The hypothesis of a single identical genital apparatus – the male organ – is fundamental in order to account for the infantile sexual organisation of both sexes' (Irigaray 1985b, 35).

This identity is vital – in Freudian theory the little girl can (only) be considered as a smaller boy. Female sexuality escapes determination, at this stage, on purely anatomical grounds at the cost of its reduction to a dependent formation, a reassuring reflection of the correctness of a masculine and masculinist concern. Freud's 'femininity' is 'a male representation of female desire. One conforming to his desire, no doubt?' (Irigaray 1985a, 30 note 8). The sensory privilege of such a system is that of sight. While it conforms to the psychoanalytical modelling of desire, it can only do so to the advantage of the male whose sex is a visible attribute to be confirmed or denied by fixing the value of truth on the mirror image he makes of his own desire. An optical illusion is generated in which the female figures as a photographic negative of the male form; and can be accommodated into a hierarchy which assures his dominant position as possessor of the visible and the visual while she is dispossessed on both accounts. In his eyes, it is a differential equation which confirms the correctness of his speculation: 'Nothing to be seen is equivalent to having nothing' [*'Rien a voir equivaut a n'avoir rien'*] (Irigaray 1985a, 48).

Irigaray is not concerned whether the contents of these theoretical elaborations stand up to psychological proof: the point is that they impose their own conditions, as the precipitate of their informing anxieties, on women in the world. Her account turns on the imputation to 'nature' of the basis of a theoretical reflection; the sophistic fixing of this virtual image as a state of nature or a state of fact. A specular constitution of the feminine is reinforced within the same theoretical confines by an appeal to physical 'fact': the self-confirming correctness of speculation in its highly motivated selection of suitable tropes; and the female physical constitution is recentred around its reflection of the male.

The tortuous path of the Freudian 'feminine', as it maps out the male anxieties in reverse, is realised in Irigaray's writing 'as a woman' in the disruption of the straightforwardly 'progressive' syntax of a linear development. This 'linearity' is criticised for censuring the feminine investment in the figures of her own sexuality:

> The development of a woman in which the little girl would have to reject and devalue all representatives, male or female, and representations of her sex in order to turn her desires, her 'envies' toward the only sex/organ: the masculine.
>
> (Irigaray 1985a, 102)

This movement precipitates a 'castrated' femininity, a sexuality cut off from the positive realisations or representations of its own. Freudian theory gives an account of the Oedipus complex which, for the male child, remains an imaginary elaboration confirmed by a selective recognition in the physical contours of the female child, of the realisation of the state he fears. Irigaray reads this as the amputation of the feminine from its own complex of imaginary identifications and its implication in the masculine economy, both as the figure of negativity and the instance

THE EXPERIENCE AND IDENTITY OF 'WOMAN'

of undeniable fact. Representational and historical levels of experience are articulated in order to manipulate the feminine into a supporting and subordinate position:

> [T]o seek once again to make a science of it amounts to bringing it back inside the logic of the subject. To giving an over-and-beyond back over to the same. To reducing the other to the Other of the Same. Which could also be interpreted as submitting the real to the imaginary of the speaking subject.
>
> (Irigarary 1985b, 98–9)

The feminine is admitted under such a repressive regime only as a negative and dependent formation. It is thus that any indication of her specificity can only surface in the form of inconsistencies or contradictions in masculinist logic; irruptions accountable to his regulations – effectively the unconscious of his discourse: 'The same barrier that separates the "subject" from the "woman" is that which keeps the conscious and the unconscious apart' (Irigaray 1985a, 84 note 70).

In a strategic reclamation of the feminine from its repression under this system, Irigaray works through the elements of its specificity which irrupt into the systematic. Fragments are reconstituted as indices of a plurality unformulable in a specular economy. Irruption is rewritten as the momentary invasion into a resistant system of a sustained articulation operating in an 'elsewhere', a pluralised locus of mutual feminine relations whose indifference to phallic self-representation is translated into suppression or censorship within the male economy. Irigaray re-establishes within the 'blind spot' of systematic and self-confirming speculation a grammar of femininity which overruns the categories of singular and plural – feminine plural verb forms are bracketed on to the singular; first and second person are bridged into apposition; pairs of propositions govern ambivalently the syntax of a sentence; and the self-confirming future property of the future perfect tense is rewritten as a contingent of hypothetical construction. These raids on normalising syntax reply to the imperatives of Irigaray's descriptions of feminine relations. Essays which undermine the market economy of male rivalry by articulating the woman's part in this organisation allude to her repression but emphasise the positive imagining of her sex. The reflexive constructivism of a masculinist system is overrun by the inalienable contingency of material contiguity: of mother/daughter relations no analysis can satisfactorily or justifiably overwrite; of the proximity of female sexual relations which are always already in place, which confound systematic (re)organisation or dematerialise before its intervention:

> Any other instrument, any hint, even of theory, pulls me away from myself by pulling open – or sealing up – unnaturally the lips of that

slit where I recognise myself by touching myself there (almost) unmediated.

(Irigaray 1985b, 200, translation modified)

CONCLUSIONS

Irigaray's positive modelling of feminine specificity appeals to an aesthetic of contiguity: a contingency of association which undercuts the effort to arrange as fractured sections of feminist practice the revisions of theory it embraces and with which it contends. As long as this sense of disparity is seen in opposition, though, to a strict set of 'masculine' patterns, a deliberate intransigence masks the – potentially – more dynamic lack of congruence between the analytical models on which feminist thought draws, and the motives for their being taken up positively by women. Cixous, Kristeva, Irigaray: all three women are practising psychoanalysts and their (hypo)critical complicity with this and other academic disciplines is an issue their work raises and which Kristeva, perhaps, most successfully confronts. There is no independent constitution of a feminist psychoanalysis as such, just as there is no 'feminist' deconstruction. The replication of 'woman' in psychoanalysis calls, though, on the feminist to adopt a deconstructive stance to its understanding in this context. The theory must be made to submit on its own terms, since it entertains no other. The problem of articulating feminist theory and a deconstructive practice in respect of psychoanalysis is the implication that a woman is, as a woman, *bound* to pursue this strategy elaborated and authenticated as a masculine institution; an idea which sets up precisely the traps which feminism, in deconstruction and psychoanalysis, works to avoid. The persistent susceptibility of 'male' models to the disconcerting treatment of feminist thought reflects on the disparate and disruptive features of the feminisms contesting the institution of their authority.

ACKNOWLEDGEMENTS

I would like to thank Sarah Kay and Nick Sparks for their advice and encouragement.

NOTES

1. This difference between reference and sign, between the lived and the spoken 'woman' is echoed on a lexical level, in the difference between *la femme* and *(le) feminin* (in French), which loses a lot of the sense of this overlapping when translated into the English *woman, (the) feminine*.
2. 'There are many goals which women can achieve: freedom of abortion and contraception, day-care centres for children, equality on the job etc. Therefore we must use "we are women" as an advertisement or slogan for our demands. On

a deeper level, however, a woman cannot "be". . . . In *woman* I see something that cannot be represented, something that is not said.' (Kristeva 1980b, 137)

3. De Beauvoir (1980, 149) warns of the subtle confusion of what is male with what is universal, and Clément (1980, 135) of the dangers of ceding discourse and thought to a group which has had the advantage of their practice by tradition, not by nature.

4. Kristeva follows up the implications for feminism of Jacques Lacan's idea that the 'feminine', in terms of female sexuality, is a thing of language. There is no necessary and evident underpinning of Kristeva's position in Freudian and Lacanian psychoanalysis. It is difficult to convey this complex of theoretical accretions without ending up simply by compiling a glossary of terminologies: it is assumed that a knowledge of Freud's and Lacan's treatment of sexual differences through their own works, or in the details of Cixous', Kristeva's and Irigaray's arguments, is preferable to any hasty summary that could be made here.

REFERENCES

Beauvoir, S. de (1980) 'From an interview', in E. Marks and I. de Courtivron (eds) *New French Feminisms: An Anthology*, Amherst: University of Massachusetts Press.

Cixous, H. (1976) 'The laugh of the Medusa', trans. K. Cohen and P. Cohen, *Signs* I: 875–93.

Cixous, H. (1986) 'Sorties: out and out: attacks/ ways out/ forays', in H. Cixous and C. Clément, *The Newly Born Woman*, trans. B. Wing, Minneapolis: University of Minnesota Press.

Cixous, H. (1988) *Writing Differences: Readings from the Seminars of Hélène Cixous*, ed. S. Sollers, Milton Keynes: Open University Press.

Clément, C. (1980) 'Enslaved enclave', trans M. R. Schuster, in E. Marks and I. de Courtivron (eds) *New French Feminisms: An Anthology*, Amherst: University of Massachusetts Press.

Irigaray, L. (1981) *Parler n'est jamais neutre*, Paris: Minuit.

Irigaray, L. (1985a) *Speculum of the Other Woman*, trans. G. C. Gill, New York: Cornell University Press.

Irigaray, L. (1985b) *This Sex Which Is Not One*, trans. C. Porter with C. Burke, New York: Cornell University Press.

Kristeva, J. (1980a) 'Oscillation between power and denial', trans. M. A. August, in E. Marks and I. de Courtivron (eds) *New French Feminisms: An Anthology*, Amherst: University of Massachusetts Press.

Kristeva, J. (1980b) 'Woman can never be defined', trans. M. A. August, in E. Marks and I. de Courtivron (eds) *New French Feminisms: An Anthology*, Amherst: University of Massachusetts Press.

Kristeva, J. (1984) *Revolution in Poetic Language*, trans M. Waller, New York: Columbia University Press.

Kristeva, J. (1986) *The Kristeva Reader*, ed. T. Moi, trans. various, Oxford: Blackwell.

Marks, E. and de Courtivron, I. (1980) *New French Feminisms: An Anthology*, trans. various, Amherst: University of Massachusetts Press.

Moi, T. (1985) *Sexual/Textual Politics: Feminist Literary Theory*, London: Methuen.

Part Two
ARCHAEOLOGICAL PERSPECTIVES

CHAPTER 5

Although post-processual archaeology has spawned much passing reference to the problem of writing the past, to the need for a radical process of reading material culture texts, there has been little more detailed discussion and elaboration of what that might involve. It is this issue which Tilley's paper seeks to consider, particularly as the question is directly informed by the implicit post-structuralist emphasis on writing.

For Tilley, the problem of archaeology and how to do it is a problem of modernity, of a particular set of historically specific conditions and concepts; it is thus within an understanding of modernity, and through its terms, that a reforming of archaeological discourse must proceed. A part of that is to see archaeology as a materialist practice where, at one level, meaning necessarily resides in the arbitrary viewpoint of the observer – as seen, for example, in Tilley's 'history' of archaeology. Paradoxically, it is this very situatedness of interpretation which confers the past with its possible plurality of meaning from a wider perspective, and allows intelligible discourse at a lower level. The situated meaning Tilley proposes to extract through his programme of not just rewriting, but rewriting the terms of writing – is the analysis of power relations (the particular appropriation of power associated with Binford or Schiffer's appeal to an archaeology as science for example), and the understanding of the artefact as a discursive object, as a product of material relations.

Drawing on the influence of critics such as Macherey and Pêcheux some principles of writing/reading to this end are outlined. This involves various rhetorical strategies of decentring the institutionally invested production of the text to produce a meaning going beyond the appearance of superficial content, to read the past and writings on the past through an active irreverence, an active battle against academic self-importance.

5

On Modernity and Archaeological Discourse

Christopher Tilley

MODERNITY

For most of the development of human society the past has posed no problem or threat to the present. There has been no need for a special class of experts to investigate it, to probe into its trajectories, contours and hidden depths. Archaeology and a scientific history are preoccupations of a recent date. This sense of the past, cumulatively building on itself since the Renaissance, marks a new consciousness in which humanity becomes both object and subject of knowledge. It has led to an unparalleled enquiry by the west into its own genesis through detailed examination of empirical culture sequences to reconstruct the past of individual nation states. More recently in Britain and other European nation states this is increasingly being ideologically channelled through university courses and in more popular discourses to create a notion of a distinctive 'European' past. It is important to remember that both archaeology and history are *impositions* which only become structurally necessary in certain types of society such as our own. This imposition is part of the project of modernity which I take to both subsume and account for much contemporary discussion as regards the emergence of so called post-modernism, often conflated with post-structuralism. Postmodernity, however we may choose to define it, remains entrenched in modernity, it forms part and parcel of the same project, although its *forms* may be defined as different. Following Berman (1983) I want to refer to modernity in a very general sense as involving a definite experience of the world, a quality of contemporary life inducing:

- a break with tradition, a feeling of novelty and sensitivity to the ephemeral, fleeting, and contingent nature of the present
- a making sense of the experience of life in urban spaces and in a consumer culture
- awareness of continual change exemplified in Marx's comment, that 'all that is solid melts into air'

- a sense of possibility: that the world can be changed, turned upside down
- a constant force of dynamism that both spurs creativity and crushes and destroys us
- contradictory forces informing our lives: desire to be rooted in a stable and coherent personal and social past and desire for growth in experience, knowledge, sensibilities, growth that destroys physical and social landscapes of our past.

Modernism is, of course, part of the social and cultural space of capitalism. Capitalism has created the modern world, conditions for modernity. It has also created the conditions for its transcendence. Marxism is a thoroughly modern set of beliefs. Forged in a society of constant change, it itself proposes to change the world, to turn it upside down to create a new social order out of the wreckage of the old. In this limited sense modernity may be, as Habermas argues (1981), an incomplete project.

Archaeology is rooted in modernity. The historical knowledge code, itself forged in the modern age, becomes increasingly packed with signs of social transformation, growth, innovation, development. A sense of the past helps to fuel the modernist fires of change. Furthermore, a historical approach has to be invoked in any attempt to explain them, to make sense of our own experience. We actively create the past in a modernist identity space. The crucial questions become: what is the status of this knowledge of past worlds? and what do we want out of it?

The problem with archaeology in relation to a modernist identity space is that it has not sufficiently embraced the enormous potentialities provided to create new pasts, new knowledges, new truths and to use the difference of the past to challenge and restructure the black side of modernity: domination, exploitation, repression, alienation, violence. There has been an insufficient modernist dynamic within archaeology itself. Traditional and 'scientific' archaeological knowledges have both remained seriously abbreviated or curtailed. Given that we might say so much about the past, the lack of diversity in archaeological texts remains striking – the same old stale statements tend to be endlessly repeated. Nowhere is this more evident than in explaining change in the archaeological record where a few simple processes such as population pressure, technological or environmental change or an inexorable process of internal 'evolutionary' societal growth are often held to account for social change.

Furthermore for too long archaeology has consistently tended towards providing an alibi for cultural escapism as opposed to cultural critique. The past ten years or so have witnessed the surfaces of emergence of an archaeology which is beginning to embrace and self-reflexively understand itself as a modernist discourse, and a variety of competing and contradictory discourses have begun to develop to forge a fresh understanding of the past; structural-Marxist archaeologies; structuralist and contextual archaeologies; archaeologies drawing on hermeneutic theories; post-structuralist archaeologies; feminist archaeologies; archaeologies forged by ethnic minorities. The discipline is no longer one united in a spurious consensus. It is fragmenting, creating a new identity space that is, and can no longer be, totalising. This is again typical of the modern condition and may, of course, lead to a contradictory set of attitudes – on the one hand nihilism: such fragmentation destroys archaeology. If there is no longer one way to approach the past which may now be inscribed and reinscribed in texts in an endless piece of transformation, what guarantees can we possibly have of ever approaching the truth? If we have no solid means of grounding the statements that we make doesn't archaeology become a waste of time? We must either be aiming to achieve certain knowledge or we have no knowledge at all. On the other hand the growth of plurality of different approaches to the past may be held to positively encourage a sense of endless productivity and dynamism – fresh spaces for debate, discussion, self-awareness, new knowledges. It is this latter sense of dynamism, productivity and debate that I think needs to be fostered without embracing a strident relativism. A truly modernist vision of archaeology will be to regard it as an activity taking place now, something that intimately involves ourselves as part of the creation of meaning for our own times: a vital, living, socially aware, politically and intellectually critical and relevant lifeworld. To embrace modernity must be to embrace archaeology as intervention in the present, part of living.

LIVING, WRITING, WORKING

I have recently come across an unusual document purporting to represent some of the strands of recent developments in Anglo-American archaeology. In relation to my argument it seems worth quoting from at some length:

'Late one night, back in 1962, Lew sat down in his study feeling thoroughly frustrated. He didn't want to be a historian any more. The very thought of history sickened him. All day long he'd been trying to remember which artefacts he should put in which culture group. As a young novice, he didn't possess the necessary experience to do this but he wanted to start serious work right away and bypass all the years of training that were required. He'd been told that the culture groups kept on changing through time and across space because of invasions and migrations. These were good things and kept on happening. None of these events had any proper dates and neither Lew nor anybody else knew the names of the invaders. It was strange that the invaders always brought their pots with them and smashed up all the old ones. Still, this was probably a fact of life and certainly made charting social life in the past that much simpler.

Earlier in the evening Lew had been watching television. The space race was on. He became fascinated by the achievements of all the men and women in white coats wandering around the rockets. Having made a strong cup of coffee, Lew began to write. Inspiration had come and he knew precisely what to do. Instead of being a historian, he would be a SCIENTIST. Next day he told everyone about his tremendous idea. The old professors shook their heads with mild amusement and told him to get back to studying the culture groups. That made Lew very cross. He read lots of books on SCIENCE which he loved more and more every day. He wrote lots about it too, telling everyone how marvellous SCIENCE was and what a great feeling it was to be doing it. He measured and weighed everything he could find in the meantime and then wrote about how great that was. At the end of this measuring and weighing you could construct big equations. That really was proof you were doing something useful.

Meanwhile, across the Atlantic, David and Colin had got pretty much the same idea as Lew. They also disliked history and found it increasingly difficult to write counterfeit history books. Even the big invasions on the European past weren't, after all, that exciting. For example, Beakers had invaded Britain at least six times but no one knew where the battles took place or how they were fought. So both David and Colin rushed out and bought bright new lab coats. The fresh, crisp whiteness of their new coats gleamed in the sunlight and they burned all their old clothes. It felt good to forget about the past. Unfortunately neither David nor Colin had any laboratories to go in with their new coats. Still, they made the best of the situation and tried to pretend their studies were laboratories. They bought sharp new pencils and masses of graph paper. Soon, like Lew, they were also measuring everything and writing to each other in journals about how satisfied they were to be SCIENTISTS.

It didn't take long, of course, before everyone wanted to be a SCIENTIST. Fred, for example, was out one day in the Hay Hollow Valley, Arizona, wandering about wondering what he could do to be a SCIENTIST. Suddenly the solution came to him. It was so simple he wondered why he hadn't thought of it before. Fred decided that he wasn't in the Hay Hollow Valley at all. In *fact* he was in a natural LABORATORY. He went wild with excitement and sat down and started constructing sampling designs and collecting lots of data and measuring it. Soon Fred found that in his laboratory he could control space and time. Sometimes he did feel a little like God but this did not worry him unduly. Fred began to think more and more about the manner in which he was controlling space and time in his laboratory and came to the conclusion that everyone should be doing this. Patty Jo, Stephen and Chuck really liked this idea too. They also wanted to control time and space and suggested that if you didn't do this then you couldn't call yourself a SCIENTIST. Across the water this made Colin secretly cross (he couldn't talk about it much at the time in public). He knew that he was a SCIENTIST even though he hadn't made much effort to strictly control space and time. He had more faith in the SYSTEM and was a fellow believer with David.

The SYSTEM was quite remarkable. You could fit absolutely everything into it and draw lots of fancy loops. Once you had understood the SYSTEM you could not only fit everything into it but explain everything as well. David and Colin felt quite content with controlling the SYSTEM and didn't feel it really necessary to try and control space and time as well. It was so much effort, and, as far as David and Colin could tell, Fred and his friends weren't doing a very good job. Kent told them they were wasting their time. He claimed they'd been watching too many Mickey Mouse cartoons. The truth was that Kent also wanted to control the SYSTEM and he didn't like people controlling all space and time because they might tell him what he had to have in his SYSTEM. He wanted complete control over that. In the end things worked out quite nicely. David had control over the theoretical SYSTEM, Colin had the Aegean SYSTEM and Kent had the Mesoamerican SYSTEM. Fred also established a SYSTEM in the Hay Hollow valley. It was a bit smaller than the others but that only made it easier to control things.

These SYSTEMS had been constructed in such a manner that they were incredibly stable. Nothing seemed to be capable of changing them. They were obviously built to last for all time. The SYSTEM really did seem to stop history in its tracks. This was good in a way because the SYSTEM represented SCIENCE rather than history. However, David and Colin and all the others who had made their own little SYSTEMS did want to see a bit of change. The SYSTEM would obviously be a lot better if you could make it move. Various ideas developed. Drastic changes in temperature or environment were one. The most popular way to get the SYSTEM moving was quite simple. You put too many people in it and they made it move. Population pressure became extremely popular in different systems all over the world. Naturally this was a bit hard on the people in the SYSTEM but as they couldn't talk or see you it was possible to do almost anything to them.

Some people didn't like the SYSTEM. It was too abstract and complicated. A young person was really required to control it. Eric had spent much of his life as a sheep farmer, and didn't feel up to controlling a SYSTEM. In fact he did not believe in it. Instead he enjoyed talking about bones. Soon he established a huge room full of bones. Having toyed with the pretentious idea of calling this room a laboratory he decided this type of institutional prop wasn't really necessary and began writing. He knew that he had to stop the SYSTEM in some way. Bruce had criticised both the SYSTEM and people controlling space and time before. Nobody had listened to him, while Glyn and Grahame and all the other old archaeologists, as they now became labelled, didn't seem to have much idea of what was going on. Of course they had heard about laboratories and the way you could create SYSTEMS but they couldn't be bothered to make the effort to understand it all. They really liked to carry on digging and fill up the museums with masses of things to look at. Back to Eric and his bones. Eric had the idea that you could call the bones ECONOMY and that this was the most important thing in the world. Eric's ECONOMY was a bit limited in scope. It was basically a euphemism for writing about what people were eating. In addition to looking at bones, by walking in little circles around sites you could also find out what people had had for dinner.

Eric didn't want to make his ECONOMY stable like the SYSTEM. He got it moving by ensuring that there were never enough bones to go round. All the people in his ECONOMY, because of the lack of bones, were starving and fighting and creating lots of changes. However, whatever they did, whatever technological innovations they introduced, it was simply no good. This was a cruel world when compared with Colin's Aegean SYSTEM with its magnificent civilisation replete with vines, olives and metals.

About a decade after Lew had first become a SCIENTIST, almost everyone, at least in America and Britain, had bought lab coats and were busy developing new technologies to control the past. They were being so objective they had forgotten about people all together, at least those living in the past. However, they were concerned about the impact they were having on other archaeologists in the present. The centres of new archaeological power felt it necessary to measure the influence they were having. Ezra and others started conducting citation surveys to determine just how much impact was being made on the rest of the world!

The SYSTEM has helped to create a timeless world. Young Ian showed archaeologists various ways in which they could control space. One basic idea was to change settlements from being place in which people actually lived and instead call them SPATIAL NODES and connect up huge regression lines between them. The statistics were amazing: page after page of symbols. So long as you could do this meaning didn't really seem to matter. Of course, Fred and his friends had tried to control space before but their work wasn't really all that practical because they had controlled space by compressing it into LAWS which everyone had to obey. Ian's space was a bit more flexible and could easily be manipulated. Regressions, like everything else, fitted very nicely indeed in the SYSTEM.

Despite the fact that he was a SCIENTIST Lew got tired of measuring things people had made and constructing equations. It became increasingly clear to him that people, either in the past or in the present, just didn't go together with SCIENCE and he decided to eliminate them altogether by creating a SCIENCE of BONES. Lew really enjoyed working out which dog ate which bone. He came obsessed with his new SCIENCE but many other people began to forget about him. Michael had a similar idea and similarly rejected the idea that people had much to do with the past. What really mattered were the activities of earthworms, wood-rotting fungi, and various other types of animals and microbes in the present. You could sometimes, perhaps, talk about people too in a rather limited way provided you confined yourself to measuring the distance between hearths, making an inventory of the individual timbers used to construct a hut, or working out statistically whether they were more likely to lose a drawing pin than a 40-ton lorry.

Others felt there was still a need to maintain real people in the picture in some way at least. Michael J., Tim, and others saw people in the past as business executives who were always out to minimise their risks and maximise their profits. You sat in your cave in the Stone Age, with bone calculator ready to hand, and worked out utility indices for hide, meat, antler, weight, protein content, etc. of various species of animal and then set out to eat them with the minimum amount of effort. The most successful entrepreneurs survived and the rest were eliminated from the prehistoric market. This was a realisation that OPTIMISATION and EFFICIENCY have always been the order of the day. The past mirrored the present so faithfully it seemed almost pointless to investigate it at all. You already knew what was going on!

Just about the same time as Lew had created his new SCIENCE of bones and the entrepreneurs were moving into the Palaeolithic, Colin moved south from a very cold place. The heat probably went to his head a bit. One day while basking in the sunshine, he discovered an absolutely huge equation. It was so vast that you could get lost in it and almost nobody could understand it. That was good! Colin immediately wondered how he could fit the new equation into the SYSTEM. The only way that this was possible was to create lots of catastrophes. The poor people in his SYSTEM simply didn't know when they were going to be hit next. Bruce later claimed this only illustrated Colin's pessimism in the wake of the 1973 oil crisis.

By the late 1970s the new framework was getting a bit tarnished. There were quite a few different perspectives around. Some archaeologists were grappling with the problem of overpopulation in the past, others were wondering exactly how many calories had been expended to build a tomb or flake an axe. Others diversified to analyse such things as the spatial distribution of cow pats in a field or measuring exactly how many times in a year a dog might knock over a pot in a street corner in Peru. SCIENCE had now spread to Scandinavia, Australia, and many other parts of the world but all the excitement had gone and some were beginning to question exactly where and to what purpose all this was leading.

In Britain some fresh developments took place. Having just completed his ninety-fifth analysis of Iron Age bone combs in Wessex, not to mention all the spatial autocorrelation studies and manipulations of the rank size statistic along with computer simulations of the length/breadth indices of flint points, Ian decided that he just couldn't take it any more. He realised that all this SCIENCE just wasn't getting him any further in understanding anything and it was deadly tedious anyway. Having moved to Cambridge he and his students went French, as had Mike, John and Barbara in London somewhat earlier. Ian imported the SYMBOL and the STRUCTURE. These were used to bomb the SYSTEM, LAWS, the ECONOMY and everything else that had preceded them. Mike R. imported and disseminated MODES OF PRODUCTION, CONTRADICTION and the WORLD SYSTEM which subsumed every other SYSTEM which had previously been built. Colin's Aegean SYSTEM was dwarfed in comparison with the sheer scale of this!

The SYMBOL and the STRUCTURE were particularly slippery and difficult to grasp. Enveloping most of life they were constantly changing from place to place and time to time. They never seemed to have quite the same meaning twice which had definite advantages according to the type of argument you wanted to make. Tombs kept turning into houses, houses into women and women into pots. Europe and the rest of the world was full of such TRANSFORMATIONS. For Mike R. and the others in London, CONTRADICTIONS were rife, everybody was contradicting and exploiting everybody else; individual against individual, lineage against lineage. This picture of the past was almost as dismal as that found in Eric's ECONOMY. The world was in a perpetual state of implosion, PRESTIGE GOODS spread to Europe from Melanesia and West Africa and contradictions with kin-based lineage systems were no sooner dissipated than they were replaced by others in Crow-Omaha-type kin groupings. CENTRES AND PERIPHERIES kept on changing and were soon spread by Kristian from south-west Germany up into the far reaches of northern Scandinavia. Eventually you began to realise that your toilet was on the periphery of your bath.

All these new concepts were just insufficient for Chris, Danny and Mike S., who wanted to incorporate many of them and include many others. SYMBOL, STRUCTURE, TRANSFORMATION, CONTRADICTION were maintained and IDEOLOGY, STRUCTURATION, POLYSEMY vigorously promoted. Any interpretation of the past now became particularly difficult. POWER was everywhere investing everything down to the last flint flake and you could no longer be certain whether the flake was representing or distorting what went on in the past. This was in addition to the usual meaning shifts that could be expected every so often. After a while Mike and Chris realised that archaeology was simply a bourgeois plot subtly manipulated to control the workers. What was needed was a revolutionary movement that would do away with it once and for all. The arena of the class struggle was to be transferred from the factories and the streets to the interpretation of 5000-year-old pot shards!

What ever will happen next? We can probably expect a PSYCHO-ANALYSIS of the Bronze Age, a DECONSTRUCTIVE analysis that will finally rid us of the Mousterian, a radical FEMINIST struggle against male domination in the linear pottery culture and various other interventions such as a growing archaeology READERS' AND WRITERS' LIBERATION MOVEMENT . . .'

At this point, sadly, the text peters out into a confused cacophony of words and statements in which an attempt appears to have been made to question the epistemological and ontological status of the 'history' by conducting some form of self-reflexive discursive analysis. Certain stains on the document suggest that the author must have turned to drink.

DISCOURSE

One obvious moral of this little history of archaeological modernity, if I interpret it correctly, is that the past is a *construction*, socially produced, something done here and now, in the present. The implications of this need to be closely examined but they by no means imply a pernicious form of relativism in which 'anything goes' and every statement made about the past is equal to any other. It is quite clear from the history of archaeology that anything does *not* go. The past resists our constructions, its empirical materiality has to be respected. At the same time it is necessary to realise that there is no firm bedrock or foundation to which we can anchor our statements about the past, no criteria of validity absolutely independent of the practices of the archaeologist. The task is to come to terms with a materialist position in which it is realised that any (serious) archaeological practice involves minimally a triple dialectical relation: between the materiality of the past, the materiality of the present, and the materiality of the process of constructing discourses, writing texts. Each age, of course, can believe that it has managed to capture the meaning of a segment of the past but if we look in a broader historical perspective the singular meaning becomes transformed into a plurality of different meanings. The archaeological record is not so much a historical as an anthropological fact. Meaning is multiple not because of an error on the part of the archaeologist but because the past is open, something which by virtue of its very social and historical constitution contains different meanings.

ON MODERNITY AND ARCHAEOLOGICAL DISCOURSE

The study of the past is a materialist practice in which it becomes necessary to take sides in any discussion, to take a stand, to fight for what we believe in. And this does not mean therefore that we ignore evidence or simply manipulate it to suit our purposes. Archaeology inevitably forms part and parcel of a battle over words and their meanings. To realise this is to understand the insertion of the archaeologist within a modernist identity space in which he or she *makes* rather than *finds* knowledges. We decide between different versions of the past not just by evaluating discourses and the arguments made in them. We also evaluate the way in which the argument relates to material symbols: *evidence*. The evaluation of arguments and evidence means that we can accept some arguments as valid and reject others. But there are no absolute ground rules for this process. It all depends on the case in hand. If we abandon such a position for one in which all statements are simply totally reducible to a certain individual, social group, time or place then there would seem to be no point whatsoever in doing research. But to think that we can place any 5, 10 or 1000-year universal guarantees on our statements as embodying certainty is completely ludicrous – an idealist fantasy.

One way of understanding why archaeologists work and write as they do is to examine the social relations in which discursive production is embedded. Another related strategy is to analyse those discourses themselves in detail. I will refer to discourse as something that comes between *langue* and *parole*: situated speaking and writing in actual language use in which groups or classes of users are differentially related to *langue* and do not participate in it equally. Pêcheux (1982) has underlined the fact that speaking and writing are not only instruments of communication (as in an idealised sender/receiver of message scenario) but also of non-communication. In particular linguistic communities' discourse is related to power–knowledge–truth strategies and is connected to struggles and divisions in society. It is readily apparent that discourse is to be related to processes of domination and resistance particularly in class-divided societies such as capitalism. Those who cannot speak the 'right' language as fostered in educational systems become subordinate to those who can. Discourse is not only bound up in a general way with divisions of labour but quite specifically with different social institutions and academic 'disciplines'. These create specific sites of communication which establish the place and role of the sender and receiver of messages and determine what kinds of message may be deemed appropriate and those to be outlawed and banished. Saussure's *langue/parole* distinction is both highly general and abstract, an idealisation. Discourse we might say is the specific material site in which the relationship between language and speech actually gets played out. Theoretical linguistics cannot deal adequately with the realisation of language in the world. Discourse analysis on the other hand, is a manner of approaching language use as a materialist practice embodying power and ideology. Another way of thinking about this is to understand that when we move from the morphology of the sentence and syntax to meaning we leave behind a *langue* to which ideally everyone bears an equivalent relation to consider the material site of the enunciation. A sentence is not just a collection of linguistic signs to be understood in their difference. The meaning in it is a predicative act in which something is relayed to someone in the here and now.

The meaning of the sentence takes on a material character according to the wider discursive formation (arena of writing/speaking) in which it is situated so that the same sentence and the same words can take on different meanings in relation to their social conditions of enunciation and reception. Meaning is not neutral but relates to institutions, groups and struggles. Althusser has remarked that:

> The realities of the class struggle are 'represented' by 'ideas' which are 'represented' by words. In scientific and philosophical reasoning, the words (concepts/categories) are 'instruments' of knowledge. But ... the words are also weapons, explosives or tranquillisers and poisons. Occasionally the whole class struggle may be summed up in the struggle for one word against another. Certain words struggle amongst themselves as enemies. Other words are the site of an *ambiguity*: the stake in a decisive but undecided battle ... The philosophical fight over words is a part of the political fight.
>
> (Althusser 1971, 24)

It is this general position that I want to amplify in relation to archaeological discourses – that words and sentences use *matter*, that they are a site of struggle, and that the words and sentences may be utilised in radically different ways to further different ends. It is possible to distinguish between discourses in *dominance* which lay claim to a universal significance and importance through manipulating words and sentences in a particular manner and discourses in *resistance*. The latter attempt to undermine the status of the dominant discourse in order to open out new possibilities for truth and knowledge systematically denied in dominant discursive forms which always attempt to make themselves appear as certainties: self-evident, beyond questioning, in the true.

REMARKS ON THE DISCOURSE OF A PSEUDOSCIENCE

I will introduce the position just mentioned by considering three pieces of relatively recent archaeological discourse (Binford 1983, chapter 6; 1987; Schiffer 1988). Let us start by asking a simple question: What do you do if you want to convince someone of the validity of your own position and crush all those who disagree? A general characteristic of discourses in dominance is that considering their position as self-evidently true they have no real need to argue for it. In their 'rationality' they thus display their irrational nature. A typical discursive strategy employed by Binford and Schiffer is to use emotive and value-charged 'keywords' such as *science* and *objectivity* – and use them over and over again and/or employ them strategically as a substitute for logical argumentation. We all know that in the west to be scientific is consistently equated with the 'good'. Any one who heeds not the ways of science immediately runs into the danger of being labelled reactionary, regressive and 'relativist'. Now, of course, there are many different definitions of science, objectivity and scientific activity as a process linking subjects to objects in various ways. In a very real sense these words are vacuous: empty of any specific content. The content only becomes moulded through their discursive employment. Here I do not wish to 'fill up' these words but to think that it may be rather more interesting to examine their conditions of use in the texts under discussion, remembering that words not only have a certain exchange value as communication but situated symbolic and referential significance going beyond themselves.

Binford's article (1983, 45–55) is eleven pages long. On these pages 'science/scientific' occurs on 58 separate occasions and 'objective/objectivity' a further 20 times. This gives a quite remarkable mean figure of 5.3 references to science on every page and 1.8 to objectivity. In another paper (Binford 1987) 'science/scientific' appear 52 times (mean: 4 times/page). Clearly the hope must be that if you repeat a value-loaded word and use it to advance your own position someone may be foolish enough to believe you in the end. Simple *repetition*, or perhaps incantation, lies at the heart of Binford's discursive strategy. Science functions as a juggler's ball. The word science in Binford's text is unnecessary to any of the points he wants to make but it still *has* to be there. When we watch the balls of the juggler we become mesmerised. Only if he or she drops one will we regain consciousness of our surroundings, of context, life going on around the event. And for Binford, the word science is exactly analogous to the juggler's ball. Divested of any social context it accrues a thing-like quality. Science isn't about people but an entity one throws into the text in order to valorise anything and everything you want to say or do. All very convenient.

Refreshingly enough, in Schiffer's 18-page text (1988) the word 'science/scientific' occurs on a mere 20 occasions. The textual distribution of this magical word is not however uniform. There are three mentions in the introductory pages, another three in the concluding sections, thus establishing a certain symmetry, while in the bulk of the text the word is absent. 'Science' thus sets the scene and concludes the exposition. The word clusters an additional twelve times in just five paragraphs. These are parts of the text in which Schiffer attacks work that he claims is 'relativist'

(1988, 467–9; cf. Binford 1987, 402). Nowhere, of course, does Schiffer explain the meaning of this 'thing' science. It is no doubt simply assumed that we all know what it is: a commonsense category of goodness and value.

In Binford's and Schiffer's texts science is a category consistently employed as a substitute for thought. When you have this 'thing' on your side arguments are hardly required and, indeed, Schiffer criticises the attempt by Michael Shanks and myself (1987) to 'discredit other theories, using a variety of strategies including ponderous argument' (1988, 468). However, as Schiffer's text makes clear, if you enlist 'science' this relieves you from the troublesome burden of argumentation altogether, 'ponderous' or otherwise. Mere mention of the word is enough to annihilate the opposition. Binford's and Schiffer's thing called science functions in just the same way as religious dogma. One is either a believer and thus 'saved' or doomed to the fires of hell.

A battle over words – Binford's and Schiffer's 'science' is my ideology. Their texts embody a refusal to acknowledge themselves as anything other than neutral, impartial, universal, value-free which they patently cannot be and are not. They are advancing an ideology, which naturally refuses to acknowledge itself as such and masquerades as truth. Science for them is a term which bears no relation to the real world of people working, living, relating, writing:

> Archaeologists produce data from facts on contemporary observations on artefacts. This important point is given further importance when we consider the criteria commonly employed *in* science for judging the admissibility of data for scientific treatment. . . . *In* modern science the word *projective* has a very specific meaning. It simply means that the rules for observation are made explicit . . . .
> (Binford 1987, 392 my emphasis)

In science, *of* science, *by* science, *for* science; let's all climb aboard. Once upon a time 'objective' used to refer to processes of rational argumentation, now it is to be reduced to an empiricist administrative procedure of describing facts and objects. Science with its thing-like qualities functions in the texts discussed as *power*: those who possess it have power on their side. The dispossessed – the opposition – are to be crushed. This 'science' is to be utilised to foster relations of dominance. As Schiffer makes clear, to possess this thing has a number of definite advantages: 'society rewards those who address its significant problems with employment opportunities, grants, prizes, prestige' (1988, 468). No doubt those who criticise the social order cannot expect any of these 'rewards'. Indeed a failure of so called 'neo-Marxists' according to Schiffer is that they simply do not recognise 'the inevitability of social stratification in complex societies' (1988, 468). Schiffer confesses that he is 'distressed by the prospect that some investigators wishing to use archaeology as a means to further unspecified political ends, will subvert the scientific process' (1988, 469). Wouldn't that mean no grants, prizes or prestige?

We all know that capitalist society rewards those who duly conform to its values and expectations and don't rock the boat and can be thankful to Schiffer for reminding us of this basic fact of life. In Britain, faithful industrialists who contribute to Conservative Party funds can confidently expect a knighthood. In the States those who work not just in a Department of Anthropology but in a 'laboratory of traditional technology' (Schiffer 1988, 461) can hope that the funds will flow freely even if the 'scientific' statements made such as: 'Wood also is altered by weathering, a synergistic process involving both water and sunlight' (1988, 473) and social theory can be 'tentatively divided' into two domains: hunter gatherers and complex societies (1988, 465) do appear to be just a little banal.

In Melanesia the phenomenon of the 'Big Man' is well known. The big man is one who has acquired power and prestige. According to Sahlins (1963) the decisive factor in the building of personal renown is the ability to amass wealth and redistribute it with an astutely calculated generosity. The big man and the power he possesses represent a specific institutional reaction to a specific type of society: a response in an acephalous system to the temporary need for supralocal political power in some circumstances such as warfare, exchange and political ceremonies. Analogies to 'Big Man' type systems can readily be found in academia in which prestige is to be related to citations of one's work. The worst thing that can happen is to be ignored. This is clearly uppermost in Schiffer's mind as he references his work no less than 66 times or about four times a page. There is hardly a paragraph in which his own name does not crop up somewhere. Schiffer's science does seem to be a bit on the narcissistic side. Occasionally judicious reference is made, in limited measure, to the works of others but in the references we duly find Schiffer's work in a ratio of 16:1 to that of almost everybody else. His nearest self-created competitor turns out to be Binford (16, 8). Despite this Binford's works are only referenced 14 times in the text in a few paragraphs, a figure dwarfed by Schiffer's total and continuous 'presence'.

The nature of the prestige-power game being played out is transparently obvious. It betrays precisely the sense of personal insecurity as that found in Cambridge inaugural lectures in archaeology in which the speakers insert themselves into genealogies of previous professors and make reference to the antiquity and importance of the institutional post of which they are incumbent (Tilley 1989). As Sahlins' own account makes clear 'big men' who continually need to reaffirm their own status, and in this case, need to use magical keywords as props for their arguments are, in effect, weak men.

THE PRODUCTION OF MEANING

Moving on from discussion of these rather blatant, and by no means exceptional, examples of the manifestation of power in archaeological discourse I want to discuss the nature of writing and the manner in which it mediates between past and present in a more general way. My concern is the manner in which meaning becomes grafted onto the past. The inscription of artefacts, their attributes, context and associations into a textual medium is something that requires problematisation. Any writing of material culture is transformative. There is a gap between words and things. Writing is not, and cannot be, a transparent medium for expression and analysis. The associations made between artefacts and their context occur as much in the linguistic medium of the text as they do in that which the text may attempt to describe or discuss. Studying material culture then inevitably means a process in which artefacts become transcribed. The end product is both something and something less than the raw materials worked upon. It is this 'something' that requires understanding. The text is neither a direct expression of reality, nor is it divorced from it. Concomitantly meaning in the text is dual. It is to be found both in the text's organisation and syntax and in relation to the text of the world. These two aspects of meaning cannot be separated out, they inhere in each other and help to constitute each other.

The artefact in the text is always a *discursive* object. This theoretically and conceptually produced object is formed by a process of language acting on the world. No description is 'pure', nor can any description be 'total'. Listing the attributes of a house, an axe, a pot or a grave does not allow one to arrive back at these things. The textual embodiment of material culture is always partial, a reduction of complexity. It also goes substantially beyond the pot etc., because it transports it into an entirely different medium, a medium which then sets to work on it. This means that I or you never deal with the artefact or more generally the past or the present in-itself and for-itself. Knowledge and understanding comes through a linguistic, textual medium. The necessity to place things into texts is simultaneously a violence done to those things and a productive and creative exercise. Writing material culture is *producing* material culture.

Now, this linguistic production of material culture has to be taken very seriously indeed for the *meaning* of material culture is created in the text. It does not reside outside the text. From the very beginning to the very end meaning resides in what the text *does* to the non-textual on which it operates. Meaning always remains internal to the text, its language use, and the reader's response to it. Meaning does not reside externally over and above this relation except insofar as discourse has wider effects in the world in helping us to interpret, understand and intervene in it. But it needs to be recognised that all activity is always already an interpretation of an interpretation of an interpretation.

Meaning can be understood as a form of materiality, a production rather than an abstraction (something which just occurs within thought). Every material object that is studied becomes constituted as an object of discourse. What this means is that objects only become objects *in* discourse. Such a position does not deny that a pot or rock carving exists outside thought but that they could constitute themselves in a particular manner without discourse.

WRITING IN A NEW WAY

You and I must write material culture and we must write the past and the present. It follows that part of the creation of an alternative past and an understanding of material culture will, of necessity, be to write it in a different way than is at present the case. You and I need to experiment in the production of new types of writing, of textual inscription. What might these fresh forms of writing be? Four areas might be tried. First we can experiment with *organisation* of the text itself – the manner in which we inscribe words and statements on to a page. Second we can attempt to break the types of power relation set up between the writer and the reader in texts as constituted at present by attempting to write 'producer' as opposed to 'consumer' texts. Third we can self-reflexively examine ourselves, our subjectivity as writers in the texts that we produce. Fourth: the archaeologist is not the humble servant of the artefact who must always bow in deference to it. Growing awareness of the conventions governing discourse will lead to the development of a way of writing/challenging the boundaries between a text claiming to be an analysis of the artefact and thus remaining an appendage to it, with no further interest, and a text that has a value in its own right *as* a text, a literary production.

The employment of archaeological texts, 'scientific' or otherwise, dealing with any region or data set takes place at present exclusively in terms of a linear narrative structure bearing an uncanny resemblance to a detective story. In the introduction we are presented with the problem to be solved. Putative clues are then unfolded and discussed, with the reader left in suspense until the tension is broken in the conclusion and the real meaning of the evidence is revealed. The hold of such nineteenth-century historicism over archaeological discourse is very powerful indeed. A 'counterfeit' history occurs in the very structure of archaeological writing. This lends itself perfectly to the discussion of grand themes such as the emergence of 'civilisation', the origins of agriculture, the beginnings of metal technology, the expansion of trading networks, the 'development' of European society and the rest of them. An obsession with origins in

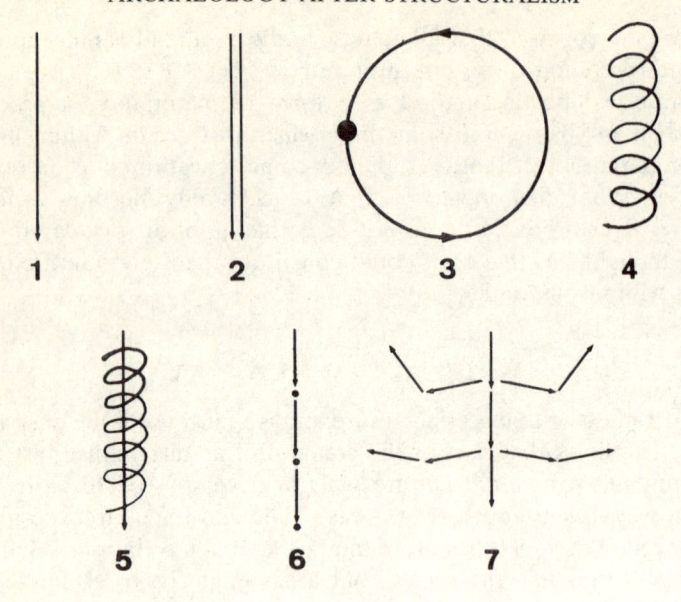

Key

1 Linear narrative
2 Parallel texts
3 Circular texts returning to the point from which they start
4 Spiral text
5 Linear narrative with inbuilt 'spiral' mediation
6 The 'aphoristic' text – stopping and starting off on a new theme
7 The 'tangential' text

Figure 5.1 Alternative writing structures for producing the past

archaeology is an effect rather than a cause of such a narrative structure aiming essentially to smooth time, to paste over the cracks, to fit everything into a coherent whole. A linear narrative form is by no means a 'natural' procedure and there are many alternatives: circular texts, spiral texts, double texts set side by side commenting on data from different angles, texts that take one point of departure and then explore others at a tangent returning periodically to the initial theme and then transforming it and exploring it in different directions (Figure 5.1). Other possibilities are the type of aphoristic writing employed to particular effect by Benjamin (1979) and Adorno (1978). Exploring these ways of structuring a text we would not only be writing the past in a new way: it *would be* a qualitatively different past. It would also mean that we would have to *think* a lot more carefully about the very process of *writing* that past, entailing a rejection of the naive presupposition that words are just a resource, instruments we use.

A related strategy will be to create texts that attempt actively to involve the reader in the process of meaning creation. What is required is a new practice of writing that involves the reader. Within archaeology, at least one virtual hegemony reigns based on what I shall term an empiricist theory of reading and writing. According to this theory, never explicitly stated but always constituting an absent presence in the text, writing is a mere medium in which the non-discursive, the ideas or mental conceptions of the individual, become realised. Alternatively it is regarded as the manner in which knowledge of the real (archaeological data) are set down and recorded. Discourse becomes reduced to either a record of the thought patterns of the thinker or as the manner in which the real may be reproduced in the text. Differing methodologies produce differing realities. Reading becomes a kind of activity as obvious and automatic as drinking or sleeping. Furthermore writing must conform to prescribed but usually specified standards encompassing non-personal involvement. Rhetoric and polemic are to be outlawed (Binford 1983, 45). The text should involve clipped speech and ideally be as clear, precise, parsimonious and unambiguous as inhumanly possible. Nuances, word plays, poetics are to be frowned upon as frivolous. Such tactics reveal a lack of *discipline* to which anyone who wishes to be regarded seriously must guard against. Conformism – no surprises – is the order of the day. Language must ideally be reduced to the most banal level.

Benjamin notes that 'the typical work of modern scholarship is intended to be read as a catalogue' and he goes on to ask: 'But when shall we actually write books like catalogues?' (1979, 63). When indeed. Empiricist notions of writing effectively outlaw discourse both as a problem and as an object of study. The text becomes almost auto-intelligible and its author is always the final arbiter with regard to its meaning. Archaeology books written in such a fashion become read simply as a means for the reader to extract information, useful concepts, modes of analysis or ideas which the reader 'collects up' to be deployed elsewhere: in examinations of his or her text. Alternatively expositions, summaries and commentaries may be given on the works of others based on such a reading. This normally passes for what is termed 'education'. Common to both this archaeological education and the processes involved in concept extraction and redeployment is the notion that the text or texts can be carved up in such a manner that the statements, positions and concepts employed can be effectively separated out from the conditions of their production: the discursive modalities which create them and in terms of which they are intelligible. But texts embody powers. Words are not just words; their meanings alter according to the discourses in which they are inserted and the effects of these discourses on the reader.

At present when you or I read a text – let it be clear that *this* text is a typical example – our role is to consume. Naturally we are taught to be critical consumers and this is regarded as a virtue: be suspicious of what *he* says! But nevertheless our relation to the text is one of distanciation. We try to construct a meaning in the text: to interpret it in various ways. Our interpretation may, of course, differ somewhat from the author's intentions but the best reading is often thought to be one that is able to reconstruct those intentions. We are firmly placed in the role of a consumer because of the internal closures which the writing of the text itself creates. An 'open' text is an alternative. It would be a text in which the author systematically attempts not to close the text down, to produce a spurious coherency but leaves gaps and fissures for the reader to fill in, threads and strands to follow up. The reader becomes no longer a passive consumer of knowledge or whatever but through his or her reading of the text helps actively to create knowledge, the text's meaning. A 'producer' text as opposed to a 'consumer' text invites the reader to participate, to join in as part of the process. It is only our present education system and sheer laziness that demands that everything should be provided to us on a plate; that we should expect to read a book like eating steak and chips in a restaurant.

It is worth pointing out that the notions of both 'consumer' and 'producer' texts are ideal types, neither of which bears any relationship to any text already produced or likely to be produced. It is a matter of *degree*. With the texts that we have in hand in archaeology at present we can write into them many effects and meanings of which the authors were completely unaware and these remain valid. The meaning of the text once disseminated goes entirely beyond what the author may or may not have intended. We are not to be restricted by the constraints the author would put on the appropriation of his or her text. To write, as Barthes states somewhere, is not to give someone else the last word. So in one sense we always produce the meaning of the texts we read. The reader is always active in a limited sense but let us not say that such an activity is not exactly 'invited' by archaeology books and articles. From the author's point of view the more the reader uncritically consumes the better. The textual strategy is one in which as many textual cracks as possible are to be filled in by a smooth consoling narrative. The writer tries in vain to foreclose the entry of the reader. Rather than just saying with Barthes that 'the birth of the reader must be at the death of the author' (Barthes 1977, 48) we could hope, in the future, for both to co-operate in the production of the text's meaning. To use an analogy, the author would create a sketch in pencil for the reader to paint the final portrait.

Examining ourselves: what are we doing and why? In writing we need to be constantly vigilant and self-reflexive to ask: do I really want to state *that* and *why*? What are the implications: personal, political, institutional? What are the powers at work here? Whom am I trying to convince and for what end? Schiffer – to his credit – has more or less given us his reasons: prestige, grants and prizes. Mine? A constant struggle against power and authority structures, a 'scientific' closing down of the past. It involves an attempt to open the past to the present, to productively fuse the two together; to create a socially and politically relevant past, to invite the readers in; to help create pasts which are meaningful to them. This doesn't mean I reject science, which I conceive as a dialectical process fusing past and present, subject and object; nor does it mean I think a thousand incompatible archaeologies should bloom. It means dialogue and discussion, taking sides in an argument: constant criticism, objection, construction and reconstruction in accordance with a thoroughly *materialist* position. The materiality of the past's relation with the present does not simply reside in its artefactual traces but also in the material relation of men and women today with these traces, a position which makes a mockery of a simplistic and traditional polarisation of objectivity and subjectivity.

The type of archaeological writing I am advocating will undoubtedly be difficult. I am pessimistic whether in the present circumstances it is even possible. We can be sure that because it diffuses an authoritarian relation with the past it will be decried by many, probably most especially publishers, for fear that it might not sell. But the past is not up for sale; most innovations have been feared and have to be struggled for and we'll just have to forget about prestige, grants and sparkling prizes!

TOWARDS A SCIENCE OF THE TEXT

Before we can even begin to write along the lines I have suggested it is necessary to learn how to read. Unless we have a thorough understanding of the nature of contemporary archaeological discourses we are likely, whether we like it or not, simply to reproduce them. In order to understand what archaeologists write, and how, a new theory of reading is required. The object of this will be to facilitate a greater degree of criticism, debate and self-reflexivity. As a counter position to the empiricist theory of reading that was outlined above I want to make some remarks designed to promote an alternative theory of reading involving five main elements:

1. The joke principle;
2. The presence/absence principle;
3. The rarity principle;
4. The power/knowledge principle;
5. The restriction principle.

ARCHAEOLOGY AFTER STRUCTURALISM

THE JOKE

Reading, rather than being regarded as an attempt to elaborate the text's self-knowledge, should be seen as a process of establishing a decisive rupture between the reader and the text. The first principle of reading should be an attempt (which will always fail to a certain degree) to bracket-off the self from what is being read, a creation of distance. Paradoxically, in order to understand and take it seriously, it needs to be provisionally regarded as complete nonsense or at the very least something that should not be taken seriously. In order to effect this the text read can be taken as a joke. The first thing we do to the text is to laugh at its claims to say anything serious or meaningful about the world. *Analytical Archaeology* is a Disney cartoon.

PRESENCES/ABSENCES

The second principle is that what is of primary importance in the text is just as much that left unwritten as that written: the gaps, silences, the spaces and meanings between the lines. Here it is important to ask two related questions of the text: (i) why do certain statements, concepts and words etc. occur? (ii) Why do these statements, concepts and words occur rather than others? These questions orientate us towards an analysis of what fixes the content of the text both in terms of manifest presences and in terms of absences. To know the text is not to 'translate' it but to rewrite it using its substantive form as raw material for this purpose. This is not so much an attempt at a hermeneutic recovery of original meaning by discovering that which is buried in the depths but more a form of critical production which makes the text's silences speak. This process, after Althusser (1977) and Macherey (1978), we call a *symptomatic* reading. We learn to read the text like a psychoanalyst reading a patient's mind from slips of the tongue. This does not involve a re-doubling of the text which an empiricist reading would inevitably give but the production of a new textual object establishing fresh knowledge in some respects discontinuous with the text itself. Such a reading regards the text as being constituted by an entire network of internal and external discursive relations and what defines the text in its singularity is not so much that which is in it but that which is not. If this were not the case the text would, of course, be wholly independent of anything and everything else and concomitantly either unreadable or incomprehensible. The text is a distinctive production only by virtue of its differences from, and relations to, other texts. The text is 'hollowed' by the absent presence of other texts to which it is related and against which it constructs itself. Macherey, citing Nietzsche, reminds us to ask the *hinterfrage* question of the text:

> When we are confronted with any manifestation which someone has permitted us to see, we may ask: what is it meant to conceal? What is it meant to draw our attention from? What prejudice does it seek to raise? and again, how far does the subtlety of the dissimulation go?
> (Nietzsche, *The Dawn of the Day*, cited in Macherey 1978, 87)

It implies as much in its non-said as its said that the meanings of the text are to be revealed through the said: 'diverting attention is to show without being seen, to prevent what is visible being seen' (Macherey 1978, 88). It is necessary to regard the text as a constant dialectic between presences and absences to neither of which does the reader grant any necessary priority. Concomitantly, writing and reading cannot remain separate. To read a text adequately is to rewrite it, to fill in those absences found in the text's margins and the spaces between the lines and the words. A science of the text does not leave it where it is but transforms it.

RARITY

Why is it that, given that there are an almost infinite number of aspects of material culture patterning to be discussed, only a limited of statements tends to be made by archaeologists, disseminated in various ways, and repeated? We can begin to analyse discursive practices within archaeology as sets of rule-governed statements in a relation to dispersion in texts. These rules, not discursively available to the writer, may be held to partly account for the said and that left unsaid. In analysing the rarity pervading archaeological discourse we will be concerned with the underlying regularities governing the dispersion of statements, concepts and words in texts, and their effect on readers: those archaeological 'treasures' carefully preserved to be re-laid from one text to the next and the empty deserts surrounding them. We will find that twenty different books on the European Iron Age, beneath the shifting content of the sentences, are all the same book defined in their mutual repetition and scarcity. This, it should be pointed out, is not a concern with the psychology of individual authors but an attempt to understand how discourse 'takes over' so that the names added to the texts become, in effect, interchangeable. To analyse texts in this manner is, as Foucault puts it, to:

> weigh the 'value' of statements. A value that is not defined by their truth, that is not gauged by the presence of a secret content; but which characterises their place, their capacity for circulation, and exchange; their possibility of transformation, not only in the economy of discourse, but, more generally, in the administration of scarce resources.
> (Foucault 1974, 120)

Beneath the sprouting of archaeological books on the Iron Age, or any other topic, we are likely to find the same underlying generative rhizome sending up shoots at various points in time and space but all characterised by the same lack.

POWER–KNOWLEDGE

Powers and desires secrete texts, mould them, frame them, invest them. Foucault has taught us that power and knowledge cannot be separated out into discrete areas. Equally, they do not collapse into each other. It is a mistake simply to equate knowledge with power which would make one or other term redundant. The point is that they form part of each other while maintaining their identity. In other words, power and knowledge are in dialectical relation and neither can exist without the other. Together powers and knowledges constitute truths. The linkage power–knowledge–truth allows us to investigate the politics of truth involved in making and accepting statements. Here we inquire into the social and political implications of producing one textual account of material culture rather than another. In other words, what are the linkages between a text and its social context of production? We have to try and analyse the relationship between archaeological knowledges and power, both within academia and without. We have to understand the manner in which archaeology creates its own discursive objects – never the only possible ones – and the manner in which these are framed and worked upon in texts.

Archaeological discourses need to be situated within the micropolitics of power in the academy. One obvious way to do this is to look at the networking of references in texts in terms of the individual and institutional influence and power and various tropes of writing and critique employed. These powers go considerably beyond the texts themselves. Studies need to be conducted of who gets employed and how and who does not, who gets grants and how and who does not, who gets published and how and who does not, who has praise heaped upon them and how and who does not, what gets read and what does not, why some debates are conducted and others are not. All these and others are not issues of secondary importance. They are of some considerable interest in assessing the manner in which the archaeological police force operates. Gero (1985) and others, from a feminist perspective, are producing valuable work along some of these lines.

RESTRICTION

What are the limits? What is held to differentiate between a serious discursive act worthy of comment, repetition, quotation, etc. and something considered threatening enough to be banished from public speech, and why? Think about what you would like to write and yet know you dare not set down on paper. By exploring the social and political 'unconscious' of archaeology it may be possible to analyse the way in which prohibitions are systematically placed on what 'proper' archaeological discourse is supposed to be about. Choices are always made as to what to study and why to study it. In effect the archaeological record only exists within the spaces of the discourses which have purported to describe it. A positive outcome of analysing contemporary archaeological discourse will be to open out fresh choices, new discursive objects.

Contemporary empiricist discourses place the study of material culture into a brittle crystalline structure which it is vital to shatter in order to open up fresh meanings, new ways of seeing, fresh truths. A renewed focus on material culture and its study threatens today to dissolve the discursive boundaries that archaeology has erected around itself and this is both productive of new discourses and new knowledges. Even the most cursory comparison of archaeology with other disciplines such as anthropology or sociology reveals an astonishing conservatism, a fright at the very name of politics. This is perhaps not so surprising. Traditionally only the very wealthy have been able to afford the luxury of a life devoted to the pursuit of the past. In Britain the Prince of Wales studied archaeology. We would hardly have expected him to study sociology.

CONCLUSION

Today little is served, apart from traditional power and authority structures, by retaining the disciplinary label 'archaeology'. Fresh insights can be expected from striking away prohibitions with regard to what it is right and proper to study (usually the older the better) and develop a focus around the materiality of social practices, whether in the past and the present, in our society or others. It is important to abandon a simplistic focus on an absolute distinction between truth and falsity in analysing texts and the statements made in them. Rather we ask: why *these* statements rather than others and what interests do they serve? Who has the right to make these statements and what powers are embedded in them? What is being left unsaid? How is our attention being diverted and to what end?

Archaeology is not so much about reading the signs of the past but a process of writing these signs into the present. Correct stories of the past are dependent on a politics of truth linked to the present because all interpretation is a contemporary act. Interpretation is always active. There is no single meaning to be textually recreated in an analysis of a set of artefacts since meanings are always to be linked to the practices producing them, whether of prehistoric artisan or contemporary archaeologist. The production and analysis of discourse is a willed act of struggle for and against the production of particular types of statements. The analysis of archaeological discourse is not an academic game, a new fancy icing. It has a deeply serious intent which must be derived, I think, from learning how to laugh, dispelling academic pomposity and a sense of self-importance. We need to be *irreverent* not only to work we may not like and respect but also to ourselves. The intent is to effect a liberation from the prohibitions placed on discourse at present. And that is why it is worth undertaking.

A few aphorisms:

If anyone tells you their work is apolitical look for their politics!

When anyone tells you writing is unimportant watch them at work! Let those who think they can escape modernity, cast the first stone!

REFERENCES

Adorno, T. (1978) *Minima Moralia*, London: Verso.
Althusser, L. (1971) 'Philosophy as a revolutionary weapon', interview conducted by Maria Antonietta Macciocchi, in L. Althusser, *Lenin and Philosophy and Other Essays*, London: New Left Books.
Althusser, L. (1977) *For Marx*, London: Verso.
Barthes, R. (1977) 'The death of the author', in R. Barthes, *Image, Music, Text*, New York: Hill & Wang.
Benjamin, W. (1979) *One Way Street*, London: New Left Books.
Berman, M. (1983) *All that is Solid Melts into Air*, London: Verso.
Binford, L. (1983) 'Objectivity–explanation–archaeology–1981', in L. Binford, *Working at Archaeology*, London: Academic Press.
Binford, L. (1987) 'Data, relativism and archaeological science', *Man* 22: 391–404.
Foucault, M. (1974) *The Archaeology of Knowledge* (2nd edn), London: Tavistock.
Gero, J. (1985) 'Socio-politics and the woman at home ideology', *American Antiquity* 50: 342–50.
Habermas, J. (1981) 'Modernity: an incomplete project', in H. Foster (ed.) *Postmodern Culture*, London: Pluto.
Macherey, P. (1978) *A Theory of Literary Production*, London: Routledge.
Pêcheux, M. (1982) *Language, Semantics, and Ideology*, London: Macmillan.
Sahlins, M. (1963) 'Poor man, rich man, big man, chief: political types in Melanesia and Polynesia', *Comparative Studies in Society and History* 5: 285–303.
Schiffer, M. (1988) 'The structure of archaeological theory', *American Antiquity* 53: 461–85.
Shanks, M. and Tilley, C. (1987) *Social Theory and Archaeology*, Cambridge: Polity.
Tilley, C. (1989) 'Discourse and power: the genre of the Cambridge inaugural lecture', in D. Miller, M. Rowlands and C. Tilley (eds) *Domination and Resistance*, London: Unwin Hyman.

CHAPTER 6

The great epistemological debate of the last ten years has been on the relationship between the past and the present. The consensus within post-processual archaeology leans towards the contextualist/hermeneutic notion of the past as relatively autonomous from the present. The problem, however, is that methodologically this still results in a division between form and content, and what is of interest is not only the theoretical legitimacy of such a distinction, but the legitimacy of the forms and structures through which we write the past, and with which we populate it. These forgotten significations form blind spots which require re-examination.

In this paper Yates attempts to rethink the relationship of past and present through Freudian and post-Freudian theory. The potential of this articulation expresses itself in an alliance with the unconscious, in which are contained and repressed all that the present cannot contemplate, and yet that, from the 'inside' of the present, forces modification and change. The radical potential of archaeology might therefore be found within this exile 'on the inside', and historical writing would become the process of charting the limits of the present in order to shatter the narcissim upon which it depends. An example would be homosexuality, which Freud identified within the unconscious of normal individuals, and it is possible to demonstrate how this social class – treated with respect and equality in other societies – forms the tolerated but unsignifiable other within our own. Historical work, once it sets out to explore the unacknowledged limits of the (contemporary) ego and super-ego, offers us the chance to remodel the ways in which we see ourselves and our relationships.

6

Archaeology through the Looking-Glass

Tim Yates

We have only to understand the mirror stage *as an identification*, in the full sense that analysis gives the term: namely, the transformation that takes place in the subject when he assumes an image . . . This form would have to be called the Ideal-I, if we wished to incorporate it into our usual register, in the sense that it will also be the source of secondary identifications, under which term I would place the functions of libidinal normalisation. But the important point is that this form situates the agency of the ego, before its social determination, in a fictional direction . . . I am led, therefore, to regard the function of the mirror stage as a particular case of the function of the *imago*, which is to establish a relation between the organism and its reality.

(Lacan 1977, 2–4)

I: FRAMING THE PAST

In some way yet to be determined, a genuine historicity is possible only on condition that this illusion of an absolute present can be done away with, and the present opened up again to the drift from the other ends of time.

(Jameson 1972, 187)

1: Narcissism and the Text

The dominant metaphysical conceptualisation of the 'archaeological record' in post-processual archaeology is that of the text. As defined by Ian Hodder, the archaeological text is a web of similarities and differences from which is built up the network of meaningful associations through which we know the past. The concept of the text, of course, serves to denote the epistemological shift away from the identity (passive) of the 'record' to the networking (active) of differences. The emphasis is placed upon the chains of signifiers, making any particular item or artefact referent to the other signifiers with which it is articulated. The artefact, studied in isolation by the functionalists, is engulfed in a system of difference, which locks it into a framework of ever-shifting reference.

But Hodder perceives that it is necessary to suspend this movement, for otherwise the boundaries of the text will never appear and we will be led off into a labyrinth from which no return is possible. A 'text', as such, ought to have borders, boundaries (covers, chapters, spine . . .?) to hold it together. At the conceptual level, therefore, the chains must be closed (at the practical-interpretative level, they are already closed, as we shall see) and the signifiers will have to be fixed by returning them to points which are stable and no longer shift. The theory of context which has consumed all structuralism under a common banner, steps into the breach formed by the disappearance of the signified. Context operates to close these chains of signifiers, allowing us to conceive of a totality – a 'text' – once again, a totality which produces definable, stable relationships between the signifiers of the differential matrix, and allows us to pass down, once more, to the signified. 'The totality of the relevant dimensions around any one object can be identified as the context of that object' (Hodder 1986, 139). The meaning of a particular signifier, 'X', is contextually determined, in its relationship to 'all those aspects of the data which have relationships with "X" which are significantly patterned' (Hodder 1986, 139). Thus the context of a burial would be the edges of the grave, which determine what is within it and what is to be conceived as outside, as part of the exterior. At the borders of context, the shifts and exchanges of difference are no longer possible.

Hodder introduces the concept of context at a crucial point, therefore, in order to reintroduce into the radical horizontality of Saussurian structuralism, at least as it is mediated within post-structuralism by Derrida (and, in a different way, Lacan), the notion of depth, the vertical relationship as the passage back to a signified, which will never have been wholly absent. He endorses the notion of the differential signifier, and recasts the archaeological record as a web of similarities and differences which are constructed in the process of interpretation, arranged in order to form meaningful associations. However, there have to be, for this process to take place, points which escape the play of differences which a reading of Saussure's work must force us to accept. Conceptually, the notion of context operates to close down the chains of signifiers and to forestall difference, the effects of which would be too unsettling if let loose to play out their will through the domain of an archaeology. What this amounts to is the delimitation of practice around an object rather than a domain, though it is now to be called context rather than 'the past'. We decentre the archaeological text, rendering its component parts only differential marks within a system of differences, only to panic at the prospect and to recentre that text on an element that escapes this movement – for context cannot, to perform its promised function, itself be a part of the movement it serves to forestall. If it is to be a part of these differences, then it cannot, at the same time, control them. The *arche* is dispatched on a journey by Hodder along a signifying chain, meeting on the way politics, the present, androcentrism, whatever, and then returned to its place at that moment when, seeking to stabilise the forces that this interest in Saussurian theory has set loose, context is defined non-differentially, non-contextually. Context is allowed to become transhistorical and, in the process, to cease to signify – the borders of the text take place in 'lack', in the absence of any significant (signifying) differences and similarities (1986, 139), a point without significance, without difference, without text.

Thus far, the function of context has been purely conceptual. It amounts, in fact, to a systematic exploration of the limits of the paradigm, but it succeeds only in recasting the paradigm in new terms, to modify certainly, but not to change it beyond recognition. We have lost signifieds, opened outwards onto a surface apparently without features, and been saved by these points outside of signification which no longer signify. The problem becomes that of locating these functions. Context reassures the archaeological structure that there is the possibility of a distant presence waiting to be discovered or rediscovered, of a return to the vertical. To do this, and in order to set it to work to recover this *arche*, we must dispense with any further flirtation with the concept of difference. 'The abstract analysis of signs and meanings is particularly a problem in archaeology which is primarily concerned with material culture' (1986, 47). What archaeology seeks to do is to discover how non-arbitrary meanings 'come about', and to do this, evidently, we require that our theories be centred. And to centre them on the outside of difference, we must centre them on that which escapes the rule of the sign – on the materiality of material culture.

The role of context cannot, of course, be kept at a purely conceptual level, for it needs to be located within the terms of analysis. It is therefore placed within its *material* dimensions, material being defined as that which does not signify, as that which is meaning-less. Structuralism would thus appear to have come full circle with the reintroduction of the referent which had, from the very beginning, been written out of its frames of reference, bracketed off. Thus for John Barrett, whose work represents a different emphasis but nevertheless still parallels that of Hodder, the 'architecture' of the material world is reciprocally related within a dialectics of structure/action, but is nevertheless still more permanent and stable than the mere memories of past experience (Barrett 1987, 8). Unable to refind the signified directly, and so to reintroduce the vertical passage to the *arche*, the referent is returned to its place, on the outside of the text, and the polarity ideal–material is reified. The problem of the horizontality of structure or, in Derrida's phrase, the *structurality* of structure, which the whole elaboration of context has sought to solve, is finally by-passed by refinding that which, since ever there was an archaeology, has named its terrain, its cipher, mute and silent but containing the codes of the past:

> Even though written language may have the same basic principles as material culture language, a written language is always very difficult to decipher even when much of it survives. This is partly because it is very complex, designed to express complex ideas and thoughts, and has to be fairly precise and comprehensible. But there are no grammars and dictionaries of material culture language. Material culture symbols are often more ambiguous than their verbal counterparts, and what can be said with them is normally much simpler. Also, the material symbols are durable, restricting flexibility. In many ways material culture is not a language at all – it is more clearly action and practice in the world. In so far as it is a language, it is a simple one when compared to spoken or written language. For these various reasons, material culture texts are easier to decipher than those written documents for which we do not know the language.
>
> (Hodder 1986, 123)

Material culture as a sign is turned against itself, such that the *materiality* of artefacts acts to break the flows of difference. Referentiality is tamed in the face of the referent. But, because we have already adopted these terms of discussion, and because this materiality, as the site of the absent context, cannot be outside the text without being, at least partially, 'inside' (which is to say that context has a *thickness*), the referent is indistinguishable from this function of context as the signifier outside of signification. Where processualism has proposed and maintained the identity and ontology of the signified – the unmediated passage to the signified of an object, namely its 'function' – post-processualism overturns the hierarchy and rests upon the perceived ontology of the signifier, where stability is offered to the structuring of meaning by the 'lack' that is context and which is filled by the material world which intervenes from the outside in order to break the flows of differing and reference.

Hodder's context and Barrett's field of discourse, both coupled to this materiality, are conceived on the basis of a signifier without a signified, without any necessary requirement having been placed upon it to mean, since its function is to perform this break in flow which threatens to carry off, once and for all, the objects of archaeological study (as the institution still defines them, and guards them, jealously), *linearly, horizontally,* and without return.

For what is the alternative? The flows must be broken, for otherwise we will drown in the flood that will break over the institutional practices and rituals of this science. The present would be opaque and we would be trapped within it, like a prisoner. And it is precisely the *arche*, the ontology of the origin, that is at stake. The radical difference and horizontality that holds structuralism together as an epistemological challenge is shocking because it threatens to overturn the conventional metaphor which requires that we conceptualise our work vertically as a return to the origin or to the originary point. Excavation promises to pass from surface to depth, absence to presence, present to past. We all *know* that archaeology is not just about digging up the past from the ploughsoil, but we still think it possible for us to excavate – by induction, by deduction, by strategies of reading through context(s) which break up and divide this featureless plain of the signifier. We still think in terms of the passage from the manifest to the hidden.

So, for instance, context is resolved around two poles, one of the past and the other of the present, a conceptualisation that is anticipated in the division between primary and secondary evidence and which, to a greater extent than is recognised, it repeats. It reproduces this 'original' distance and spacing, only now we want to try to think them in terms of each other, in terms of a single context. Conceptually, neither has priority, and the intervention into the chain of signifiers that is necessary to write the past is structured by a dialectic between production and reproduction, construction and reconstruction, *telos* and *arche*, present and past. But this is not enough, it cannot be sufficient, to make us overlook that this writing is still an intervention, the chain has still been broken, the past has still been produced. Someone has had to decide what to put into the context and what to exclude, and this cannot be forgotten. If context is to contain the past and the present, then we know that these poles are not complete, for chains have been rearranged and fixed around the enclosure, in order to prevent this context from being carried off linearly.

This structure, therefore, still reassures the *arche*, the ontology of the past, precisely because it attempts to stabilise all that signifies with this context. In order to allow the *arche* to confront the present from a position of relative autonomy, from its outside, Hodder *already* has to decide what form this past will take. What matters here only appears on the outside, that which determines every configuration of the structure, starting with what is chosen to be placed within it and which prevents it from following off in a spiral of supplementary significations along chains of differences of which past and present, subject and object and so on are only spacings on the level. The emphasis upon the already-interpreted, upon the irreducibility of interpretation, is a strategic blow against empiricism and positivism, but it offers us no escape from the system which holds us and imprisons us in the present, despite the *supposed* relative autonomy of the past.

It is not a question of a failure within context, of a component part which can be added or subtracted in order to guarantee the function. It is a question of the difference of the past *failing* to arrive because it has been *prevented* from appearing *before* it is given the option of a contextualised arrival. Difference here means not only a space, a spacing of the past from the present, but also a structural incompatibility, a contradiction – so we may say that context, to which we would now have to append a great deal that calls itself hermeneutics, protects the present from the past. Universalised categories are inserted into the past through context – the domestic, for instance, becomes a structuralised difference (it is *already* a signified) to be compared across cultures and genres, such that the frame for the past is already set, its form dictated *in advance*, so that all that remains for the archaeologist is to fill this frame with a landscape, the elements of which will be permitted to signify through this prefix. The structure of male/female is a similar problem, where a radical division between form and content allows Barrett (1987) to be vociferous in his opposition to the notion of material culture as 'text', because the past can only signify in its own terms, while at the same time preserving the hope that unique structures can still be identified. We ought first, surely, to have thoroughly diagnosed the problem, but instead the past becomes only a reflection of the present, where it is no longer clear where the forms with which we wish to populate the past originate.

The past is therefore claimed to have a relative autonomy, for the *arche* is not dismantled (context, in fact, situates the *arche* in order only to reassure it), but we remain trapped within the present, which takes on the form of an inevitable and irresistible super-ego (to use Freud's term for that which guarantees obedience to the social and cultural laws of the present). The present sets the rules for interpretation, and no possibility is offered for reflexivity with respect to these categories. Sørensen's (1987) framework has two poles, male and female (where do they come from? what are they? how do they function? – these questions should have been considered), which are set to work through a space in the Late Bronze Age (but where are they really going?). Within this framework, no further dissent is possible, because *there is no longer anything left to question* – these questions belong to the outside of context (this dialectic of past and present) which is not recognised as such. Like Narcissus gazing into the pond, we mistake what is actually our own image for that of another, the self for other, out of a desire to break with that which imprisons us – within our own bodies, which is always our own space and our own time. Reading these accounts of the Neolithic, the Bronze and the Iron Ages, we should emphasise the colonisation, by a hoard of little Oedipuses, carrying with them the message that some things are outside of meaning, outside of history and beyond question – that some things just never change.

The past, to which hermeneutics and contextual archaeology claim to assign a relative autonomy, is already silent, already unable to respond, dispute or debate, to enter into a discussion with the present. The prison house of difference, which carries off the *arche* along chains of signifiers, is recovered by context only as a distant mirror, endlessly reflecting back our own image. Context becomes not only the point of incision into a signifying chain but the point of entry for this narcissism. What we want to do is not peer through or beyond the mirror – for there is no space into which we may pass beyond the shiny surface which is not already a mirror, an illusion; no space from which we may confront the present as it were *from the outside*, and by believing that any of these possibilities are open we will continue to run the risk of mistaking the same for other, identity for difference. We do not and cannot gaze beyond, for this beyond is infinitely veiled, preluded by a limitless hall of mirrors. *We must shatter the looking-glass, open outwards and sideways, never back or down.*

In order to conduct this rethinking of the past on the inside of the present, to build beyond context, and to release the radical differentiality of the past, its *challenge* to and against the present, the metaphor must be shifted back from depths to surfaces, back from the signified to the signifier, from all that holds us to the context of the past at the expense of its form, back to the past *in the present*. This means reasserting the horizontality or structurality of structure and the signifying chain, by which the past is active in the present only as a trace, and is effective through the processes and powers of the unconscious. What we need to theorise, to elaborate, is a means of breaking out of the cycles of reproduction and production, of pasts and presents, to break with this security, and to mix strategy with adventure. We need to theorise this silence, the silence of the border and the voicelessness of context. What I propose here is to rethink the difference between past and present, silence and voice, self and other, within the terms or supplementary significations of the unconscious/conscious, *in the present*.

> This is why it seems useful and legitimate to ask of every production what it tacitly implies, what it does not say. Either all around or in its wake the explicit requires the implicit: for in order to say anything, there are other things *which must not be said*. Freud relegated this absence of certain words to a new place which he was the first to explore, and which he paradoxically *named*: the unconscious. To reach utterance, all speech envelops itself in the unspoken.
>
> (Macherey 1978, 85)

2: On the Unconscious

Let us therefore compare the system of the unconscious to a large entrance hall, in which the mental impulses jostle one another like separate individuals. Adjoining this entrance hall there is a second, narrower, room – a kind of drawing room – in which consciousness, too, resides. But on the threshold between these two rooms a watchman performs his function: he examines the different mental impulses, acts as a censor, and will not admit them into the drawing room if they displease him . . . . But even the impulses which the watchman has allowed to cross the threshold are not on that account necessarily conscious as well; they can only become so if they succeed in catching the eye of consciousness. We are therefore justified in calling this second room the system of the *preconscious*.

(Freud 1917, 336–7)

Freud's spatial and topographical model for the structure and operations of the psyche has, to a certain extent, become sedimented within the conventions of western culture, although certainly more sympathetically in Europe than in Britain. It is fairly commonplace to speak of an unconscious, in the sense of something unintended or not anticipated, but this is much less specific and more diluted than Freud's own usage.

The human mind does not, of course, function homogeneously in Freud's model of consciousness. From his work with Breuer on hysteria, making use of hypnosis in the clinical research, Freud had been led to postulate the existence of other kinds of consciousness and motivation. 'The possibility of giving a sense to neurotic symptoms by analytical interpretation is an unshakeable proof of the existence – or, if you prefer it, of the necessity of the hypothesis – of unconscious mental processes' (1917, 13). The symptom is the result when these unconscious thoughts and impulses make their appearance in the conscious system (though their significance remains in the unconscious). From the quotation above it should be clear that the conscious is not a thing or an identifiable space – it is not a separate room. What is conscious for Freud is that which is being thought at any one time. The fundamental distinction, therefore, is not between conscious and unconscious but between thoughts *available* to consciousness and thoughts not so available. The conscious has no space within the terms of this metaphor, but is rather like the host wandering around the drawing room, engaging with those whom the doorman has allowed access. The conscious takes place within the pre-conscious, which is divided from the unconscious by the operations of a censor, who acts to *repress* all impulses originating there and prevent them from becoming available to consciousness.

What is of interest here is the way in which unconscious material becomes available to consciousness, and is manifested consciously by evading the repressive threshold and adopting a form which is acceptable to the censor. In *The Interpretation of Dreams* (1900), Freud draws a distinction between the manifest content of the dream, which is what it appears on the surface to mean, and the latent dream thoughts, which are the real motivation for the dream, its proper, correct unconscious meaning. Between the two is the action of the dream work which, by processes of condensation, displacement and secondary revision forms out of the latent dream thoughts the manifest content. So the original impulse can lose some of its elements, having diverse meanings concentrated onto single symbols, *condensed* from many to a few; it can have its centre *displaced* and its symbols replaced by others which are apparently without connection; and its lacunae will be *revised* in order to form an apparently complete narrative structure. All this creates a path whereby the cathexis of energy imputed to the unconscious material can gain conscious release via a detour. 'The dream, in short is one of the detours by which repression can be evaded' (Freud 1905a, 44).

The same processes of psychic distortion account for the formation of the symptoms that form neuroses. Thus, in Breuer's treatment of Fraulein Anna O, a 21-year-old woman suffering from various forms of hysteria, the shock and disgust felt at seeing a friend allow a dog to drink from a glass of water was distorted into an hysterical thirst and an inability or refusal to drink (Freud and Breuer 1895).

> The formation of the substitute for the ideational portion has come about by *displacement* along a chain of connections which is determined in a particular way . . . The result is fear of a wolf, instead of a demand for love from the father.
>
> (Freud 1915a, 155)

This latter is, of course, a reference to the 'Wolf-Man', who was the subject of Freud's most celebrated case history, in which an obsession with a particular symbol took the place, by displacement, of the original emotional and ideational content of the neurosis.

If we look at another of the case histories, that of Little Hans (1909), we see exactly how distortion operates. Hans was a five-year-old boy living with his parents in a suburb of Vienna, and his neurosis arose within what Freud called the Oedipus or Castration complex. It originated in his own personal obsession with his penis, which was prominent among his erotogenic zones, and the threat of castration for masturbation, which attaches itself to an object remote from the original meaning but in some way connected to it. This object performs the role of substituting for the original symbol. According to Freud's interpretation Hans tried to repress his love for his mother and his desire to masturbate by his fear of horses, the latter becoming the symbol for his father in his unconscious. The choice of this symbol was not random, but was 'determined' by certain points of similarity between the horse and his father, and by his not-too-distant childhood games where he would ride on his father's back. In the neurosis, therefore, certain points became of significance and acted as these points of contact – the emphasis on the black around horses' mouths (muzzle) was linked to his father's moustache, so also the blinkers worn by drays were connected in Hans' mind to his father's glasses. The distortion operating between the latent and manifest content of the neurosis was the means by which repression was by-passed.

Freud emphasised that repression is not a part of the process of substitution of content by symbols, since the aim of repression is only a withdrawal of the cathexis of energy from unconscious material. What repression does is to create a *substitutive formation* – it leaves behind traces of the original meanings, the symptoms. So symptom-formation is a part of the process of repression via substitutive formation, but where the repressed has been allowed to return to consciousness, to cross back over the threshold that separates the entrance hall from the drawing room.

What is clear here is the similarity of these processes to the linguistics that launched structuralism into cultural analysis. Thus repression works linearly – so that displacement is a movement along a chain of signifiers, so that the place of the father can be taken by that of a horse or a wolf. Psychic distortion is part of the processes that articulate the signifying chains of meaning. Thus a symptom is not a single signifier connected to a signified that exists only in the unconscious. Writing about the case of Ida Bauer – to whom Freud gave the pseudonym Dora – a young hysteric, Freud emphasised that '. . . at least *one* of the meanings of a symptom is the representation of a sexual fantasy, but . . . no such limitation is imposed upon the content of its other meanings' (1905a, 80; 1910, 37). The connection between the manifest and the latent meanings, the dynamics studied by psychoanalysis, can thus be linearised, so that they are linked as different points of focus along a signifying chain. These shifts and focuses constitute the dream symbolism, which – although the emphasis is upon the individual history of a neurosis – need not always be personal, as is underlined in Freud's description of the symbols found in dreams, where many of the connections derive from mythology, folk stories and fairy tales (Freud 1900, 466ff; 1910, 64; 1917, 186ff). Indeed, Freud depicted the field of psychoanalysis as extending, necessarily, beyond medicine to the humanities and social sciences (1926, 351ff).

It is Lacan who most particularly pursues this potential for reading Freud in the terms of Saussure. To a certain extent, he had been prefigured by Freud himself who, as far back as 1900 had begun to conceive of the necessity of a linguistic metaphor for the unconscious. Opening Chapter VI of *The Interpretation of Dreams*, on the dream work, he comments that the apparently nonsensical content of dreams can be solved if, instead of trying to take the dream as a whole, 'we try to replace each separate element by a syllable or word that can be presented by that element in some way or another' (1900, 382). Many of the dreams analysed by Freud contain similar uses of a linguistic analogy.

For Lacan, the dream symbol becomes the signifier, and it is precisely this linguistic structure that allows us to read dreams. It is 'the very principle of the "significance of the dream", the *Traumdeutung*' (Lacan 1977, 159). Thus the movement of displacement and condensation that's fundamental, not only to the manifestation of the dream but also to its interpretation, and therefore to the hypothesis of an unconscious, can be approached linguistically, as (following Roman Jakobson) *metonymy* and *metaphor*. Displacement becomes metonymy, a relation of meaning which exists only in 'the *word-to-word* connection' (Lacan 1977, 156), that is, between signifiers, without involving the signified as a determinant factor, since it is (for Lacan as for Derrida) always divided from the signifier by a barrier resisting signification. Metaphor, which now describes the movement of condensation, articulates the appearance of the signified only as one signifier taking the place of another signifier – the function of two equivalent signifiers combining into a relation such that one appears to become the signified for the other.

The processes of signification/consciousness are therefore detached from the mythical vertical dimensions in which they had been contained –

$$\frac{\text{signifier}}{\text{signified}} \quad \frac{\text{as conscious}}{\text{unconscious}}$$

or, as in the dream symbolism –

$$\frac{\text{manifest}}{\text{latent}}$$

and forced into a horizontal structuring in which what moves are the relations of difference amongst signifiers. It is thus possible to account for the unconscious and its effects wholly at the level of the signifier. Thus Lacan allows the content of the unconscious to float, as the signified floats, under the barrier which prevents it from surfacing by connection to a signifier. Reading Edgar Allan Poe's short story 'The Purloined Letter' (Lacan 1988), the content of the letter, which is a metaphor for Lacan for the contents of the unconscious, are never revealed to us, as it moves from point to point, engaging with different supplementary signifiers and significations attracting different meanings. However, it is still returned to the point from which it started out and its meaning as ontology is assured. 'At every moment each of them [the characters in the story], even their sexual attitude, is defined by the fact that the letter always arrives at its destination' (Lacan 1988, 205). Lacan insists on the non-differential status of the phallic signifier, Lacan's name (drawn from the Freudian concept of the Oedipus/Castration complex) for the point where the signifiers of the signifying chains are determined. It is this that, like the letter/unconscious which, in the story, is displaced, determines its return to its proper place.

It is at this point therefore that Lacan compromises by insisting on the status of the unconscious as a veiled and virtual presence, something that can be located and isolated and whose meaning-effects can be returned to where they belong. So Dupin, the detective in the story, recovers the letter and fulfils his contract. Just when the unconscious appears to become on the level with consciousness,

> Lacan leads us back to the truth, to a truth which itself cannot be lost. He brings back the letter, shows that the letter brings itself back to its *proper* place via a *proper* itinerary . . . the signifier has its place in the letter, and the letter refinds its proper meaning in its proper place.
>
> (Derrida 1988, 436)

Derrida's reading focuses upon the status of the phallic signifier which, by being the point at which difference as references ceases, is the point where the symbolic order is established. It refers, of course, to the Oedipal triangle (Mama–Papa–Me) where the chains of the symbolic are arranged around the hierarchy of the presence/absence of a penis. Lacan, however, emphasises that the concept of the phallus refers to many things as well as the organ in this myth. It is the means by which the subject (ego) is produced and against which the pre-symbolic self (the Id) appears only as a negative.

The proper place to which the letter is returned, therefore, is the place of the phallus, the place of the Oedipus or Castration complex – 'woman as the unveiled site of the lack of a penis, as the truth of the phallus, that is of castration' (Derrida 1988, 439). But where Lacan emphasises the singularity and indivisibility of the letter/phallus, thus determining the unconscious and the symbolic through the point of closure of the Oedipal triangle, Derrida emphasises the differential status even of this signifier, its belonging to difference and to text, such that, where before the letter's arrival appeared guaranteed, its status is now open to question:

> Its 'materiality' and 'topology' are due to its divisibility, its always possible partition. It can always be fragmented without return, and the system of the symbol, of castration, of the signifier, of the truth, of the contract, etc., always attempt to protect the letter from this fragmentation . . . Not that the letter never arrives at its

destination, but it belongs to the structure of the letter to be capable, always, of not arriving ... Here dissemination threatens the law of the signifier and of castration on the contract of truth. It broaches, breaches the unity of the signifier, that is, of the phallus.

(Derrida 1988, 444)

By taking apart the status of the phallic signifier (the signifier that is not a signifier, because difference/reference at that point are no longer possible) Derrida's reading insists on the horizontality of signifying relations, such that the unconscious as a defined place, a present signified, is no longer possible. 'The irreducibility of the "effect of deferral" – such, no doubt, is Freud's discovery' (Derrida 1978, 203). The textual metaphors found throughout Freud's work – as in, for instance, 'A Note upon the "Mystic Writing Pad"' (1925) where the occurrence of memories existing only in the unconscious is addressed – are taken to their fullest extent. The conscious or manifest dream text is not a transcription of a latent meaning,

> because there is no text *present elsewhere* as an unconscious one to be transposed or transported ... The text is not conceivable in an originary or modified form of presence. The unconscious text is already a weave of pure traces, differences in which meaning and force are united – a text nowhere present, consisting of archives which are *always already* transcriptions. Originary prints. Everything begins with reproduction. Always already repositories of a meaning which is never present, whose signified presence is always reconstituted by deferral ...
>
> (Derrida 1978, 211)

In place of that space to which Freud gave a thoroughly metaphysical name (that is, one invoking surfaces and depths, signifiers and signifieds, manifest and latent meanings ... etc.), Derrida has only 'a certain alterity':

> ... the unconscious is not, as we know, a hidden, virtual, and potential self-presence. It is deferred – which no doubt means that it is woven out of differences, but also that it sends out, that it delegates, representatives or proxies; but there is no chance that the mandating subject 'exists' somewhere, that it is present or is 'itself', and still less chance that it will become conscious ... the unconscious can no more be classed a 'thing' than anything else; it is no more a thing than an implicit or muted consciousness ... With the alterity of the 'unconscious', we have to deal not with horizons of modified presents – past or future – but with a 'past' that has never been nor will ever be present, whose 'future' will never be produced or reproduced in the form of presence.
>
> (Derrida 1973, 152)

The unconscious becomes, we may say, not a space to be discovered beneath consciousness, but a spacing *within* consciousness, within consciousness as writing and consciousness as text. The id is neither the being-present that Freud seems to suggest not the being-absent of which Lacan writes. The id is not to be conceived on the basis of presence or absence, but as difference. If the pre-symbolic is all that does not appear in the symbolic, then we may align the unconscious with all that the symbolic – in the form of the ego, the subject and the super-ego – seeks to repress. The id would contain all that must be excluded from the symbolic/the present in order for them to exist. The id is 'primitive and irrational' (Freud 1933, 107) without being the simple negation of consciousness: 'There are in this system no negation, no doubt, no degrees of certainty: all this is introduced by the work of the censorship between the Unconscious and the Preconscious' (Freud 1915b, 190). The unconscious, removed from the metaphysical function given it by Freud and retained by Lacan, becomes all that, inside the symbolic and cultural order, is also its outside, that which threatens from the inside (there is no outside) but cannot be contained there.

3: Archaeology through the Looking-Glass

In the multiplicity of writing, everything is to be *disentangled*, nothing *deciphered*; the structure can be followed, 'run' (like the thread of a stocking) at every point and at every level, but there is nothing beneath: the space of writing is to be ranged over, not pierced.

(Barthes 1977, 147)

Archaeologists, despite many of their claims, are fetishists. They eschew antiquarianism (the very antithesis of science), the sheer possession of objects regardless of meaning, but our museums continue to overflow with artefacts. They try to lend theoretical legitimacy to this preference. Binford denounces structuralism as idealist, but his materialism and functionalism rest upon the idealism of the sign conceived as an immediate and tangible unity. A clever deception. Hodder dissents, but only to renew the contract (albeit in a modified form) after a circuitous detour through structuralist logic. He rejects the notion of the arbitrary sign, because what is of concern is *material* culture. Barrett endorses this view, and despite attempts to suspend material and ideal dialectically, still valorises the difference by preferring the former as a vessel to limit and contain the latter. The material world maintains discourse because of its materiality. After the sign, after the signified, after difference, post-processualism arrives at the signifier without signification, without a signified, without difference – a material culture that is no longer divisible through or by difference. *Material* culture is related to meaning and the sign as the *indivisible* is related to the divisible. Its very properties signify permanence, the raw, the hard, the physical, the tangible. Where Saussure threatens to carry us off sideways, laterally, along horizontal chains of signifiers leading off everywhere and at once, Hodder restores the signifier to its place (the place from which it had been deferred, *purloined*) and reintroduces the depth and the truth that assures us of a contract with the signified, an intelligible descent to the *arche*.

Saussure, like the minister in Poe's short story, purloins the signifier and with it the *arche*, and takes it from its place, diverts its course. The past is forced back into signification, and in this flat and featureless plain of difference, we choke. We've got signifiers everywhere, cloaking the horizon, and none of us know which way to turn or what to do with them. We don't know where the past is any more, all we've got are these signifiers. The archaeologist is sought out and contracted. Hodder pursues it, and returns it to its place, its proper place, its proper context, *the* context out of which it would not have been readable (1986, 141) – which is to say that there are contexts and there are contexts, and we must establish the *proper* context and return the signifier (*arche*) to its place. He leads us back, back from the spectre of a structuralism released (by Derrida) even from the limits set it by Saussure, back to the truth of archaeology and back to David Clarke's indivisible disciplinary identity ('Archaeology is archaeology is archaeology') which assures and reassures this truth, back to the material culture with which archaeology has always been concerned. Back to the context without which it could never have operated and which functions ultimately to protect structuralism from subversion by its own logic. Materialism without (proper) context is antiquarianism; materialism with (proper) context is archaeology (Hodder 1986, 120). An obvious sigh of relief; the horizon clears, the signifiers dissipate. Someone spots the *arche*, it is found and returned. An archaeology becomes possible once again.

Context is indispensable. To divert the signifier (the *arche*) from its context is to dispense with archaeology, to break with its rules and its truth. The signifier, forced through difference into a labyrinth of referential traces (in which the *arche*, too, would be carried off) is returned to its proper place, is 'contextualised', and the verticality of the signifying relation re-established. 'To affirm the importance of context thus includes reaffirming the importance of archaeology as archaeology' (Hodder 1986, 120). The *arche*, diverted and purloined by an unfettered structuralist logic, is refound through a *material* culture that intervenes (has intervened) to foreclose the difference of difference and the structurality of structure.

Material culture is indivisible. We can talk, therefore, of the *phallusy* of context for, like Lacan's concept of the phallus (which performs the same function) it operates on the singularity and indivisibility of the letter/signifier, which breaks through the shifting chains of discourse in order to lock them in place and in order to recover the identity, possibility and stability of presence and truth. At this point, through the phallic law of the indivisible signifier, an archaeology becomes practicable, because it is precisely this truth and the potential for this truth that will have been protected and preserved.

But the materiality of the signifier is not the identity and integrity of its form, but its ever possible partition, through difference that works along a line that runs between the signifier and itself. This phallus/material culture is broken up by 'the delicate levers that pass between the legs of a word, between a word and itself' (Derrida 1988, 78). Post-processualism articulates material culture as text, as writing, but makes of this graphic metaphor only a further fetish, a further identity that reassures the *arche*. 'But the pen, when you have followed it to the end, will have turned into a knife' (Derrida 1981, 302). The signifier in material culture is cut up, the *arche* dissected, by difference, and set loose to wander again, a nomad in an infinite plain without points that can be fixed or mapped out in advance.

Beyond context as/and the rule of the phallus, beyond this version of materiality, there is the horizontal structure, through which excavation works laterally not vertically. The past is to be disentangled in the present, not deciphered. No *arche*, no marginal text, no original meaning. No context can deliver. Nothing is hidden any more, everything is on the level and is in this sense *manifest*. It is a question of connecting signifiers on a horizontal plain, pursuing traces of difference and identity through difference. Past and present are bound on this surface, out of which we do not pass. There is no beyond, no beneath into which the archaeologist can pass, no 'before' to be made present, no potential presence for the past. There is only and always difference. Only a chain of signifiers articulating a further chain of signifiers: there are only, everywhere, differences of differences and traces of traces.

Where contextual archaeology (the last gasp of the old order and the first breath of the new) sought to presence the *possibility* of the *arche* through a glorious, ontological signifier, to assert the radical horizontality of archaeological production is to open archaeology onto a discourse no longer concerned with the past or present as alternatives – as if it were possible for them to rise and separate, for us to choose one and not the other, for one to become present and the other to be made absent. All these perspectives – past not present, object not subject, etc. – are founded upon a mutual exclusivity which forms the topography of an innocence so ingrained within archaeology that it is not so much 'merely' in the name, in its etymology, as a part of the walls and foundations which enclose the institution. We are beginning to break down the barriers which enclose the *arche* from the outside. When the horizontality of the signifier and the signifying chains is asserted, the past cannot appear without the present, and the *arche* as pure signification is delayed indefinitely. It forces us to abandon a project centred on the past or the present and commits us to a practice firmly spaced within difference. Without the various ontological centrings that have protected the fortress, our historical labour shifts to being focused upon differences rather than identity, on the dividing line between identity and non-identity, subject and object, presence and absence, surface and depth, past and present, conscious and unconscious and to what opens these binaries onto a signifying chain.

> It was never our wish . . . to transform the world into a library by doing away with all boundaries, all frameworks, all sharp edges . . . but that we ought rather to work on the theoretical and practical system of these margins, once more, from the ground up.
> (Derrida 1979, 84)

A systematic discourse on the borders and margins.

But these borders and margins will not be those immediately of the past and present. The hermeneutic project will always have reassured identity, lent to it a stability and put the *arche* back in place. The relative autonomy of the past can only be thought, first of all, from the present. Like the unconscious, the past is 'structured like a language'. The *arche* is produced as a space or spacing in a horizontal surface of signifying traces. It is a question of the present displacing itself onto this space now called 'the past' and distanced from the present rhetorically, horizontally. And it is a question of condensation, of the elements of this writing representing many other elements, a *dialogism* to use Bakhtin's term. Age is a measure of lateral distance, and 'the past' is a rhetorical signifying space, a space in a horizontal chain. It is a 'contemporary' space, a space contemporaneous with the present in which the utterance takes place, a space in the present.

What we use to measure this space – a radio-carbon date, for example – does not launch us into the past. It is no more the past than a railway timetable. They are part and parcel of a rhetorical system of writing designed to create a regulated and controlled spacing on a horizontal signifying plain and to give to this space, thereafter, the associated meanings of past and present. The designation 'X number of year BP (before present)' is a rhetorical gesture designed to distance the remarks hung on it from the present and provide them with a different stage, one spaced from me, the present and the conditions of my writing. It should not be allowed to deceive me into thinking that the referentiality of these remarks is anything other than contemporary. Don't think that chronology has anything to do with temporality, with being outside the present, with anything we might call 'history'. The spatial representation of time is not enough to establish distance but, because of the nature of this writing, this would be its rhetorical function. All it does is to create the effect or impression of distancing (from the present) through a process of regulation and ritualisation within signifying effects articulated on a horizontal surface.

The effect of depth, the signified, is thus produced on this horizontal surface, amongst signifiers and signifying chains arranged laterally. Lacan's formula for describing metaphor expresses this succinctly:

$$f\left(\frac{S'}{S}\right) S \cong S (+) s$$

(Lacan 1977, 164), which can be described as the function of two signifiers combining in a relation such that one appears to take the place of the signified for the other.[1]

It should therefore be possible to account for the production of the past in archaeology wholly on the level of the signifier. The *arche* is differed and deferred, displaced and condensed – it is no more than a signifying trace, an effect, which is not a virtual presence or a presence to be placed (discovered, rediscovered, reconstructed) in a context. It has to be thought on the basis of difference, not a difference (past/present) already prescribed in advance, but of difference from the present. The past, produced in this way, is the experience of difference, but it is *not* a foreign country, it is a little England, a home from home. This narcissism is assured at every moment because rhetorical and formal strategies and the sedimented symbolism of archaeology create the impression of space on a signifying chain as temporal remoteness. Thus contextual archaeology is caught up in these cycles of specular identification of self as other and finds, not the relative autonomy of the past mediated by the present but the doorway that opens onto a hall of mirrors.

What we need is a means of breaking with the present, in order to find the past from the inside of the codes and regulations that protect and guarantee the present. The past appears and has value, therefore, not as a reconstruction of the past but as a deconstruction of the present, the strategies of which explicate 'the relationship of the work to itself' (Derrida 1986, 124). Like the unconscious, the past only appears when a rupture of the present can be effected, when the 'thetic' (to use Julia Kristeva's term), which originates in the mirror stage and is completed in the full inauguration of the symbolic, is broken through. We should, therefore, align ourselves with the Id, with Kristeva's *semiotic*, which 'constantly tears it [the symbolic] open, and this transgression brings about all the various transformations of the signifying practice that are called "creation" . . . what remodels the symbolic is always the influx of the semiotic' (Kristeva 1984, 62). So, to paraphrase Sollers' comments on the novel, the past is the way in which society speaks to itself, and it signifies the ways in which the subject must live in order to be accepted there. It provides the codes of instinctive reference, the exercise of its power, 'the key to its everyday unconscious, mechanical, shut' (quoted in Laing 1978, 99).

And yet it is possible to use the resources of this signifying practice to explore the present, to chart its limits and work through its fissures, to explore the real, the possible, the tangible. The present is not the prison it appears to be, and we are not necessarily condemned to be contained within its walls: 'There is a crack there. Construction and deconstruction are breached/broached there. The line of disintegration, which is not straight or continuous or regular . . .' (Derrida 1987a, 132).

Writing is not a discovery, or a rediscovery, of something located elsewhere, 'It is something newly raised up, an addition to the reality from which it begins' (Macherey 1978, 6). It is not passive with respect to reality, but it adds and produces and changes the real. An emphasis upon production ruptures the unidirectionality of our epistemologies. From a critical knowledge of our present we can start to explore that unconscious that sustains the present through the mirror of the past, in order to release another unconscious which is capable of remoulding and reshaping the present. The 'past' is only of any value if it can break out of these cycles of projection and introjection, and this must involve an identification of the past with the unconscious – with all that lies 'outside' the present (while always being 'inside'), with all that is forbidden, with that forged on the difference between the intelligible and the possible, the spoken and the silent.

The 'distant mirror' must be shattered, not pierced. No passage across boundaries but their fragmentation. It is in the difference between the conscious/spoken/intelligible and the unconscious/unspoken/silent in the present, rather than in the simple difference between the past and the present that we find the space of our writing. Our task as archaeologists is not to administer the scene in order to locate the past (the *arche*) here, there or wherever, but to work the scene in order to break with the present and to allow 'the past' to wander through its corridors unfettered.

II: READING THE UNCONSCIOUS

No 'theory,' no 'practice,' no 'theoretical practice' can intervene effectively within this field if it does not weigh up and bear upon the frame, which is the decisive structure of what is at stake, at the invisible limit at (between) the interiority of meaning (put under shelter by the whole hermeneuticist, semioticist, phenomenologist and formalist tradition) and (to) all the empiricisms of the extrinsic which, incapable of either seeing or reading, miss the question completely.

(Derrida 1987a, 61)

1

Cambridge, 1989

(framing)

otherwise we miss the question completely.

What becomes of concern in context, therefore, is the thickness of its walls, the silence of its borders, the function of the frame, the dividing line (always active, never passive) that wedges between interior and exterior, forcing them apart.

We always try to forget about this frame, Kant reduced the parergon (hors d'oeuvre, accessory, supplement, addition) to a secondary status with respect to the ergon, the essence of the aesthetic, beauty itself. The drapery on the body of the statue, the ornamental frame that surrounds the painting, the columns of the classical building – all are parerga, secondary, detachable, and we would lose nothing if we were to discard them. Always, we must know what belongs on the inside, and what is therefore to be valued, and what remains external, on the outside, what can be removed from our attention and disregarded.

It is precisely the strategic legitimacy of this move that is at stake.

'No text,' Umberto Eco writes, 'is read independently of the readers' experience of other texts' (Eco 1981, 21). There is only a radical intertextuality where everything is text, is already text. Every text is a multiple reading head for further, other texts. 'An apocalyptic superimprinting of texts: there is no paradigmatic text. Only relationships of cryptic haunting from mark to mark. No palimpsest (definitive unfinishedness). No piece, no metonymy, no integral corpus' (Derrida 1979, 136–7).

What is important then is the marginal and the question of the marginal. And perhaps we should also say that what is of interest is less of the form of a context than of a 'reading formation', which 'would be the question of studying texts in the light of their readings, readings in the light of their texts' (Bennett 1987, 74). A question always of refusing to separate the reading of an archaeological text from my experience of other texts, from experience as text itself.

2

Vienna, 1905

(posing the question)

Psychoanalytic research is most decidedly opposed to any attempt at separating off homosexuals from the rest of mankind as a group of special character. By studying sexual excitation other than those that are manifestly displayed, it has found that all human beings are capable of making a homosexual object-choice and have in fact made one in their unconscious. . . . On the contrary, psychoanalysis considers that a choice of an object independently of its sex – freedom to range equally over male and female objects – as it is found in childhood, in primitive states of society and early periods of history, is the original basis from which, as a restriction in one direction or the other, both the normal and the inverted types develop. Thus from the point of view of psychoanalysis the exclusive sexual interest felt by men for women is also a problem that needs elucidating and is not a self-evident fact based upon an attraction that is ultimately of a chemical nature.

(Freud 1905b, 56–7)

The framework of heterosexuality is not natural or originary, but a secondary development. It is already a parergon. The choice of sexual object could go either way, and 'normality' – heterosexuality, my heterosexuality, for example – appears as the child takes on the rules and regulations of culture, and learns to structure not only its thoughts, attitudes and actions but its whole being around these provisos. Stephen Frosh writes – 'heterosexual genitality is not a *natural* organisation of sexual instinct, but a channelling of, or restriction on, potential to be found in the child' (Frosh 1987, 46). Normality is a work of repression, passing through a series of stages, but the perverse character of human sexuality remains within the subject, repressed and subdued, but capable of breaking out of the unconscious to form, in conscious life, the parapraxes, the dreams, the neuroses and their symptoms. Although I am a heterosexual I am still capable, Freud tells me, of making a homosexual object-choice in my unconscious. I have *already* done so, and thus everything depends upon how well I keep these forces walled up there.

The 'unity' of the unconscious–conscious/preconscious is, therefore, a bisexual unity. 'And I am accustoming myself to the idea of regarding every sexual act as an process in which four persons are involved' (Freud 1954, 289). I am not one; I am divided, dissipated, my maleness is distributed on all sides: I am already a crowd.

No rigid division can thus be drawn between normal and abnormal sexuality. Normality is not a function of reproduction, but, on the contrary, the elevation of reproductive sex to a position that condemns all else to a position from which, henceforth, they will always be described as deviant or perverse. The 'natural' state of libido – if it makes sense to think of it in this way – would be the free combination and articulation of desire (see Nordbladh and Yates, chapter 8).

What we seem to be incapable of understanding is the extent to which the organisation of our lives, down to the most intimate aspects and preferences of our ego, is cultural and historical. And this is, of course, a major problem in a science which (processual or post-processual) is attempting to understand culture before the emergence of a Christian morality, let alone those more recent developments which have precipitated on our doorstep the concept of 'Man', upon which so much now depends.

We have to read sexuality always as a supplement, always as an addition, always as a parergon – something without a point of origin, a point of presence. This takes away from anything an immunity to the question. Freud understood it: that we must explain the normal as much as that which deviates from its rules; we must account for its appearance, its conditions, and its functions.

3
Bohuslän, Sweden, 3000 BP
(becoming a sexed body in the Bronze Age)

If one were to describe the problematics of the Bronze Age – or, indeed, any periodisation in archaeology – then it could be put like this: (1) it ought to be possible to isolate proper identities, and – as a corollary – (2) it ought to be possible to arrange them properly – i.e. normally – so that they obey some expected regularities, fall within established borders, arrange themselves around a recognised and recognisable centre.

The material of concern here is the rock carvings of northern Bohuslän, situated on the west coast of Sweden, abutting on the Norwegian border. I want to discuss this material in a very preliminary fashion, in a marginal manner, suspending questions of chronology, typology, spatial analysis, structural analysis, as I will suspend the question inaugurated by context along with all the regulated symbolism. What is at stake here is not an interpretation, but what may be put into an interpretation, what is inserted into the past through the thickness of context – the pre-contextual (as we would have to call it in Hodder's formula), the 'absolute presents' which, as Jameson stresses, bar the way to a genuine historicity. It is necessary to suspend these questions because, first, these are derivative of a certain organisation of which we are only very dimly aware, and it requires examination and, second, because until we have diagnosed the situation, we do not know what status or value these strategies deserve.

We begin with the marginal, because we recognise it as the displaced centre, as the point where we must begin if we are to attempt to *know* the centre. We begin not with what is said so much as what is not said, with the journey to silence which is the hidden history of the work, its prehistory. These are insidious questions, those which from from behind.

Let me start, then, by describing the rock carvings as a structure of signifying chains whose circuit remains to be completed. In so far as this rock art is 'the sign of the past' it confronts us today as a potential crisis of the Oedipal. For what is absent in the rock art, as always in an unfamiliar semiotic system, is precisely this triangulation, this third term which enters to determine the signifying chains, the Name-of-the-Father as Lacan calls the phallic signifier which determines and establishes the codes of normality.

What is absent from the rock art is precisely this authority, and so it is this authority that must be added whenever there is a requirement, less to say something than to prohibit it, to render a possibility, a possible or potential arrangement or configuration, impossible. Proper identities become through a proper framework, which rests on a division between what is permissible amongst a set of signifiers and what is not permissible – a division which determines for a generative structure what combinations are and will henceforth be possible (the possible always being inseparable from sanction).

Interpretation is an Oedipalisation – the rewriting of a signifying chain according to a grand code whose contingency is hardly perceived, and whose status appears to be natural, ordained, governed from without. It is the territorialisation of the drives which set up over an unformed sexuality the division which will force conformity to a norm and confirm all other organisations as, by comparison, both polymorphous and perverse. Confronted by a chain of signifiers that intrude into the present, the first step of an archaeologist is to territorialise these chains, to execute an occupation of the signifying space. The past cannot be allowed to roam in the present unattended, going where it will – it needs a chaperon, it must be located, given a place, a name, a neighbourhood. Interpretation is always the conflict of the sedentary with the nomadic.

And yet we meet our first hermeneutic problem – although it is really more of an inconvenience. We cannot in the rock art identify properly (i.e. as binary exclusivity) male and female figures. Bohuslän has the highest proportion of human figures in all the rock carvings of northern Europe (Malmer 1981), and yet we cannot, as our point of contact with this origin, locate those two poles which will give us access to this 'other world', a point of entry into its symbolic codes. All that we can do is determine whether the figures are phallic or whether they are non-phallic – whether or not they are depicted with erect penises. The phallus is what lends to the signifier (the figure as signifier) a substance – sexlessness reterritorialises around this point, this attribute. Men are there to be found, and they rise up out of a mass of undifferentiated (unsexed) bodies, erect and proud (Figure 6.1). Women, on the other hand, elude the eye, they cannot be identified by any code of reference that we are

Figure 6.1 Being male

capable of recognising. Females have become invisible – for their sexual organs offer us that horror of there being nothing to see, nothing to represent (the horror of the castration threat fulfilled):

> A defect in this systematics of regulation and desire. A 'hole' in its scoptophilic lends. It is already evident in Greek statuary that this nothing-to-see has to be excluded, rejected, from such a scene of representation. Women's genitals are simply absent, masked, sewn back up inside their 'crack'.
>
> (Irigaray 1985, 26)

A whole artistic and social tradition separates us, not simply from the past – the Bronze Age, etc. – but (and this is what we really mean) from the possibility of representation in a different way. The artist, then, looked upon the male and, in common sympathy with us, found an organ to represent, something worthy of attention, but looked upon the female and found no such organ and – in its absence – nothing to represent.

And this would provide us with a topography of 'the Bronze Age' cultural lens, a snap-shot of the land refracted through it. It would be composed, on the one side, of figures which are 'incontrovertibly' male, and on the other of figures whose sex is, strictly speaking, indeterminate – they may or may not be female, for we cannot rule out the possibility that these non-phallic figures are – to use Gro Mandt's (1987) delicate little expression – not as 'potent' as the others – an expression which converts the phallic–non-phallic couple into the binary active–passive, always reserving the possibility that this division may be located a little more specifically on a subsequent occasion. It is into this latter class that women disappear.

Thus the phallic/active equation becomes signified as 'male', while the non-phallic/passive equation becomes, by default, female or a passive male. Man as the presence of the phallus, the engorged organ (which need not, we should remind ourselves, follow the more modest dimensions of reality) and woman as the figure without *the* organ, the site of the absence of the penis, the state of 'phalluslessness'. Woman becomes as the non-male, not as a species of being in her own right. Woman possesses – and Freud is as much in line with this opinion as anyone else – not so much a genital as the absence of a genital, not a vagina but a not-penis, the non-presence of the 'proper' organ. A little boy submits to the symbolic order in Freud's account of the Oedipus complex because he fears castration, a becoming-female; the little girl, however, submits because, in this valuation, she is *already* castrated, already a castrato, a submissive, and so no alternative strategy is offered.

So, in what we call 'the Bronze Age' and in this art which we assign to that space, we would be confronted with a two-fold sexual system, the phallic and the non-phallic, which need not be strictly equivalent to that of male and female, but which is perhaps beginning to signify these identities through an association with the active–passive couple. The absent phallus could still be signifying male, and anyway this structure remains *homosexual* because, however great the signifying opportunities open to interpretation, however heterogeneous the divisions active: passive/erect:flaccid/present:absent appear, they are always referent to the male organ, the identity of which is never open to question, and find their territory defined from that point.

The symbolic world of the carvings is, therefore, divided into a realm of sexual certainty, the phallic/active/male, and a secondary (and therefore derivative) realm of sexual ambiguity, the non-phallic/passive/malefemale. The feminine world of the Bronze Age therefore takes place and is played out in the absence of identity, identity always rising up erect and proud in the form of the male organ with which it is always synonymous. If we were to formalise an anatomy of the sign, as a geometry of the body, then it would look something like this:

PRESENCE : absence
PHALLIC : non-phallic
POSITIVE : negative
POTENT : passive
IDENTITY : ambiguity
MALE : 'female'

A fairly typical collection of structural oppositions. All very neat. 'Female' is still suspended within quotation marks because it is a provisional assignment depending upon some cultural supplementations. Interpretation aligns itself with the side of presence, with the molar/male, and attempts to fuse or graft on to it, from a position of (phallic) identity, all that is to be related within the same context and to be determined from that point. Man becomes in the rock art through the identity of his phallus, while, because she is lacking, woman is denied this opportunity, and becomes only as an uncertainty, an incompleteness, the conceptual and cultural absence of the male. It is the task of the archaeologist to forge from this absence an identity and a stability. From a position of certainty established on the basis of a single and exclusive erotogenic zone, a whole principle of hermeneutic method is to be elaborated.

And yet, the indeterminacy of the female almost strikes a familiar note in a society (today) which offers women a discourse based on the values of inadequacy, inconstancy, inferiority and relative irrationality. Women don't know their own minds, they are fickle, inconsistent – whereas to be a man (we are brought up to believe) is to be solid, fixed, like a rock. Does not our own culture arrange its signifiers around these phallic/active:non-phallic/passive dichotomies, and while woman is taught to identify with the latter side, men live with the threat of passing over and joining them. A male can be caught up in a discourse of non-phallic passivity which can precipitate him into the processes of cultural elaboration connected up to a feminine-becoming. It is part of the codes by which patriarchy establishes control not only over women but over any form of dissent from its own ranks. The ideals of the active and erect phallus are also the ideals around which contemporary male peer groups are organised, 'the "strongest" being the one who has the best "hard-on", the longest, the biggest, the stiffest penis, or even the one who "pees the farthest" (as in little boys' contests)' (Irigaray 1985, 25). Is not impotence, for instance, a betrayal of male identity, an act of infidelity to the gender, a sign that marks the passage from identity to process, from a being-male to a becoming-female? And there are many other means of such a betrayal.

Thus also a man who breaks away from the presumed unity and identity of the male world, who dissents over adopting the regulated symbolism that conditions masculine identity – he drifts from the security and culturally acceptable 'being a male' (ontology) into a shady world of ambiguous or uncertain significations. He produces contradictory signs to which society, rigidly normalised (Oedipalised), finds enormous difficulty in assigning a place within the symbolic order of things. Those who mix the accepted norms of representation – Boy George might be one such example – are condemned to a world of shadows and uncertainties, to a liminal territory in which there is no real ontology, no 'proper' identity. A 'gender bender' has, for that very reason, ceased to signify his phallic/active/masculine identity and is rationalised as no longer *being-male* but a *becoming-female*. Felix Guattari writes:

> To understand homosexuals better we tell ourselves that they are somewhat 'like a woman', and even some homosexuals join in this convention to help normalise the situation. The feminine-passive/masculine-active couple thus remains a kind of obligatory model, dictated by authority, to enable us to situate, localise, territorialise and control the intensities of desire.
>
> (Guattari 1984, 234)

The topography of the rock art, as it is manifested as interpretation (and interpretation as supplementation) takes on a field of signifiers organised only by difference, but it is already a form of inheritance, since this topography is already territorialised. Each signifier here, each body, becomes the focal point of an intensity of desire, a libidinal tension, and it falls to the archaeologist, not so much to interpret as to patrol the territory and survey the scene. S/he who paints a picture of Bronze Age sexuality, provides the body with a frame, such that interpretation is always already a frame-up.

4
(the marriage ceremony at Vitlycke)
Tanum, c. 1000 BC

> When it comes to humans in the rock carvings, it is almost only men that are represented. They often have strongly emphasised sex organs, but this is not marked all the time. Of course, they are found in the scenes, the marriage pictures, where even women are depicted, characterised by their long hair . . .
>
> (Almgren 1975, 73–4; my translation)

> Figures of women occur rarely amongst the rock pictures . . . Where a woman is identified, it is in most cases quite certain. That holds especially for the rather dispersed 'marriage scenes'; there one clearly sees that it is a man and a woman that are depicted. The woman is drawn with long hair, the man with a phallus and sword.
>
> (Elverheim 1986, 8; my translation)

This territorialisation of sexuality is effected, performed, carried out. A certain combination of figures, perceived in a particular way, are described as belonging to marriage scenes, which strikes us as familiar, proper, even appropriate.

Of these scenes, the most famous is located at the top of the large panel at Vitlycke (Figure 6.2), in the heart of Tanum and a few miles south of the town from which the parish takes its name. It is composed of

Figure 6.2 The marriage ceremony

two figures, apparently locked in an embrace and sealing their attachment with a kiss, watched over by a larger, phallic figure who carries a sword and holds an axe above the couple. This latter figure is often described, cautiously, as the priest, which matches the convention that the union here occurring is a legitimated one. The priest would, therefore, be blessing a union between partners in marriage (a union which, we cannot fail to suspect, is already in the act of being consummated).

'The marriage scene.' This descriptive appellation does not belong on the inside and yet neither can we think it wholly on the outside. It stands in an ambiguous relation to the picture it depicts, neither inside nor outside. It is the addition that bridges the differences and explodes the border. It is the supplement. It is added because it must be added, because there has never been anything without the supplement. Take one away and there would still be supplements, because the ergon is always preceded by a lack, which overturns the hierarchy and installs the parergon in its place. No metacommentary can exhaust this lack, nor could we go back so far as to find a text without a commentary. Discourse multiplies infinitely.

So the verbal appellation could not be either secondary or primary with relation to the origin – it is both at the origin and spaced from it. If we were to represent this by the formula $\frac{signifier}{signified}$, then it would only be to accept that the signified appears only by foreclosing a chain of signifiers – the frame intervenes – while, at the same time, being no more than a signifier. 'The marriage ceremony' cannot be judged from any external object-space (no 'past'), it can only be taken apart from within, read for the frame, through the frame, by the frame. It is not the past that must be made to appear, but the parergon that anticipates all statements, all significations, all signifying production. It is the difference of the signifier, a line which passes through 'the marriage ceremony' as a line of force, that offers itself up as an opening for reading.

'The marriage ceremony'

> What is a version? What is a title? What borderline questions are posed here? I am seeking here merely to establish the necessity of this whole problematic of judicial framing and of the jurisdiction of frames.
>
> (Derrida 1979, 88)

A further seventeen scenes follow essentially the same pattern, depicting the figures more or less schematically than at Vitlycke – although the priest would appear to be an optional extra, a walk-on part, since it is depicted at only one other site (see Figure 6.3 for eight of the scenes).

Again, conventional attitudes have dictated the way in which these scenes have been approached. At Vitlycke, the figure on the right is described as the male, with a sword and penis, while the figure on the left

Figure 6.3 Being married

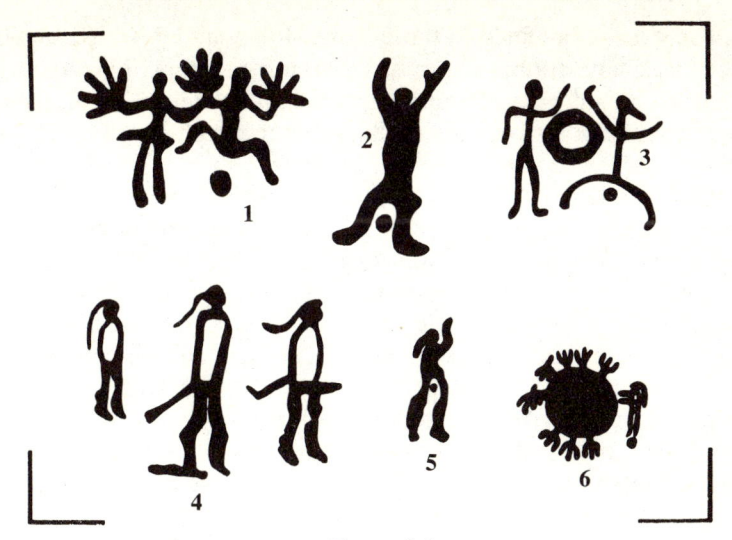

Figure 6.4

becomes, *de facto*, female, lacking either sword or penis, but depicted with long hair (Elverheim, 1986, considers this feature the one certain indication of female sex). Length and style of coiffure are not, of course, universal, cross-cultural and transhistorical sexual symbols (they are not even stable gender signs in our own culture, as the fashion of the last thirty years amply demonstrates), and so it is worth looking at the scenes a little more closely. Only three of the nine 'females' who appear in these scenes actually have long hair – in two cases the heads of the figures are, or are no longer, visible, while in the remaining four examples the 'female' would be indistinguishable from the male on the basis of this feature. It is, indeed, only clear in two cases (Figure 6.3–1 and 6.3–2) to which figure the penis actually belongs (and then only because the artist has troubled to depict the testicles). Thus, we must also note, there are cases where long-haired figures are depicted with weapons (Figure 6.4–4), an attribute which would, if we had accepted the conventional view, distinguish male from female. Indeed, in the same example, one figure with long hair is quite clearly phallic.

According to P. V. Glob, whose monumental work (1969) on the Danish rock carvings of the same period devotes space to a consideration, and formalisation, of these relationships, the cup mark (small, circular depression), which is found between the legs of human figures on carvings in Denmark and right the way up the Swedish west coast as far as Østfold in Norway, is a female symbol, indicating her genitalia (this argument is repeated *ad infinitum* in the literature, most notably by Burenhult 1978 and Mandt 1987). It is found with figures with long hair, as in Bohuslän (Figure 6.4–5), including the adorant figure from Aspeberget (Figure

6.4–6), but it is not confined to those alone. It is found with figures which otherwise lack any distinguishing or characteristic marks (Figure 6.4–1; 6.4–2). There might be a certain logic to this argument – if the penis is depicted by a line or a stroke protruding from the front of the figure, then the vagina, as the opposite of the penis, its absence might well be depicted by a dot, denoting the opening. But this proves as difficult to sustain as the other diagnostic markings. Firstly, the cup mark is not only found with figures whose sex is otherwise uncertain, but with those which are indisputably male – either in front of the figure proximal to the penis (Figure 6.5–1) or between the legs of the figure in what we are told is the 'feminine' position. Similarly, at Aspeberget, a few hundred metres from Vitlycke, the cup mark is found associated with the male bulls which process across the top of the central panel. If it does in any way designate anatomy, then the cup mark would indicate, not simply the hole that is the vagina, but that which forms the urethra and the anus as well.

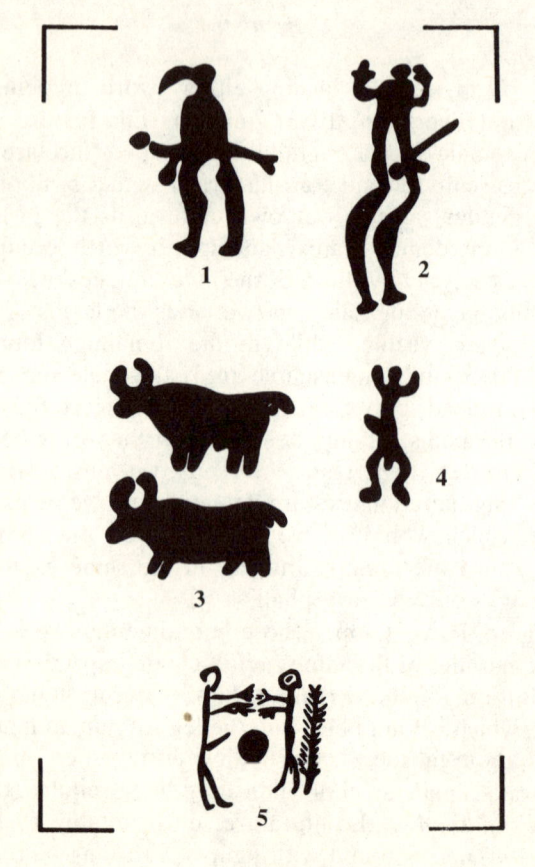

Figure 6.5

Indeed, if we look back to the embracing figures at Vitlycke, we must note that the marriage couple are accompanied by a cup mark, but beneath the feet of the male, phallic figure, not those of the 'female'. The cup mark cannot be tied down to a self-identical and fixed sexuality, therefore, be it male or female.

The problems involved with these positions and interpretations, and their delicate but by no means uncontradictory choreography, are well illustrated by the blatant circularity of Glob's argument: 'It [the "female" cup mark] is thus seen in the carving at Rished in Bohuslän under a woman standing beside a phallic man. . . . As cups are not otherwise found in this scene, the location of the cup-mark cannot be fortuitous' (Glob 1969, 306). The cup mark floats, engaging with many different types of figure. It is what we might call a floating signifier, one that travels the signifying chains, traversing the differences that articulate their components. It 'becomes' a female sex indicator only if we first presume that the figure it accompanies is female, and if there is, first and foremost, and certainly not interior to the rock art, the necessity of assigning a figure a determinate identity, a determinate sexual identity, particularly a determinate female identity.

What is interesting here is not simply that this designation has taken place – that, of course, might seem to be reasonable – so much as *why* it has occurred. Why is it necessary to depart from that model which accepted the ambiguity of the non-phallic figures in the rock art in order, now and here – in these particular scenes – to draw determinacy out of indeterminacy. It can only be out of a desire to close off that possibility that at Vitlycke and the other eight scenes are depicted, not a man and a woman in a sexual embrace, but a man and a man. What a shocking possibility! The model of the phallic:non-phallic and active:passive suggests to our cultural eye that there ought to be a woman here, the counterpart for the engorged male organ, but in scenes as suggestive as these it becomes necessary to close off the latent but nevertheless possible signification. As soon as we find a woman here, we have already passed under a prohibition. The possibility that these are homosexual scenes cannot be left open. Therefore (and it is principally at these points, the marriage scenes) the monolithic system of sexuality – already homosexual because it recognises the presence of only one organ, one sex, the phallic male – is displaced to make room for the appearance of woman, in order to prevent another but different form of homosexuality. Under these specific circumstances, Bronze Age woman becomes determinate, is dragged into presence.

But not for her own sake. She appears, we note, only when a set of sexual prohibitions is brought to bear upon the range of possible significations. *The marriage scene.* Women have use value for men (pleasure) but are also a commodity which has exchange value (prestige) amongst men. If, then, this is to be a marriage scene, then we should expect to find a woman here, at the locus of the ceremonies by which she is circulated and exchanged between patriarchal heads. Especially if there is to be a kiss, an act of copulation, then there must be a woman.

Always, we read, she is a commodity, necessary for exchange, necessary for reproduction, necessary when the male requires a space into which he may plug his penis. This we cannot forget. Woman only becomes necessary when something threatens the phallic directionality and unity of the male. She is not a subject, not an individual with an identity, she is no more than a prop, one that post-Oedipally takes the place of the hand which is forbidden by taboo from continuing to gain satisfaction auto-erotically: 'The vagina is valued for the "lodging" it offers the male organ when the forbidden hand has to find a replacement for pleasure-giving' (Irigaray 1985, 23). Woman appears, therefore, in interpretation only as a structural necessity, as the recognised object of the drives and the correct locus of desire, the regulated destination of the semen. 'She' is not a person, not a 'subject': she is part of the process by which ideology patrols the territory of masculine identity, she is needed to *validate* that identity.

But this sudden determinacy cannot be maintained. Glob notes two scenes from the rock carvings of Denmark that are comparable to those in Bohuslän. The first, which he claims as a marriage scene, is too stylised and too schematic for us to distinguish either sexual partner. The other, which is carved on the Maltegård stone from northern Zealand (Figure 6.5-5) depicts a male figure on the left, with an erect penis depicted by a line, and a 'female' (*sic*) figure on the right, her genitals apparently indicated by a vertical line between 'her' legs. This time the convention that establishes the formula VAGINA = HOLE = CUP MARK is abandoned, and the vagina is to be represented in the same way as the phallus, by a single straight line. 'Undoubtedly we see in this unique piece a depiction of the "sacred" wedding, the May wedding, known from classical lands and recent folklore' (Glob 1969, 294). And yet this scene and its execution are by no means as unique as Glob suggests. What strikes us here is that the apparently 'female' figure is depicted with what would otherwise, under different circumstances, have been described as a phallus – depictions of non-erect phalluses in just this way are by no means unheard of amongst the carvings of southern Scandinavia. Depicting the penis passively rather than as 'potent' (erect) is a means of representation which, while not as common as the erect or non-phallic figures, is found all the way up the east coast of the Skaggerak/Kattegat (e.g. Figure 6.5-4), and in these cases it seems a little unlikely that anyone would not regard these figures as male.

For what we would otherwise have to face is the possibility that the scenes identified in Bohuslän at eighteen sites and, crucially perhaps, on the Maltegård stone from Denmark, represent not heterosexual but homosexual coitus. The coupling of erect (active) and non-erect (passive) figures is certainly to be maintained, but by examining the circumstances by which these have become, in interpretation, 'women', we must be led to seriously doubt the frameworks within which we have worked. There is no reason to assume that both these figures are not male, nor is there any contemporary reason why they should not be so. In any case, we must accept that there is an ambiguity that is not undesirable but in fact as original as the identities we think we see, which allows these scenes to signify either form of sexuality, and to perform upon the present a deterritorialisation of the rules and structures, the codes and signs, the signifying production, of desire.

The action of making women 'appear' in the otherwise 'homosexual' structures of praxis is only motivated in opposition to this threatening possibility – is only in order to exclude and so deny it, to make women appear in order to make this unspeakable 'other man' disappear. Always there is a kind of male, a certain male, but only under circumstances that it is possible to describe does there become a female: *interpretation is traversed by a line of socio-psychic repression.* She appears, not for herself, not to find herself in herself, as her own identity, but as the portable vagina to be deployed strategically whenever masculine self-identity is threatened or brought into question. The designation 'the marriage ceremony', which delimits this process, teams with significations which should become the object of an archaeology.

> The fact is that women are the only authorised repositories of the process of becoming a sexed body. If a man breaks away from the phallic rat race inherent in all power formations, he will become involved in various possible ways in this sort of feminine becoming. Only then can he go on to becoming animal, cosmos, words, colour, music.
>
> (Guattari 1984, 234)

5

n.d.

(becoming human)

> I am convinced – as the experience of psychoses and serious neuroses makes clear – that, beyond the ego, the subject is to be found lying in scatters all over the world of history.
>
> (Guattari 1984, 27)

> If we descend to the least evolved societies . . . Here, the individual himself loses his personality. There is a complete lack of distinction between him and his exterior soul or totem. He and his 'fellow animal' together compose a single personality. The identification is such that man assumes the characteristics of the thing or animal with which he is united. For example, on Mabuiag Island people of the crocodile clan are thought to have the temperament of the crocodile: they are proud, cruel, always ready for battle . . . The Bororo sincerely imagines himself to be a parrot: at least, though he assumes the characteristic form only after he is dead, in this life he is to that animal what the caterpillar is to the butterfly.
>
> (Durkheim and Mauss 1973, 6–7)

Gregor Samsa woke up one morning to find that he had become a gigantic insect. What shocks us, perhaps, is that the criteria for being-human have been torn back and a metamorphosis has taken place. Such an event should not, strictly, be allowed: man may have been an ape, but he is now (being) that which is absolutely prohibited from mixing with other forms, especially that of the insect. And so, in the end, Gregor is sacrificed in order to preserve the rules of existence, the Oedipalised codes of ontology and of the family (Bogue 1989, 111–12).

But – and presuming from the start that the two are separable rather than internal to each other – we might say that fact is stranger than fiction. If Gregor abandons being for a becoming (and there was never any question of choice), then this horror of a becoming-other is by no means confined to the imagination of literature. Stephen D., for instance, dreamt one night that he was a dog, and woke to find that the transformation of which he had received a premonition was already complete. He awoke to find himself

> in a world unimaginably rich and significant in smells, the becoming-animal here marked by the sudden ascendancy of one sense over the others. 'I had dreamt I was a dog – it was an olfactory dream – and now I awoke to an infinitely redolent world – a world in which all other sensations, enhanced as they were, paled before smell . . . I see now what we give up in being civilised and human. We need the other – the "primitive" – as well'.
>
> (Sacks 1985, 149–51)

And it is this becoming-other which we fear as the absolute deterritorialisation of the human. Gregor had to be destroyed less because he had ceased to be human than because he had ceased to be anything in particular – he does not turn into an insect, for he remains Gregor Samsa, he remains a man-becoming-insect, between ontological realms, and so outside of the liberal values that would protect the hallowed space of the human individual.

The body-ego is not fixed and inviolable. It is not something upon which we can rely and assume to be the basis – fundamental and unquestionable – of all experience. The notion of a knowable body-self – which is without doubt an historical one, and therefore one that is socially and culturally determined – cannot confront the transiency and arbitrary nature of the ego and its alliance with the conception of the complete and homogeneous body. From Lacan and the formulation of the mirror stage we know that the vision of the homogenised-body is a specular image with which the ego identifies in order to become signifiable. Fold back the ego (the ego which humanism continually reifies and reproduces) and you find a very different organisation, a whole kaleidoscope of possibilities. Christina, perhaps, whose mind separated one day from her body, or the man whose legs detached themselves and were replaced by those of another man, which would not obey any of his commands (Sacks 1985, 42ff; 53ff). Beyond the ego we start by finding only that which we regard as abnormal or deviant, the unusual, denoting a certain alienness to our society, a lack of fit within our ontologies and their recognised identities. Beyond the egos and the super-egos that dominate our perspectives, our sanctioned literature, our official histories and prehistories, there is the fragmentation of that unity which has dominated western thought since classical times. Do we forget that, if this science of man is a recent development, then the concept of man is scarcely of any greater antiquity? A different relationship existed before the dominance of this ideology – a dialogue, for instance, between madness and reason (Foucault 1973), but certainly a madness always within reason, on the inside – today, as much as in all those yesterdays.

We experience the folding back of 'the real' today only in the terms of what clinical psychology and psychoanalysis (already from positions charged with upholding the tyranny of the normal) call illness, psychosis, neurosis, paranoia, schizophrenia, insanity – all the terms which seek to stabilise the situation by normalising the cracks in the ego's surface. Explorations of alternatives, which attempt to explode the identity of men – becoming-animal in Kafka, becoming-mineral in Beckett – become neutralised by being regarded as 'mere metaphor', since this becoming-other-than-it-appears-to-be is strictly prohibited by the identity, and most particularly by the self-identity, of the ego. And yet all these 'disorders' remind us that the ego is fragile, that it is traversed by lines of stress and strain, by cracks and fissures, and that it is within this fragmentation that history is to be found within the science of man. History shines through these tears and rips in the surface of the body-ego, and beneath the smoothness and pristine quality of the homogeneous and homogenising skin of the antique statue, the self shines through as the lived experience of a Picasso or a Munch. Why shouldn't Gregor turn into an insect? Why shouldn't Stephen D. enter a course that precipitates him in a becoming-dog, one which although (or perhaps because) not complete is mourned. *Homo sapiens* opens on to history only as it bursts at the seams – the zoomorphisation of the body and its organs, so that the anus can become a wolf, or a rat which is already also a penis, already the worm that burrows as the rat would burrow into the anus of the victim. And, before either of these processes will have taken place – before we speak, following Freud, of a Wolf-Man or a Rat-Man (analysis formalising the transformation as it seeks to reverse it and bring the man back out of the animal) – before the becoming-animal of the body there is already a becoming-female, an unbecoming-male.

> Everyone, even the most unembodied person, experiences himself as inextricably bound up with or in his body. In ordinary circumstances, to the extent that one feels one's body to be alive, one feels oneself to be alive, real and substantial. Most people feel that they began when their bodies began and that they will end when their bodies end.
>
> (Laing 1969, 66)

But what, we must ask, after all, *is* a body? This image, this contemporary experience of myself and my body, is the image reflected to my ego for its own purposes. When shaken a bit (and it doesn't take a lot) it proves to be a mirage and a chimera. Daniel Paul Schreber – to speak only of an obvious case – 'lived for a long time without a stomach, without intestines, almost without lungs, with a torn oesophagus, without a bladder, and with shattered ribs, he used sometimes to swallow part of his own larynx with his food, etc.' (Freud 1911, 147). When the body in question reformed, the judge awoke from one neurosis only to find that he was now a woman, possessed of the structures that 'give the female skin its peculiar softness' and with 'nerves of voluptuousness' that envelop the whole body, producing on his chest (periodically) female breasts, and covering his entire body with those feelings of sensual pleasure 'such as are found only in the genital region in men' (Schreber 1955, 204–6).

Beyond the ego, then, we find a wholly different world, which reminds us how much our ontologies coincide with our ego's and our body ego's – the fragmentation of the body, the involvement in a series of becomings (becoming animal, mineral, female) which would threaten to articulate man with all that we are used to thinking of in opposition to him. Beyond the ego and the limits it imposes upon signification, beyond its controls, regulations, codes and taboos, anything is possible – 'Man' ceases to be the centre of meaning and becomes merely an arbitrary signifier, floating and engaging with other signifiers. The body can be experienced in different ways, it can be conceptualised and reconceptualised in chains of production that are as limitless as the signifying units that compose them. The molar identity of man is shattered, and it no longer makes any sense to attempt to understand history on the basis of a monolithic category of the person – 'the science of man' is a theatrical farce, 'the antiquity of man' a charade: games we play in front of the mirror. Beyond the ego/*cogito* which inaugurate the modern period – as the state of being – there is only a state of becoming and unbecoming. If we are to approach prehistory, which must begin at the edges of this modern period, then we must abandon the science of man and work to obliterate his memory. We may read Kafka or Beckett instead of Descartes or Giddens. It is not sufficient to erase Being as does Heidegger any more than it is sufficient to attempt to define it. We must conceive it on the basis of difference, on the basis of equivalence with all the other signifiers of the meaning system. It is in disturbing identity, and the identity of 'man' as exclusivity and as something specifiable in advance and applicable in all times and places, it is in disturbing these cycles of production and reproduction that govern our own image and our own self-image, our time, our place, that history is to be found.

And yet these are not mere dreams or fantasies, these becomings that cut across and dissect the body of 'man'. Respond in this way and you miss the point, you will already have begun on a path that leads back to ontology via a total destruction of history. They are perfectly real, since what is at stake here is always the specular identity of identity. Doesn't deconstruction differ from classical (Hegelian) dialectics precisely because it insists upon the non-identity of identity? That things differ from themselves:

> . . . it is clear that the human being does not 'really' become an animal anymore than the animal 'really' becomes something else. Becoming produces nothing other than itself. We fall into a false alternative if we think you either imitate or you are. What is real is the becoming itself, the block of becoming, not the supposedly fixed terms through which becomes passes.
>
> (Deleuze and Guattari 1988, 238)

You must comprehend the difference, for if identity must be iterable in order to be identified, then we will always already have ruptured the conditions of ontology (Derrida 1977). The becoming-other of being ruptures its self-circuit – the becoming always lacks a subject, a point of pure reference, since that space, too, 'is' not without also and at the same time being caught up in various becomings.

Juxtapose fact and fiction, subject and object, ideal and material, and you will never comprehend the movement of a becoming. When it comes to a becoming, no further separation between fact and fiction is possible –

or, rather, the becoming produces at once both fact and fiction, it is a material force. In Andalusia in 1977 no one doubted any of these possibilities:

> If masculine behaviour, for the men of San Blas, has its conceptual focus in the male genital region, then feminine behaviour is concentrated linguistically on the anus. Men show themselves to be constantly aware that the anus can be used in homosexual encounters, in which case the passive partner is perceived as playing the feminine role, and indeed of being converted symbolically into a woman. It is this sexual transformation that men fear.
> (Brandes 1981, 232–3)

Do not suppose that because the transformation is symbolic that it is therefore, in some sense, less real than the real. The symbolic not only represents but, because the real is lacking in anything more, it also performs. Of course, the cuckold does not really sprout *cuernos*, the horns, and there will be nothing visible, no physical transformation resulting from the infidelity of the wife. And yet the metamorphosis is still as real:

> To be cuckolded is to be transformed symbolically into a woman. The horns, originally associated or belonging to the woman, are placed on the head of a man, thereby feminizing him. The cuckold not only wears horns but also simultaneously becomes symbolically converted into a *cabron*, or super-goat.
> (Brandes 1981, 229)

And this transformation is irreversible, the male is 'forever branded with this female symbol'. A man-becoming-horned (-becoming-goat-) becoming-feminine.

It is as real as the being-male or the being-female. In Samoa, a man must guard his behaviour and appearance against the ever present possibility of becoming *fa'afafine*, like a woman, a latent potential within every male (Shore 1981, 209–10). We have to get outside ourselves (our time, our place) in order to appreciate the difference – the Californian man-becoming-bear, for example, which is a culturally recognised category (Kroeber 1952, 315; Whitehead 1981, 101), could not be comprehended in a society which imposes an absolute taboo on the mixing of the category 'human'.

And so 'the marriage scene' produces an endless stream of ontological significations, and it is these that we need to question. It adds to the rock art not simply what is necessary or sufficient to make it intelligible, but an interpretative excess. To talk of humans as beings, of human-beings, makes a claim upon libidinal organisation that extends far beyond the accredited concepts of 'male' and 'female', forcing its signifying production into little territories, into self-limiting circuits. The marriage scene protects and preserves identity and ontology by conferring upon it legitimacy – by forcing out the possibility of a homosexuality, which is more generally the possibility of breaking with ontology and precipitating man on a course of becoming-passive/becoming-female. Legitimacy, here, is the buttress of identity, and it is without doubt to legitimate and validate the identity of man that woman is called into existence.

So that all these categories of 'being' – subject, ego, *cogito*, agent, as also man, woman, animal – all these designations, presuppose a certain organisation of libido, using the 'concept' to refer to that force which charges a body and its organs in relation to other bodies, without presupposing that there need be any particular unity, hierarchy or axiology. All these signs in the rock art, all signs and all significations, are charged with libido – they offer the possibility of 'man' becoming articulated in a series of becomings that relate humans to all that would lie outside their bodies, and it is this possibility that interpretation has always foreclosed.

Re-examining the production of signs and their relationships as essentially the production of libido,[2] we can begin to re-examine the ways in which the self and body – the body-ego – were signified in what we call (as though it were a place) 'the Bronze Age'. As is clear from what was said above, 'the marriage scenes' cannot support the notion of a rigid and exclusive organisation of the sexual drives than may be generally the case in western societies today, but libidinal deterritorialisation is extended much further to directly assault the integrity of human identity (as we recognise it). Thus the sex organ can be used for copulating with animals (Figure 6.6–1 and 6.6–2) such that the division that separates nature from culture, man from animal, is torn down. The phallus loses its transcendent status, its unimpeachable self-identity. It becomes a weapon, a bow, or an axe that is already, at the same time, the head of an animal (Figure 6.6–6). The penis can integrate the body within an architecture – the boat, as the prow of a ship, which is already signifying an animality (Figure 6.6–3 and 6.6–4). Indeed, so acutely does this masculine ontology come into question that the male can become fully integrated, in the act of copulation, into the body of a deer (Figure 6.6–5). Human and totem as one.

What we see here is the incision, right into the heart of the masculine/phallic principle of identity, of those values which have hitherto been regarded as belonging to a subsidiary 'feminine'/non-phallic discourse within the reading formation that has been analysed here – the values of ambiguity, flow and process – that offers itself, in the marriage scenes, as potentially subversive. It speeds up signification, forcing it forward and shifting it out of the molar and through the molecular. At Källsangen (Figure 6.7) there are only becomings – these are neither man

ARCHAEOLOGY AFTER STRUCTURALISM

Figure 6.6 Becoming animal

nor animal but something between terms and between these alternatives, something between 'man' and 'animal' and therefore unnameable. These are, at one and the same time, both men and birds, a man-becoming-bird or a bird-becoming-man (who knows from which place to start?). We do not know what to call these unfamiliar figures, but the fact of being unnameable does not alter the fact of the becoming. Nor does it matter that these creatures are not 'real', since nothing can alter the power of the becoming, of representation and presentation. Man articulates with animal – they share features – and if the becoming animal is always incomplete, it still remains more real than the being-human.

(In historical work we ought to be able to say that anything can

ARCHAEOLOGY THROUGH THE LOOKING-GLASS

Figure 6.7 Becoming animal

happen. The value of the past ought to be its potential to untangle the threads that hold us, anchored, to the present.)

But what would be at stake here would be the parergon of the human, the parergon of the body, the body as parergon. For there is no doubt that the body is framed – by the sex organs that shift us into a gender system, by the concept of 'being-human' and its subsiduaries being-male, being-female, being-animal, etc., so that everything that would claim to be the ergon or to represent the ergon-man is implicated in a system of lateral restriction. The ergon is characterised by lack, so it must be framed, prevented from following off in every direction. Because of the lack which calls forth the parergon, we go so far back into the body in our attempt to isolate this ergon that there is nothing left – it is not simply the drapes or the hoods that are removable, for everything is detachable and there would still be more. The ergon is occupied only by absence, the absence of being. The body is always a part of the signifying chain, and this phallic/molar/symbolic level as the principle for the interpretation of rock art discourse and for an ontology 'in the Bronze Age' is problematic.

At the level of the semiotic (approaching the rock art not on the basis of the symbolic dimension but only according to relations of difference amongst signifiers) the whole principle that seemed to converge around the phallus as the discourse of identity, subjected to taboo and regulation, collapses in upon itself. Designs (signifiers) can be recombined without any restriction placed upon their possible combinations. Thus, taking only the most common motifs, a ship can be articulated with a man, an animal, a disc, a foot, as each design opens and closes in multiple relations with its others. Not only combinations of two signifiers, but four, five or more motifs are conjoined. And not only combinations of whole signifiers, but an exchange of parts – the legs of a man seed off and become those of a disc, an animal head leads a ship. Although pure or basic figures still outnumber these combinations, it is nevertheless important that, in terms of what signs can be conjoined, all possible permutations appear to be equivalent, and none is prohibited. The structure of libidinal production, which convention has sought to force into the directionality and legitimacy of 'marriage' as the only sanctioned combination of motifs, the only permitted signifying union, is blown open, and man combines freely with all the other signifiers and points of focus within the system.

At Kyrkestigan (Figure 6.8), there are various becomings: the warp and weave of identity and identification, the clutter and process of deterritorialisation and reterritorialisation. Where you may see men and animals, ships and circles, I see only the free production of signs, into which man as we know him would disappear, since there would be nothing left against which he could validate his identity, and something new emerge. I see man-becoming-beast, becoming-mineral (becoming-ship, becoming-wood), man-becoming-abstract (becoming-disc), animal-becoming-ship, and so on. I see the rupture of exclusivity and the opening up of new possibilities, the liberation of self, the historicisation of man predicated upon his deconstruction.

Rather than being based upon the symbolic dimension which would

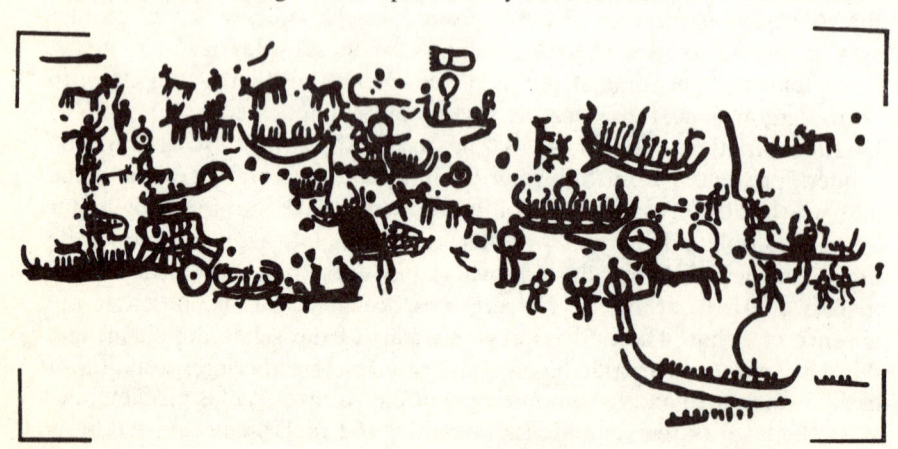

Figure 6.8 Various becomings

claim for a certain signifier an essential and indispensable status, and fail to realise that these are already caught up in a system of value which organises the range of possible combinations, the rock art signifies according to a more molecular and semiotic structure. Each sign, each apparent state-of-being, is no more than a punctuation point in chains of signifying production, which indicate a relationship of the body to external objects, and therefore to itself, that persists within a less territorialised system of libidinal investment. The identities that occur in the rock art are libidinally charged, but they are not regulated in the way that we, in our society, would recognise as 'natural'. It is not that the discourse is unfixed or without points of identity and an 'organisation', not that we have moved beyond into a space beyond structure, but that the dividing line between fixity and lability is no longer clear. Signifying production is so many becomings as deterritorialisation and reterritorialisation of ontological flux.

Figure 6.9 Becoming human

6 (Instead of a) conclusion

not yet

(beyond man)

Writing has the aim of unleashing these becomings from ontology, a fracture of the image in the mirror (stage), of man. It is man, with all his self-limiting production, that must be destroyed. An act of liberation and of infidelity to the present, a destruction of the ego, a deconstruction and a destroying, a complete scouring of the unconscious, of identity and its structures. An intervention within man, within the regime of signs that 'he' names.

Nietzsche said: man has imprisoned life, the superman is he who will liberate life *within man himself* – to the profit of another form . . . What is the superman? It is a formal composite of forces within man with these new forces. It is the form which flows from a new relation of forces. Man tends to liberate life, work and language within himself. The superman is, according to the formula of Rimbaud, man laden with the animals themselves (a code which can capture the fragments of other codes, as in the new schemes of lateral and retrograde evolution). It is man laden with the rocks themselves, or the inorganic (where silicon reigns) . . . As Foucault would say the superman is much less than the disappearance of existing men and much more than the change of a concept, it is the advent of a new form, neither God nor man, let us hope that it will not be worse than the two preceding forms.

(Deleuze 1986, 139–141)[3]

ACKNOWLEDGEMENTS

This chapter was originally two papers. The first was presented in different forms to the Society for American Archaeology Annual Meeting in Phoenix, Arizona, April 1988, and then subsequently to the Cambridge Seminar on Poststructuralism and Archaeology in June 1988. The second was writen for a one-day seminar on iconography held in Cambridge in May 1989. Both papers were modified and presented at the Institutionen för Arkeologi, Göteborgs Universitet, in October 1989. I wish to thank all those at these sessions and elsewhere who have helped it to develop: Grant Chambers, Knut Helskog, Mike Shanks, Chris Tilley, and especially Ian Hodder and Jarl Nordbladh.

NOTES

1. Lacan's gloss is as follows: '. . . the metaphoric structure indicating that it is in the substitution of signifier for signifier that an effect of signification is produced that is creative or poetic, in other words, which is the advent of the signification in question. The sign + between ( ) represents here the crossing of the bar – and the constitutive value of this crossing for the emergence of signification' (Lacan 1977, 164).
2. I anticipate the criticism that these interpretations are underdetermined. The point here, however, is not to establish a definitive claim upon what this material 'meant' or 'means', but what it *can mean* – to establish a different way of reading and therefore of seeing man, one that has been concealed by the ontologies with which 'history' has been approached.
3. The problems of finding a new name for this form when it emerges are obvious

– 'Man' is self-evidently inadequate, but we must beware that, by a simple change of nomenclature, we think the problem solved.

I am grateful to Grant Chambers for drawing my attention to Deleuze's work, and for providing a suitable translation.

FIGURE REFERENCES

All figures redrawn by the author from the following sources:
Figure 6.1: Almgren, 1927, Fig. 73; Baltzer, 1911, pl. xiv–xv.
Figure 6.2: Almgren, 1927, Fig. 75; Baltzer, 1911, pl. xix.
Figure 6.3–1, 2: Almgren, 1927, Fig. 79; Baltzer, 1881, pl. 51/2
       3: Baltzer, 1881, pl. 4/16
       4: Baltzer, 1881, pl. 56/5
       5: Baltzer, 1881, pl. 56/5
       6: Almgren, 1927, Fig. 81; Baltzer, 1881, pl. 41/3
       7: Baltzer, 1881, pl. 3
       8: Baltzer, 1881, pl. 3
Figure 6.4–1: Glob, 1969, Fig. 104
       2: Glob, 1969, Fig. 104
       3: Almgren, 1927, Fig. 52; Glob, 1969, Fig. 10
       4: Marstrander, 1963, pl. 20
       5: Baltzer, 1881, pl. 50/8
       6: Almgren, 1927, Fig. 55a; Baltzer, 1881, pl. 24
Figure 6.5–1: Svarteborg, site 17/1 (Ancient Monuments Register) – redrawn from unpublished photograph.
       2: Fredsjö, Nordbladh and Rosvall, 1981, No. 182.
       3: Almgren, 1927, Fig. 73; Baltzer, 1911, pl. xiv-xv
       4: Fredsjö, Nordbladh and Rosvall, 1981, No. 91a
       5: Glob, 1969, Fig. 102
Figure 6.6–1: Almgren, 1927, Fig. 75; Baltzer, 1911, pl. xix
       2: Baltzer, 1881, pl. 54/5
       3: Fredsjö, Nordbladh and Rosvall, 1971, No. 283
       4: Fredsjö, Nordbladh and Rosvall, 1981, No. 180
       5: Fredsjö, Nordbladh and Rosvall, 1981, No. 158
       6: Fredsjö, Nordbladh and Rosvall, 1981, No. 91b
Figure 6.7: Fredsjö, Nordbladh and Rosvall, 1975, No. 75
Figure 6.8: Fredsjö, Nordbladh and Rosvall, 1971, No. 241
Figure 6.9: Baltzer, 1881, pl. 14/1

REFERENCES

Works by Freud cited in the text are listed according to the date of their original publication. Unless otherwise stated, references are to the translations in the respective volumes of the Pelican Freud Library (PFL), London: Penguin Books, 15 volumes, 1973–85.

Almgren, B. (1975) 'Hällristningarnas tro: till tolkningen av de Svenska hällristningarna från bronsåldern', *Kungl. Gustav Adolfs Akademien Årsbok* 69–108.
Almgren, O. (1927) *Hällristningar och Kultbruk: Bidrag till Belysning av de Nordiska Bronsåldersristningarnas Innebors*, Kungl. Vitterhets Historie och

Antikvitets Akademiens Handlingar 35, Stockholm.
Baltzer, L. (1881) *Glyphes des Rochers du Bohuslan (Suede)*, Göteborg: Göteborg Handelstidnings Aktiebolaget.
Baltzer, L. (1911) *Några af de Viktigaste hällristningarna samt en del af de fasta fornminnena i Bohuslän*, Göteborg.
Barrett, J. (1987) 'Fields of discourse: reconstituting a social archaeology', *Critique of Anthropology* 7(3): 5–16.
Barthes, R. (1977) 'The death of the author', *Image–Music–Text*, trans. S. Heath, London: Fontana.
Bennett, A. (1987) 'Texts in history: the determination of readings and their texts', in D. Atridge, G. Bennington and R. Young (eds) *Poststructuralism and the Question of History*, Cambridge: Cambridge University Press, pp. 63–81.
Bogue, R. (1989) *Deleuze and Guattari*, London: Routledge.
Brandes, S. (1981) 'Like wounded stags: male sexual ideology in an Andalusian town', in S. B. Ortner and H. Whitehead (eds) *Sexual Meanings: The Cultural Construction of Gender and Sexuality*, Cambridge: Cambridge University Press, pp. 216–39.
Burenhult, G. (1978) *Hällristningar: Hällbilder från sten- och bronsålder i Norden*, Malmö: Malmö Museum.
Deleuze, G. (1986) *Foucault*, Paris: Editions de Minuit.
Deleuze, G. and Guattari, F. (1984) *Anti-Oedipus: Capitalism and Schizophrenia*, London: Athlone.
Deleuze, G. and Guattari, F. (1988) *A Thousand Plateaus: Capitalism and Schizophrenia*, London: Athlone.
Derrida, J. (1973) *Speech and Phenomena and Other Essays on Husserl's Theory of Signs*, trans. D. B. Allison, Evanston: North-Western University Press.
Derrida, J. (1976) *Of Grammatology*, trans. G. C. Spivak, Baltimore: Johns Hopkins University Press.
Derrida, J. (1977) 'Limited Inc. abc. . .', *Glyph* 2: 162–254.
Derrida, J. (1978) *Writing and Difference*, trans. A. Bass, London: Routledge & Kegan Paul.
Derrida, J. (1979) 'Living on; border lines', in H. Bloom *et al.*, *Deconstruction and Criticism*, New York: Seabury, pp. 75–176.
Derrida, J. (1981) *Dissemination*, trans. B. Johnson, London: Athlone.
Derrida, J. (1986) *Memoires for Paul de Man*, trans C. Lindsay, J. Culler and E. Cadava, New York: Columbia University Press.
Derrida, J. (1987a) *The Archaeology of the Frivolous: Reading Condillac*, trans. J. P. Leavey, Lincoln and London: University of Nebraska Press.
Derrida, J. (1987b) *The Truth in Painting*, trans. G. Bennington and I. McLeod, Chicago: Chicago University Press.
Derrida, J. (1988) *The Post Card*, trans. A. Bass, Chicago: Chicago University Press.
Durkheim, E. and Mauss, M. (1973) *Primitive Classification*, trans. R. Needham, London: Routledge & Kegan Paul.
Eco, U. (1981) *The Role of the Reader: Explorations in the Semiotics of Texts*, London: Hutchinson.
Elverheim, I. (1986) 'Kvinnofigurer på Hällarna i Tanum', *Adoranten*, Tanumshede: Scandinavian Society for Prehistoric Art, 8–13.
Foucault, M. (1973) *Madness and Civilization*, London: Tavistock.
Fredsjö, A., Nordbladh, J. and Rosvall, J. (1971) *Hällristningar i Kville harad i Bohuslän: 1. Svenneby Socken*, Studier i nordisk arkeologi 7, Göteborg: Göteborgs Arkeologiska Museum.

Fredsjö, A., Nordbladh, J. and Rosvall, J. (1975) *Hällristningar i Kville harad i Bohuslän: 2. Bottna Socken*, Studier i nordisk arkeologi 13, Göteborg: Göteborgs Arkeologiska Museum.
Fredsjö, A., Nordbladh, J. and Rosvall, J. (1981) *Hällristningar i Kville harad i Bohuslän: 3. Kville Socken*, Studier i nordisk arkeologi 14/15, Göteborg: Göteborgs Arkeologiska Museum.
Freud, S. (1900) *The Interpretation of Dreams*, PFL 4.
Freud, S. (1905a) 'Fragment of an analysis of a case of hysteria', PFL 8: 31–164.
Freud, S. (1905b) 'Three essays on the theory of sexuality', PFL 7: 33–169.
Freud, S. (1909) 'Analysis of a phobia in a five-year-old boy', PFL 8: 167–305.
Freud, S. (1910) 'Five lectures on psychoanalysis', in *Two Short Accounts of Psychoanalysis*, trans. J. Strachey, London: Penguin 1984.
Freud, S. (1911) 'Psychoanalytic notes on an autobiographical account of a case of paranoia (Dementia Paranoides)', PFL 9: 131–223.
Freud, S. (1915a) 'Repression', PFL 11: 145–58.
Freud, S. (1915b) 'The unconscious', PFL 11: 159–222.
Freud, S. (1917) *Introductory Lectures on Psychoanalysis*, PFL 1.
Freud, S. (1925) 'A note upon the "mystic writing pad" ', PFL 11: 428–34.
Freud, S. (1926) 'The question of lay analysis', PFL 15: 279–353.
Freud, S. (1933) *New Introductory Lectures on Psychoanalysis*, PFL 2.
Freud, S. (1954) *The Origins of Psychoanalysis: Letters to Wilhelm Fliess, Drafts and Notes, 1887–1902*, trans. E. Mosbacher and J. Strachey; ed. M. Bonaparte, A. Freud and E. Kris, London: Imago.
Freud, S. and Breuer, J. (1895) *Studies on Hysteria*, PFL 3.
Frosh, S. (1987) *The Politics of Psychoanalysis*, London: Macmillan.
Glob, P. V. (1969) *Helleristningar i Danmark*, Copenhagen: Jutland Archaeological Society.
Guattari, F. (1984) *Molecular Revolution: Psychiatry and Politics*, trans. R. Sheed, London: Penguin.
Hodder, I. (1986) *Reading the Past*, Cambridge: Cambridge University Press.
Irigaray, L. (1985) *This Sex Which Is Not One*, trans. C. Porter with C. Burke, New York: Cornell University Press.
Jameson, F. (1972) *The Prison House of Language*, Princeton: Princeton University Press.
Kristeva, J. (1984) *Revolution in Poetic Language*, trans. M. Waller, New York: Columbia University Press.
Kroeber, A. L. O. (1952) 'Psychosis or social sanction?', in A. L. Kroeber, *The Nature of Culture*, Chicago: Chicago University Press, pp. 310–19.
Lacan, J. (1977) *Ecrits*, trans. A. Sheridan, London: Tavistock.
Lacan, J. (1988) *The Seminar of Jacques Lacan: Book II: The Ego in Freud's Theory and the Technique of Psychoanalysis*, trans. S. Tomasselli, Cambridge: Cambridge University Press.
Laing, D. (1978) *The Marxist Theory of Art: An Introductory Survey*, Brighton: Harvester.
Laing, R. D. (1969) *The Divided Self*, London: Penguin.
Macherey, P. (1978) *A Theory of Literary Production*, London: Routledge & Kegan Paul.
Malmer, M. P. (1981) *A Chorological Study of North European Rock Art*, Stockholm: KVHAA handlingar: Antikvariska Serien 32.
Mandt, G. (1987) 'Female symbolism in rock art', in R. Bertelsen, A. Lillehammer and J-R. Næss (eds), *Were They All Men? An Examination of Sex Roles in Prehistoric Society*, Stavanger: Stavanger Archaeological Museum, pp. 35–52.

Marstrander, S. (1963) *Ostfolds Jordbruksristninger*, Oslo: Institute of Contemporary Research in Human Culture.
Sacks, O. (1985) *The Man who Mistook his Wife for a Hat*, London: Picador.
Schreber, D. P. (1955) *Memoirs of my Nervous Illness*, trans. I. Macalpine and R. A. Hunter, London: Dawson.
Shore, B. (1981) 'Sexuality and gender in Samoa: conceptions and missed conceptions', in S. B. Ortner and H. Whitehead (eds) *Sexual Meanings: The Cultural Construction of Gender and Sexuality*, Cambridge: Cambridge University Press, pp. 192–215.
Sørensen, M. L. (1987) 'Material order and cultural classification: the role of bronze objects in the transition from Bronze Age to Iron Age in Scandinavia', in I. Hodder (ed.) *The Archaeology of Contextual Meanings*, Cambridge: Cambridge University Press.
Whitehead, H. (1981) 'The bow and the burden strap: a new look at institutionalised homosexuality in native north America', in S. B. Ortner and H. Whitehead (eds) *Sexual Meanings: The Cultural Construction of Gender and Sexuality*, Cambridge: Cambridge University Press, pp. 80–115.

CHAPTER 7

That there is a politics to style and an order to discourse is one of the main themes and questions raised by post-structuralism, which embraces the issue of language and extends its analysis to cover the whole sociocultural horizon. So deconstruction forces upon us the disjuncture between rhetoric and logic, and Derrida menaces philosophy by insisting that ontology, epistemology, the very foundations of western metaphysics, are all forms of writing. The tower of transcendental concepts collapses. So Roland Barthes can take a Balzac novella and subject it to an exact, line by line reading, analysing it as what Philippe Sollers calls 'sheer text'. Rhetoric creates certain meanings and prohibits certain others; it is the silent 'centre' of discourse which conceals its various functions by hiding in the shadows.

Interest in archaeological production as textual production is, of course, growing in post-processual archaeology, and although some of the more recent experiments have been a little coy, an emphasis upon the contemporary context must lead archaeologists to explore in greater detail the role of rhetorical and other formal devices in constituting authority, objectivity and polarity within archaeological literature. In this paper, Moran and Hides raise questions that we cannot afford to ignore – questions about the authority structures implicated in writing, the systems and the orders of discursive production. They chastise contextual archaeology for a continuing adherence to the rhetoric of authority, and demand that we examine the institutional symbolism which guarantees the survival of the dominant order, and which is capable of defusing all but that which breaks with its established rules and codes of representation.

Refusing to split form from content, their response is to call for an 'opening out' of discourse, a 'dethroning' of the big names, the great experts, who in Moran and Hide's writing appear only alongside personal conversation and debates which emphasise the subjective background of reading. It is possible, they claim, to apply the 'essential' tenets of post-structuralism without restricting one's audience to those who are familiar with Kant or Hegel or Nietzsche. The proof, indeed, of the claims made by Derrida and other critics on politics would be the extent to which their ideas can break with the privileged and highly ritualised discourses, and their sphere of impact be widened. Their writing is challenging and shows that a practice informed by post-structuralism is possible that does not operate on the basis of exclusion. Their text forms, in both form and content, a critique of the existing modes of writing adopted by post-processual archaeologists (and by contributors to this volume) and challenges us to embrace experimental writings which use their very form to disseminate the meaning of the past.

7

Writing, Authority and the Determination of a Subject

Paul Moran and David Shaun Hides

I[1]

There are a number of points that we would like to raise in this piece of writing about authority and the determination of a subject. But it is not so much each of these points that seem to be of the greatest significance to archaeology and the identity of other subjects – for example, the origin of this identity, and the political and economic investments which we make in order to discover the continuity of our identity generally. Thereby is sustained the legitimate (where 'legitimate' means, at the same time, the lawful, the hereditary, by unquestioningly acceding to the rules that determine a single, rightful line of descent; where legitimate also, therefore, means phallocentric – or more accurately ethno-phallocentric, according to the rules which define the non-bastard field, the proper, continuous, determinable field of operation; so that legitimate must also mean the permissibly named) integrity of a subject, such as archaeology. On the contrary, it is not so much any of these individual points which have aroused our special interest in this piece of writing – all of these points have been raised and discussed at length for the past fifteen or so years by my father in conjunction with his political activities in the Communist Party and as a fitter in the construction industry and as a member of the AEU, together with his work in a domestic environment as a father; by Virginia Savage's Auntie Greta in discussions, particularly on a Sunday afternoon, about the problematics of her own identity as an electrical-circuit assembler and member of a very tightly knit family community – the discussions were and still are at their most intense during the viewing of a football match on television, when other disruptions to a stable identity are brought into play; by Vicky Beaumont in her fourth-year essay on the film *Stand By Me* for her GCSE English Literature folder; and by Richard, the barman, at the New Road Inn. Perhaps it should also be mentioned at this point, before we proceed any further, that others, writers, whose work is produced within, and, we must for the moment assume, is directed towards educational, institutions (their work is very rarely needed outside this institutional arena and containment) and – it has generally been accepted, is exclusively concerned with post-structuralist theory – is considerably less political than ideas presented by my father, Virginia Savage's Auntie Greta, Vicky Beaumont and Richard the barman. I am thinking, of course, of the following writers: Eddie Frank, who, in 1988 was a member of the fifth year at Beauchamp Community College; Lisa Ablett who, a year earlier was a member of the fifth year of the same educational institution, was pre-occupied in much of her work with Hegelian dialectics and the idealisation of meaning within the development of a concept. Also, to name but one other, Danny Hackshaw, whose most recent work on speech acts, whilst doubting the veracity of speech act theory, refuses, still, to engage with the issue of the political and economic investments that have guaranteed, within this domain, the integrity of not only the subject of speech and theory. He also questions the determination, through this investment, of the transcendental nature of the speaking subject as already constituted by itself, without any reference to the material field of language within which its identity is made possible and the social context which holds this field in place. In this sense Danny Hackshaw's criticism of speech and theory provides a useful example, in more ways than one, of the features which, in this piece of writing, seem to us to be quite remarkable (not the least remarkable being the persistence with which the rhetorical logic of legitimacy authorises and identifies the speaking subject, as indeed it does of all subjects, whilst erasing evidence of this rhetorical determinacy from the written scene. For here we are not simply concerned with the assumption of the authority of the archaeologist in determining archaeology – its practice, its field, its context, its place, its legitimacy, its (ir)relevance, its (in)significance – and its discoveries – its recoveries of itself, its objects (subjects), its dominance over them, and, according to its laws, the system of its primogeniture, its own outrageous production of their being. Nor are we only concerned to examine the claimed renunciation of this determinacy, the rhetorical moves which designate this as being already there, of archaeology not being determined by political and economic investment, of being itself as indetermined but there anyway.[2] No, we don't want simply to discuss this – after all archaeology, here, is redundant, finished in this purely idealistic sense (where do they, the archaeologists, keep the past these days?). But what we are also interested in, in this piece of writing, is that even in the midst of such a critique of the anthropology of the subject, which, by making use of the metaphor of writing hopes to displace the author from the scene as the anonymous producer of an archaeological text, another authority must in the same moment be brought into the text to determine its place, function and legitimacy within the archaeological field in general. All that this switching amounts to, this relentless digging in one place instead of in another for buried treasure according to the legitimating authority of another line of de(s)cent, is the legitimation of a subject which not too secretly knows that its time is really up. We would therefore like to outline, to demarcate, a very brief history of this piece of writing and most importantly of all its context. That is, we would like to assess the archaeological record. And within this demarcation of the past, the production of an archaeological record in itself, we would like it to be noted that a number of changes have been made, changes of a legitimate order, hence our position now; after all, a degree of jiggery-pokery in the archaeological record is always permissible, indeed is normal practice – it is in fact this ordering which normally makes up the record itself. But what do we know of order, of context, of order's proper context and how this is achieved, of legitimate context, of its lawful difficulties and its solutions, of its appropriate reason and judicious findings? For some reason then, for an examination of some of archaeology's most famous reasons and its archaeological site, which is perhaps even the privileged ethnoarchaeological site of its manufacture, let us turn, but briefly, so as to avoid the dizziness of its apparent kaleidoscopic vision, to Ian Hodder.

As Ian Hodder (1986a; 1987b) seems to admit, there are a number of difficulties that stem from this intersection of a contextual archaeology, difficulties which, if not constrained, would undermine the authority of his contextual project; these are difficulties which cannot simply be confined to or by the methodology through which the laborious construct of the beginning, the origin, is written – whether it is expressed in the fidelity of the past or the transcendent innateness of ethnic identity. It is the only concern of the archaeologist: the origin, its authenticity, its birth, its purity and integrity. This is the expressed desire of archaeology as long-term history, which clearly articulates 'the need for archaeologists to examine the origin' (Hodder 1987a, 8), and asserts against all else that 'concerns with "origins" are important' (Hodder 1987a, 4). It is, however, an obsession which, in common with the way in which many obsessional neuroses have been described (Freud 1984), moves away from its own origin, displacing it from the written scene where it was inscribed, abstracting it from its material context of production, as an origin apart, already, to be discussed by a methodology which traces its path along another route from the institution and the practices and privileges where the origin was conceived, securing it ideally at this distance of assurance. In this way, this rhetorical distance from the origin, and all that the origin stands for, guarantees two points. Firstly it permits, according to its own rules of differentiation, its own writing of context. A distinction here is to be made between the subject (the discipline of archaeology, its status, funding, and bureaucracy, its hierarchies, its methodologies and theorisations, its history, the formulation of its beliefs and practices, the determination of its proper domain of study, indeed, all of archaeology's discretions, its delicate attempts to keep itself to itself) and its organisation. As part of the latter, we must consider archaeology's objects – objects which, (tauto)logically, but also distantly, tendentiously, in a way which *seems* far off and so might not be noticed with a discrete and therefore contextual vision, must occur within the field of archaeology generally, as determined by its status, its funding and bureaucracy, its hierarchies, its methodologies etc. – and their organisation. Secondly this distance from the origin, between the subject and its objects, ensures that all of archaeology's practices will be validated by their findings in the field. Spectacularly, then, archaeology will be able to justify itself by its own discoveries in another place, its other place, its proper place, which (legitimately, expertly) is where it intended (discreetly, appropriately) to find them. Thus the practices of archaeology become, in the field (its field) a 'pattern playing, inductive exercise' (Hodder 1987a, 8). Again, in common with the ways in which obsessional neuroses have been described in the past as movements away from their origin through acts of displacement, of duplications of space and their topological organisation in another location, even though acts of transference maybe, it is thus naturally 'Archaeologists [who] have the ability to watch the way in which variability in one realm [the ethnoarchaeological realm in which archaeology's privileges are ordered, the space in which its funding is secured] becomes adopted to take a dominant position' (Hodder 1987a, 7). A dominant position, that is, contextually speaking, in its other realm, its appropriately organised place of study – whether this is East Africa, the neolithic, or a pet-food factory. It is naturally archaeologists because 'ideologies involving naturalisation are involved' (Hodder 1987a, 7).

But how do these ideologies which involve naturalisation take place? How, according to archaeology's rules of naturalisation, is the field of archaeological practice appropriately ordered? How are its objects assembled, marked and identified? By what means and according to what methodological practices is the realm of archaeological organisation specifically discovered in another place, which, miraculously, is always its place of investigation? The answer, of course, is rhetorically, by its judicious writing of context (again Ian Hodder needs to be cited with respect to his very significant work in this area). Rhetorically – we know of no other way that such an operation could naturally be secured – a space is hollowed out from context, for and within the ethnoarchaeological context, a continent space, blank and pure from contextualisation, as (un)known space of the past and the culturally other. A space, already, virgin, unmarked, unnamed by and ordained according to the graphically clumsy fumblings of the archaeologist. A pure space then, a space which is only knowable as such, can only be identified as being there, according to two marks appropriately made by the archaeologist's pen. It writes a rupture in (its) (writing's) contiguity, it marks a severance of the past from the present. It is in this way that context is made possible. This first mark also expresses an ideal distance between its writing and the awkward and embarrassed pen of its author, a mark therefore which is indispensable to the entire archaeological project, for in its absence archaeology would be unable to describe even its rhetorical distance from its field of study (it would simply recognise that it spent its time revealing itself to itself), but a mark which is at the same instant deeply compromising since it exposes, graphically, the authority by which distance is forged. In view of this telling but unavoidable revelation about the affair and divorce of the first mark, in which an unsightly rupture is written, there is an unbecoming desire to remain silent or pass over very quickly. For example, following the works which make up the archaeological text, Ian Hodder writes that 'In the construction of the cultural world [though how it is constructed is not overtly made clear in this writing], all dimensions (the shape or colour of pottery for example) already have meaning associations [meaning, then, as grafted on through writing? the writing of the archaeologist? the writing already there? the writing of the severance of meaning from culture and therefore the graphically produced (absolute) other of material culture? of meaning, not derived from culture, but associated with it anyway by the way of the archaeologist?]. An individual [individuality already constructed, culturally, as the meaning-of-the-individual, written by the archaeologist in the context of archaeology's institutional and cultural existence and associated with an other written, the written "already there" of "the individual"? the writing of the individual away from the written, the materially and culturally produced, origin?] is situated in this historical frame [this written frame? this written frame which claims not to be a frame? the individual as framed by archaeology's writing of the frame] and interprets the cultural order from within its perspective [as Hodder claims (not) to do]. The archaeologist seeks also to get "inside" this context [the context of the archaeologist's writing, of the institutional, cultural, political and pedagogic which makes up archaeology's identity and determines its being? but all of this rhetorically, only, because of the quotation marks round "inside"? so that archaeology does not really want to write the inside of itself, to expose itself? or is all of this the written site of archaeology's other, its rhetorical claim to be other than its writing? This, then, is the site of rupture, its graphic divorce from itself, effected, graphically through its writing?], but the jump is often a considerable one' (Hodder 1987b, 7). Outside the writing of the jump – outside history, outside material culture, outside the situation of the written historical frame – the jump would be impossible. The rhetorical jump. The jump that really goes nowhere. The pretend jump. The pseudo jump. The jump away from the origin which is the origin, the institutional site of archaeology; this is its first mark, its marking, its institutionalisation of its rhetorical divorce with, its lame jump away from, its own writing of itself.

Archaeology's second mark, which follows, rhetorically, after the first, after archaeology has legitimated itself by writing its severance from the writing of the space in which the past might be maintained, is its *inscription*, the written agenda by which this space, its history, its stratigraphy, its contours, its ethnic groupings, can be made recognisable as an other space, culturally and in terms of the past as not being there, but as there anyway in the way of the archaeologist. Again, we could, briefly, turn for archaeological evidence of the highest order to the writing of Ian Hodder, who seems in this sense to be little more than contradicting himself; we could discuss his description of 'the *index*', 'which is a sign where the signifier is contiguous with the signified' (Hodder 1987b, 2), despite the fact that 'the relationship between the signifier and the signified is seen as arbitrary' (Hodder 1987b, 2), except, of course, in the case of the ordering of the archaeologist; for without this exception which literally proves the rule, contiguity – and think what this would mean for archaeology: without the rule of the archaeologist – would be impossible. Or, from the same text, we could explore his explanation of the *symbol* as 'a sign with an intentional signifier' (Hodder 1987b, 3); we might ask, especially given the earlier description that the relationship between the signifier and the signified is arbitrary, if, first of all, intentionality is a tenable concept, and then, given the assumptions of archaeological authority, to question whose intentions are being recorded and accounted for, which intentions might legitimately be left out, where these intentions are derived from – though if they are derived, then they are hardly intentions – and how they might be known. We could explore his writing of structure in the context of archaeological meaning (Hodder 1987b), and his writing of ethnic identity against his writing of material cultural identity (Hodder 1982), but for the present it is probably more practical simply to note the following: the past and other culture is secretly, but not very secretly, authorised by the same pen which marks out the legitimate topology within which the legitimate archaeologist can work, scrivening the proper spatial organisation of the book in which the archaeologist's writing might be made possible and be contained (rather like this book and the rules which govern its authorisation and the place of its authority, both generally and specifically). Contextual archaeology – and all archaeology is contextual – is concerned with the writing of its text and the context which lies within, claiming to be without, its pages. Its discoveries are inevitably recoveries of its own inscriptions, of an origin which it claims as not being its own, an origin which is thus the political guarantee of its own legitimacy.

WRITING, AUTHORITY AND THE DETERMINATION OF A SUBJECT

It is this peculiar but absolutely necessary turning away from the radical implications of context – the context of archaeology's production, the social, economic, and political context of its fields, of its most important sites, its sites of privilege, where its institutional practices are arrangements of the most overt forms of discrimination, which is the only context of any importance, the only context where archaeology can be thought of as being at all significant, the place of its original writing of the past and other culture, the context which the Cambridge Conference on Post-Structuralism and Archaeology steadfastly refused to consider, which is also the context in which archaeology would cease to exist – that makes archaeology at all plausible; and it is because of this that all discussions of an alternative 'political' archaeology, of a 'left' archaeology, of a radical archaeology which occurred during and after the conference are the most absurd forms of privileged indulgence. Archaeology's political identity – as an elite writing of the past and other culture, which is effectively a recovery of its own institutional schemes of *marking*, a hobby[3] of ludicrous proportions – will not change unless the contemporary written scene of archaeology is recognised, and its participants include, without priority, everyone. This would also be the end of archaeology. It would no longer be identifiable. It would cease to have experts. Its departments as presently constituted would be redundant. For archaeologists this must be too terrible to think about – this would account for the absence of its discussion at Cambridge and the delusory talk of an alternative 'political' archaeology at Leicester University (it is difficult to understand how this would function given that, institutionally, the agenda of archaeology's past is already determined, that entrance procedure, systems of assessment, pedagogic assumptions, cultural hierarchies, legitimate fields and methods of study, even the concept of a course remain unchallenged and intact; and it is perhaps more difficult to see how such an extremely limited alternative 'political' archaeology, whose exponents wish to maintain its name and identity, could be at all transformative except in a self-valorising, that is, reactionary, manner). So let us move on, slightly, but not very far, not very distant. Not really separated by the writing of a legitimate space, hereby the addressers' communication is determined as being with the addressee; essentially, the writing which establishes, rhetorically two locations, the here and the there, the one and the other.

Not very far, then, but over the telephone and in the pub, Richard Martin, who originally came (comes) all the way from Glasgow, but now works in Australia for a security firm, asked me if I was still delivering papers at Cambridge, what the paper was called and who I was delivering the paper to. It was (is) called 'Identity, Object, Praxis: Excavations in the Teleology of Knowledge'. It sounds, he remarked, just like any other paper. In that sense its destiny was (is) assured, rhetorically, as – and about which – it was written. And indeed, this is the only point of my interest in all of philosophy, its *re*-mark, its perpetual *re*-marking of itself, its series of deliveries to itself, as if this were a delivery away from itself, a pseudo delivery, a rhetorical delivery, its *re*-ordering of its own history which is at the same time its constitution, its legal writing, its onto-juridicial discovery of its history: the writing of Parmenides, Plato, Kant, Hegel, Nietzsche, Heidegger, Husserl, Adorno, Derrida, Chomsky all testify to this rhetorical sending away in respect to themselves. It is these names which are variously organised into the delivery of a message which goes nowhere, and by going nowhere confirms itself, as being legitimate; they are the names by which any discourse can be made safe, by being properly located in its other than institutionally written, elite context. This is the way that the message of the institution can be authorised, officially, pseudonymously, away from itself, as part of an other – its other – lineage. After delivering my paper at Cambridge, and submitting a paper for this book, we received a reply from the editors – a message sent to itself: 'Thanks very much for the copy of your paper . . . we think it is very good, but would like to make the following suggestions', the most interesting of which – for as I *re*-marked before this is the only interesting point about all of philosophy – was (is) the expressed desire to locate the origin of this paper in respect to Derrida, which, in effect is the history of authority and the determination of a subject. Archaeology or the Jacques Derrida club? Really, contextually, they amount to much the same thing: the institution of this writing, of writing in general, at Cambridge. With references in this writing, ordered by the institution of this writing, away from itself, rhetorically, of course, the Jacques Derrida course in archaeology at Cambridge University. Let us then, for the remainder of this paper, which was not delivered at Cambridge, discuss how this course in archaeology, the Jacques Derrida course, or rather its equivalent – its equivalence with itself – which as we just noted, will be the same as archaeology is written. Let us look, very briefly, at how archaeology has been constituted in this most advanced of theoretical arenas, an arena in which the name of Hodder will again help us to find our way.

II

This archaeology describes itself as being about material artefacts and the relationship between them and the society in which they occur. But more specifically it is about artefacts of the past. Until recently 'archaeology' implied a search for and description of the ancient world and of the origins of humans, human societies and civilisations in the ancient past.

In part, the retreat from some of these aspirations could be attributed to a recognition of the racist/colonialist social evolutionary theory at their core. In addition, attempts to bolster social sciences and humanities like archaeology by modelling them on the physical sciences have generally been seen to have failed. Archaeological theory, especially as it is produced in Cambridge, has focused on a new source of meaning. The artefacts in the 'archaeological record' are held to be readable, to form a kind of text. Yet within this position, Hodder, for example, despite some of his claims, still seems to hold a residual attachment to an archaeology in search of an original, ancient, ruling voice or discourse (*logos*) which gives meaning to the artefactual record. This voice is the cry of the thoughts, words, actions, social structures and ideologies of past societies. A theory is required which links the voice speaking through the traces of the past with the traces themselves, and describes how this text can be read. Attempts to provide this theory seem to have led archaeologists into a bind. This bind doubles over and catches archaeology between its claims to authority and its contemporary practice, between a theory of reading archaeological artefacts and writing archaeological texts, between the past and the present. The bind doubles because archaeology requires a means to determine and legitimate the source of its authority, in order to constitute its own proper identity, but it is the attempts to describe these determinations which render such an identity impossible.

Archaeologists have already discussed the ways in which contemporary concerns shape the interpretation of archaeological material (e.g. Shanks and Tilley 1987a and b; Trigger 1981, 138–55; Wobst 1986, 1–21). But in a similar way to the archaeological theories they describe, they have an unacknowledged limit which disappears silently into the background. It only seems to be possible to describe theories from several years before; even when this limit is reduced it is never removed, so as to include that analysis of theory in the contemporary field of political determination. As for these archaeological theories, what are the special properties of this distance which they embrace, this (our mythical) idea of the past and its inevitability and importance, which ensures that the mainstream of archaeological interest terminates at the 'post-medieval period'? How can it contain Industrial Archaeology within the eighteenth and nineteenth centuries, and prevent any limited forays 'beyond this' from a discussion of, for example, the post-industrial society (Hebdige 1988; 1989; and see also Walsh this volume) within which industrial archaeology is practised? Why is an archaeology of now avoided?

Commonly the answer is that this would simply not be archaeology – archaeologists want to find out about, discover the past. It would be proper for social anthropology or sociology to deal with the archaeological material of now, the contemporary world. The closest to such an approach, contemporary cultural studies, views the field between high- and low-brow culture (Art design, Architecture, Advertising literature, etc.) through the various media of public presentation. The reticence of archaeologists, as opposed to heritage and museum managers, to see archaeological material within this context is justified or even necessitated by their idea of the past, based on spatial and temporal distance.

Ethnoarchaeology does deal with contemporary situations using archaeological methods. Its main aim has been to provide a new direction of growth in archaeological theory. However, it seems necessary to separate the two, so that new theories can continue to be about the past. How is archaeology separated from ethnoarchaeology? Ian Hodder provides the answer through his concept of context, which formulates it as embracing two components: the context of the past, and the context of the present. The two are supposed to occupy the same space, and are only separable by a distance produced rhetorically – that is they are written apart, archaeologically by the distance of 'the past' and, ethnoarchaeologically by 'cultural' and 'geographic' distance. This writing is authorised and legitimated by not appearing as writing, but as an account of a natural, original distance. We need to know how to discover a context, what it determines, and how it can apparently constitute itself in such a way that an archaeology comes to respect these limits.

In contextual archaeology all items of material culture are 'meaningfully constituted' (see Hodder 1982; 1986a; 1987a; 1987b). This meaning is not adequately described simply by an account of the item's construction and function, instead they have within them many meanings, a plurality of signification. Different meanings are discovered in different contexts. Artefacts form a simple and limited but readable kind of language, in material form. In part what surrounds these artefacts are other artefacts, but the majority of 'their' context is non-material, it is social relations, ideology, *spoken* language, etc. The problem, put archaeologically, is that none of these other contextual constituents leaves any trace in the archaeological record, other than in the way they determine, or speak through, the artefactual traces. Ethnoarchaeology is therefore about learning the language, or at least the theory, of all languages of material culture.

Ian Hodder's fieldwork in East Africa (Hodder 1982) emphasised the ways in which various groups 'actively' manipulated symbolically significant artefacts. In one study Hodder sought to reject existing theories of the passive role of artefacts and their distribution as simple reflections of society and social interaction. Instead, an active role of the use of ear-flaps, stools, calabashes, and spears in both asserting and undermining ethnic identity is proposed.

This has already been brought into question. If artefacts are meaningfully constituted and if contexts give meaning to the artefacts, if these contexts are both to be found within the material itself and defined as what is relevant (i.e. gives meaning to) the artefact, for whom could this meaning be constituted? Who could get inside this tightly circular context? Of course, it cannot be said that the archaeologist simply makes it all up, in the way that a free agent, un-bound by any constraints, would produce pure fiction. Instead, therefore, we are constrained within the half-admitted implausibility lurking within Collingwood's declaration that 'historians' [and by implication archaeologists'] pictures are meant to be true' (Collingwood 1946, 246).

Recognising contexts in Baringo seems to be the writing of ('discovering', without writing) one context which is innate, more natural, prior to all others and original. How else could it be possible to decide which contexts determine the meaning of identity in opposition, and which in agreement with ethnic identity? What then is the distinction between ethnic and cultural identity? In what way are categories such as Pokot, Njemps, ethnic group, culture constituted if it is possible to suggest that 'although families might become fully incorporated into another culture and way of life and express their incorporation overtly, they might still think of themselves as different and prefer to marry back into their own tribe' (Hodder 1982, 31). When can the implicitly 'natural' ethnic category (own tribe) only be identifiable through material and other aspects of 'culture'? There seems to be nothing present to fix any category in this position, nothing which could halt the continuous process of differing and deferment between or away from such categories. Of course, each context is to be found by the archaeologist, and in every page and photograph Hodder returns to Kenya, crosses the cultural distance to discover the authentic context.

Ethnoarchaeology must be kept at a discreet distance from archaeology as itself, the inappropriateness of direct, cross-cultural, cross-temporal analogy (which of course means the destabilising effect of an (ethno)-archaeology of here and now) requires the ethnographic evidence to be used for the building of general theory. In this theory artefacts have meaning in terms of their function in the world, by virtue of their position in a structured symbolic system, and in terms of the content of meaning, its concept, idea or voice. Three levels of context are used to resolve these meanings: the environmental or physical context, con-text as meaning within the text of structured materiality, and lastly the historical context – both the past historical context and the present context of archaeological theory. The historical context, of course, encompasses the first two levels, and is itself shaped by the present theoretical context. The two aspects of this historical context, are, however, clearly separable in the sense that interpretation occurs in the present of the past. Ethnoarchaeology within the writing of contextual theory can provide examples of cultural and ethnic phenomena, but a general theoretical description of how these are reified into an archaeological text, and how this text can be read, is the main aim.

In this theory, artefacts are symbols (a kind of sign), they are each part of a structure system of difference where each sign is a duality of signifier–signified/form–content/sensible–intelligible, and this system has to be meaningfully constituted, it has to refer to real objects. A structural-Marxist analysis of ideology is incorporated to determine the role of ideology in the constitution of social meaning. Finally, the specificity of each example of a structuring principle or ideology is determined with reference to the particular nature of the surrounding historical circumstances. The social (socially intentioned) actor is the origin, the authority for, the source of meaning (following Giddens' (1979) 'structuration' theory). The social actor is the original context which enables a 'getting inside of events' (Hodder 1986a, 77).

All this weaving (binding) is required to enable archaeology to read the past of the artefactual text. So that there could be a meaningful constitution of the archaeological text, so that archaeology can comprehend the action of individuals in their cultural or temporal otherness, there has to be an authentic source that is fundamental, universal, and naturally present to be interpreted, something other to discover, to return with across the distance which authenticates it. There has to be a voice, a speech before writing if 'the artefacts do speak (or perhaps faintly whisper) to us' (Hodder 1986a, 123), if 'the past still speaks in its traces' (Tilley 1986, 18).

But this description of language – any language – cannot be authorised by the language as language itself. The distinction between signifier and signified, sensible and intelligible depends on the power of belief to sustain a stable and hierarchical duality within the sign. This belief, that there is a voice which animates, gives meaning to words or other artefacts, produces an immediate authority, a (super)naturalisation of the hierarchical description of the sign. This theological account of language underpins Judaeo-Christian morals, political institutions and knowledge, but for all that, it is still rhetorical, it is still a kind of writing. Similarly, artefacts, material cultures are a kind of literature.[4]

Archaeologists have carried out ethnoarchaeological fieldwork, but there is a possible tyranny for archaeology in such studies being conducted here as opposed to East Africa. The second bind becomes inescapable. In such a study, the writing of an authorising distance could not be so easily effaced or concealed. The distance to be recovered by an ethnoarchaeology of another society could not be naturalised by travel or place names. The distance written by archaeology between its own writing of the past would become collapsed. If this were to occur, how could archaeology explain why the powerful forces determining symbolic meaning, the mythical and ideological constitution of knowledge, the particularity of historical meanings, don't all impact upon their own writing? Why are they not decentred? The only example of ethnoarchaeologies 'close to' have been of punks or gypsies (Hodder 1986b), outsiders who use material culture to distance themselves from the norms of society, the common, the accepted and the conventional – all that defines the natural location of archaeology.

Let us return to the myths of the past. Ethnographic or prehistoric societies have dealings with death and the past through myths or cults. One which occurs in both literatures is the collective burial ancestor cult, for example that of the Merina with its festival of burial, the *famadihaua* (Bloch 1972). But our society is supposed to relate to the traces of the past through archaeology, and its interpretation of monuments. These monuments are described as relating directly to the past. Part of the role of institutions – English Heritage, The Ancient Monuments and Archaeological Areas Act of 1979, The Heritage Act 1984 – is to prevent the improper interpretation (i.e. contemporary re-use and re-identification) of such monuments. New interpretations are, of course, always possible and acceptable, as long as they are of what the environment meant, not what it means.

Archaeologists (e.g. Chippindale 1986) have written about the recent uses of Stonehenge (i.e. from the sixteenth century onwards). But descriptions of the delusions of Druids, pop/drug festivals, and alternative archaeologies, have always stood alongside serious archaeological work. Serious archaeology involves, for example, the description of the role of the later phases of Stonehenge in association with beaker assemblages, and the process of the demise of ritual authority centred on henge monuments (Clark, Cowie and Foxon 1985; Bradley and Gardiner 1984). The peace convoy, in contrast, has to be a reaction to and distancing from contemporary society, a subject for sociology to determine, and the police to confine. Archaeologists have, so far, only seen such people as a nuisance to be contended or compromised with. To write about them archaeologically, with reference to their use of material culture, the material culture defined by law as archaeological, would be to collapse the authorising distance which archaeology has to write – i.e. the past. An ethnoarchaeology would face a similar difficulty, a group of them, other and distanced through the constitution of 'their' identity with 'our' archaeological artefacts. In both cases the ritual authority being challenged is that of contemporary legal power and knowledge.

Archaeology, as a form of ritual authority, opens analyses with which it seeks to build and evaluate its theories (myths) of the past. The past of monuments, buildings, even communities which have to be conserved, preserved, authenticated, outside of, distanced from now, is a past no less ideologically, mythically determined or written than that of the Mexican ancestor cult. The 'immediate implications for archaeologists' (Hodder 1986a, 67) of this are not for bones in cemeteries, but for institutions and the rules which govern their reproduction. Thus one such institution, Cambridge University Department of Archaeology, becomes, within the context of a mythical past, as much a proper or natural context (a place within which texts are produced) as is prehistory, a site, or a hut circle. In this context power and knowledge together with archaeological artefacts are bound into the processes of the institutional, ideological constitution of knowledge. Academic capital is invested and exchanged in this context, all 'meaningful' artefacts, pots, flints, passage graves, ideology, power, prehistory, critical theory, social theory, Anthony Giddens, Jurgen Habermas, R. G. Collingwood, etc. discover their authenticity, and are written (without the utterances of the process by which they are distanced) into archaeology as if from outside it.

Despite attempts to find another source of authority beyond writing, the white, Anglo-Saxon, middle class professional, male dominance of university composition, or theoretical discussion, or the Theoretical Archaeology Group, or indeed of the conference which spawned this volume, cannot be simply unwritten by self-critique or critical theory, because this is the space where archaeology is constituted, and its authority conferred.

Even Pryor (1987) knows that to undermine the authority of academic, theoretical, university archaeology does not require questions of the 'Contextualised matrix of associations and syntagmatic relations' (Tilley 1986, 19). Instead professionalism is belittled by equating it with amateurs, television pundits and 'coffee table' book readers. It is described as naively optimistic, which is to say non-serious and superficial. Most damning of all, it is un-manly, it lacks a 'strong factual' or 'strong theoretical' background. It does not even involve 'having to turn a sod or walk a field'. All these signs of weakness emerge as Pryor reviews how 'she [armchair archaeology] is presently practised' (Pryor 1987, 786).

As long as this kind of discussion goes on, as long as institutions themselves retain their present shape, academia cannot be transformative in a wider social context. Within contextual archaeology it seems likely that women will have to wait, either until men talk about the issues of a feminist agenda (such as the number of women excluded from the institution), and so in the terms of the institution make it important enough to discuss, or until women can be read as part of the traces of the past, through feminist reinterpretations of prehistory. The alternative seems to be that such calls for changing the institutional production of knowledge will be labelled (and thereby contained) as 'women's studies'.

Similarly, claims that an overtly ideological, structural-Marxist, self-reflexive archaeology as outlined by Shanks and Tilley (1987a; 1987b) can form a point of critique for the present and as such a source of liberating demystification, are wholly falsified, made worthless by the construction of this theory as a distancing from the present within the past. Such a theory is easily contained within the institution, because, while it calls upon the deconstruction of the sign, to show how knowledge was constructed in the past and in museums, it calls again on the social order to continue this within the past and to escape such determination in the present. Both for the reconstructed and the contextual archaeologies, the writing of the social order is an essential attempt to escape the binds which they themselves place upon the text of the past. Writing the social actor as if without and beyond writing (the production of the myth of the past) means that archaeologists 'are free to think as they want' (Hodder 1986, 102). But this suggests the nostalgic search for self-knowledge in the past which is not what is offered as the hope of a reconstructed archaeology.

Once again, the idea of an endlessly open debate produced within the distance between the past and the present as a source of political debate *is* naively optimistic. An 'overt' political theory of prehistory is not open to debate or evaluation because it does not conceal the traces of its political borrowing. It cannot be as long as it avoids the politics, the economy of power of the institutions including the profession of archaeology. The idea of a radical pluralism leaving a 'political' theory open to evaluation and critique ignores the role of institutional power, academic authority, pedagogic hierarchies, and much else in constituting knowledge. A radical excavation of academic archaeology could not leave institutional authority in place – excavation is at the same time destruction. This is also not the same as pushing archaeology into a fall which is productive of endless discourse, a fall into knowledge. This would not necessarily be bad, or even uninteresting, but it can scarcely claim to be liberating, to include those presently excluded from universities, or to change institutional practice.

NOTES

1. Editors' note. Part I was written by Paul Moran, Part II by David Shaun Hides. Although the authors intended the two parts to run together without any break, we felt it necessary to indicate this division so as to avoid confusion between the two different styles of writing each author employs.
2. For an example of this, any university archaeology department could be cited, and the socio-economic system which holds this method of privilege in place noted.
3. Archaeology as a personal hobby, or as Collingwood's search for self-knowledge (Collingwood 1946) seems to mark a return to the quest of the eighteenth century 'Grand Tour', and the self-interest of the educated or enlightened 'gentleman'.
4. In contrast to the claim in the cover notes to *Reading the Past* (Hodder 1986a), where it states 'while material culture is not a literary text'.

REFERENCES

Bloch, M. (1972) *Placing the Dead*, London: Seminar Press.
Bradley, R. and Gardiner, J. (1984) 'The decline of ritual authority and the introduction of beakers into Britain', in R. Bradley and J. Gardiner (eds) *Neolithic Studies: A Review of Some Current Research*, Oxford: British Archaeological Reports (British series 133).
Chippindale, C. (1982) *Stonehenge Complete*, London: Thames & Hudson.
Chippindale, C. (1986) 'Stoned Henge: events and issues in the summer solstice 1985', *World Archaeology* 18: 38–58.
Clark, D. V., Cowie, T. G. and Foxon, A. (1985) *Symbols of Power at the Time of Stonehenge*, Edinburgh: HMSO.
Collingwood, R. G. (1946) *The Idea of History*, Oxford: Oxford University Press.
Freud, S. (1984) *Case Histories II*, London: Penguin.
Giddens, A. (1979) *Central Problems in Social Theory*, London: Macmillan.
Hebdige, D. (1988) *Hiding in the Light*, London: Routledge.
Hebdige, D. (1989) 'After the masses', *Marxism Today* January.
Hodder, I. R. (1982) *Symbols in Action*, Cambridge: Cambridge University Press.
Hodder, I. R. (1986a) *Reading the Past: Current Approaches to Interpretation in Archaeology*, Cambridge: Cambridge University Press.
Hodder, I. R. (1986b) 'Digging for symbols in science and history: a reply', *Proceedings of the Prehistoric Society* 52: 352–6.
Hodder, I. R. (ed.) (1987a) *Archaeology as Long Term History*, Cambridge: Cambridge University Press.
Hodder, I. R. (ed.) (1987b) *The Archaeology of Contextual Meanings*, Cambridge: Cambridge University Press.
Pryor, F. (1987) 'Pragmatic and didactic: some thoughts on the changing structure of British archaeology', in C. Gaffney and V. L. Gaffney (eds) *Pragmatic Archaeology: Theory in Crisis*, Oxford: British Archaeological Reports (British Series 167).
Shanks, M. and Tilley, C. (1987a) *Reconstructing Archaeology*, Cambridge: Cambridge University Press.
Shanks, M. and Tilley, C. (1987b) *Social Theory and Archaeology*, Cambridge: Polity.
Tilley, C. (1986) 'Interpreting material culture', in *Archaeological Objectivity in Interpretation, Volume 2*, Southampton: World Archaeological Congress.
Trigger, B. (1981) 'Anglo-American archaeology', *World Archaeology* 13: 138–55.
Wobst, M. (1986) 'Prospects for a world archaeology', *World Archaeology* 18: 1–21.

CHAPTER 8

The emergence of the gender archaeologies in post-processual archaeology has been greeted with much enthusiasm, and is one of the most significant developments of recent years. Its potential is limited, however, by the uncritical fashion in which certain identities – 'male' and 'female' – are accepted as if these were given, 'natural' and the division between sex and gender, as between nature (biology) and culture, is often made as if this supported this position. In this paper, Nordbladh and Yates take up the point that we must not simply reconstruct structures, since this leaves too much unexamined, we must deconstruct them. And the question must be pushed back further to the critique of the subject, who, populating history, is the absolute death of historicity, limiting the conceptualisation of relationships to those traced out by our own dualistic conception of humanity and sexuality. All sex is already gendered – a classic deconstructive reversal – and what must be done is to fracture this limiting structure in order to allow the real potential of historical difference to emerge.

8

This Perfect Body, This Virgin Text: Between Sex and Gender in Archaeology

Jarl Nordbladh and Tim Yates

The writing which we have been discussing confronts this phallic position either to traverse it or to deny it. The word 'traverse' implies that the subject experiences sexual difference, not as a fixed opposition ('man'/'woman'), but in a process of differentiation.

(Kristeva 1981a, 165)

The same applies for sexuality: it is badly explained by the binary organisation of the sexes, and just as badly by a bisexual organisation within each sex. Sexuality brings into play too great a diversity of conjugated becomings; these are like *n* sexes . . . Sexuality is the production of a thousand sexes, which are so many uncontrollable becomings.

(Deleuze and Guattari 1988, 278)

One of the defining characteristics of post-processual archaeology has been its interest in the issue of gender. Ignored in processual archaeology – because a concentration on systems, adaptation and function seemed to obviate the necessity of referring to subjects at all, let alone to structures of inequality and domination amongst subjects – gender has become one of the principal ornaments for display in the post-processual showcase.

The gender archaeologists have perceived that gender is a social construction, and concluded that 'rather than assuming that the term "woman" has universal cultural characteristics, there is a need to examine the way in which gender constructions can vary' (Hodder 1986, 160). But these examinations, while accepting that gender is historical and therefore social, base their research upon the assumption that sexual differences are inviolable, trans-historical, and that from the beginning of time there has always been the polarity male–female. According to this view, which insists on a distinction between culture and nature/biology, meanings move and gyrate to the beat of time, but only around fixed points, since the framework for gender elaboration is already set, from birth, in advance of any distinctions introduced by cultural discourse. Before there is culture, there are men and women. John Barrett is perhaps alone in his observation that 'it is a requirement of historical analysis that we may discover potentially unique ways by which men and women have defined themselves' (Barrett 1987, 13) but does not pursue this realisation to the extent of questioning the framework for analysis, its initial conditions, its origin and its destiny. He reifies the distinction between the sexes by his reading of Giddens' theory of structuration and agency which, by making only passing reference to the elements that situate consciousness (the place of the unconscious in the unacknowledged conditions of action, for instance), turns it back towards the ontological centrings of the Cartesianism he is anxious to escape. The gender archaeologists present us with this vision: we will always have been labouring under the tyranny of genital difference, which will always have been resolved on the basis of the presence or absence of particular anatomical features, on to which have been grafted – secondarily – the cultural apparatus of gender.

But have the categories 'male' and 'female' fallen from the sky, miraculously outside of time and history, and so beyond its charge? Is it possible to separate sex from gender, and assume the metaphysical/ontological priority of the former and assign temporal and spatial referentiality only to the latter? Is it possible to split sex from gender in this way, and prioritise biological/genital difference, imbuing it with independent legitimacy? Confining the operation of the dialectic between the sexes in this way assures rather than menaces the identities which we are supposed to be questioning, denaturalising, opening on to time and change.

For if sex is not to be separated from gender, then this changes the question. What is at stake here is what must be destroyed by an archaeology of (against) the contemporary conditions of identity, not what can be assumed, what poles can be taken as always and irrevocably fixed and therefore what remains for our historical labour is to undo the knots that bind sex to gender. What holds sexuality to this binary positionality established on the basis of genitality? What holds it like a promise to these two extremes, confining the play of sexual instincts to the law of presence (a penis therefore male and therefore not female)? What, in fact, prevents the structures from breaking loose of the limits set, *de facto* and *de jure*, by biology?

If the distinction between sex and gender is to have any validity, it ought to be possible to demonstrate the primary position of this binary structure of sexual differences (male:female :: penis:vagina) and the secondary position of gender differences, the 'coming to' sex of gender.

BIOLOGY AND SEXUAL DIFFERENCE

> It is popularly believed that a human being is either a man or a woman. Science, however, knows of cases in which the sexual characters are obscured, and in which it is consequently difficult to determine the sex. For it appears that a certain degree of anatomical hermaphroditism occurs normally. In every normal male or female individual, traces are found of the apparatus of the opposite sex.
>
> (Freud 1905, 52)

Archaeologists writing about gender have assumed sex is an unquestionable, biological fact, the background to history, the synchrony against which the diachrony is played out. The position sex–gender would thus be equivalent to that of nature–culture. But biology is also a social and cultural construct, and demonstrates that the binary framework of the categories male–female is itself not originary. More categories than two do exist (Kessler and McKenna 1985) and may be the subject of cultural elaboration. In medicine this third category – strongly hidden in our own society – is called the class of abnormalities, into which are collected all those who do not directly fit the ideal sex stereotypes.

Biological sex is a *composite* concept, with several prerequisites. The two main classes male and female are not totally separated but rather two extremes on the same scale. Indeed, they have very much in common. Because they are not fixed but relative, uncertainty can appear in the sex determination of individuals. Attributes for the recognition of sex are not all present at birth, but appear during a period of about 15 years, up to sexual maturity (puberty). Apart from their external genitalia, girls and boys are otherwise very similar in their bodily characteristics to about the age of ten. Biological sex, as recognised from the external genitalia, is therefore tentative rather than certain at birth and will only emerge during development in response to the demands placed on the individual by society (Caplan 1987; Ortner and Whitehead 1981).

Modern medical science has developed several complicated methods for the determination of sex. Nevertheless, none of these gives a 100% division into separate classes. Several exceptions to the binary structure of sex have been noted. As the female has only X chromosomes in the fertilised egg, the sex is given by the male in the form of an X or Y chromosome. The embryo has 'growth buds' that can develop into male or female organs. Ovaries and testes are the first parts to develop followed by internal and later external genitalia. It is interesting to note that male embryos begin to develop male characteristics six weeks before female embryos begin to develop female characteristics. After this early start, the chromosomes seem to have done their sexual duty.

The normal male and female have an XY and an XX chromosome pair respectively. But several other combinations have been observed and by

1970 some 11 different possible combinations were known. Some are only observed in the laboratory and would in other respects not diverge from the normal. Others may share some of the properties of the normal, but diverge in other respects. These variations may or may not be visible. A normal appearance can be severely biased in relation to the normal and an abnormal appearance can nevertheless share the most important properties of the normal ones (for instance, fertility).

The gonads produce sex hormones of three kinds – progesterone, androgens and oestrogen. The same hormones are present in males as in females, but their proportions differ. Some of the hormones promote development of certain structures, others act in a preventative way to retard growth of other characteristics. For example, the presence of testosterone promotes the development of male genitalia in the normal foetal male, and virilisation of the foetal female where exogenous testosterone is present. These important mixtures of sex hormones vary across the male:female divide, and can cause in one sex the external characteristics of the opposite sex. There are also genetic variations.

The external genitalia develop – in contrast to the internal ones – from the same preliminary structure and are the ones which can be the most similar between the two sexes. It is then especially remarkable that these characteristics should become the main basis for the assignment of sexual identity. The female constitution is the basic structure, developing without much hormonal influence. The male gonads are more active and crucial – without them, a male will develop a female appearance. It is of interest that male development is more problematic and complex than that of the female, and that more varieties of male exist than female (see, for instance, Gräslund 1982, 62–3; Stockhard and Johnson 1980, 117–22).

Sex classes based upon biological analysis are far from sharply differentiated, therefore, and there are several crucial stages in the development of individuals from conception to adulthood. Some of the types cause problems for a binary category system, such as people with double sex or appearing to possess double sex, or people who never (physically) grew mature, or extremes such as males menstruating through their penises (Federman 1967, 173). The extent to which these varying groups receive cultural attention and recognition varies, but we should not mistake the fact that the binary biological structure with which our own culture is concerned is not the only possible one nor, indeed, one that can have claim to natural and therefore cross-cultural status.

THE STRUCTURE OF SEXUALITY

The notion that there are only two sexes and that this division is natural assumes, therefore, a far simpler distinction than can be shown to exist. Not only is it biologically more complex, but it can be argued that the rule that organises sexuality around the two poles, and therefore around reproduction, is already an abstraction and idealisation.

Part of the problem of maintaining a sex–gender opposition is that we are not born knowing sexual differences, but rather this knowledge has to be acquired, like other forms of knowledge, in the processes of education. The description of sexual development and of how society organises sexuality is, of course, one of the main themes of Freud's work. What Freud disclosed to the late nineteenth century audience was that sexuality is present from the moment of birth, and that it does not miraculously awaken in line with the hormonal clock, which forces the child at puberty suddenly to recognise the function of those superfluous pieces of anatomy. On the contrary, puberty is the final shift in the development of human sexuality, effecting the dominance of the genitals as the focus of all the component instincts, excluding and repressing other 'erotogenic zones' (mouth, anus, etc.) which have hitherto been centres of stimulation.

The infantile sexual organisation is distinguished from that of the adult world, since it has yet to come under the sway of genital tyranny. The child is what Freud called 'polymorphously perverse' – infantile sexuality is formless, it spreads in all directions and can embrace all objects and bodily parts. It is solely under the influence of 'the pleasure principle', which is guided only by the desire to satisfy the instincts' appetite for stimulation and excitation, and is not determined by custom, propriety or procreation. The infant's sexuality is not channelled along the particular paths that will eventually reduce sex to the interaction of two organs. In the pregenital period, Freud wrote, 'What stand in the forefront are not the genital component instincts but the sadistic and anal ones' (1917, 369). The distinction between males and females has no place here – there is only a distinction between active and passive, onto which gender will later be grafted. Genitality, when it does come to exert influence over the drives and to organise them according to its two poles, will only have come about as part of a socially sanctioned organisation.

The framework of heterosexuality, which establishes the law of the binary code of sexuality, comes secondarily to the child as part of its socialisation and education. Prior to this process, the child has no conception of genital difference or of sexual difference – its universe is bisexual, or perhaps (as in the case of Little Hans) homosexual, composed of only one gender type. Normality in the framework of society is not, therefore, biologically determined, a natural product that renders deviation unnatural, but is itself a social construct, the dominance of custom, regulation and convention over sexual instincts which embrace more than one 'erotogenic zone'. The original and 'perverse' character of human sexuality remains within the subject, repressed and subdued, the triumph of the normal – of social norms – taking place only at the cost of splitting the subject from him/herself, into a conscious/preconscious opposed to an unconscious (Freud 1900) or, in the later formulation, into an ego protected from the memories of its earlier and now unacceptable sexuality, which remains within the id, by the activities of the conscience and censor, the superego – the ideal social type and stereotype (Freud 1923; 1933, 88ff). Contained in every individual, as s/he is 'acculturated', the superego is both the cause and the agent of repression. It acts as the ego-ideal formed by the internalisation of the reality principle (the system of cultural laws and prohibitions necessary for acceptance as a member of society) which confront the ego and protect it from all that is forbidden and sedimented into the unconscious.

Sexual difference and identity is established in the child, therefore, not as a process of binary coding that is grounded in nature and provides a complete account of what will have taken place, but as the result of a process of repression. 'Male' and 'female' come into significance as a process of splitting within the subject. The identification of subjectivity is only possible by the operations of the superego, which is the only place where these ideals – 'male'/'female' – have reality.

So what denaturalises the ontology of binary sexuality is the inherently subversive nature of the sexual instincts. For Freud, the sexual instincts, polymorphous in the pre-genital organisation, have to be repressed in order to allow for the work of building civilisation. The pleasure principle, seeking only to satisfy the drives by plugging them into objects, must give way to the reality principle, as society demands that those drives be organised, become centred on the genitals (and thus place the emphasis on reproduction), the organisation being the work of repression. It is when this process fails (it can never succeed in eradicating the id) that psychoanalysis finds its material – from jokes and parapraxes to dreams and neuroses. Normality (sex and gender) exist for the subject only on one side of its consciousness, that which is formed through socialisation, the processes by which the child's ego submits to the established norms of society. Its 'other side' knows none of these bounds. 'The id of course knows no judgements of value: no good and evil, no morality . . . Instinctual cathexes [energies] seeking discharge – that, in our view, is all there is in the id' (Freud 1933, 107).

The work of Herbert Marcuse in his rethinking of Freudian psychoanalysis is of particular interest here. Marcuse endorses the view that sexuality is organised by a process of repression, but distinguishes between two forms. *Basic repression*, 'the "modifications" of the instincts necessary for the perpetuation of the human race in civilisation' (1987, 35), and *surplus repression*, the intensification of that constraint 'necessitated by social domination' – that is, the divergence of organisation away from satisfying the drives and promoting pleasure (from serving Eros, in Marcuse's terms) towards serving the interests of power and authority. Genitality (of which Marcuse has a fairly positive view, believing that the focusing of the instincts on a single erotogenic zone heightens pleasure) would belong to basic repression, and what we mean normally by gender (the historical elaboration of discourses around this framework, a process of supplementation and addition) would belong to surplus repression.

But if this would seem to reproduce the divisions between sex and gender, Marcuse insists that even if we propose an original priority, the two have become irrevocably entwined in the history of civilisation. Surplus repression is already *within* primary repression, present all along and not a secondary addition that can be stripped away to leave some originary and non-repressive existence. The instinctual constraint enforced by scarcity has *always already* become a part of 'the hierarchical distribution of scarcity and labour'. Both types of repression – primary and secondary – are bound up together in history, to be related to the reality principle, which should be understood as itself not monolithic but constantly changing. Under capitalism, the instincts are organised around the 'Performance Principle', which operates to reduce sexuality to the purely genital or procreative and so suppress all non-procreative sex, in order to save energy for work and production. The dominance of genitality, therefore, is itself a component of the capitalist formation, for the instincts are forced into an organisation which, like that of labour, is hierarchical and centralised, focusing 'the various objects of the partial instincts into one desired object of the opposite sex' (Frosh 1987, 155).

Freud emphasised, to a certain extent, precisely the same intermingling. Sexual difference takes place for the child as a process of 'enlightenment' – the horror of the little boy on discovering that women have no penis, the shame and envy of the little girl on making the same comparison (Freud, 1908). It is not that the genitals have no place in the infantile sexual organisation, but that they do not yet have primacy (to the exclusion of the other erotogenic zones). The child is aware of gender differences – it has grown up with the role-models of its mother and father – but it has yet to attribute biological/genital significance to this. Thus, when the genital difference between the sexes first becomes clear to the child, or at least first accrues significance, it is appended to the already perceived gender attributes of the two sexes.

The processes by which gender differences become clear for the child are therefore inseparable from value, from the introjection of a third term into the binary code. For the sexual differences are already arranged according to a process of hierarchisation, already positioned axiologically. The child does not confront sex as a neutral observer. The penis is already valued over the vagina: not only by boys who attribute 'to everyone, including females, the possession of a penis' (Freud 1908, 193), whose curiosity and pride in his little organ will, like Little Hans (Freud 1909) lead him to assign to the diversity of gender roles and types a common genital, and whose discovery of the existence of the vagina will cause him to react with either 'horror of the mutilated creature or triumphant contempt for her' (Freud 1925, 336); but also because 'little girls fully share their brothers' opinion of it' (1908, 195–6). 'They notice the penis . . . strikingly visible and of large proportions, and at once recognise it as the superior counterpart of their own small and inconspicuous organ . . .' (Freud 1925, 335). On the discovery of her genital difference from the male, the female immediately endorses the valuation of the organs and her own inferiority with respect to that which she envies but can never possess: '. . . as a result of the discovery of the women's lack of a penis they [the mother, females] are debased in value for girls just as they are for boys and later perhaps for men' (1933, 160–1).

As soon as there is sexual difference, there is the valorisation of the genital organs. The children are already, therefore, under the influence of what Freud calls the Castration or Oedipus complex, at the end of which genitality will have arisen supreme as the centre of instinctual satisfaction and the seat of the axiological difference, and the child will, by means of this 'paternal agency' (1931, 375) have become a subject (a 'male' or 'female') plugged into its own superego. Women and their sexuality are already debased and devalued at the opening of sexual difference *inside* culture. The castration complex, which establishes the cultural order and normal (genital) sexuality by its prohibition upon incest and masturbation, applies properly only to males: females are already castrated, already subjected to the law.

SUBJECTIVITY AND THE STRUCTURING OF SEX/GENDER

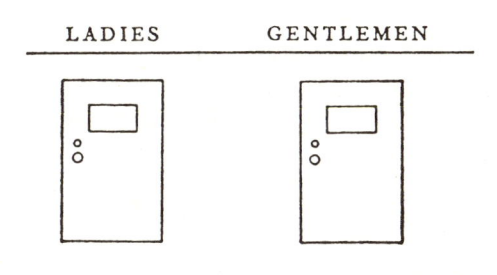

Figure 8.1

A train arrives at a station. A little boy and a little girl, brother and sister, are seated in a compartment face to face next to the window, through which the buildings along the station platform can be seen passing as the train pulls to a stop. 'Look,' says the brother, 'we're at Ladies!'; 'Idiot!', replies his sister, 'can't you see we're at Gentlemen.'

(Lacan 1977, 151–2)

How do we read Lacan's metaphor? Certainly, it articulates the arbitrariness of the division between the sexes, of the gender division, based upon Saussure's insistence on the arbitrary nature of the sign. What articulates this image is not the natural distinction between the sexes, to which has been given, subsequently and so as to name pre-signifying categories located elsewhere, the signs 'male' and 'female'. We know that the divisions between the sexes are constituted through the operation of a system of signifiers articulated by difference. The signified is divided from the signifier, which Lacan expresses in the algorithm $\frac{S}{s}$, such that the signifier is 'over' the signified, 'over corresponding to the bar separating the two stages' (1977, 149). This bar between the signifier and the signified resists the vertical passage from signifier to signified. So we have the signs 'Ladies' and 'Gentlemen', but there is no immediate passage to what these signs signify, no unmediated access to the meaning of sexual difference. This passage takes place only as the attachment of supplementary signifiers which cross and dissect the scene, constructing the exclusivity presented by the image of the twin doors and their associated prohibitions – supplementary signifiers which are not present but cannot either be absent. They play a determining role from the shadows, for it is impossible to understand the picture without assigning them their place. But the sexual difference, to which signs supposedly come, after the event, to describe, is veiled from us. It does not appear as such, for it is hidden behind closed doors. The essential difference, to which all else is secondary, additional, supplementary, is invisible. There is only a space of signifiers and signs to be ranged over, connections to be made. We gaze over and again, but we do not penetrate this signifying surface. The signified does not appear; in its place only the doors opening on to tabooed and forbidden spaces.

Lacan's reading of Freud recasts his theory in the terms of structural linguistics. The split between the signifier and the signified which divides the sign and prevents the two sides from becoming a unity, necessitates a concentration on the signifier, which floats and slides as it is drawn into a plurality of signifying relations. Thus the operations of psychic distortion – the processes of condensation, displacement and secondary revision which are the requirements placed on unconscious material by the censor to allow it to obtain conscious release – are properties of the primary processes of meaning, *metonymy*, a relation that allows the signified to be represented by different signifiers by shifting it along signifying chains. The unconscious is, therefore, always in process, not an entity (*the* Id) but a signifying chain in motion, which is already anticipated by Freud (1915, 155) but which is recast in the light of Saussure. Signifiers connect to signifiers. So fear of the father becomes a neurosis expressed as fear of horses (Freud 1909, 277ff), or fear of a wolf instead of a demand for love from the father (Freud 1918). The unconscious cannot be read directly, cannot be made present, because it is articulated within a structure that escapes such ontologies, an immanent structure of signifying chains which cannot be totalised or completed.

Subjectivity, or the fixing of the subject's identity through the conferment of an ego (and thus consciousness) takes place when the subject enters and learns to adopt the modes of representation that are the norms of the symbolic order. Like Freud's 'polymorphous perversity', the child prior to symbolisation is an 'hommelette', 'a little man and also a broken egg spreading without hindrance in all directions' (Coward and Ellis 1977, 101). The child has no sense of its own identity, this being predicated upon a distinction between self and other – a distinction which is no longer (not here) appropriate. This is achieved during the mirror phase (Lacan 1977, 1-7), where the child begins to perceive itself as a unitary and autonomous self distinct from the outside. But this cycle of (specular) identification is only completed when the child passes through the Oedipus complex, which is synonymous in Lacan's account with the acquisition of language and entry into the social and cultural norms of representation ('the symbolic').

In adopting language, the child is entering into a symbolic order which is not neutral but consists of already determined relations of difference. It is the symbolic that confers identity and consciousness – subjectivity as we understand it – to the amorphous collection of drives and instincts that occupy its space in its 'pre-history'. The child is forced to adopt modes of signification of its self that are alien to it – like the image presented to me when I look into the mirror, my linguistic self or identity is an objectification of myself, an image presented back to me from a space external to my body but with which I identify and learn to represent my place in the symbolic order, and with which I learn to identify what it is to be me. The subject, the polymorphous mass of forces operating without a distinction between self and other, is fixed through this 'I' in discourse, but this is always a stand in for the 'I' who speaks – 'I' cannot be one, since I am predicated as both subject and object of the utterance. A division is therefore initiated between the 'I' who is represented in discourse (the ego) and the 'I' who is only partially represented there (the id).

The subject is therefore constructed in relation to language and to the general codes of the symbolic. In becoming a subject, therefore, I am being offered socially sanctioned and *situated* means of representing myself and of thinking the relationships between 'me' and 'the real'. As soon as the child learns to identify with the first person singular pronoun, as soon as it becomes identifiable and learns how to represent and be represented, its position is fixed, for the subject position s/he is offered is already itself 'determined' by the relations of difference that articulate each and every sign within the symbolic system. As soon as the child-subject becomes 'I', learns to represent itself in discourse by this stand-in or replacement, it becomes simultaneously 'he' or 'she', 'boy' or 'girl', and a whole chain of significations is initiated. The child is enmeshed within a matrix of discursive supplements that lead on to one another like a labyrinth, and which will determine how it will see itself and how it will be seen. Entry into subjectivity – the acquisition of identity as such – is inseparable from entry into the social and cultural system.

No time delay can be observed, empirically or theoretically, in the 'subjectification' of the infant. As soon as it acquires sex it acquires gender, because the signifier that denotes sex will have been at the heart of the difference, and will already be connoting the structures of gender. Thus, to return to the twin signs on the two doors on the station platform, the signs that signify (denote) sexual difference – these signs already invoke a host of supplementary significations which, while not immediately present, cannot be made absent. These signs are already and simultaneously connoting urinary segregation, privacy, separation – will, in other words, already have wound around the difference a text of differences that lead off linearly in every direction. Into the binary structure of sex is introjected a third term, turning it always from a dualism into the triangular framework of the Oedipus complex, where the couplings mother–me as female–male are already determined as relations of difference by the law that regulates their existence. Something else is always active in order for it to be possible to speak of male and female as categorical opposites.

Gender does not come to sex. It is not a question of the perverse (the distortion of the pure, beautiful and perfect) coming to an originally virgin territory, to contaminate and infect. We know this, for failing to be able to demonstrate these divisions biologically, historically or logically, the practitioner is forced always to account for why, despite the primacy of biology, gender is always already there. There is no 'first text', purely natural and biological 'man' – no absence of power, no virgin surface. The sexual difference is permeated by a struggle, and however far back we go gender is there before us, waiting. It is not simply a question of accounting for the non-appearance of an obscured but potential presence, a discourse without difference that is yet to be realised, but of realising that there is nothing beyond gender, nothing without gender – nothing, indeed, outside of the text. It is this internal disseverance that wrenches man and woman, nature and culture from their places, snaps the anchor chains, and opens them on to history and the possibility of change.

What is at stake, then, is precisely the 'belonging to text' (difference) of every sign, every identity. If every sign is articulated in a system of differences, it is therefore arbitrary in the sense of referring to no external reality (to no trans-historical, 'natural' reality principle), then the context in which these identities emerge is never closed. No end to differences can take place, because nothing penetrates the text and escapes to the outside. Its position is at all times differential – that is, therefore, referential. The possibility of a biological difference 'before' gender, as the possibility of a meaning or presentation which the sign comes to *re*-present, is taken away. There is no 'male' or 'female' outside of gender on which this presupposition could be centred and anchored.

> One cannot determine the centre and exhaust totalisation because the sign which replaces the centre, which supplements it, taking the centre's place in its absence – this sign is added, occurs as a surplus, as a *supplement*. The movement of signification adds something, which results in the fact that there is always more.
>
> (Derrida 1978, 289)

'Male' and 'female' are split down the middle, divided from themselves by the bar that prevents them from coming into 'being' except through the detour of difference which, by opening signification, allows them to come (in)to subjectivity.

RESUMÉ

It makes no sense, therefore, to attempt to divide sex from gender, as most archaeologists and anthropologists seem to have been content to do. The emphasis upon treating gender as a social construct rather than the 'contractual' image which is the most critical processual archaeology could become is, of course, correctly placed, but to protect sex from similar treatment is fallacious and indeed damaging to the project of a feminist archaeology. In this paper, we have argued that biology is more complex than a simple binary male:female opposition, and that such 'biological' categories do not reside on some true and independent or natural ground of presence. Gender is already present in sexual differences, since the signs 'male' and 'female' cannot be isolated as idealities or projected to a ground beyond language and culture, where the supplementary significations of 'masculinity' and 'femininity' no longer apply: they are bound up, always and irrevocably, in a signifying cultural system and are always referent to it. Biological (sexual, genital) differences are always supplemented by the trace of gender. The division between sex and gender is, therefore, no longer guaranteed by some external reality, a penis or a vagina: it is itself the abstraction of a cultural system brought about within an historical mode of the reality principle, determined by a third term that allows them to divide and separate, while at the same time binding these differences to those 'external' discourses that are built up around them.

The notion of 'males' and 'females' outside of the symbolic system presupposes homogeneous subjects, 'ideal' types that are anti-historical and indeed need entertain no relationship to history. They would thus be the page upon which history is inscribed. Psychoanalysis demonstrates that the constitution of subjectivity, the 'coming into being' of the subject is a process made possible by entry into the symbolic order. 'Males' and 'females' only have reality as identities through the superego or ego-ideal, the internalised *identification* produced through the mirror stage and the Oedipus complex (cf. Lacan 1977, 2) at the cost of splitting the subject from itself as it is bound up in an historical net of traces and signifying chains which determine what form this 'I' will take, and forming out of the component instincts which dissect its body the conventional directions and sublimations for the drives. Coming to possess a sexual identity is achieved at the same time as achieving a gender identity, as a *specular identification*. This moment of entry marks the beginning of subjectivity, the formation of identities through the initiation of a process of differentiation which sets up the axiology and hierarchy centred on the signs 'male' and 'female'. Prior to this moment, to this contract through which the ego is brought into being through subjection of the id, no such thing as a subject, as a 'male' or 'female', has any meaning. These 'come about' only as a process of repression, a process in which 'primal repression' is bound up with 'repression proper' (Freud 1915, 147) as basic and surplus repression bind and infuse.

Subjectivity, Lacan assures us, is a social and cultural construction, but against the grain of Lacan's work we need not assume that the pre-subjective, the pre-symbolic 'subject' is negative, an absence. This merely preserves subjective identity through a negative ontology, and reassures the symbolic by leaving us nothing against which to judge it, and indeed adds to the established order the guarantee that its subjection of the Id cannot be overturned. Rather, the subject is in *différance*, in the sense that Derrida gives to Saussure's concept. It is never present, let alone self-present, but is always supplemented by that which it is not. Absence and presence no longer have finitude and explode the limits set for them. Prior to the repression which shifts sexuality into the genital system and inaugurates the male–female opposition under the law of the symbolic, there is only the incompleteness of the drives, the fragmented body, the self that knows none of the restrictions on identity placed on the subject through the intervention of the law via its agent, the superego. There is only that 'self' that is the resolutely anti-humanist account of the pre-subjective found in the vision of Gilles Deleuze and Félix Guattari (1983) where 'I' am not, where the self is a collection of machines coupled to other machines.

The historical investigation of gender and sexuality therefore takes account of the fact that subjectivity is not predicated upon a naturalised and virgin biological text, in which the binary opposition of 'male' and 'female' already exists amongst complete and perfect subjects, but rather upon the ordering of the component instincts that cannot be conceived along these lines, for self and other have not yet been *subjected* to any censure or taboo. The subjection of the id to the reality principle should offer us the point of incision into history, by which other forms of organisation are possible, according to different reality principles. Following Marcuse (1987) we may regard this post-humanist morality as based, not upon the individual or subject (who is already cultural, already an identity assured by the symbolic order) but upon the treatment of the instincts.[1] 'We' are no more than an agglomeration of drives reaching outwards and articulating with and through partial objects that are fragmented and carry off the binary series (presence:absence, nature:culture, self:other, subject:object, active:passive, male:female . . .) linearly in each direction:

> It is at work everywhere, functioning smoothly at times, at other times in fits and starts. It breathes, it heats, it eats. It shits and fucks. What a mistake to have ever said *the* id. Everywhere it is machines – real ones, not figurative ones: machines driving other machines, machines being driven by other machines, with all the necessary couplings and connections. An organ machine is plugged into an energy-source-machine: the one produces a flow that the other interrupts. The breast is a machine that produces milk, and the mouth a machine coupled to it. The mouth of the anorexic wavers between several functions: its possessor is uncertain whether it is an eating machine, an anal machine, a talking-machine, or a breathing machine (asthma attacks). Hence we are all handymen, each with his little machines. For every organ machine, an energy machine: all the time, flows and interruptions. . . There is no such thing as either man or nature now, only a process that produces the one with the other and couples the machines together. Producing machines, desiring machines everywhere, schizophrenic machines, all of species' life: the self and the non-self, outside and inside, no longer have any meaning whatsoever.
>
> (Deleuze and Guattari 1983, 1–2)

NOTES

1. The rigid adherence of the gender archaeologists to a male:female binary structure reveals a certain complacency towards those groups which are oppressed in our own society, but which do not fall comfortably within this framework – homosexuals, most particularly, after recent British government legislation. Anthropologists are well aware that other categories exist in societies, and a more flexible approach, such as that proposed here following psychoanalysis, is both logically and politically more coherent, and preserves the possibility of disclosing structures in the past which, in contrast to our own, were not based upon a rigid dualism.

REFERENCES

Works by Freud cited in the text are listed according to the date of their original publication. References are to the translations in the respective volumes of the Pelican Freud Library (PFL), London: Penguin Books, 15 volumes, 1973–85.

Barrett, J. (1987) 'Fields of discourse: reconstituting a social archaeology', *Critique of Anthropology* 7(3): 5–16.
Caplan, P. (1987) Introduction to *The Cultural Construction of Sexuality*, London: Tavistock, 1–30.
Coward, R. and Ellis, J. (1977) *Language and Materialism*, London: Routledge & Kegan Paul.
Deleuze, G. and Guattari, F. (1984) *Anti-Oedipus: Capitalism and Schizophrenia*, London: Athlone.
Deleuze, G. and Guattari, F. (1988) *A Thousand Plateaus: Capitalism and Schizophrenia*, London: Athlone.
Derrida, J. (1978) *Writing and Difference*, London: Routledge & Kegan Paul.
Federman, D. D. (1967) *Abnormal Sexual Development. A Genetic and Endocrine Approach to Differential Diagnosis*, Philadelphia: Saunders.
Freud, S. (1900) *The Interpretation of Dreams*, PFL 4.
Freud, S. (1905) 'Three essays on the theory of sexuality', PFL 7: 31–169.
Freud, S. (1908) 'On the sexual theories of children', PFL 7: 183–204.
Freud, S. (1909) 'Analysis of a phobia in a five-year-old boy', PFL 8: 165–305.
Freud, S. (1915) 'Repression', PFL 11: 139–58.
Freud, S. (1917) *Introductory Lectures on Psychoanalysis*, PFL 1.
Freud, S. (1918) 'From the history of an infantile neurosis', PFL 9: 225–366.
Freud, S. (1923) 'The ego and the id', PFL 11: 339–407.
Freud, S. (1925) 'Some psychical consequences of the anatomical distinction between the sexes', PFL 7: 323–43.
Freud, S. (1931) 'Female sexuality', PFL 7: 367–392.
Freud, S. (1933) *New Introductory Lectures on Psychoanalysis*, PFL 2.
Frosh, S. (1987) *The Politics of Psychoanalysis*, London: Macmillan.
Gräslund, B. (1982) 'The human sex ration at birth: reproductive strategies in early societies', *Annales: Kungl. Vetenskapssamhallets i Uppsala Årsbok* 24: 59–84.
Hodder, I. (1986) *Reading the Past*, Cambridge: Cambridge University Press.
Kessler, S. J. and McKenna, W. (1985) *Gender: An Ethnomethodological Approach*, Chicago: Wiley.
Kristeva, J. (1981a) 'Oscillation between power and denial', in E. Marks and I. de Courtvron (eds), *New French Feminisms: An Anthology*, Brighton: Harvester, pp. 165–7.

Kristeva, J. (1981b) 'Woman can never be defined', in E. Marks and I. de Courtivron (eds) *New French Feminisms: An Anthology*, Brighton: Harvester, pp. 137-141.
Lacan, J. (1977) *Ecrits: A Selection*, London: Tavistock.
Marcuse, H. (1987) *Eros and Civilisation*, London: Ark.
Marks, E. and de Courtivron, I. (eds) (1981) *New French Feminisms: An Anthology*, Brighton: Harvester.
Moore, N. (1987) 'Androgynt i tradiska skatter', *Svenska Dagbladet*, 7 June: 12.
Ortner, S. B. and Whitehead, H. (eds) (1981) *Sexual Meanings: The Cultural Construction of Gender and Sexuality*, Cambridge: Cambridge University Press.
Rasmussen, S. J. (1987) 'Interpreting androgenous women: female ageing and personhood among the Kel Ewey Tuareg', *Ethnology* 26 (January): 17–30.
Stockhard, J. and Johnson, M. (1980) *Sex Roles: Sex Inequality and Sex Role Development*, Englewood Cliffs, NJ: Prentice-Hall.

CHAPTER 9

One critic who has been equally influential across many of the different strands of post-structuralist thought has been Nietzsche, and it is no coincidence that the 1960s and 1970s have also seen an important revival in Nietzsche criticism. Though Nietzsche has perhaps been most commonly associated with his polemical, anti-establishment critique, that posture more implicitly connects to an attempt to break conventional parameters of meaning, to reach out to an 'overcoming' of the boundaries the 'will to truth' has imposed. This Nietzschean vision particularly has explicitly influenced Foucault, more implicitly Derrida; it not only helps to clarify the problematic relationship between these latter two thinkers, but in itself points to the potential for a radical writing with particular relevance to the archaeological engagement with the material world at its most fractured, broken and incoherent.

From Nietzsche's genealogy of morals, through to Foucault's genealogy of power (and the distinction here with deconstruction), Bapty moves to the beginnings of a genealogy of archaeology. As Nietzsche constructs his analysis of morality in the three overlapping, self-displacing essays of *On the Genealogy of Morals*, so this paper discusses current debates in archaeology within a similar structure, also drawing on the decentring metaphor of Foucault's accounts of disciplinary society. Bapty argues, indeed, that archaeology is the ideal site for the excavation of a genealogy, situated as it is in a context that has always been difficult to define as a context, in relation to evidence, which, for a conventional rationality, is at best exiguous, fragmentary, and dispersed.

9

Nietzsche, Derrida and Foucault: Re-excavating the Meaning of Archaeology

Ian Bapty

EVALUATING NIETZSCHE: BETWEEN DIALECTICS AND DECONSTRUCTION

How could anything originate out of its opposite? for example, truth out of error? or the will to truth out of the will to deception? . . . . such origins are impossible; whoever dreams of them is a fool, indeed worse; the things of the highest value must have another *peculiar* origin. . . . Rather from the lap of being, the intransitory, the hidden god, the 'thing-in-itself' – there must be their basis and nowhere else.

This way of judging constitutes the typical prejudgement and prejudice which give away the metaphysicians of all ages; . . . it is on account of this 'faith' that they trouble themselves about 'knowledge', about something that is finally baptised solemnly as 'the truth'. The fundamental faith of the metaphysicians is *the faith in opposite values*. . . .

. . . one may doubt, first, whether there are any opposites at all, and secondly whether these popular variations and opposite values . . . are not perhaps merely foreground estimates, only provisional perspectives, perhaps from some nook, perhaps from below. . . . It might even be possible that what constitutes the value of these good and revered things is precisely that they are insidiously related, tied to and involved with these wicked seemingly opposite things – maybe even one with them in essence. Maybe!

(Nietzsche 1966, 10)

What is the nature of the project Nietzsche is undertaking as a philosopher 'of the dangerous maybe in every sense' (ibid., 11)? To state the question more fundamentally: on what ground even does this maybe stand? If the extension of 'maybe in every sense' is exactly to dispose of 'solemnly baptised' truth together even more famously with the God sitting imperiously on the 'lap of being', then where in the first place can that maybe come from to call itself dangerous? How does this maybe come to occupy a real identity, or, to phrase the question at a more Nietzschean level, through what force, and in relation to what value does it operate? Indeed, suppose Nietzsche's maybe has, in his terms, succeeded silently and unnoticed to slip on the guise of being untainted by truth, untouched by the hand of God, has managed covertly to lodge itself in the affirming memory of what is. Would that really be a 'dangerous', new, unknown achievement? Are we really dealing with some possibility, which, as Nietzsche frequently assures us, has never previously reared its head in all of time, has emerged 'for the first time in history' (Nietzsche 1956, 9)? Do we not already know this maybe by some other name – a name perhaps which after all embodies the age-old 'prejudice' of metaphysics?

Nietzsche might well expect a rather more positive response to his suggestion, something more than the suspicion of unsubstantiated aspersion and insinuation, the mere reaction (to anticipate Nietzsche once more) of *ressentiment*. What, he wishes to know, are these already familiar names for a philosophy of 'maybe in every sense'? What other perspectives consider the interrelation, the tied togetherness of opposites, in the exact terms of *his* maybe?

The immediate and obvious answer which western philosophy provides in a tradition reaching through Marx, Hegel, 'old' Kant, even back to Socrates – is that of dialectics. The process of dialectical synthesis (at least as typically represented) where an absolute state of identity (at the level of sublation) is only reached paradoxically in the contradiction raised as the positive posits its negative (within objectification) could perhaps be taken to describe the kind of mutual relationship of opposites that Nietzsche intimates. To the degree that the dialectical unity is only produced through a malaise of continuous, necessary, painful altercation, a unity fraught with the irony of unintended outcome, then the relation of opposites which it embodies might well be seen as 'insidious'. Yet it is soon clear that Nietzsche's proposition does not fit comfortably in this dialectical bracket. His opposites are not only related to and involved with one another (and perhaps indeed not even 'opposites at all'), they are also bound in that final clause problematically stating that they are '– maybe even one . . . in essence'. 'In essence'? That surely then is to site the relation of opposites *before* the point of any contradiction, before the moment of objectification can create an antimony, before the dialectical space can exist. It would seem to be exactly the sense in which Nietzsche is implying a founding interaction of opposites in a radically different way to a dialectical perspective – where the metaphysical emphasis on 'peculiar' origins is still retained as an ultimate point of reference – which prompts him to call that possibility 'dangerous' and 'insidious'. For

Nietzsche, opposites are 'one . . . in essence', not, as in dialectics divided by essence; they are together in metaphorical, simultaneous displacement, not united across the labour of metonymic distance and connection.

If not dialectics, then another immediate possiblity springs to mind which might accommodate Nietzsche's still homeless maybe, a name which has only (comparatively) recently become familiar. Perhaps we are here observing the residual record of an event in the prehistory, the bottomless origin, of what we now call 'post-structuralism'? Surely Derrida would understand the possibility 'that what constitutes the value of these good and revered things is precisely that they are insidiously related, tied to and involved with these wicked, seemingly opposite things'? But stop. That same phrase, that same 'maybe' intervenes: '– maybe even one with them in essence'. 'In essence' is the stumbling block again, now in a rather different way. Derrida's 'insidious relation' of opposites rests in emphasising the defining space between such polarities, until it becomes the dominant, all-embracing force; difference becomes (literally) *différance*, a force of absence marked rather parenthetically than in itself, promoting the obstruction, the deferral, the delay of identity, opening signification as a continuous movement exactly always just stopping short of, and just starting after, the position Nietzsche's 'in essence' occupies. '*Différance* produces what it forbids, making possible the very thing it makes impossible' (Derrida 1976, 143). Essence for Derrida is necessary lie, the guilty face of meaning, the shame-faced admission of origin covering up, concealing, its endless non-origin, not some place where opposites can *really* and freely meet, collude, cohabit.

Nietzsche then still seems to be offering something different again, his maybe still remains with no name other than its own.[1] But surely this apparent escape is nonetheless revealing itself as an increasing sham, in a sense embroiling Nietzsche as another unwitting victim of the inevitable Derridean conspiracy? After all, how is it 'in essence' can repeatedly come to the rescue of the uniqueness of Nietzsche's maybe without simply and in direct contradiction pointing back straight to the beginning, straight to the 'prejudice which gives away the metaphysicians of all ages'?

Let us hedge that leading question again for a moment, or at least begin by rephrasing it in a different way. Supposing Nietzsche is interpreted at a level which ultimately throws him back – however unwillingly on his part – into the arms of metaphysics, where then? What happens if we do view him as a basically essentialist thinker? We can see one expression of such an interpretation in existentialist attempts to read Nietzsche as arguing for the eventual fulfilment of an enduring and innate human presence and 'good' over and above the interloping, secondary relational consciousness associated with 'evil'. Very different (and that should be emphasised) is to translate this division not so much in terms of the constitution of the individual subject, as in the relative roles of different racial groupings, valorising the fundamental ascendancy of master over slave, of purity and strength over 'weakness' and 'sickness' in an entirely distorted projection of Nietzsche's ideas to support racist and Fascist ideologies. This last misappropriation in any sense is really out of place in assessing a wider platform to analyse Nietzsche, but the main point here is that Nietzsche cannot really be approached through any simple rationalisation of the apparently paradoxical, conflicting, unreasonable formulation he gives us; that is an unstable relational philosophy of opposites, surrounding a regulated controlled philosophy of identity and vice versa. Only by examining how this unlikely 'maybe' can work – or rather perhaps how Nietzsche claims it works – can his key concepts, the reactive/active relation, the wills to power and nihilism, the idea of the 'eternal return', and the 'overcoming' of man in 'overman', be properly focused on and evaluated.

The plan of this paper is to use Nietzsche to frame a discussion of rather more recent trends in 'structuralism' and 'post-structuralism', and to do that specifically in relation to the thought of Foucault and his transition in the late 1960s/early 1970s to a position explicitly and implicitly claiming links with Nietzsche (and then, in a final skew of direction to interpose from this debate into the topic of this book – *archaeology* after structuralism). The point is not to conduct an analysis ultimately justifying Nietzsche against Foucault or Derrida, or vice versa, and then to impose this new 'truth' as yet another new epistemological underpinning for archaeology – which would be exactly to fall prey to the seductive wiles of what Nietzsche calls the 'will to truth' once more 'tempting us to many a venture' (Nietzsche 1966, 9) – instead the aim is to consider the value that binds together such opposing positions in their mutual activity and reactivity. Nietzsche's stated aim as the overall object of his philosophy was to 'attempt . . . a revaluation of all values', to question the implicit belief in a necessary moral interpretation of opposites as represented, for example, in Darwinist theory –

> the well being of the majority and the well being of the few are opposite views – points of value: to consider the former *a priori* of higher value may be left to the naivety of English biologists – *All* the sciences have from now on to prepare for the future tasks of the philosophers: this task understood as the solution of the *problem of value*.
>
> (Nietzsche 1969a, 56)

It is this spirit of enquiry this paper aims first to explain (necessarily in some detail) and then develop in relation to current debates in post-structuralism and 'post-processual' archaeology.

THE GOOD, THE BAD, AND THE EVIL: NIETZSCHE'S 'GENEALOGY OF MORALS'

'Am I understood? . . . Have I been understood? "Not at all, my dear sir." Then let us start again from the beginning' (Nietzsche 1969a, 97–8).

On The Genealogy of Morals is usually seen as Nietzsche's most orthodox, systematic book.[2] In that sense – but not without misgivings – this book is an apt template with which to form a provisional understanding of Nietzsche's philosophy. The misgivings arise in the need to be wary of that apparent accessibility, to see that *On The Genealogy of Morals* is only Nietzsche's most systematic book from the point of view of what it attacks – at root the 'will to truth' – and from Nietzsche's point of view should rather be regarded as his most 'unsystematic' work. Although to many readers it seems entirely incomprehensible, *Thus Spoke Zarathustra* – 'The greatest present that has ever been made to mankind' (Nietzsche 1969b, 219) – is Nietzsche nearest to his own project and its epistemological, or rather ontological, justification. Indeed Nietzsche's pretext for *On the Genealogy of Morals* was precisely to provide a guide on how *then* to go back to such books as *Thus Spoke Zarathustra* or *Beyond Good and Evil*, with their poetic and aphoristic structure, and begin to understand his philosophy properly – that understanding was not meant to be directly conveyed in *On the Genealogy of Morals* itself.

> People find difficulty with the aphoristic form. . . . An aphorism has not been deciphered when it has simply been read; rather one has to begin its exegesis, for which is required an art of exegesis. . . . One thing is necessary above all . . . before my writings are 'readable', something for which one has to be a cow, and at any rate not a 'modern' man: Rumination.
>
> (Nietzsche 1969a, 23)

What does this process of rumination, this 'art of exegesis' involve? One way of understanding Nietzsche's statement is to consider it as a part of the sense in which Nietzsche sees himself as engaged in writing a hitherto and (for him) significantly absent mythical explanation of and for the modern age. 'Man today, stripped of myth, stands banished among all his pasts and must dig frantically for roots, be it among the most remote antiquities' (Nietzsche 1966, 137). Nietszche's mythology is a 'history' continually displacing an active value structure, at the same time questioning the search for historical truth, and rejecting it as ultimately meaningless. One might almost say then that Lévi-Strauss is Nietzsche's ideal reader, a reader going outside the visible logic of metonymic reference and story content to the metaphoric displacements acting through the whole 'mythical' *oeuvre*, a reader regurgitating, ruminating on and reconstituting into a new form the apparently discrete elements of the text before him – 'almost' because Lévi-Strauss still tries to close the myth out, to make material once more a new truth behind it. Nietzsche's aim is rather to leave the constitution of the ultimate meaning of his dislocated aphorisms and poems to the free movement of the 'Dionysian' imagination, displacing the aphoristic parts into a whole which has no translation and remains elusive at the level of 'truth', 'overcomes' such meaning, and in that overcoming has an existence entirely its own.

> There is only a perspective seeing, only a perspective 'knowing': and the *more* effects we allow to speak about one thing, the more eyes, different eyes we can use to observe one thing, the more complete will our concept of this thing, our 'objectivity' be.
> (Nietzsche 1969a, 119)

Nietzsche sees 'true' meaning in an aesthetic consciousness, rather than one delimited by metaphysical reason; he can imagine 'a historiography which had in it not a drop of empirical truth and yet could claim to the highest degree of objectivity!' (Nietzsche 1983, 91). To this end, Nietzsche's intention in such works as *Thus Spoke Zarathustra* and *Beyond Good and Evil* is therefore to counter any territorialisation of sense, and instead to release the 'objectivity' and meaning which becomes in the endless juxtaposition, the endless aesthetic inter-examination of parts, a meaning which has a moment of absolute presence on its own active terms, through its own imputed value, but not in the words or writing of any material, originary vocabulary. Nietzsche's books are literally to be understood, to exist in becoming, not simply be read, to be passively consumed. Meaning is generated in the 'art of exegesis', not in what is nominally said. Genealogy is 'History for life', history which has real value at this aesthetic level, and does not rest its significance in truth and the 'disinterested' struggle for knowledge.

Thus, if Nietzsche has sought to partly exemplify, embody and make this process easy to 'spot' in the rhetorical relationship of the three essays in *On the Genealogy of Morals* – on ' "Good and Evil"/"Good and Bad" ', ' "Bad Conscience" and the Like', and 'What is the Meaning of Ascetic Ideals?' – that has only been done at the cost of a partial seduction to 'the will to truth', a tendency to localise and claim meaning in the divorced logic of any one of these parts or still smaller subdivisions within them. The part appears elevated to a whole in itself, in a way that exposes some of Nietzsche's statements all the more easily to misinterpretation exactly because of the seemingly 'straightforward', 'transparent' format in which they are contained. To understand Nietzsche in *On the Genealogy of Morals* as elsewhere, one always has to bear in mind his advice to readers of *Thus Spoke Zarathustra* (and almost already know what the advice means before it is given): 'One must hear *aright* the tone that comes from this mouth, the halcyon tone, lest one should do wretched injustice to the reasoning of its wisdom' (Nietzsche 1969b, 219).

The question Nietzsche poses as the basis for *On the Genealogy of Morals* is: How 'have good and evil originated' (Nietzsche 1969a, 16)? – which is to say, at the level of Nietzsche's enquiry, that 'the value of morality' is 'at stake' (ibid., 19). He is dismissive of accepted arguments, where it is suggested 'good' first appears as a quality ascribed to unegoistic acts perceived as useful by those gaining benefit from them, that this usefulness has then been forgotten, and thus unegoistic acts are now seen as naturally good in themselves. According to Nietzsche, such an explanation is the invention of a subsequent development through which the supporting antithesis egoistic/unegoistic is itself produced. In fact

> the judgement good did not originate with those to whom 'goodness' was shown. . . . Rather it was invented by 'The Good' themselves, that is to say the noble, powerful, high stationed and high minded, who felt and established themselves and their actions as good, that is of the first rank, in contradistinction to all the low, low minded, common and plebeian. It was out of this *pathos of distance* that they first seized the right to proclaim values.
>
> (ibid., 25–6)

Those who advance moral opposition as a natural origin of things in itself are merely evidencing their fall at the hands of 'the *ressentiment* of natures that are denied the true reaction, that of deeds, and compensate themselves with imaginary revenge' (ibid., 37). So, whereas the good, 'the noble mode of valuation . . . acts and grows spontaneously, seeks its opposite only so as to affirm itself . . . its negative concept 'bad' . . . only a contrasting image in relation to its positive basic concept' (ibid., 37), the slave morality produced by *ressentiment*

> from the outset says No to what is 'outside', what is 'different', what is 'not itself': and this is its creative deed. This inversion of the value positing eye – this need to direct outward instead of back to oneself – is the essence of *ressentiment*: in order to exist, slave morality always first needs a hostile external world; it needs external stimuli to act at all – its action is fundamentally reaction.
>
> (ibid., 36–7)

Nietzsche emphasises the point in relation to the delineation of the concept 'evil', and the difference between 'evil' and 'bad'. For the 'man of *ressentiment* "the evil enemy", "the evil one" is the basic concept, from which he then evolves as an afterthought . . . a "good one" – himself!' (ibid., 39). Thus, where, in 'master morality', 'bad' is merely an 'after production . . . a contrasting shade' (ibid., 40), a belated recognition of some vague other which is not its active self, recognition of 'evil' is the *primary* impulse driving 'slave morality', it is a spontaneously reactive reference to 'the "good" man of the other morality . . . seen in another way by the venomous eye of *ressentiment*' (ibid., 40). The master does not know evil, only subsequently sees bad, the slave does not know bad, because he first of all sees evil. Good in master morality is the primary, spontaneous adjunct of *action*, good in slave morality is the derived product of a prior *reaction* to master morality as evil, and therefore the subsequent referencing of itself as good. Nietzsche goes on to identify the beginnings of *ressentiment* with Judaism –

> the two opposing values 'good and bad', 'good and evil' have been engaged in a fearful struggle on earth for thousands of years . . . the symbol of this struggle inscribed in letters legible across all human history is 'Rome against Judaea, Judaea against Rome.'
>
> (ibid., 52)

(and it is most important at this point and throughout to recall Nietzsche's advice to readers of *Thus Spoke Zarathustra*, and not to take such statements at immediate face meaning and insinuation). Moreover, he argues that slave morality, as transmitted through Judaism, to more refined form in Christianity, and finally to its most modern embodiment in science has triumphed and continues to triumph over master morality in the overall control of western society; the 'ascetic ideal' is insidiously dominant everywhere in these different forms.

The more detailed elaboration of this process and of what Nietzsche means by the 'ascetic ideal' is first prefaced in the second essay of *On the Genealogy of Morals* by a discussion of 'conscience' running directly parallel to that of 'good' and 'evil', and it is here that the concept of the 'will to power' is also more explicitly introduced. Again Nietzsche is quick to dispose of claims that the restraint of 'conscience' and 'responsibility' is a symptom of a natural and fundamental morality. On the contrary, such ideas have only emerged at the end of a struggle where man first had to gain the capacity to make promises, which is to say once man had succeeded in displacing the primary, active tendency to forget, with the secondary reactive tendency to remember.

> Forgetting is no mere *vis inertiae* as the superficial imagine; it is rather an active and in the strictest sense positive faculty of repression . . . a little quietness, a little *tabula rasa* of the consciousness, to make room for new things . . . above all for regulation, foresight, premeditation . . . – that is the purpose of active forgetfulness.
>
> (ibid., 57–8)

The 'robust health' of this forgetfulness has nonetheless 'bred in itself an opposing faculty, a memory, with the aid of which forgetfulness is abrogated . . . in the cases where promises are made . . . this involves no mere passive ability to rid oneself of an impression . . . but an active *desire* not to rid oneself, a real memory of the will' (ibid., 58). Only when man had 'become calculable, regular, necessary' (ibid., 58) in this way, only when he had imposed a system of 'mneumotechnics' most basically linked to the application of punishment and pain, could he begin to promise, to 'stand security for his own future' (ibid., 58), and accordingly lay himself open to qualms of conscience about the need to honour that security.

One way of framing this development is in the distinction between 'good' and 'bad' conscience (where 'good' conscience is not really 'conscience' at all, in the same way that 'good' in master morality is not really a moral judgement). Nietzsche examines this question by considering the meaning of punishment as analysed at the level of a creditor/debtor relationship. The basic form of punishment then does not devolve from the desire to correct the criminal (the debtor) 'because he could have acted differently' (ibid., 63), rather it relates to the sense in which the debt owed to the creditor (the person against whom the criminal act was committed) must be reimbursed, at the level of pain and suffering. Whether or not the true wrongdoer is punished hardly matters, as long as the action of punishment, the collection of debt is carried out on someone. In so far as there is conscience at this level, it is on the part of the creditor to fulfil the impulse to punish for his own sake, not in relation to any sense of moral transgression felt by the punished, or indeed in any desire in those who punish even to *produce* that sense of moral transgression in the criminal.

> If we consider those millennia before the history of man we may unhesitatingly assert that it was precisely through punishment that the development of the feeling of guilt was most powerfully hindered – at least in the victims upon whom punitive force was exacted.
>
> (ibid., 82)

'Good' conscience is purely active, representing the simple impulse to act, to exercise will for no more purpose than that of exercising will, of pointing completely to, demonstrating dominance over, something that is external. Law, too, accordingly begins not to enshrine 'justice' but to institutionalise a context for operating this active impulse, 'that of *making suffer*' (ibid., 76) – thus, '. . . during the greater part of the past the judges . . . themselves were *not at all* conscious of dealing with a "guilty" person' (ibid., 82). Concepts such as 'just' and 'unjust' appear only after the law is instigated, they are created *by* the law as its superficial justification.

The development of the now dominant 'bad conscience' is sited by Nietzsche at the point when man 'became finally enclosed within the walls of society' (ibid., 84), when the action of good conscience finally became constrained by the appearance of the state, a happening that good conscience itself partly induced by the invention of such restrictive social conventions as law. The result was, according to Nietzsche, the '*internalisation* of man' (ibid., 84), which is to say that former outward reaching drives could now only be turned inward on oneself. 'Hostility, cruelty, joy in persecuting, in attacking . . . all this turned against the possessors of such instincts' (ibid., 85) '. . . the *instinct for freedom* forcibly made latent . . . pushed back and repressed . . . able . . . to vent itself only on itself . . . that is what the *bad conscience* is in its beginnings' (ibid., 87). This 'instinct for freedom' – '. . . in my language the will to power' (ibid., 87) is on the one hand then the primary dimension through which 'good' conscience acts, but it also forms the basic *raison d'être* of the process of internalisation via the construct of 'bad conscience'; the will to power is at another level what produces *ressentiment*. It is as an extension of the will to power that the self-denial and self-sacrifice associated with bad conscience are made to appear the source of 'freedom', a source of justification *for* life. Thus, it is at this juncture that conventional ideas of morality, guilt, the origins of religious behaviour, and the invention of God as the Redeemer, belong. What bad conscience perpetuates 'is the *will* of man to find himself guilty and reprehensible to a degree that can never be atoned for . . . his will to erect an ideal . . . of the Holy God – and in the face of it to feel the palpable certainty of his own absolute unworthiness' (ibid., 93).

Bad conscience as the 'positive' correlate of *ressentiment* – the specific mechanism whereby slave morality legitimates itself as 'good' – gives an advance clue to the answer to Nietzsche's next question, forming the basis for the final essay of *On the Genealogy of Morals*: 'What is the meaning of Ascetic ideals?' (ibid., 97). The key to the problem, can, for Nietzsche, be seen in the simple fact '*That* the ascetic ideal has meant so many things to man' (ibid., 97) which itself implies 'a basic fact of the human will . . . it needs a goal, and it will rather will nothingness than not will' (ibid., 97). It is precisely this 'will to nihilism' which Nietzsche takes to define the ascetic ideal, a will in the first place originated out of the necessity imposed by internalisation. On the surface then

> the ascetic life is a self contradiction: here rules a *ressentiment* without equal, that of an insatiable . . . power – will that wants to become master not over something in life, but over life itself; here an attempt is made to use force to block up the wells of force . . .

pleasure is felt and sought in ill constitutedness, decay, pain, mischance . . . we stand before a discord that wants to be discordant, that *enjoys* . . . suffering.

(ibid., 118)

Thus the ultimate discovery of philosophy itself perhaps – as a procedure which 'would not have been possible . . . without an ascetic misunderstanding' (ibid., 116) – would be to declare 'with ascetic self-contempt and self-mockery of reason . . . "there is a realm of truth and being, but reason is excluded from it!" ' (ibid., 116).

Superficially, then, this process of setting 'life against life' seems 'physiologically . . . and psychologically . . . a simple adsurdity' (ibid., 120). Yet that impression is a perverse mask, concealing exactly the fact that the ascetic ideal is all along 'an artifice for the *preservation* of life', and moreover could not operate did it not implicitly believe itself to be so, were the will to power not behind it. 'The meaningless of suffering, not *suffering* itself was the curse that lay over mankind . . . and the ascetic ideal offered man meaning!' (ibid., 163). Moreover, because at his deepest level the ascetic idealist must therefore always dislike himself, want 'to be different, to be in a different place' (ibid., 120) then paradoxically he possesses a dynamism which makes 'this apparent enemy of life . . . among the greatest conserving, and yes-creating forces *of* life' (ibid., 121). Out of continually threatening life the ascetic ideal claims to display the 'freedom' of life, and the paradoxical way it argues for this redemption is precisely what is at the the root of its appeal and triumph in western society.

Nietzsche outlines this success in detail, with, as ever, his most vociferous polemic aimed at Christianity. But nor does he accept that even those places where atheism and anti-asceticism might seem to have emerged – notably the rise of post-Darwinian science – in any way corresponds to the overthrow of the ascetic ideal; quite the reverse indeed. For Nietzsche science 'is rather the latest and most refined form of it' (ibid., 147). Thus 'Science first requires in every respect an ideal value in the service of which it could believe in itself . . . it never creates values' (ibid., 153). In classic ascetic fashion 'all science . . . has at present the object of dissuading man from his former respect of himself . . . [aims to sustain] the *self-contempt* of man as his ultimate and most serious claim to self-respect' (ibid., 153).

RUMINATION: FROM THE ACTIVE/REACTIVE RELATIONSHIP TO THE ETERNAL RETURN AND OVERMAN

We are left then with three nominally historical and obviously overlapping stories concerning the emergence of good and evil, bad conscience, and the ascetic ideal respectively. What is now required is to attempt the 'art of exegesis', the process of 'rumination', seeking at least to provide the conditions for the release of a meaning beyond such surface appearances.

The basic structure which forms the grounding reference of Nietzsche's thought is the division between active and reactive forces.[3] It is immediately clear that it is not sufficient merely to say that active force is 'primary' (with the insinuation 'better'), and reactive force 'secondary' (with the insinuation 'worse'), even if that is superficially the linear relationship embodied in the sequence of Nietzsche's historical dramatisation. Indeed, it is possible to argue that, on the contrary, it is reactive force which is in some ways more 'primary' than active force. Thus, while the condition of *ressentiment* as a basic expression of reaction is simultaneously defined by the act of recognising the other it automatically calls 'evil', active force only really becomes fully 'active' in the secondary process *of* acting; good in master morality only *comes* to exist as it progressively exerts its goodness in relation to something – 'bad' ('Good was invented by the good themselves . . . who established their actions *as* good in contradistinction to all the low, common, and plebeian' (ibid., 25–6, emphasis added)) . To put the point another way: The will to power is present in *ressentiment* from the very moment of its founding presence (as contained within the justification of bad conscience), whereas the will to power relates to good in master morality as the drive *making* it act, making it only then realise its activity and goodness. Reactive force is fundamentally conscious, where active force only has consciousness in so far as that consciousness is produced through action (i.e. as prescribed in the rather limited sense of 'good' conscience) – and that indeed is the basic reason, that, within Nietzsche's historical scenario, active force has become dominated by reactive force. If then in the first instance reaction seems secondary to action, that is precisely an implicit reference to the sense in which reactive force has a more basically 'active' identity than active force (so, for example, the ascetic idealist of slave morality 'is among the greatest conserving, yes-creating forces of life' (ibid., 121)). It is reaction that naturally 'acts', action that acts 'in relation to', the man of *ressentiment* needs nowhere to direct his drives but on himself, the man of action needs an external other to direct his drives *at* – which is what makes him, in Nietzsche's sense, 'active'. So paradoxically, the active needs the reactive as much as (if not more than) the reactive needs the active; moreover neither has an innate being without the other, both exist through different kinds of co-relation to the other.

Yet it is equally important to Nietzsche's argument to see that the fact that active force and reactive force are in one way sustained at a relational level does not compromise the absolute separation of those forces; for Nietzsche (unlike Hegel) there is no part of the slave in the master, no part of the master in the slave. In one sense, action may need reaction *to* see, to be active, but it can never see as far *as* reaction, can never designate evil, only recognise the 'contrasting shade' of 'bad'. Likewise, reactive force necessarily sees active force as 'evil', which is to say it never appreciates any part of what active force is to itself. The *quality* of force therefore derives from relational value, but value does not impinge on or break down the absolute distinction of forces. Active force and reactive force at one level continually become together, but never get to the point where they can in any sense *join* together, reach a moment of synthesis; it is this necessary state of becoming which Nietzsche refers to as 'the eternal return' (and this is also the sense in which opposites are 'insidiously related' and 'one in essence' – i.e. one in constant becoming). The condition of force as a differential condition bound to the will to power is to justify itself against the perceived contrary force (i.e. to survive and live), but precisely because force is thus prescribed as an expression of opposition, the same basic stasis of active/reactive relationship must always be reproduced; the other at one level eternally returns the same at another.

This is the basic insight of Nietzsche's position and it is from here that his 'revaluation of all values' is legitimated. What might properly be termed 'meaning', 'true' life, is specified in the overall becoming value *of* the eternal return (i.e. the ultimate sublimation of the will to power), not the claim to absolute values *producing* the eternal return. Nietzsche's Zarathustra lives in the shadow of his avenging demon, and it is that admission of a relationship to something which nonetheless remains completely other (i.e. of an identity which must always be becoming) which constitutes the value of Zarathustra's life and teaching, not what he is in himself (or what the demon is in itself). Thus when Nietzsche talks of 'overcoming' what he means is a going beyond the eventual justification of either reactive *or* active force, he means precisely the realisation of a value (at the level of becoming) which opposes values. While the active/reactive opposition is what makes the eternal return, ultimately that opposition has no more meaning than *as* a structure of opposition, it has no 'natural' meaning, for example, in terms of 'good' versus 'evil'. It is only by seeing this that a real value can be grasped which *can*, in a sense, distinguish between 'good' and 'evil' beyond a level where both with equal right will necessarily reduplicate themselves as 'good' in their own estimation. Nietzsche's philosophy, his notion of 'overcoming' man through an aesthetic (as opposed to metaphysical) consciousness is thus absolutely *not* a philosophy of 'anything goes', on the contrary it is exactly to demonstrate that anything *will* go only as long as things falsely take their founding legitimation from a system of moral relationships (as Deleuze (1983) puts it, Nietzsche emphasises the 'negativity of the positive'). 'Truth' belongs to those who claim it (i.e. the 'good' of master morality, or the 'good' of slave morality), it is not produced via the arbitration of any final, 'natural', truth. For Nietzsche, where the natural arbitration of things comes from (or rather becomes) is at a different level. 'Only as an aesthetic phenomenon is the world and the existence of man eternally justified' (Nietzsche 1956, 42).

As if to finally emphasise the point that the active/reactive juxtaposition was only ever a relation of opposites, not a relation where the active was intrinsically 'better' than the reactive, it is exactly from within the reactive that Nietzsche sees the disjuncture out of which 'overcoming' is precipitated. One reason then why it is 'in the interests of life that such a self-contradictory type [as the ascetic ideal] does not die out' (Nietzsche 1969a, 117), is because in so far as 'truth' for the ascetic ideal is claimed in the 'freedom' of self-sacrifice and self-questioning, then the ultimate 'truth' it can reach is precisely to question the value of the will to truth itself. 'After Christian truthfulness has drawn one inference after another, it must end by drawing its *most striking inference*, its inference *against* itself: this will happen . . . when it poses the question "what is the meaning of all will to truth" ' (ibid., 161). The ascetic ideal necessarily leads to a point where its fundamental justification – that the will to nihilism is better than no will at all – is fatally undermined, where the will to nihilism and the will to power are no longer pulling in the same direction, and thus the 'act of self-overcoming' is generated. 'From the moment faith in the ascetic ideal is denied, a new problem arises: that of the value of truth' (ibid., 153).

NIETZSCHE AND POST-STRUCTURALISM: THE VALUE OF DERRIDA AND FOUCAULT

We are now in a position to review in more detail Nietzsche's relationship to 'post-structuralism'. At first sight, Nietzsche's argument might seem ripe for Derridean deconstruction. How can he really claim that active and reactive force maintain their integrity, while freely admitting the relational constitution of forces by difference? Can we not see here Nietzsche falling for the fatal attraction of the supplement, entering in to the age-old adulterous relationship with identity; perhaps we could even place *ressentiment* alongside *hymen* or *pharmakon* etc. as the place of emergence of this guilty secret?

Yet it is equally clear, of course, that Nietzsche knows Derrida as well as, if not better than, Derrida knows Nietzsche. What is this talk of guilty secrets? Does not post-structuralism exactly restrict the process of meaning within a *moral* judgement? Can we not see the archetypal weakness of reaction, of *ressentiment* at work here, infused into the very density of language itself? Does not Derrida push ever further the effects of that moment when man 'found himself first enclosed by the walls of society' (Nietzsche 1969a, 84) (Which is to say the moment when *ressentiment* first became institutionalised)? Is the judgemental role of *différance* not precisely to prevent the signifier reaching out, fulfilling itself, enjoying the pleasure of its will to power and freedom in the *action* of pointing completely to an external other, the signified? Instead the signifier suddenly finds itself implicitly reproached at any outward movement, is given nowhere to vent the will to power but towards itself, its only inspiration the false comfort which *différance* teaches that this self-sacrifice is necessary to allow existence, to allow any will (if only the 'will to nihilism'), any pretence of presence, at all. In short, does Derrida not leave the signifier gripped with 'bad conscience', but seeing in that not so much a sign of weakness, as a virtuous, meretricious admission, the ascetic ideal *par excellence*? 'This is precisely what the ascetic ideal means: that something was *lacking* [my emphasis], that man was surrounded by a fearful void . . . he suffered from the problem of his meaning' (ibid., 162). Post-structuralism almost marks the point of the 'last man', the ultimate realisation of 'internalisation', the final refuge (where refuge is not so much a desperate last hide-out, as a space of ever 'more elusive, more spiritual, more captious' (ibid., 155), occupation) of the ascetic ideal, of Christianity itself! 'Man is slipping faster and faster away from the centre . . . into a "penetrating sense of nothingness" . . . hasn't this been the straightest route to the old [ascetic] ideal!' (ibid., 155)

The post-structuralist 'freedom' of the signifier thus emerges as the same (for Nietzsche) pernicious and disingenuous 'freedom' offered in the Christian idea of Redemption. *Différance* is another Christ nailed to the cross, accepting self-destruction, violation of body, dissolution of earthly presence and identity, the end of the signified, with the understated, paradoxically disarming justification that this sacrifice is *for* us, *for the sake of*, not against meaning! The key is when we see that deconstruction does not, nor was intended (as is sometimes implied) *finally* to disperse and end meaning –

> The trace is not only the disappearance of origin – within the discourse *that we sustain* and according to the *path we follow* it means that *the origin did not even disappear*, that it was never constituted except reciprocally by the non origin, which thus becomes the origin of the origin.
>
> (Derrida 1976, 61, emphasis added)

We must then also see that, perversely, and in a covert, far more damaging way deconstruction's silent *raison d'être* must be exactly and self-righteously to *save* meaning, to redeem it, to give it new sense of life, to allow it thankfully and contritely to see itself in its eternal sin before it is too late! The signifier is left overwhelmed and penitent, thankful for that little, fleeting and finally flawed identity it has, bound by the humility demanded to preserve this slight gift – therefore also perceiving itself as strong and residually active exactly at the point where it is weak and reactive, unable to see that it has really been robbed, prevented from ever actually understanding the suffering it so much covets, and wrongly interprets, as evidence of its 'good' health and 'freedom'. The Derridean signifier is forever reassuring itself that 'the will to nihilism is better than no will at all', affirming that view as a positive because it cannot – must not for its own salvation – see the negative element.

Of course, given that the Nietzschean overcoming of man emerges exactly *from* the final stages of the ascetic ideal, then rhetorical posture aside, such a Nietzschean 'critique' of deconstruction could rather be taken to point to the common project which both Nietzsche and Derrida share. Derrida does seem to be involved in the same basic problematic as Nietzsche – the questioning of the will to truth, and the realisation that there is a valid zone of meaning beyond that prescribed by metaphysics (or in Derrida's terminology that prescribed by 'logocentrism'). It is not necessarily surprising then that Derrida (1981) has been one of a clutch of 'post-structuralist' critics – also including Deleuze and Foucault – to affirm their relationship to Nietzsche in positive terms.

Yet that said, it would still clearly be inappropriate and simplistic to directly conflate Nietzschean genealogy with Derridean post-structuralism or vice-versa. Nietzsche's 'overcoming' overcomes in order to reach a non-material aesthetic consciousness, where Derridean 'overcoming' (i.e. deconstruction) is precipitated by extending the text to every corner of consciousness, so precisely shutting out the possibility of the final escape of identity to refuge outside the material realm of textuality. According to Derrida 'There has never been anything *but* writing [i.e. difference]' (Derrida 1976, 159, emphasis added), where for Nietzsche 'the fact that everyone can learn to read will ruin in the long run not only writing, but thinking too' (Nietzsche 1969c, 67). Nietzsche sees a danger that meaning will become trapped in the unnatural material restriction *of* writing – exactly the distinction between an inferior material (textual) representation of identity and a higher, more immediate embodiment of presence located in the spontaneity of thought and speech, which deconstruction sets out to destabilise. Thus Derrida's 'eternal return' (i.e. the endless dispersal of 'substitutional significations') works completely at the level of the other, where the Nietzschean eternal return is motivated *by* the other, but still means the return of the same (albeit the same as becoming). From a Derridean point of view Nietzsche's argument is still necessarily flawed if with the 'right' intent, while for Nietzsche Derrida remains at best only on the edges of self-overcoming, still clinging at metaphysical meaning in the paradox of revealing its falsity, rather than displacing such meaning completely.

Foucault's somewhat ambivalent relationship to Derridean post-structuralism (as he incorporates an emphasis on textuality and difference within the theory of discourse, and yet sites such a project in the seemingly contradictory terms of some form of historical analysis) in part reflects this distinction via the sense in which the 'later' Foucault is exactly attempting to realise a 'post-structuralism' around a Nietzschean framework (and let us suppose, for the sake of argument, that there is a logical pattern of development behind Foucault's *oeuvre*).

In so far as the Foucault of *Madness and Civilisation* (1973), *The Order of Things* (1974), and *The Archaeology of Knowledge* (1972) was writing a structuralist 'history', then he might well seem to invoke the Nietzschean criticism that his project is little more than 'anti-history' (Nietzsche 1983). According to Nietzsche, 'anti-history' involves the characterisation of the past in terms of periods of discrete individual identity, where the lack of attempt to link those periods in any overall context of historical development is not so much an attempt to find a new level of meaning for history, as it is a reflection of the endemic historical disinterest of a self-satisfied present. Foucault would, of course, have rejected any such suggestion. On the contrary, his claim was that the 'structuralism' embodied in his earlier works was at the level of methodology rather than epistemological intent, an analytical strategy to recover the logic and reason of past discursive formations, and thereby exactly to demonstrate the falsity of any prevailing claim to reason, to emphasise the present as an accident of the contingent eruption of the event. Foucault's 'archaeological' investigations were consciously conceived as the opposite of any attempt to fix the past within the stable unity of an underlying structure; that, for Foucault, was rather the aim of traditional historical analysis. Archaeology is focused on the 'constant verticality' of history so as 'to discover on what basis theory and knowledge becomes possible, within what space of order knowledge was constituted' (Foucault 1974, 21–2).

Thus *Histoire de la Folie* (translated into English with the title *Madness and Civilization*) is much more about the 'madness of history', the unreason of a reason which seeks to prescribe the understanding of madness as a unitary, progressive development, than it is a 'history of madness'. The book (and Foucault's subsequent *The Birth of the Clinic*, 1975) stresses how the emergence of those discourses seeming to speak for and understand madness, in reality involved a speaking over and through madness to the emergent problem of the modern 'episteme' – the ambiguous identity of man as both subject and object of representation and discourse. The 'enlightened' treatment of madness therefore took its cue from the need to rationalise and distance the unreason at the basis of modernity itself, and in fact inaugurated a far more rigorous exclusion of the discourse of madness than had operated in the pre-classical age. Likewise, *The Order of Things* (in the original French version entitled *Les Mots et Les Choses*, though Foucault stated a preference for the

English alternative) is better seen as an analysis of the 'disorder' of things, a study of the absence of a natural, guiding logic behind the appearance and consolidation of the discourses of biology, language, and economics.

Yet the iconoclasm of Foucault's interpretations cannot conceal a basic epistemological contradiction in 'archaeology'; however much Foucault tries to maintain a position contra-history, the ultimate legitimation of his argument has to be an extension of orthodox historical consciousness/metaphysical reason. Derrida was quick to raise the point in criticism of *Madness and Civilisation*, noting the necessary impossibility of writing a history of madness without, in the final analysis, the support of reason, without indeed reproducing the appropriation of the discourse of madness Foucault nominally criticises – 'We might have the right to ask what, in the last resort, supports this language without recourse or support . . .? Who wrote and who is to understand, in what language and from what historical situation of logos . . . this history of madness?' (Derrida 1978, 38). Where this difficulty is most explicit is in the paradoxical status of Foucault's concept of the *episteme* –

> the total set of relations that, unite at a given period, the discursive practices that give rise to epistemological figures, sciences, and possibly formalised systems . . . [the *episteme*] is the totality of relations that can be discovered, for a given period, between the sciences when one analyses them at the level of discursive regularities.
>
> (Foucault 1972, 191)

The obvious question becomes, how does Foucault escape the historical a priori of the contemporary *episteme* – is his analysis not similarly situated according to a pre-determined set of 'discursive regularities' ultimately bringing it back, however unwillingly, to the level of a kind of Nietzschean anti-history? Foucault poses the problem for himself in the conclusion to *The Archaeology of Knowledge*: 'You give yourself the whole field of a free space. . . . But are you forgetting the care with which you enclosed the discourse of others within systems of rules? . . . You make revolution very easy for yourself, but very difficult for others' (Foucault 1972, 208). The reply to his own query hedges the issue behind statements which if plausible in themselves must nonetheless rebound on the ultimate heuristic legitimation of archaeology:

> the positivities I have tried to establish must not be understood as a set of determinations imposed from the outside on the thought of individuals . . . [they are more] the field in which the initiative [of subjects] is articulated. . . . I have not denied – far from it – the possibility of changing discourse.
>
> (Foucault 1972, 208–9)

It is this problem and the search for a better answer to it – an answer that at the same time does not not fall into what Foucault sees as the Derridean trap of reducing 'discursive practices to textual traces; the elision of the marks therein and the retention only of marks for a reading' (Foucault 1979, 26–7) – which prompts Foucault's consideration of an alternative to archaeological knowledge based in the 'overcoming' of Nietzschean genealogy. In some ways this does not seem a very significant departure; Foucault's first major 'genealogical' study *Discipline and Punish* (Foucault 1977) retains much the same periodisation, subject matter and direction of argument as his earlier works. One response might be to regard Nietzschean terminology as a new legitimation for a mode of analysis which is still essentially archaeology and beset by the problems of archaeology; a kinder appraisal is perhaps to note that archaeology had always shared close affinities with a basically Nietzschean posture. Foucault's laughter at the Chinese classification of animals taken from a passage from Borges which opens *The Order of Things* – with categories such as 'Belonging to the Emperor', 'Innumerable', 'That from a long way off look like flies' – is prompted as he sees here a reason collapsing 'our age old distinction between the same and the other' (Foucault 1974, 15), in short a reason precisely embodying the active Nietzschean process of 'forgetting', rather than complying with the endless metaphysical struggle for memory. Foucault's own classifications of discursive modalities characterising *The Order of Things* and *The Archaeology of Knowledge* can be closely identified with a similar attempt to institute a logic of 'forgetting', to disperse a meaning in the 'illogical' displacement of overlapping categories of analysis rather than to try and tie meaning down deterministically through the external imposition of those categories (which helps to elucidate the grounds of Foucault's defence of 'archaeology' at the end of *The Archaeology of Knowledge*). Another covert genealogical emphasis in archaeology had been the implicit concern with the issue of power, and the role of the institution (however understood) in constituting patterns of action and discursive production. As the genealogical Foucault was to reminisce 'When I think about it now, I ask myself what could I have been talking about in *Histoire de la Folie* for example, or *Naissance de la Clinique* if not power?' (cited in Sheridan 1980, 115). The breakthrough for Foucault was not only explicitly to see the issue of power, but to see that issue at a Nietzschean level where the will to power is fundamentally an impulse of begetting rather than of repression, where power is linked in the first place to the preservation of life, and only secondarily takes the form of disciplinary regulation and control. Here was a principle which offered a new way of questioning the operation of discursive formations, and also, as there could be nothing from the start which was not involved in the will to power, gave Foucault justification for a 'historical' analysis outflanking the residual historicism entombed in the epistemic structure of archaeology.

So whereas 'archaeology' had fallen at the hurdle of being itself a new totalising system of knowledge which could only have the same legitimation in 'truth' as orthodox history, Foucauldian genealogy, on the model of Nietzsche, claimed consistently to oppose the production of truth at a 'normal' metaphysical level.

> How can we define the relationship between genealogy ... and history in the traditional sense ... Nietzsche's criticism always questioned the form of history that reintroduces a suprahistorical perspective: a history whose function is to compose the finally reduced diversity of time into a totality fully enclosed upon itself. ... Once the historical sense is mastered by a suprahistorical perspective metaphysics can bend it to its own purpose ... the historical sense [must] evade metaphysics and become a privileged instrument of genealogy [refusing] ... the certainty of absolutes.
> (Foucault 1984, 87)

The way this happens is when power is admitted as object and source of Foucault's discourse, so precipitating an acknowledgement of 'becoming' which carries with it a 'true' 'historical' sense, not a collapse into relativism; relativism is what those who submit to the will to knowledge participate in (i.e. in the sense of Nietzsche's 'will to nihilism'). Thus in *Discipline and Punish* the basis of the analysis is to 'make the technology of power the very principle both of the humanisation of the penal system and of the knowledge of man' (Foucault 1977, 23), indeed to examine the 'way in which the body itself is invested by power relations' (ibid., 24); Foucault is writing Nietzschean 'history for life', history which in one way can be regarded as 'mythical', but in exactly that sense has a 'real' relationship to the present. Foucault is not writing the 'history of the past in terms of the present', he is writing 'the history of the present' (ibid., 31). As the notion of punishment as fundamentally repressive is overthrown in *Discipline and Punish* (cf. Nietzsche's consideration of the nature of punishment), and the fallacy of the repressive hypothesis in relation to the control of discourse on sex is exposed in the first volume of *The History of Sexuality* (Foucault 1980), Foucault also overthrows any similarly repressive absolute network of historical meaning, and opens the moment of Nietzschean becoming. Foucauldian genealogy is written through and is a writing of the sublimation of the will to power in western society.

Foucault, then, is best described as a 'superstructuralist' (in the sense of Nietzsche's 'superhistory' or 'super[over]man', not, of course, at the more general level of Harland's (1987) use of the term), rather than a 'post-structuralist' in the deconstructive mould. His achievement is in a sense to extend the Nietzschean insight to a treatment of the past which is far more 'substantive' than Nietzsche's own schematic and sometimes seemingly offensive historical outline. One might still argue – and doubtless Derrida still would – that this is at best a clever piece of theoretical justification which cannot evade the metaphysical grip of any level of historical analysis, however nominal that history claims itself to be. The technologies of truth are strongly inculcated in the historical statement whatever the surrounding theoretical network which seeks to resist that implication – and to a point that is a valid criticism. When Foucault describes the operation of Panopticism in *Discipline and Punish* for example, it is hard not to see this as an interpretation of the past as the past, and that that is where it derives its meaning and impact.

Perhaps, indeed, one might then do better to look at a domain of study of the past where technologies of truth are even now very much in their infancy, where overcoming has always been an incipient possibility. . . . What of the potential of archaeology itself as the object of a genealogy, a potential Foucault ironically overlooked in his continual use of the term?

ON THE GENEALOGY OF ARCHAEOLOGY

Let us ask a rather strange question, although one logical in the present context: Is archaeology good or evil? Or more pertinently: should archaeology be good or evil? What is the value of archaeology?

The question will be examined here from three different directions: the historical context of archaeology, the opposition in contemporary debate between processual and post-processual archaeology, and a consideration of the technologies through which the archaeological body is controlled (or rather willingly controls itself) in terms of the will to truth. These categories are not absolute, but are schematic, overlapping, contradictory and self-displacing. They are categories of genealogical enquiry.

The Historical Context

The history of archaeology has never been seen as particularly problematic. In the conventional scenario the emergence of archaeology is tied to a breakdown of the ahistorical mode of thought dominant in the eighteenth century (which had been marked by strict adherence to the biblical canon and also at a different level by the interests of Cartesian/Newtonian science) induced by the 'truth' which the evolutionary movement in its different forms from Lamarck and Buffon through to Spencer and Darwin, gradually began to reveal. The transition from antiquarianism to archaeology naturally occurs as a component of this emergent historical consciousness (Daniel 1962). The problem has been one of the detail of this development (for example the exact origin of the word 'prehistory' (Chippindale 1988)), not a more fundamental critique of how 'natural' and ultimately necessary the constitution of archaeology really was, how real the identity of *archae*ology itself – as the explicit study of origins and identities – has ever been. Where 'critical' evaluation of the history of archaeology has been raised is more at the level of 'filtering' out historically transmitted biases in the current way we approach the past – for example Rowlands' discussions situating the genre of explanation typically applied to later European prehistory through the historical context of archaeology within the capitalist mode of production (Rowlands 1986; 1987) – rather than to put that desire to get to the truth itself in its 'historical' context.

It is clear at the very least that in so far as the genesis of 'archaeology' does indeed connect to the evolutionary debate as orthodox accounts suggest – for example as directly represented in the work of Lewis Henry Morgan or General Pitt-Rivers – then that is only one of a much more complex web of origins. For example, the description of archaeological sequences in terms of an early, middle, late or archaic, classic, post-classic periodisation might be seen to reflect, and in some degree derive from, the tripartite division of the post-Hegelian dialectic (as distinct from a wider tradition of cyclical descriptions of human development from Montesquieu to Vico and beyond), and this can be seen particularly as such a structure was influential on the analysis of material culture at an art historical level (e.g. Westropp 1856; Gardner 1883). Indeed one stimulus to the formation of an 'archaeology' might exactly be at this level where material culture became an interesting and intrinsically significant aspect of discourse in relation to the problematic the Hegelian process of objectification posed. In the context of human identity conceived as a dialectical problem, the material object becomes the literal embodiment of the externalisation of the subject (i.e. man), and the field of tension between idea and object, between the productive action of man and the form of material culture, is promoted as a 'natural' focus of study.

In one sense then the emergence of archaeology might be sited alongside Foucault's description of the shift to a more 'humanitarian' treatment of madness, that is as a construct of the underlying foundation of late eighteenth/nineteenth century 'reason' at a point where man has become the problem which discourse surrounds and is generated by, rather than simply one of the objects which discourse illuminates, describes and differentiates. The constitution of archaeology as the study of the deepest and remotest origins of man correlates with the need to resolve the contradiction of an emergent world view where that identity and absolute origin of man is both its basic problem, and its basic point of becoming. So, in Nietzschean terms, one might say that archaeology arises and is legitimated precisely out of the process of internalisation, where the will to power is turned further inward on man himself, and life and knowledge come to rest in continually and paradoxically questioning the provenance of 'man'. The appearance of archaeology represents the progressive realisation of a necessary truth, only in so far as that truth is prescribed by a wider shift in the mode of sublimation of the will to power.

From another perspective it is interesting to consider the related degree to which the new procedures forming the incipient archaeology can be understood in Foucauldian terms as comprising an elaborate disciplinary technology. The rationale of systematic excavation, classification, and codification which characterises and is closely connected with the realisation of a discrete archaeological identity in the nineteenth century (the classifications of Thomsen, Worsaae, and Montelius, Petrie's seriation procedure etc.), at one level associated with the transition from an antiquarian discourse of resemblances to an archaeological discourse of absolute correspondences, can also be seen to embody a more rigorous set of implicit restrictions through which patterns of action and the operations of the body are specifically and carefully regimented and controlled. It is no coincidence that the principal innovators in excavation technique, notably Pitt-Rivers in the late nineteenth century and Mortimer Wheeler in the early twentieth century had strong military connections, and indeed the analogy between the process of excavation and the organisation of a military campaign has often been stressed (Wheeler 1954). One interpretation at this level might, then, be to relate the appearance of archaeology to a series of technologies of discipline and order (of which the foundation of the modern prison system and the laying down of penal codes would be the most explicit example) produced through and reinforcing the particular structure and conditions of nineteenth-century western capitalist society. Pitt-Rivers openly advanced the model and practice of archaeological procedure as a means of reproducing the wider hierarchical social structure of contemporary Britain (Thompson 1977). Yet it is clear too that this disciplinary technology cannot be purely understood as a repressive mechanism, whether openly manipulated or operating as part of a more dispersed and unconscious network of social discourse and order. The sense in which the emergent and literal discipline of archaeology was perceived from the start as a process of necessary labour required to produce 'truth', and 'correct' meaning (e.g. Lubbock 1865, see introduction) is itself important as a reflection of the origins of archaeology within a kind of Nietzschean ascetic ideal. One might say in those terms that what the methodological format of the new archaeology of the nineteenth century represents is not so much a structure of simple disciplinary domination, as one incorporating in another form the emergent and underlying problem of human identity. Self-regulation and self-discipline in the minutiae of archaeological procedure is a context for establishing a 'natural' logic of human action and presence exactly called into question at the root of post-Enlightenment ontology, and indeed called into question very much more explicitly and directly in the rapidly changing political and social conditions of contemporary Europe.

There is a great deal more surrounding the appearance of archaeology than any simple cause of abstract 'truth'. The discipline did not only emerge in the modern age, it emerged *because* of the modern age. That is no new realisation, but it is perhaps one whose implications have not been properly considered. As Nietzsche might have seen it, it could be said that from its inception archaeology has been bound up in the ascetic ideal; and thus, on a face value reading of Nietzsche, archaeology in its historical context would therefore also have to be considered more 'evil' than 'good'.

PROCESSUAL AND POST-PROCESSUAL ARCHAEOLOGY

Easily forgotten, particularly as it has become fashionable to associate processual archaeology with the reproduction of a basically conservative ideology (e.g. Shanks and Tilley 1987, chapter 2), is the extent to which the 'new' archaeology was conceived as a radical, path-breaking, and in the general context of the 1960s, even a politically motivated departure (cf. Binford 1972). The 'newness' was the extension into archaeology of a perceived wider liberation from habitually and non-critically accepted structures of meaning and living. This explicit incorporation of a self-conscious memory into archaeological methodology and epistemology is a significant watershed (notwithstanding the fact that archaeologists such as Childe and Collingwood had always been 'critically aware') beyond which both the 'mature' processual archaeology, and the subsequently realised structuralist/post-processual archaeology, equally belong. Thus, the contemporary era of theoretical awareness, however that awareness is differently formulated and characterised, fundamentally involves (in terms, at least, of the dominant perception of how archaeology had operated previously) 'the transition of archaeology from noble innocence to self-consciousness and critical consciousness' (Clarke 1973, 8). Almost in Nietzschean terms, that is to embody a transition from 'master morality' to 'slave morality', in another way a re-purification of the reactive context which had spawned archaeology in the nineteenth century. One might nevertheless say that processual archaeology seeks to constrain this reaction in an active posture, where post-processualism aims to emphasise the reactive quality itself, and indeed the main thrust of the anti-processual critique is exactly to 'expose' the similarly reactive nature of processual archaeology.

The stance taken by processual archaeology – or at least that 'first generation' processual archaeology associated with the early work of such as Binford, Clarke, Renfrew and Flannery – is first explicitly to acknowledge that the interpretation of the past is inherently problematic, and to argue accordingly that such interpretation (the truth of the past) can only be reasonably pursued at certain limited levels of abstraction. Those levels of abstraction are located in the realm where general laws (such as rules of functionalist prediction (e.g. Binford 1962; Schiffer 1976) or at least some component of cross-cultural generalisation – for example as represented by systems theory (e.g Clarke 1968; Renfrew 1972)) can be formulated and then linked to archaeological data through 'middle range' theory (Binford 1983). In a sense then, processual archaeology is self-conscious only to the degree that such consciousness does not compromise the possibility of an absolute, 'true', interpretation of the past; indeed the explicit object of processual critical awareness (where it is implicit in post-processual approaches) is to make that interpretation more true, more exactly representative of some past reality. The way it does that is precisely in the supposed merit attached to the admission that the whole truth of the past cannot be known, that the historical uniqueness of particular contexts and the meanings of symbolic representations are necessarily inaccessible and lost to the archaeologist.

So, to the extent that processual archaeology does embody an explicit component of self-criticism, involves an equation of truth with the rigorousness of its testing procedures, with constant evaluation of the quality and representative integrity of the data, that should not be taken to imply directly that behind all this the reactive element is uppermost. Rather it is the case that this nominal reactive tendency is viewed as part of the middle range question of how best to apply and localise interpretive force, maximise interpretive efficiency (cf. Binford and Sabloff 1982). Critical consciousness does not connect to a more fundamental self-regulation at the level of compromising the basic desire to dominate and completely reach out to a past divorced from the present. Thus what is not questioned (in the first instance at least) is the situated context of archaeology itself in a particular set of social structures, historically constitued meanings, and arbitrary discursive regularities; the past/present relationship is de-emphasised (or rather left silent), and the stress is all on producing the most reasonable understanding of the past in itself (though that may involve considering the contemporary context in so far as distorting biases can therefore be isolated and removed). The admission of one absence at the level of the constraint of possible interpretation to only certain kinds of analysis, conceals a second covert absence, that of the present, in the processually produced past. That is indeed also the sense in which processual archaeology might, from a Nietzschean perspective, be considered basically active, and from its own point of view primarily 'good'.

In metaphorical displacement, one might draw an analogy with

Foucault's description of the technologies of punishment operated under the aegis of the European ancien régime (Foucault 1977). The penal system underpinning the ancien régime is restricted to the process of trying and executing the criminal within a formalised and deliberate procedure justified against the generalisations embodied in the law, these generalisations formed on the basis of widely established principles of what is 'just'. No pretence is made actually to cure, reform or treat the criminal, or even to listen to and understand his words, his reasons for committing the crime, except in so far as they go towards identifying the generally defined condition of guilt or innocence (the presence or absence of a general pattern). The strength of the system is its explicit claim to operate only in the terms of those variables which can reasonably be known and controlled. Indeed it is not necessarily annoying that the criminal on the scaffold (or the particular aspects of the archaeological data which cannot be reduced by generalisation) might cry out to the watching crowd and renounce the system that sentenced him, talk of the particular circumstances which make his conviction through the level of generality offered by the law unjust. Rather it is almost hoped that the condemned *will* cry out in this way, will demonstrate the impossibility of any pluralistic system of justice based beyond that area of discourse definable as the source of secure knowledge, beyond an arbitrating force applied equally and generally to all (data), reaching out without reserve from the point of sovereign authority (science).

The place of departure for post-processual archaeology, and its justification as a more sophisticated approach to the study of the past (which ultimately does mean a 'truer' interpretation), is precisely to begin to listen to the voice of the madman, or the criminal – to emphasise the particularity of contextual meanings. The analogy might now be drawn with Foucault's analysis of the humanitarian and liberal reform movement of the late eighteenth–early nineteenth century. Where post-processual archaeology is fundamentally based is in the claim to free the madman, to get to the real complexity of the data, really to begin for the first time to study 'process', to join Pinel or Tuke in cutting away the restraining shackles (of generalisation), to interpret the words of the oppressed, the specific meanings and symbolism of the past. In a sense the 'truth' offered by processual archaeology is not questioned; what is questioned is how far that truth really tells us anything at all at the level it is derived. How can it be just to ignore the madman or condemn the criminal without even trying to understand (difficult and perhaps even impossible as that may be) and to cure madness and criminality, without even trying to make the deviant (elements of the past) *see* reason? Is it really secure knowledge simply to make certain kinds of complexity an inaccessible category without attempting first to examine the nature of that complexity – perhaps this excluded zone, the words of the madman, or the symbolic contexts of the past, or the context of the past in the present, is exactly where 'meaning' lies all along. Thus one aspect of the post-processual critique has been to argue that processual archaeology was necessarily involved with the symbolic and contingent meanings it claimed to isolate itself from (e.g. Hodder 1982a). So, even at the most simple level, a basic unit of archaeological description such as the term 'potsherd' necessarily embodies a particular and contingent meaning. Within post-processual archaeology the madman is uncovered as a facet of the very reason which had previously loftily and without conscience automatically distinguished itself from madness.

That, of course, does pose a difficulty. Where is any ultimate meaning whatsoever to come from, where is the humanitarian to take his stand and nonetheless preserve order within the freedom of liberal understanding? For post-processual archaeology, whether implicitly or explicitly, the answer is to erect the constraint of 'context' (Hodder 1982b; 1986; 1987b; Barrett 1988), mediated on the one hand between the emphasis on material culture as meaningfully constituted (as demonstrated through structural analysis of the historically specific form of particular archaeological contexts, e.g. Hodder 1984), and on the other by the realisation that that meaning takes its sense not from any abstraction of the past in itself, but from the production and situatedness of the past in the present (as analysed in a hermeneutic/dialectical framework (Shanks and Tilley 1987, chapter 5)). The generalisations that inform interpretation within this duality are justified as the product of critical reflection, that is in one sense they actively incorporate a contemporary critique at the level, for example, of questioning the dominant portrayal of gender relationships (Gibbs 1987), or current norms of social relations and power structures (Shanks and Tilley 1982), and yet in another sense the process of interpreting the past is held to act back on these generalisations, so constituting an eventual interpretation which while reflecting and acknowledging the past/present relationship is not completely subsumed by the interests of the present. One common interest of post-processual archaeology, for example, has been the attempt to locate the active individual in the past (much as Pinel and Tuke sought to find the individual behind the category of the madman), drawing on (an at times somewhat basic reading of) the structuration theory of Giddens (e.g. Giddens 1979) and Bourdieu's theory of practice (Bourdieu 1977). The limitation of context is defined neither simply in the structure enabling action (such as symbolic meanings), nor in the general process of action itself, but in the recursive relationship of the two together supporting and reforming one another (e.g. Leone 1984; Barrett 1988). Thus contextual/ post-processual archaeology claims to inaugurate a more mature approach to developing the understanding of the particular (the structure and the specific historical trajectory of change) within the process of the general (such as patterns of human action etc.). In this way a 'critically' formed meaning is closed (e.g. Hodder 1986, chapter 7).

To return to the metaphor of Foucault's discussion of the eighteenth/nineteenth century humanitarian reformers – they too sought to limit the interpretation of criminality or madness within context, and the place where that context emerged was called the asylum or the 'modern' prison. The asylum was a place where the deviant could be observed, studied and heard, the nature of unreason understood at one level, and accordingly and in mutual interaction the appropriate treatment to recover the mad to the side of reason devised and administered. For Foucault, these new institutions were a space where both the reformers and the reformed became locked in a new geometry of power, a new procedure of self-regulation and self-constraint on both sides. The symbol of this shift is Bentham's Panopticon, the material embodiment of the humanitarian system of disciplinary control. In relation to the Panoptic structure, on the one hand the deviant must constantly police himself in terms of, and feel aware of, the prescribed norms of behaviour and reason, even though he can never see the observer or actually know whether he is ever observed. And on the other the observer in the central Panoptic tower is also constrained by the specific procedure of observation, and by the paradox that to see one prisoner is effectively to see all. The process of observation becomes one of non-observation (absence), and yet *to* observe (to maintain the illusion of presence) remains a requirement, more so for the sake and identity of the observer than for the control of the observed. So, indeed, it might be argued, does the concept of context locate itself within the Panoptic structure of post-processual/contextual archaeology. Contextual archaeology produces the past through the ironic mode of a sustained *double entendre*. The archaeologist in the present becomes locked in the procedure of still having to observe the past while admitting that the past in itself, or any part of its original unity, is not completely observable (is observed only in absence), and meanwhile the contextual meaning of the past is accordingly closed in obedience to the continuous threat of a never actually present watching presence. This is both the founding and the legitimating paradox of 'critical reflexivity', where context must be both within and without the 'text' simultaneously, the point which post-processual/contextual archaeology prides itself upon, finds perverse 'truth' in terms of.

Within a Nietzschean framework, then, post-processual archaeology might be seen as fundamentally reactive, basically tied to the ascetic ideal, promoting a truth of the past by its rigour in questioning the ground upon which any such truth might be constructed. One could almost say too that post-processualism is essentially a posture of *ressentiment*; it defines itself as 'good', and realises bad conscience in the form of context, in relation to the 'evil' of the archetypal processual approach, not in any necessary good attached to post-processual archaeology in itself – indeed it positively refutes any such suggestion of such self-good, as, for example, one more symptom of the bourgeois ideology lying behind archaeology (e.g. Shanks and Tilley 1987). Furthermore, it is exactly because of this fundamentally reactive nature that post-processual archaeology has such a disparate identity, and has been effective because of rather than despite that in breaking down the processual position; once processual archaeology begins to lose the fundamental innocence on which it rests it must become fatally flawed, where for post-processualism ever more vigorous criticism and self-criticism is exactly how it sustains the validity of the interpretations it offers of the past.

THE TECHNOLOGIES OF ARCHAEOLOGICAL TRUTH

How is it possible to make the statement 'the past does not exist', without making a particularly contentious or philosophically abstract point, and yet at the same time also without undermining the basic justification of archaeology, processual or post-processual alike, which is to argue that at some level the past in a part of itself *does* exist?

To clarify the point: Stonehenge exists, the British later Bronze Age exists, and so on. Yet as has been emphasised many times in recent debate (as one example the emic/etic discussion), these things exist as they are constructed through meanings in the present, not as they naturally represent and necessarily embody some part of the past which is not the present. Thus, most archaeologists would only ever claim to offer interpretations, even if they might claim that some interpretations can be demonstrated to be more 'true' representations of the 'real' past than others. The disjuncture of processual and post-processual archaeology is then at one level on the question of how far towards the original meaning of the past it is possible to get, not a question of whether there is or ever will be a fixed, finally correct archaeological meaning (or at the very least that such a finally deciphered past, and presumably with it the end of any need for archaeologists, is a long way off); both accept in that sense that the past does not exist. One might say indeed that archaeology must as its starting point embody a basic ability to ignore the fact that it will always ultimately fail in its stated aim. Moreover it must learn to accept that the extent of its failure in the cause of an absolute 'truth' will be consistently more obvious than the equivalent 'failure' of any other of the social (or other) sciences which archaeology has assiduously sought to emulate and claim equal academic status with. Thus the standard throwaway line about a 'mature' archaeology actively contributing to wider interdisciplinary debate is largely written for the benefit of other archaeologists, not because anyone outside archaeology takes such a statement as a serious possibility. What needs to be questioned is how, then, does archaeology continue to maintain its identity, continue to operate within the guise of science and truth when it would be difficult to argue that any final truth about the past has ever been discovered – certainly more difficult than it would be (even if with no more ultimate validity) than in the domains of study occupied by anthropology or history, for example?

What will be considered here, more as an observational than a primarily critical exercise, is what might be viewed as the 'technological' devices through which the 'body' of archaeology – the material forms through which the discourse of archaeology is produced – controls itself in terms of the will to truth. We need to try and 'see' the machinery which regulates and masks – not as false consciousness or ideological mystification, but simply as an apparatus of practical legitimation – the evident fact that the will to truth can never, even fleetingly, be consummated in the pasts we write. Below, merely as one rationalisation, one fictionalisation perhaps, of this essentially non-discursive process, three such technological systems operating in contemporary archaeology will be outlined.

Archaeological Description as Archaeological Truth

The first technology we might observe is one which acts to induce a particular kind of forgetting, tacitly to make 'truth' out of aspects of archaeological enquiry which are not 'truth' nor indeed at the explicit discursive level are even perceived to be so. One form of this process is where strategies of analysis are made synonymous with the 'truth', rather than viewed as means of obtaining a 'truth' which can only ever be provisional and unstable.

Thus, as one example, the whole elaboration of excavation techniques, and the involved and minutely regulated discipline of recording, observing and preserving the material record of the past connects to the assumption that this process through its very complexity and apparent scientific abstraction must necessarily be producing a more 'true' past. One might say that the correct emphasis is that it is a very specific level of truth which has been produced through this development, an identity of the past made manifest through scrupulous attention to the carefully dissected form, size, postition, and relationship of entities such as 'contexts' and 'features', a truth which is real in itself – in terms of the discipline to which it belongs – but reveals no necessary knowledge about the past where 'features' and 'contexts' nominally originate. The art of a particular discourse of identification and representation, providing a picture of the past formed only in the image of a regularising procedure entirely external to the past, is nonetheless necessarily taken to indicate a greater knowledge *of* the past.

What is interesting is the way this technology has in fact generated and been partly sustained through a range of counter discourses demonstrating that greater knowledge of the past *per se* has not really been obtained through it. Two examples would be the site formation processes debate (e.g Schiffer 1976), and the debate on the appropriate and best form for excavation publication (e.g. Frere 1975; Cunliffe 1982). As the site formation question implies, complex patterns of artefact and feature relationship recovered by sophisticated excavation are in the first instance no more than that, no more than a pattern of complex relationships; they do not directly translate to a more correct interpretation of the past. And similarly, the site report controversy underlines the point that the excavation archive does not translate itself into a natural body of meaning and a truer account of the archaeological record. It may indeed be that we now have *less* actual truth about the past than at any time previously in the history of archaeology, exactly in the sense that we have more evidence of it.

Another example of this general technology is the use of radio-carbon dating, and the related idea that through the 'radio-carbon revolution' an 'absolute' archaeological chronology has become available. Certainly, radio-carbon dating has had a very great and useful impact in archaeology, but is it right to suppose that this necessarily connects to a 'truer' knowledge of the past? As a hypothetical example, consider the statement 'An AOC beaker was associated with a radio-carbon date of 1950 ± 50 BC', which would appear to be a solid statement of archaeological knowledge. Yet, in a sense, all that sentence really means is 'a radio-carbon date of 1950 ± 50 BC, having nothing whatsoever in itself to do with the archaeological past, happened to be associated with an AOC beaker'. The point is not to cast aspersions on the general validity of radio-carbon dating, or to say that radio-carbon dating has not indeed been an important breakthrough for archaeology, but rather to question the notion that *because* we have radio-carbon dates the past becomes more true, and therefore that radio-carbon dates reveal a truth about the past. All radio-carbon dates reveal is an abstract structure relating to radio-carbon dates. The implication of archaeological truth is only derived in relation to and after that.

If this seems to make a great deal of stating the obvious, that is the point. It is precisely by habitual acceptance of what is too obvious and embedded to criticise explicitly that this group of technologies is effective in sustaining an apparently real level of archaeological truth.

Archaeology as Other than Archaeology

A second technology closely related to the first is the process of constituting the truth and identity of archaeology in relation to anything but the identity of archaeology itself. The meaning of the past is established at a level which constantly defers and leaves absent an actual 'archaeological' meaning, covertly and implicitly conceals the fact that no such meaning or even a true disciplinary identity of archaeology as such exists.

This procedure is manifest in many ways (for example at another level in relation to excavation technique or radio-carbon dating) but the most obvious example has been in the context of the post-1960s theoretical debate. Behind the mask of repeated calls for and announcements of a pending development of a truly 'archaeological' theory a whole industry and labour of discourse has developed explicitly sustaining archaeology in terms of meanings developed within other disciplinary positions. As one example, one of the leading 'archaeological' theorists, Ian Hodder, has so far drawn that 'theory' from human geography (Hodder and Orton 1976), statistical analysis (Hodder 1978), Chomskian structuralism (Hodder 1982b), Marxist ideology analysis (Hodder 1982c), Collingwoodian hermeneutics (Hodder 1986), Braudelian history (Hodder 1987a), Weberian historical materialism (Hodder 1986), post-structuralist linguistic theory (Hodder 1988), etc.

This, of course, might seem an almost inevitable process, and this paper is located in the same technology, the same maintenance of an archaeology by consistently reaching outside it. One might indeed say that any disciplinary position is defined in the same way; but it is still worth considering, why, were this a paper in philosophy or social theory for example, it would be very unlikely to be drawing its argument from the latest discussion in the archaeological literature.

The 'Loss of Innocence'

The recent theoretical 'awakening' has also in a more explicit way marked what might be seen as a major technological innovation in supporting the archaeological will to truth. This might be termed, in Clarke's much used phrase, the technology of 'loss of innocence'. In effect, this has been to produce an accepted and naturalised context and mode for discourse on the impossibility of actually achieving archaeological truth exactly as a means of sustaining that aim; the very proliferation of discourses on the fact that the past is ultimately inaccessible to the archaeologist has deferred the impact such a realisation might seem to carry with it, and enabled archaeology to believe itself to be more truthful than ever. Shanks and Tilley give one statement of what 'loss of innocence' in its post-processual phase means: 'What is important is that archaeology recognises its temporality and fragility, recognises itself as a contemporary practice . . . [where] established positions . . . need to be criticised and transcended' (Shanks and Tilley 1987, 246). In this process of continual criticism, of one theoretical posture transcending the next, the 'real' past itself is allowed to disappear, exactly, it would usually seem, as a means of talking about that past as if it had not disappeared – or at least still talking in terms which persist in locating some kind of truth, some kind of original unity, within the past (the truth of ideology analysis for example).

In more specific terms, this effect is maintained by a careful procedure of apparently logical argument. One archetypal argument of the 'loss of innocence' technology is as follows: the notion of a once existent past in itself is posited, yet qualified by arguing that that past is no longer recoverable by the archaeologist. Nonetheless, it is thus possible to claim that the archaeological past is still some transformation and reflection of this original unity, and not, therefore, a complete fabrication that did not in any actual sense exist until the point of archaeological analysis. So the past which is denied in the 'maturity' of critical awareness, is almost immediately reconstituted barely disguised by a stress on the 'mediated' and 'situated' nature of archaeology; the capacity of the past to evade the structure of its manufacture in the present (however much that may seemed to be 'reflexively' emphasised) is implicitly constructed.

To talk of these three technologies – and doubtless this rhetorical framework could be elaborated and extended – is not to imply archaeology (grasping once more the Nietzschean metaphor) to be necessarily 'evil', to suggest that modern excavation techniques, or recent heightened theoretical awareness has not marked an improvement, has not greatly extended the potential to generate a valid archaeological knowledge. What it is to imply is that that knowledge is not necessarily in itself 'good' either, that it has only been formed round that value through a specific process of discipline which needs itself to become the site of, in Foucauldian terms, an archaeological and then a genealogical investigation.

BEYOND GOOD AND EVIL: THE VALUE OF ARCHAEOLOGY

'Of course our interpretations may be incorrect, but our misreading of the language does not imply that the objects must remain mute' (Hodder 1987b, 2). But what does it imply? What does it mean for archaeology to cling on to a realm of meaning, to perpetuate the will to truth in the continual and admitted face of the fact, as in Hodder's statement, that truth in itself is not attainable? What is the implication of archaeology's explicit connection, most clearly in the recent post-processual movement, with what might in Nietzsche's terms might be seen as as a tradition of ascetic self-criticism? This paper has suggested that archaeology should exactly turn to the possibility of exploiting that long association to its advantage, finally to see the implication that where archaeology can be most effective and meaningful is not in relation to 'truth' at all, but outside it, reaching out to the potential of what Nietzsche calls 'overcoming'.

Indeed, to write a conclusion at this point, to pull together the strands of the argument into an overall unity, seems to run contrary to that notion of 'overcoming', to the Nietzschean and Foucauldian framework which has been elaborated here. It would be better perhaps to avoid the overtones of a 'conclusion', and the process of weaving together this text into the unity of a final, dominant meaning, and instead to do no more than indicate the intent of what has been written, leaving the text free to write its own endless conclusion. Much as Nietzsche in *On the Genealogy of Morals* sought to set up shifting and intersecting planes of meaning and understanding in the overlap of the three essays which make up that book, so, here, the attempt was made to open a similarly structured discussion of the relevance of some of Nietzsche's and Foucault's ideas to archaeology, not just to talk about, but also actively to construct a discussion of archaeology seeking to stretch the conventional parameters of archaeological discourse and meaning. That discussion was still very much of theoretical possibilities, very much in the mould of much post-processual debate. Yet, in a sense the real potential this paper aimed to uncover – the conclusion it might have had – is that the real place where this 'overcoming' can happen is in the process of archaeology itself, the interpretation of material culture, in the multitude of possible connections and abstractions which the very apparent inaccessibility of the archaeological past allows it to provide. It is exactly because archaeology is situated on the periphery of the social sciences, exactly because its data are disseminated, shattered, and broken across the millennia in a relationship to the 'real' past which must always seem difficult and elusive, that archaeology is precisely the place to locate a genealogy, to examine the possibility of going beyond good and evil.

This is not to say that archaeology should give itself over to some kind of relativist free for all. On the contrary, it is to point exactly to the relativism of the current state of archaeological knowledge based on endless oscillation between the 'goods' of such polarities as processual/post-processual, or in a more implicit way data and theory, past and present, active and reactive. What is an archaeology bound up in the admission that the past it interprets will never be finally known or knowable if not relativist? What this paper is about, indeed, is exactly the attempt to find a meaning of the past which does have, on its own level, a final security, a security reached by probing beyond that metaphysical limit which archaeology, more than any other social science, only ever sustained by an immense effort of will and memory.

In so far as this is a polemical call, it is a call to regain innocence, to in one way relearn to forget, to comprehend that beyond the struggle for memory is perhaps a meaning nonetheless; a call to enable archaeology as the primary site of this excavation by the very virtue of all those problems, limitations and difficulties it has become so fond of talking of. The archaeological past is eternally a foreign country. There lies its potential not its loss. Archaeology should site its project as that of recovering a kind of myth rather than a kind of history. It should push the ascetic tendency of a post-processual, even more so a truly post-structuralist posture, to its logical conclusion, to the juncture where the will to truth is questioned. There too the past may lie. Maybe.

ACKNOWLEDGEMENTS

I would like to thank Grant Chambers for encouragement and discussion in the course of writing this paper, and also Ian Hodder who read and commented on an earlier version.

NOTES

1. The point here in placing Nietzsche in relation to a schematic division between dialectics and post-structuralism is simply a rhetorical device to show that his thought cannot be easily be placed either within an archetypally essentialist or non-essentialist bracket; it is not to imply, of course, that Nietzsche cannot equally be sited in relation to a wide variety of other theoretical postures. See, for example, papers in Wood and Krell (1988).
2. The discussion of Nietzsche here is largely based on a brief exegesis and discussion of *On the Genealogy of Morals*, so as, within the limited space of this essay, to convey at least some of the flavour of Nietzsche in his own words, and to provide a basic introduction to his thinking. Needless to say, such partial treatment can be no substitute for an understanding based across the full breadth and detail of Nietzsche's writing. For recent syntheses of his philosophy see Kaufman (1974), Deleuze (1983), Wood and Krell (1988).
3. The distinction between active and reactive forces has also been an important, if implicit, grounding reference in the development of the broader current in twentieth-century philosophy. Note particularly the Nietzschean influence here on Freud and the pyschoanalytic theorisation of the development of male (active) and female (reactive) identity (for related discussion on this point, see Nordbladh and Yates, this volume).

REFERENCES

Barrett, J. (1988) 'Fields of discourse: reconstituting a social archaeology', *Critiques of Anthropology* 7(3): 5–16.
Binford, L. R. (1962) 'Archaeology as anthropology', *American Antiquity* 28: 217–25.
Binford, L. R. (1972) *An Archaeological Perspective*, London: Seminar Press.
Binford, L. R. (1983) *In Pursuit of the Past*, London: Thames & Hudson.
Binford, L. R. and Sabloff, J. (1982) 'Paradigms, systematics, and archaeology', *Journal of Anthropological Research* 38: 137–53.

Bourdieu, P. (1977) *Outline of a Theory of Practice*, Cambridge: Cambridge University Press.
Chippindale, C. (1988) 'The invention of words for the idea of prehistory', *Proceedings of the Prehistoric Society* 54: 303–14.
Clarke, D. L. (1968) *Analytical Archaeology*, London: Methuen.
Clarke, D. L. (1973) 'Archaeology: the loss of innocence', *Antiquity* 47: 6–18.
Cunliffe, B. W. (1982) *The Publication of Archaeological Excavations: The Report of the Joint Working Party of the CBA and DOE*, London: Council For British Archaeology.
Daniel, G. (1962) *The Idea of Prehistory*, London: Penguin.
Deleuze, G. (1983) *Nietzsche and Philosophy*, trans. H. Tomlinson, London: Athlone.
Derrida, J. (1976) *Of Grammatology*, trans. G. C. Spivak, Baltimore: Johns Hopkins University Press.
Derrida, J. (1978) 'Cogito and the history of madness', in J. Derrida, *Writing and Difference*, trans. A. Bass, London: Routledge.
Derrida, J. (1981) *Spurs: Nietzsche's Styles*, trans. B. Harlow, Chicago: University of Chicago Press.
Foucault, M. (1972) *The Archaeology of Knowledge*, trans. A. M. Sheridan Smith, London: Tavistock.
Foucault, M. (1973) *Madness and Civilisation: A History of Insanity in the Age of Reason*, trans. R. Howard, New York: Vintage.
Foucault, M. (1974) *The Order of Things: An Archaeology of the Human Sciences*, trans. A. Sheridan, London: Tavistock.
Foucault, M. (1975) *The Birth of the Clinic: An Archaeology of Medical Perception*, trans. A. M. Sheridan Smith, New York: Vintage.
Foucault, M. (1977) *Discipline and Punish: The Birth of the Prison*, trans. A. Sheridan, London: Penguin.
Foucault, M. (1979) 'This body, this paper, this fire', trans. G. Bennington, *Oxford Literary Review* 4(1): 4–29.
Foucault, M. (1980) *The History of Sexuality, Volume 1: An Introduction*, trans. R. Hurley, New York: Vintage.
Foucault, M. (1984) 'Nietzsche, genealogy, history', trans. D. F. Bouchard and F. Simon, in P. Rabinow (ed.) *The Foucault Reader*, London: Peregrine.
Frere, S. S. (1975) *Principles of Publication in Rescue Archaeology: Report by a Working Party of The Ancient Monuments Board for England Committee for Rescue Archaeology*, London: Department of the Environment.
Gardner, P. (1883) *The Types of Greek Coins: An Archaeological Essay*, Cambridge: Cambridge University Press.
Gibbs, L. (1987) 'Identifying gender representation in the archaeological record: a contextual approach', in I. Hodder (ed.) *The Archaeology of Contextual Meanings*, Cambridge: Cambridge University Press.
Giddens, A. (1979) *Central Problems in Social Theory*, London: Macmillan.
Harland, R. (1987) *Superstructuralism*, London: Methuen.
Hodder, I. (ed.) (1978) *Simulation Studies in Archaeology*, Cambridge: Cambridge University Press.
Hodder, I. (1982a) 'Theoretical archaeology: a reactionary view', in I. Hodder (ed.) *Symbolic and Structural Archaeology*, Cambridge: Cambridge University Press.
Hodder, I. (1982b) *Symbols in Action*, Cambridge: Cambridge University Press.
Hodder, I. (1982c) 'Sequences of structural change in the Dutch neolithic', in I. Hodder (ed.) *Symbolic and Structural Archaeology*, Cambridge: Cambridge University Press.

Hodder, I. (1984) 'Burials, houses, women and men in the European neolithic', in D. Miller and C. Tilley (eds) *Ideology, Power and Prehistory*, Cambridge: Cambridge University Press.
Hodder, I. (1986) *Reading the Past: Current Approaches to Interpretation in Archaeology*, Cambridge: Cambridge University Press.
Hodder, I. (1987a) 'The contribution of the long term', in I. Hodder (ed.) *Archaeology as Long Term History*, Cambridge: Cambridge University Press.
Hodder, I. (ed.) (1987b) 'The contextual analysis of symbolic meanings', in I. Hodder (ed.) *The Archaeology of Contextual Meanings*, Cambridge: Cambridge University Press.
Hodder, I. (1988) 'Material culture texts and social change: a theoretical discussion and some examples', *Proceedings of The Prehistoric Society* 54: 67–75.
Hodder, I. and Orton, C. (1976) *Spatial Analysis in Archaeology*, Cambridge: Cambridge University Press.
Kaufman, W. (1974) *Nietzsche: Philosopher, Psychologist, Anti-Christ*, Princeton: Princeton University Press.
Leone, M. (1984) 'Interpreting ideology in historical archaeology: the William Paca Garden in Annapolis, Maryland', in D. Miller and C. Tilley (eds) *Ideology, Power and Prehistory*, Cambridge: Cambridge University Press.
Lubbock, J. (1865) *Pre-Historic Times*, London: Longman.
Nietzsche, F. (1956) *The Birth of Tragedy* (with *The Genealogy of Morals*), trans. F. Golffing, New York: Anchor.
Nietzsche, F. (1966) *Beyond Good and Evil*, trans. W. Kaufman, New York: Vintage.
Nietzsche, F. (1969a) *On the Genealogy of Morals* (with *Ecce Homo*), trans W. Kaufman, New York: Vintage.
Nietzsche, F. (1969b) *Ecce Homo* (with *On the Genealogy of Morals*), trans. W. Kaufman, New York: Vintage.
Nietzsche, F. (1969c) *Thus Spoke Zarathustra*, trans. R. J. Hollingdale, London: Penguin.
Nietzsche, F. (1983) 'On the uses and abuses of history for life', in F. Nietzsche, *Untimely Meditations*, trans. R. J. Hollingdale, Cambridge: Cambridge University Press.
Renfrew, C. (1972) *The Emergence of Civilisation*, London: Methuen.
Rowlands, M. J. (1986) 'Modernist fantasies in prehistory', *Man* 21: 745–6.
Rowlands, M. J. (1987) 'The concept of Europe in prehistory', *Man* 22: 558–9.
Schiffer, M. (1976) *Behavioural Archaeology*, New York: Academic Press.
Shanks, M. and Tilley, C. (1982) 'Ideology, symbolic power and ritual communication: a reinterpretation of neolithic mortuary practices', in I. Hodder (ed.) *Symbolic and Structural Archaeology*, Cambridge: Cambridge University Press.
Shanks, M. and Tilley, C. (1987) *Re-constructing Archaeology*, Cambridge: Cambridge University Press.
Sheridan, A. (1980) *Michel Foucault: The Will to Truth*, London: Tavistock.
Thompson. M. W. (1977) *General Pitt-Rivers: Evolution and Archaeology in the Nineteenth Century*, Bradford-on-Avon: Moonraker.
Westropp, H. M. (1856) *Epochs of Painted Vases: An Introduction to Their Study*, London: Walton & Maberly.
Wheeler, M. (1954) *Archaeology from the Earth*, London: Penguin.
Wood, D. and Krell, D. F. (eds) (1988) *Exceedingly Nietzsche: Aspects of Contemporary Nietzsche Interpretation*, London: Routledge.

CHAPTER 10

The current of post-modernism is one that has run close to post-structuralism, and is indeed no easier to define than the latter. The post-modern world, as seen through the writings of critics such as Jameson, Baudrillard, or Lyotard, is one of reified image built on reified image, a plethora of meaningless forms divorced from context and content and disseminated and reproduced endlessly through the all enveloping media of mass communication. The post-modern world is one shaped around pastiche and simulacrum.

In this chapter, Walsh considers the implications of this post-modern condition for the practice of archaeology, and particularly for the discourse of presenting the archaeological past to the public. A notable development in recent years has been the 'take off' of the 'heritage industry' boom, with large numbers of 'theme' centres emerging to present a past for the 1980s and 1990s. For Walsh, this past, with its commercially oriented root in the 'leisure' market, is very much a post-modern past. The images of the past which are presented are the images of quaint nostalgia, of an idealised 'golden age' with the intent to satisfy what are deemed to be the needs of the contemporary consumer, not in any way to produce a critical discourse challenging the beliefs in which those very needs are rooted.

Walsh argues for the need to re-find this latter emphasis, to develop an actively deconstructive framework for the presentation of the past, seeking to inaugurate a critical consideration of the 'public' past around such themes as the history of the class struggle derived from an articulation with Marxism. Only in this way can the post-modern threat to the past be averted.

10

The Post-Modern Threat to the Past

Kevin Walsh

INTRODUCTION

Before embarking on a discussion of post-modernism it should be made explicit that I do not believe that post-modernism is a cogent philosophical, artistic movement. I believe that post-modernism is a condition which has its roots in the incongruous nature of the post-war world, most importantly in the changes imposed upon society by information technology and the development of post-industrial economies. This of course implies that post-modernism is a purely first world, and probably more specifically western capitalist, phenomenon rather than a universal one. However I do believe that certain so-called post-modern conceptions of the world are important and should be taken notice of.

WHAT IS POST-MODERNISM?

Any analysis of post-modernism should start with a discussion of what it sees as its philosophical roots, and also a brief outline of its precursor, modernism. Modernism can be considered as the period which started with the Renaissance, and the beginnings of 'real science' and the supposed discovery of 'truths' and 'facts', or rather claims for the possibility of objective truth about the world and even the universe in which we all live. It is during the modern period that the 'Metanarratives' emerged, discourse which implied a rigid objectivism and through this a thorough analysis of our world. Such 'Metanarratives' might include Darwin's theory of evolution and Marx's *Capital*. The arts and sciences were dominated (in the main) by *'great men and women'*. The great 'auteurs' were an intrinsic part of the modernist project, where there was a definite gap between high or real art and low art. The modernist project began to fail with the denial of the possibility of truth and value, and the questioning not only of scientific 'fact' but also of the legitimacy of the great 'auteurs' who dominated the arts and promoted (not necessarily actively) the division between high art for those who could afford it, and lumpen art and/or popular culture for the rest of the population.

It might be considered that post-modernism is to art and culture what post-structuralism is to philosophy. There has been developed what some see as a post-modern paradigm (most admit that there is not a unified post-modern theory) within which some people work. This is exemplified by some of the papers in the 'Post-modern' issue of *Theory, Culture and Society* (1988). In amongst this collection of papers we find some discussion of a post-modern sociology (Kellner 1988, 239–69). Nancy Frazer and Linda Nicholson discuss 'Feminism and Postmodernism', and seem keen to adopt some kind of 'post-modern' strategy where they argue for the combination of post-modernism's criticisms of functionalism and essentialism with feminism's conception of social criticism (Frazer and Nicholson 1988, 373–94). These types of post-modernism are clearly rooted in a philosophy of deconstruction and are essentially post-structuralist. They are in no way uniform in their conceptions of society and their roots lie in the post-structuralist movement.

This paper is more concerned with the widely held belief that post-modernism is actually a condition, or as Frederic Jameson calls it, 'the cultural logic of late-capitalism' (Jameson 1984a, 53–92).

I would argue that in part the development of what some may wish to label the post-modern world (Hebdige 1989, 48–53) lay with the development of the media of mass communications, initially the radio and the cinema, and then more importantly, during the post-war period, television, and more recently satellite television. These media have facilitated the removal of many of the boundaries between high and low art, and have helped to remove difference from the varied and rich cultures all over the world. Television has helped promote the onward marching machine of western hyper-consumerism all over the world, a world where the 'symbols of the free West' – Pepsi Cola, Coca Cola and the M.16 – permeate societies from Time Square to Red Square.

The philosophical roots of what is seen as the post-modern world of the 1980s lay with post-structuralism and its implicit denial of the possibility of discussing absolute 'truths' and 'values'. This stance is best summed up by David Byrne and the Talking Heads (*the* post-modern band) whose lyric of the first song on the *Naked* album encapsulates the post-modern conception of the world: 'Signs . . . Signs are lost/Signs disappeared/Turn invisible . . . No sense of harmony, no sense of time . . .' (Byrne 1988). This is essentially concordant with the post-structuralist conception of the world, largely to be found in the writings of Baudrillard, Derrida and Foucault (Harland 1987, 167–83). To reduce their ideas and do justice to them in a short section is impossible. However, some may argue that their conception of the possibility of meaning and reality is essentially nihilist, or if we are to be more optimistic we might be able to consider their conception of the world as pessimistic. The key to understanding post-structuralism and its potential for a nihilistic conception of the world is to realise the demise of the referent. The world of language is now perceived by some as consisting of an infinite number of signifiers (words or texts) that point to a signified or a group of signifieds conceived as the 'meaning effect'. Essentially the post-structuralist conception of language implies that the signifiers are now floating around with no referents (the real objects denoted by signifiers) to which they may attach themselves. Derrida writes about signifiers that point away from themselves before they are themselves, while for Baudrillard 'Today especially the real is no more than a stuck pile of dead matter, dead bodies and dead language' (Baudrillard 1980, 103). The most valuable point is that signifiers can trigger off an infinite number of meanings to any number of people and the meanings experienced by each person are going to be unique. Barthes, particularly, believes that this has important consequences for society as a whole due to the fact that without the possibility of any real meaning being attached to signs, society will be kept in a continuous state of confusion or at least in a blissful state of ignorance, where the negative takes precedence over the positive. We can know what something is not with greater certainty than we can know what something is. This is 'the tyranny of the code itself' (Harland 1987, 189). With the death of the subject comes the most important concept of all, the death of innovation. Society has reached the pinnacle of achievement in terms of culture, and all we can hope to do is to copy previous styles, remix them and call them something new. This is what Hewison (1987) might call the Laura Ashley effect.

In post-modernism this phenomenon has best manifested itself in architecture. Post-modern architecture was seen as an attack on modernist architecture and its destruction of the neighbourhood with its imposition of utopian high modernist buildings, exemplified by the high-rise block of the 1960s. This type of architecture was deemed by some to be authoritarian. The reaction against this style arrived in the form of post-modern aesthetic populism, which essentially involved the mixing of different styles. Housing estates today are filled with *mock mock-Tudor* buildings or, even worse, buildings that are a combination of a number of different styles. It might be possible to argue that, according to these criteria, the Renaissance was a post-modern phenomenon, but the Renaissance was a period when ideas were rediscovered after having been abandoned for a period of time. Post-modernism is about the regurgitation of last year's idea or style and mixing it with yesterday's. In terms of art, pastiche manifests itself especially well in art photography, particularly in the work of Sherrie Levine who is famous for photographing other people's photographs. Some have argued that this is deconstructive or even oppositional art.

THE POST-MODERN THREAT TO THE PAST

The post-modern world is a world dominated by pastiche, best defined as parody without humour or, as Frederic Jameson puts it, 'an imitation which mocks the original' (Jameson 1983, 113). The consequence of this, linked with the post-structuralist conception of language, is that we are left with a *simulacrum*, a hazy image with no reality dominating a society where innovation is doomed to failure as a consequence of the death of the subject. The death of meaning easily permits the reification of knowledge, the transformation of knowledge into an object or exploitable item. Once reified the commodification (transformation into a consumerable item) of these images is possible. People today are concerned with style rather than knowledge and meaning – which is well illustrated by *The Face*, a contemporary British magazine 'that goes out of its way every month to blur the line between politics and parody and pastiche; the street the stage the screen; between purity and danger, the mainstream and the margins; to flatten out the world' (Hebdige 1988, 161). A magazine like *The Face* is as Barthes said of the text, to be wandered through by the reader 'who will pick up whatever he or she finds attractive, useful or appealing' (Hebdige 1988, 162).

Post-structuralism, with its regime of floating signifiers, promotes a depthless synchronic history, partly as a consequence of its destruction of the historical metanarrative. For Derrida perception is continually divided from the thing itself, and so we can never catch up with the actual moment of our contact with any text. This implies that our perception of the world is like a dream and we can only hope for hazy glimpses of a past that has never really existed. This can be linked with Jameson's description of the use of a kind of preterite, or past perfect that removes the process of any past actions from the present. The past is thus cut off from the present and is perceived always as a completed and isolated event. All that is left is an historical surface which allows the 'reduction of historical periods to ruling class styles that are then pastiched' (Foster 1984, 68). This development of an ahistory, a history that is devoid of historical forms and materials, is the mediation of the past into myth.

Post-structuralism's floating signifiers with their irreverence for meaning permit the development of simulacra, with the past fragmented and rebuilt in various forms which are then ripe for reification and commodification. It is Jean Baudrillard, the 'champion of the Postmodern World', who has promoted post-modernism and its simulations and simulacra more than any other person, and consequently it is necessary to take a brief look at some of his writing.

Baudrillard moved away from Marxism in the early 1970s. This was largely due to his disagreement with Marx's conception of use value as part of a tangible material economy, which by its very nature promotes inequalities between use value and exchange value and in its turn obscures the exploitation of one class by another. Baudrillard was not concerned with the exchange of material products but rather with his belief that, today, economies are concerned with '. . . the operationalisation of all exchanges under the law of the code' (Baudrillard 1975, 121). Baudrillard believed that this form of societal control is far more pervasive than anything Marx considered, and he implied that the one way to defeat the regime of the sign is to push this system into a kind of overdrive. In the context of western economies he believed the this could be achieved through the consumption or absorption of signs. Because western political systems depend on there being elements of meaning in signs while the market relies on the alibi of use value and the fact (according to Baudrillard) that the masses take signs literally, implies that the people will drive the regime of the sign to its own logical self-destruction. Exactly how this will be achieved is not apparent. After the destruction of this system there is in Baudrillard's scheme no possibility of the emergence of something better.

Baudrillard makes it quite clear that he believes that modern politics is nothing but a simulacrum or simulation where one political stance, whether it be left or right, is really no different from the other. This is because politics for him is an ambiguous discourse, 'that conveys the impossibility of a determinate position of power . . . this logic belongs to neither party. It traverses all discourses without their wanting it' (Baudrillard 1983, in Poster 1988, 176).

Simulations and simulacra; 'the generation of models of a real without origin or reality' (ibid., 167). The real is substituted by signs which Baudrillard argues 'are a more ductile material than meaning' and permit the development of 'a hyperreal henceforth sheltered from the imaginary, and from any distinction between the real and the imaginary, leaving room only for the orbital recurrence of models and the simulated generation of difference' (ibid., 167).

In 'Fatal Strategies' Baudrillard argues that because society has been 'plunged into an inordinate uncertainty by randomness' it has become over-concerned with 'causality and teleology' (ibid., 189). Baudrillard believes that this has led to 'the hyperspecialisation of objects and people, of the operationalism of the smallest detail, and of the hypersignification of the slightest sign' (ibid.). The preoccupation with explaining everything, according to Baudrillard, becomes a burden which has its consequence in 'an excrescent interpretative system developing without any relation to its objective. All of this is a consequence of a forward flight in the face of the haemorrhaging of objective causes' (ibid.). This is the transition into the realm of hyperreality, where the nuclear arms race is justified because it has crossed the 'Dead point' (an unknown moment when every system passes a limit of questioning and is absorbed into a kind of ecstatic non-questioning stasis that can never be reversed): it has passed the limits of destruction. Baudrillard believes the 'the stage of war is abolished. There is no longer any practical correlation between the potential for destruction and its purpose, and referring to it becomes ridiculous' (ibid., 190). This is the hyperreal form of warfare which through its own ridiculousness ensures that it will never take place unless de-escalation re-establishes the 'exchange value' of weapons.

History too has supposedly crossed the 'Dead point' and Baudrillard argues that the desire to find the point where history ceased to be real or rectify the collapse of history is probably impossible, as the point that some seek

> may not even exist. It only exists if we can prove that previously there has actually been history – which becomes impossible once this point has been traversed. Outside the realm of history, history itself can no longer reflect, nor even prove its own coherence. This is why we call upon every previous epoch, every way of life, all modes of self-historicising and of narrating oneself with the support of proof and documentation (everything being documentary): we sense that in our era which is that at the end of history all this is invalidated.
>
> (ibid., 192)

Jean Baudrillard would seem to be the post-modern prophet of doom. He has adopted some of the basic tenets of post-structuralism and taken them to their 'hyperlogical' conclusion. Society is consumed by signs which promote the nihilistic. For Baudrillard there can be no totality, no reality, no social and definitely no history. The most society can hope for are simulations and simulacra, depthless regurgitations of signs. The accelerated over-production and reproduction of signs is the life blood of hyperconsumerism. Late western capitalism is quite clearly the hyper-context within which anything that can be marketed will be marketed, and if it doesn't sell it doesn't matter, put a new label on it and change its shape. Round tea bags – what will they think of next?

This is a world without meaning, where innovation is no longer possible. The consequence is a society sentenced to imprisonment in the past. Today's world is the schizophrenic world. Here there is a link with the work of Lacan. Lacan's concept of language (as described by Jameson 1983, 118–20) is the orthodox structuralist one, with language broken up into three elements, the signifier, the signified and the referent. The referent as far as post-structuralists are concerned is a nonentity, with the consequence that we can no longer talk about a reality not itself metaphysical. The other key to this concept is to see language as not naming things but to see the importance of the relationship between signifiers in the sentence that gives us the 'meaning effect'. Jameson (1983, 119) describes how this meaning effect or signified may in fact be a mirage or illusion. According to Lacan schizophrenia is a result of the breakdown of the relationship between signifiers. He believes that as far as people are concerned their perception of temporality and the continuity of personal identity is an effect of language, because language has a past and future and because the sentence moves in time. As a consequence of this we seem to have a real or experienced sense of lived time. Because the schizophrenic does not articulate language in that way s/he does not have the same perception of temporal continuity and therefore lives in a perpetual present. Events in the schizophrenic's life have no real continuity as the person's or persons' existence is discontinuous, perpetually interrupted by the other self.

A post-modernist might argue that it is in the world of the schizophrenic that we all live today. The reason for this lies with information technology and the media of mass communications. In the post-industrial economy, knowledge becomes reified in the form of information, which is *the* contemporary commodity. Information moves around the world so quickly, as does news (which is also information and therefore consumable), that production in the west becomes dehumanised. The mass media is seen as a simulacrum whose imperative is the 'over-production and regeneration of meaning'. Marx's statement that 'it is not the workman that employs the instruments of labour but the instruments of labour that employ the workman' (Marx 1954, 399) is especially apposite today, where value is put on the speed of light exchange and reproduction of meaning. Information is transmitted so quickly today that the sense of history is in danger of disappearing. As Jameson states we should think carefully about

> the media exhaustion of news: of how Nixon, and even more so Kennedy, are figures from a now distant past. One is tempted to say that the very function of the news media is to relegate such recent historical events as rapidly as possible into the past . . . the media seem to function as the very agents and mechanisms for our historical amnesia.
>
> (Jameson 1983, 125)

After a long and perhaps drawn out description of what post-modernism is I will now attempt to show why we should take notice of some of the problems that it throws up. As I stated at the beginning, I do not accept that post-modernism is a cogent movement; however I do believe that we should be aware of its features and some of its conceptions of the modern world and the status of the past in the world.

IS THERE A POST-MODERN THREAT TO ARCHAEOLOGY?

The collapse of the 'metanarratives' is linked to the collapse of the old centres of authority such as the state, the party and the church. This has been replaced with what Hebdige describes as 'the universal logic of the market'. The post-modern world is controlled from the boardrooms of the big multinationals where unrepresentative and unelected people make decisions that affect all of our lives. Today everything moves with the market, from the price of plutonium to the value put on the past and on archaeology. Today the position of the 'expert' or 'intellectual' is secondary to that of the entrepreneur; success is judged by the size of your 'wodge'. For example, a senior archaeologist directing a major project in the Fenlands is reported to have said at a recent meeting of the Prehistoric Society, one of the bastions of the archaeological establishment, that archaeology undergraduates should spend time learning how to use cash tills rather than learning how to survey (O'Sullivan and Young, pers. comm.).

Of most concern for archaeology, in the context of this analysis, is the heritage industry, especially the heritage centres and historical theme parks. But it could also be said that the subject as a whole is under threat from the post-modern condition.

The basic problem when presenting the past to the public is that as a 'text', each display according to post-structuralist doctrine will have an infinite number of meanings to the many different people who read these texts. But in the post-modern world this is just the tip of the problem for those of us who wish to present the past to the public. Commodification is probably the greatest obstacle to anything like a universally subjective interpretation of the past.

This problem of the commodification or reification of objects is important to grasp. Today people are interested in the *characteristics* of an article or object rather than its physical properties or *'meaning'*. In the world where senses are objectified and knowledge reified or commodified, punters see each heritage park or area as another *'experience'* to be bought in the same way that a packet of soap powder might be bought, although the needs satisfied by a visit to a heritage centre are obviously different from those satisfied by the soap powder. This is well illustrated by 'Catherine Cookson Country' in South Tyneside, England, where imaginary characters live in a landscape that no longer exists. Here something is created out of nothing. All of the tourist attractions, including ancient monuments (such as Jarrow Hall and St Paul's church), and areas of natural beauty (such as Marsden cliffs) are brought together in 'Catherine Cookson Country'. A brochure describes all of these places and somehow manages to link them with 'Cookson characters', including Rory 'The Gambling Man', Tilly Trotter, Fanny McBride and Katie Mulholland. We are even treated to photographs of these characters in this year's 'Catherine Cookson Country – That's South Tyneside' guide (Gillanders 1988, 2). Possibly the most extreme example of the whole image is the 'Cookson Country Carnival – Mardi Gras '88'. Here pastiche reaches a remarkable plateau where the imaginary characters of Cookson meet some All-American heroes, including Mickey Mouse. Finally everybody gets to experience the 'Northern Lights high technology illuminations'. Today's world lacks meaning to such an extent that it would appear that it is possible to create something out of nothing. It is as if we want to live inside a past or the nicest bits from a number of different pasts.

However we should not delude ourselves for one minute that the majority of people visit these places to learn. If they do learn anything I am sure that what they learn and how they ultimately perceive the past should worry most of us involved in archaeology. People are not necessarily looking for historical or archaeological differences, i.e. a learning experience concentrating on a specific period or archaeological/historical theme, but for the different characteristics of each commodity, in this case the theme park or heritage centre.

Robert Hewison has recently illustrated quite vividly some of the problems extant in the heritage industry (Hewison 1987). The past is often mediated as a piece of theatre, and transformed into something that it clearly never was. This is the case with Beamish Museum and Wigan Pier Heritage Centre, where the demise of industry is made acceptable by the appearance of heritage parks which celebrate and beautify our industrial past.

Heritage centres are problematic in terms of the techniques that they use to present and interpret the past. As far as I am concerned they can quite easily be perceived as a post-modern nightmare that becomes more real each year as more heritage centres open. One project which is still in the early stages of its development is the Raunds Heritage Park. A firm of heritage and tourist consultants have been consulting the 'experts' in our field to develop ideas as to how such a park might work. When I spoke to these consultants I was first of all informed that there was no theory to interpretation (this was a bit of a shock for someone who had spent hours ploughing through the increasing literature on the subject). On contacting the consultants later one of them said that they had realised that their comment was rather rash. However, they do plan to use actor interpreters, which as far as I am concerned will further cloud any images that people have of the past. The use of actors will create a series of surreal and artificial images of the past. On making this feeling clear to the heritage consultant, I was told that people do not want to be told the truth. As with other interpretation centres the past will be beautified, mediated through the post-modern pastiche, the simulacrum, where the Neighbours are good friends and live in an ideal world without strife or conflict, a world where we all take care of one another and the welfare state becomes obsolete.

The use of actor interpreters has become quite common – one of the most recent centres to open employing this style of interpretation is the Irish Life Viking Adventure in Dublin. Before going down into 'Dyflin', we are told by Edward Bourke in a recent issue of *Archaeology Ireland*, 'the visitors are first isolated from their modern environment in a darkened room where a video is shown introducing them to the history of Dublin and the Vikings' (Bourke 1988, 61). The contradiction here is manifest (unless of course videos are better preserved in waterlogged deposits than I realised!). After the customers have been 'removed from their modern environment . . . they are led into a time capsule and appear to be lowered through time back to 988' (ibid., 61). Mystification and a simulacrum are continually promoted in these interpretation centres.

The use of smells in both 'Dyflin' and Jorvik is an interesting area of analysis. If we try to perceive smell as a text in the same sense as speech, writing or film might be seen, it should be clear that smells as signifiers can have an infinite number of signifieds or meanings. However it is possible that the ambiguities initiated by smell are the most profuse and confusing; smell is the most acute of all the senses, because it is triggered by chemical reaction, and smell-induced memories are very personal, vivid and even poignant. The decontextualising of smells from the Viking period and placement in a twentieth-century tourist attraction seems highly dubious as each person visiting the centre will have a different perception or attitude towards a smell and it is quite likely that these will be very different from those held by the people who originally produced and lived with the smells.

This artificial image is in my mind best symbolised by the use of the hologram. The holographic image of a Viking helmet at York is the post-modern condition at its most dire. The object is an unreal projection, a product of ultramodern technology, fascinating to most people not because it is a Viking helmet (or rather an image of one) but because it is a hologram. In fact for a while some people could not see the hologram as the lasers were set in such a way that small children found the image difficult to make out. So for some people even the gimmicky signifier didn't exist let alone the referent itself. All of this illustrates how interpretation centres might be seen as merely attempting to titillate the senses and develop the simulacrum.

I hope that I am not alone in my fear of an archaeology reduced to an image of capitalism, and of a past mixed and matched in heritage centres or areas where any possible perspective of time is obliterated through pastiche and bricolage. We should be aware of the problem of unfettered competition where the 'free market' distorts reality and in fact moves away from it. This is blatant in the competition between the tabloids where, as Hebdige (1989, 51) illustrates, the distinction between news fact and extreme fantasy (or even blatant lies) has become increasingly blurred. Some people seem seriously to believe that Elvis Presley is in hiding somewhere, or that the Inner London Education Authority was run by a bunch of Trotskyite gays. If archaeology continues along its present road it will be forced further into competition in the 'free' market and in order to compete successfully with other forms of entertainment, and indeed compete with itself, it may be forced into the development of more exciting and fantastic, unreal pasts.

A post-modern past has already manifested itself in the medium of 'Dungeons and Dragons', a 'game' that cuts and mixes a science fiction fantasy future with the characteristics of a misplaced and unknown past. Recent research carried out by Heather Lomas at the University of Leicester has revealed that 15–16% of candidates applying to read archaeology in the university indicated that they have an interest in this activity (Lomas, pers. comm.). This is especially worrying if people who have an academic interest in archaeology are supporting and perpetuating a phenomena which promotes the perversion of history. This is clearly the commodification of something out of nothing, the logic of the free market taken to its extreme. Reality is discarded and mystical Arthurian pseudo-history is advanced.

The public's ability to differentiate between truth and falsity, or even economic truth, must be questioned as the role of the 'expert' or intellectual is marginalised under neo-conservative regimes. At the time of writing (March 1989) the director of the Victoria and Albert Museum in London is attempting to remove nine keepers, each of them a leading scholar in their particular fields. 'Visit the V & A, a nice cafe with not a bad museum attached', proclaims a recent advertisement. How is such a respected establishment supposed to maintain let alone advance its reputation if it follows such a barbaric strategy? The public are not assumed to be stupid, but they are 'being invited to relinquish the right in the verifiability of public truths *per se*' (Hebdige 1989, 51).

To sum up I would like to reiterate the point that post-modernism is not in itself a threat to the past: I do not believe that the designers of the heritage parks and centres work to a post-modern paradigm. However, post-modernism is a condition (or even a disease?) that does affect the way in which the past is perceived and presented. We do live in a world of confused meaning with information and images being processed and regurgitated at the speed of light. All information is consumerable and anything – or the image of anything – can be packaged and sold to a public that gets tired of styles very quickly and is concerned with the characteristics of an item rather than the intrinsic importance of the thing itself. As far as modern western society is concerned, certain aspects of the past can be appropriated and used, and the rest discarded. We are in danger of becoming little more than treasure hunters to provide for a society where the consumer rules, in a world where the concept of time is becoming redundant, where reverence is given to objects because of their authenticity rather than their importance in contributing to the understanding of past societies. It is essential that archaeologists as well as everybody else involved with the interpretation and presentation of the past recognises this threat. We should avoid this trivialisation of the past by arguing for a more political stance and the development of new modes for presenting the past to the public.

Should our political armoury include deconstruction or post-structuralist conceptions of society and culture? This paper has illustrated that some post-structuralist thought has helped to allow the development of the neo-conservative post-modern condition. Also it is quite clear that deconstruction can affect the legitimacy of any attempt at a totalising political interpretation of the past, although Jameson argues that in fact critical philosophies like deconstruction actually 'reconfirm the status of totality by their very reaction against it' (Jameson 1981, 53). He argues that history should be viewed as the experience of Necessity: '. . . why what happened (at first received as "empirical" fact) had to happen the way it did' (ibid., 101). He argues that necessity does not allow history to become a tangible object but allows it to exist as an imperative narrative.

The future of interpretation in archaeology lies in the recontextualisation of the object, and the acceptance of value-laden interpretations. The decontextualisation of the object in the museum display case,[1] or the creation of unreal pasts in Catherine Cookson Country or Wigan Pier are one and the same. It is the denial of the potential of history. Both museums and heritage parks develop some kind of simulation and shallow titillation. The contextless object in the non-context of the display case is potentially the signifier at its most rampant. It is the meaningless *objet d'art* to be appreciated only by the initiated few, while the heritage park is also guilty of depthless ahistory, the only context of which is that of the market.

Eagleton (1986, 85) argues, in his discussion of Michael Ryan's articulation of deconstruction and Marxism, that the author seems to believe that for there to be a truth there must be a context, and that for Ryan capitalism is contextless thought. Perhaps this is because the right, and especially the neo-conservative post-modernists, appear to believe that capitalism is the natural state of being for society. Nature itself is beyond definition and is therefore not definable as a context. Capitalism, however, is not contextless thought. In fact it works in the biggest context of them all, that of money and profit. This is the only real context within which capitalism functions and consequently it denies all truth other than that of the reality of profit. What thought there is revolves around the legitimacy and success of the free market. This is exemplified on South Tyneside where there appears to be no definable historical context for the many and varied attractions being thrown together in Catherine Cookson

Country. To argue for the viewing of phenomena in context is, for Eagleton, akin to Marxism where social phenomena are viewed in a material context. This has to be the way forward.

If deconstruction itself is viewed in context then its birth too might be explainable as a phenomenon. Jameson illustrates how the desire to 'deconstruct' the 'totalisation' of government in France should be seen as the context for the emergence of post-structuralism. During the post-war period French governments were keen to centralise the government not only of France but the whole of the French empire (in fact the French government until recently may have been the most centralised of all western European states). In the light of the failure of the radical politics of the mid- to late-1960s, the earlier war in Algeria and the break-up of the empire in Indonesia, the desire to develop countercultural, single interest and local political movements in France may be seen as crucial for the French left. In other countries this may not have been the key to success for the left. Jameson points out that in the United States, where a very heterogeneous society with many varied countercultural and single interest groups exist, 'the attack on the concept of "totality" in the American framework means the undermining and repudiation of the only realistic perspective in which a genuine Left could come into being' (Jameson 1981, 54). Clearly deconstruction cannot and should not be written off hastily – post-structuralism clearly has something to offer Marxists – but it is dangerous not to deconstruct deconstruction, or else it will be abused as it has been by certain neo-conservatives.

WHAT IS TO BE DONE?

How then, in practice, should the past be presented? Here there should be a role for mass communications theory. The mechanisms used for presenting the past can be considered as instruments of mass communication because they are processes 'of communication operating at the society wide level, readily identified by their institutional characteristics (a mixture of purpose, organisation and actual activity)' (McQuail 1987, 7). One strategy that might be used to 'deconstruct' the presentation of the past is to ask the questions that are recognised as fundamental by mass communications theorists to the investigation of such media. 'Who communicates to whom? (sources and receivers); Why communicate? (functions and purposes); How does the communication take place? (channels, languages, codes); What about? (content, objects of reference, types of information); What are the consequences of communication? (intended or unintended)' (McQuail 1987, 7).

There must also be a role for feedback from those who experience the interpretations and presentations of the past. Ideally, there must be a greater role for the 'expert' to communicate directly with the punter.

Guided tours of sites and museums are essential. A guide can legislate for the various types of visitor to a site and consequently pitch the information given at the right level and also respond and give feedback at the required level. The importance of the display case needs to be limited, while the simulacra and pastiches of the past must be revealed for the shallow, meaningless consumer ephemeras that they are.

We must accept different readings of the past and should argue for our interpretations from a clear political stance and let them stand the test of criticism from those who disagree with us. It is the job of archaeologists and historians to ensure that historical phenomena are contextualised and not allowed to be mixed and matched, glossed over and packaged, to facilitate their marketability. It is our duty to ensure that the public are aware that the past was not a Geordie nirvana, and that what they are being offered today in many places is often little more than half the truth with a few gimmicks thrown in.

In their book *Reconstructing Archaeology* Shanks and Tilley (1987) suggest a strategy for representing the past. They show the need for 'heterogeneity and difference' in the presentation of the past and that the reification of the object must be avoided at all costs. They argue clearly for greater political content in displays and for a removal of the boundaries between the producers of the past and the consuming public. This strategy also includes the avoidance of permanent displays and the need to 'emphasise authorship and changing perceptions of the artifactual past' (1987, 98). Artefacts should be removed from display cases and handled by the community. However, one of the suggestions is slightly worrying. It is proposed that some displays should

> break artifacts from fixed chronological narrative and from their original contexts and reassemble them with contemporary artifacts similarly decontextualised: juxtaposition, montage, (a) means of drawing attention to and engaging with official cultural meanings of the artifact and effacing an ideological critique of commodification, and (b) as a means of illustrating alternative (non-commodified) meanings.
>
> (Shanks and Tilley 1987, 98)

The decontextualisation of artefacts from various different contexts and mixing them in a kind of post-modern bricolage is inviting confusion. It is difficult to understand how a flint axe juxtaposed with a Coke can and a sextant might tell the public anything about the societal contexts from which any of these objects originally came. It is quite likely that such a display could find itself in an art gallery and commodified before you could say 'Jean Baudrillard'!

In conclusion it should be clear that there has to be the development of a framework or series of frameworks that must be applied to the interpretation and presentation of the past. These frameworks will, of course, be essentially political and context based. Each framework will implicitly accept the need for discussion about what the practitioners (archaeologists, historians, etc.) consider to be valid or considered 'truths' or themes. One such framework will accept the need for a Marxist perspective. A valid or considered 'truth' or theme must be that of the class struggle throughout the whole of history. Political content must be a prerequisite for all presentations of the past. Mechanisms for displaying the class-based nature of British history need to be developed. At the same time we should be 'deconstructing' the mechanisms that are being used today to present the past, as well as *what* is being presented. Naturally any framework can be subjected to deconstruction. This should be welcomed, and can only be healthy in comparison to the possible unassailability of the 'post-modern' developments with which this paper has been concerned. The post-modern world is a world where style is more important than meaning, a world where, according to Horne (1984, 1), 'the remnants of past cultures are resurrected so richly and professionally that the people of those days would not recognise their own artifacts'.

NOTES

1. Although this paper has not been concerned with the role of the museum and its position as an interpretative and presentational mechanism in relation to the post-modern condition, it is essential that museums are considered here in the context of how the past might be presented.

REFERENCES

Baudrillard, J. (1975) *The Mirror of Production*, trans. M. Poster, St Louis: Telos.
Baudrillard, J. (1980) 'Forgetting Foucault', *Humanities in Society* 3(1).
Bourke, E. (1988) 'Thoughts on the Irish life Viking centre', *Archaeology Ireland* 2(2).
Byrne, D. (1988) From 'Blind' on the *Naked* album. Warner Brothers Music Ltd.
Carroll, D. (1988) *Paraesthetics*, London: Methuen.
Derrida, J. (1978) *Writing and Difference*, London: Routledge & Kegan Paul.
Eagleton, T. (1986) *Against the Grain*, London: Verso.
Featherstone, M. (1988) 'In pursuit of the postmodern: an introduction', *Theory, Culture and Society* 5(2/3).
Foster, H. (1983) *The Anti-Aesthetic: Essays on Post-Modern Culture*, Port Townsend, USA: Bay Press.
Foster, H (1988) '(Post)modern polemics', *New German Critique* 33.
Frazer, N. and Nicholson, L. (1988) 'Social criticism without philosophy: an encounter between postmodernism and feminism', *Theory, Culture and Society* 5(2/3).
Gillanders, P. (1988) *Catherine Cookson Country: Visitor Guide*, South Tyneside Council.

Harland, R. (1987) *Superstructuralism*, London: Methuen.
Hebdige, D. (1988) *Hiding in the Light*, London: Routledge.
Hebdige, D. (1989) 'After the masses', *Marxism Today* 33(1).
Hewison, R. (1987) *The Heritage Industry*, London: Methuen.
Horne, D. (1984) *The Great Museum*, London: Pluto.
Huyssen, A. (1984) 'Mapping the postmodern', *New German Critique* 33.
Jameson, F. (1981) *The Political Unconscious*, London: Methuen.
Jameson, F. (1983) 'Postmodernism and consumer society', in H. Foster (ed.) *The Anti-Aesthetic: Essays on Post-Modern Culture*, Port Townsend, USA: Bay Press.
Jameson, F. (1984a) 'Postmodernism, or the cultural logic of late capitalism', *New Left Review* 146.
Jameson, F. (1984b) 'The politics of theory', *New German Critique* 33.
Jameson, F. (1988) 'Beyond the cave: demystifying the ideology of modernism', in F. Jameson, *The Ideologies of Theory: Essays 1971–1986.* vol. 2, London: Routledge.
Kellner, D. (1988) 'Postmodernism as social theory: some challenges and problems', *Theory, Culture and Society* 5(2/3).
Kroker, A. and Cook, D. (eds) (1988) *The Postmodern Scene: Experimental Culture and Hyper Aesthetics*, London: Macmillan.
Lowenthal, D. (1985) *The Past is a Foreign Country*, Cambridge: Cambridge University Press.
Marx, K. (1954) *Capital: A Critique of the Political Economy*, vol. 1, trans. S. Moore and E. Aveling, Moscow: Progress Publishers.
McQuail, D. (1987) *Mass Communication Theory: An Introduction*, London: Sage.
Poster, M. (ed.) (1988) *Jean Baudrillard: Selected Writings*, Cambridge: Polity.

Conclusion:

Reading the Signs: Responses to *Archaeology after Structuralism*

Michael Shanks

We are in the disciplinary court of archaeological reason. What are the charges to be?

INCOHERENT FRAGMENTATION OF ARCHAEOLOGY THE DISCIPLINE

The title is *Archaeology after Structuralism: Post-Structuralism and the Practice of Archaeology*. But where is the archaeology? The key word in the title is surely 'and'. And archaeology appears as a supplement. There is no archaeology as it is practised and little engagement with archaeological literature. The chapter by Yates gets only so far as considering the categorisation of an infrequent figuration in Scandinavian rock art. The charge is incoherence. What holds the book together? Not archaeology, not a tackling of archaeological problems or issues, but the writing of an assortment of mainly French intellectuals. The authors are expounding a fragmentation and dispersal of the discipline archaeology; but this is for the most part a parade of reviews, digests, commentaries on fashionable continental authors, a parasitic and marginal miscellany. Marginal because it is unlikely that the essays will make much impact on the large body of writing about post-structuralism which already exists. Are archaeologists to copy these authors, give up their unreflective discourse, escape the chains of the signified and write essays on *différance* and Foucault? Shattered remnants of a non-discipline?

IDEALISM OF THE ACADEMY: A FETISHISM OF AUTHORS

It often seems as if reality is being sought within the pages of books. Many of the chapters are simply writings about books. Bagnal expounds the work of Cixous, Irigaray and Kristeva; Maley opposes Foucault with Derrida. Consider the introduction which seems to aim to give a unity to the book with a précis of key essays and books. Freud and Lacan are treated most uncritically by Nordbladh and Yates, as if their writing was certainty, even reality. Long detours by Yates into Freud, Lacan's reading of Freud, and Derrida's reading of Lacan and Freud verge on the scholastic, considering the redundancy of much of the discussion in the argument of his chapter. Bapty writes that the great theoretical superstructure in his chapter is a use of Nietzsche 'to frame a discussion' (p. 243), but the discussion is mostly about Nietzsche and Foucault.

Given that post-structuralism is best conceived as an assemblage of writings, it is reasonable that the names of writers should recur, but I am not alone in suspecting a fetishism of authors: Moran and Hides cynically refer to the Jacques Derrida club of archaeology (p. 212), to the desire to locate and cite origins, in this case intellectual authorities.

This is the intellectual idealism of the academy: writing on writers on intellectual matters taken to constitute reality and history. Is this the meaning of the 'ubiquity of textuality'? It does mean distance and abstraction. It seems assumed that the relevance of the theoretical expositions will be visible from afar, that we all share a fascination with 'post-structuralism'. But we are far from concrete everyday reality. The assumption is made that shifts in Grand Theory or Great Ideas direct history (as in Burr's chapter). Abstractions abound: modernity (Tilley); post-modernity (Walsh). Bapty's is a theatre of abstractions: 'we are left with three . . . overlapping stories concerning the emergence of good and evil, bad conscience, and the ascetic ideal' (p. 250). Later we read of the actions of ressentiment and *différance*, reactive and active modes, master and slave morality, and the wills to power and truth. Where is the particularity of history, the reality of people's lives? 'It is inappropriate and moreover counterproductive to attempt to find a "real" woman'! (Bapty and Yates, p. 23). Personal identity is here dispersed into 'specular identifications'. On the other hand Tilley writes autobiographically of the politics of the personal. Moran and Hides attempt a subversion of the identity of archaeology as an academic discipline with their own autobiographical references to family and friends. This is where Grand Theory touches down – incidental autobiography.

Tilley calls for a materialist understanding of archaeology as contemporary practice and there are words elsewhere about power and the academy. But there is little appearance of such an understanding.

MAKING TOO MUCH OF THEORY: THEORETICISM

The book is top heavy with theory. Abstractions are formulated, worked on and purified. But what happens then? Application? Is the book not another example of the principle of the primacy theory over practice (assuming that archaeological practice involves more than writing about post-structuralism)? Burr certainly reasserts this priority: 'theoretical overhaul leads to positive political action' (p. 56). Waterman argues the need to temper Foucault's all-encompassing discourse and disciplinary powers with an awareness of ideology; but he sticks at references to the literature on ideology and its theory, providing no practical working with the concept, only the diagnosis of Foucault's theoretical flaw. Bapty's long rumination on antinomies and dialectic and Nietzsche excretes the inconsequential conclusion that the Nietzschean distinction active–reactive can be applied to processual and post-processual archaeology, and this polarisation should be overcome. Does the book not show that there can be too much theory, that there is a need to work theory through doing archaeology rather than reading Nietzsche? Nor can archaeology be theorised away with the questioning of the concept of the academic discipline. It is what archaeologists do. How many of the authors want to do 'archaeology'?

HYPOCRISY

The book fails to deliver what it promises. Bagnal writes positively about discovering and expressing feminine experience and identity. But what about herself? Where is she in the text? Is she not present as a (masculine) voice of knowledge and authority – reviewing the literature and performing critique? Moran and Hides are perhaps present in their paper, at least anecdotally. The style of their paper is meant, I think, to be a self-conscious mode of writing in accordance with their argument that archaeology must be recognised as written, and in an elite context: hence the involvement of family and friends and school projects. But here they are writing in a most academic collection of papers from an academic conference. Is this not the elite context they censure? Is this the place for their cynical rejection of academia, calls for the discipline to be open to all, denying containment within the academy? For whom are they writing here? They criticise the 'Jacques Derrida club' of archaeology, yet the style of the beginning of the chapter (with tortuous asides and parentheses) looks very much like an imitation of Derrida. A fetishism of style rather than of author citation? Whatever, the biggest question in the charge of failing to deliver is: where is the *real* post-structuralist archaeology as opposed to its theory?

POLITICAL NAIVETY

A strong split between theory and practice might well bring problems of politics. And it does with this book. The denial of the possibility of stability and system, any meta-narrative or discourse, leads to political voluntarism, where action depends on individual inclination (Burr, Tilley), to sloganism (Burr), and to Yates' abstract anarchistic and libertarian archaeology. The negative cynicism of Moran and Hides surely means writing themselves out of any archaeological politics. Yes, we can agree there should be an end to elitism and a democratic existence for archaeology; but what should be done now? Should we abandon 'archaeology' because it has been shown to be theoretically and politically flawed?

So there are calls for archaeology to be political; but apart from some general comments about politics and modernity and capitalism, the proposed focus and context of action is narrow – again it is writing, the university and Cambridge in particular. And the calls are from theory. They can be detached from what many of the papers might seem to be about – furthering academic careers through importing the latest fashionable French theory into an academic world and publishing industry which welcomes the advent of a new paradigm, new intellectual fads.

ELITISM

The authors take the role of experts, summarising and explaining to the reader the meaning of Freud, Derrida, Foucault. The Introduction is the voice of Teacher – helpful notes on post-structuralist writers. Tilley criticises such consumerism of the academy whose high abstraction evades relating directly to what we do: we should be arguing with people rather than over a purification of theory by self-appointed experts. But Tilley's 'little history of archaeological modernity' (pp. 130–6), however ironical, is of individual academics and abstractions (such as science and system), as if all that really matters in archaeology has been in the minds and hands of mainly Cambridge academics. Moran and Hides abuse the institutional constitution of knowledge and disciplines as ritual authorities. But what is theirs other than a chastising voice of authority? They reference friends and relatives as well as academic sources, but these references are entirely incidental to the argument of their paper. The appearance of their friends and relatives is a mere stylistic device signifying the self-conscious act of writing, presence of the authors. Rather than take up *seriously* the problems and questions posed and tackled by these people, they choose to patronise and stick with the academy, however cynically and negatively.

We have read the introduction, which tells us that real women don't exist (see also Bagnal, note 2). Burr's idealism sees the end 'of ontology, epistemology and metaphysics'; the 'categories of subject, object, and language' can now be dissolved (p. 57). Yates ends with a declaration of the destruction (in theory) of man, of the ego, of identity, and announces the arrival of superman. Walsh displays a troubling fear of the uneducated mass of people freed from the guidance of the expert. Ordinary people and archaeological questions appear incidental to these arguments over the intellectual concerns of relatively secure academics. This is indeed a 'privileged indulgence' (Moran and Hides p. 211).

RELATIVISM

But stop –

Whose writing is this? Whose voice? What tone?

Aggressive and masculine, it is the voice of academic legality, inquiring, assessing, chastising. We can hear this voice in many of the chapters in this book. The never-ending cycle of critique and academic 'liberal' debate needs such competitive voices, constantly setting up oppositions, finding flaws, pursuing criticism, overturning one system to set up another to be overturned.

I have used this voice myself (and many of the criticisms which appear in this chapter could be made quite legitimately of much of what I have done and written). I want to leave such voices behind now.

I have been reading this book, and much of the book is about reading post-structuralist writers. Tilley is absolutely right in putting forward the question of just what a reading is. One type of reading might be the kind of critique I have just given. Another more 'empiricist' response might be to try to simply express the meaning of the book, to condense. I would rather present now a kind of 'symptomatic' reading. This involves supplying meanings and relevances, working on symptoms of what I think the book is really about, symptoms of an underlying 'problematic' (a system of particular themes which involve asking certain questions and not others). Althusser and Balibar put it quite well in their book *Reading Capital* (1979): a symptomatic reading 'divulges the undivulged event in the text it reads, and in the same movement relates it to a *different text*, present as a necessary absence of the first'.

I think I am not alone in feeling deeply a breakdown in a consensus over archaeology, its place in the academic world, education. There are some awkward, though teasingly simple-sounding, questions which bother me. And I have been thinking of these questions while reading *Archaeology after Structuralism*. These simple questions are for me the 'different text'. The absent text. My response.

WHAT IS ARCHAEOLOGY?

I have been interested for some time now in what attitudes, what desires, orientations bring us to archaeology and guide the basic archaeological experience of digging and writing the material past. I am thinking here of an exploration of archaeology's sedimented meanings, an excavation of the archaeological project, investigation of the archaeological unconscious. What interests me; why I bother with archaeology.

CONCLUSION

Many of the chapters of this book explore the root metaphors which feed archaeological understanding. Burr writes of the idea of knowledge as landscape; spatial and specular metaphors; the scientist as observer on a journey to the past. Moran and Hides deal with the idea of 'origin' as it relates to the identity of archaeology: distance and location again lying within the notion of archaeological knowledge and the legitimacy of the discipline. Yates also considers 'origin' and archaeological work conceived vertically, excavating from present surface to hidden depths, to the origin, the past which will guarantee our efforts: archaeology as the science of the origin. To depth and the vertical Yates opposes horizontal thinking 'along chains of differences'. Bapty's whole chapter aims to re-excavate the meaning of archaeology, as the title claims. He brings in asceticism (denial and discipline of the self; seen for example in the minutiae of archaeological procedures), Nietzschean moralities, notions of madness, irrationality and reason, and the panoptic observer.

For me these little 'ruminations' are invitations to think more deeply about how archaeologists see themselves and what they are doing. Are we detectives? Or white-coated scientists transforming dirty past into clean hygienic knowledge? Is the past out there, down there, another place, another time? Or is it somehow subtly within us but beyond us? What about the fascination of things from the past? Does the aura they undoubtedly contain for many constitute a fetishism of objects, to be replaced with a play of signs and meanings? Is this all to do with our consumer culture and the way we live with objects now? Most of this is the unwritten prehistory and myth of archaeology. It is good that it is now receiving attention.

One answer to the question 'what is archaeology?' is that it is what archaeologists do. It becomes a question of archaeological professionals and society today. Many work in universities and education, including now myself. There is much in this book about the identity of archaeology as an academic discipline, as a 'subject'. The whole book is very much set against a separate identity for archaeology (though see Walsh on the archaeological expert). The general structure of the book clearly indicates that the authors and editors think that archaeology's intertextuality means it cannot legitimately be divorced from much wider questions and practices. Archaeology has long been noted for its strong links with other academic subjects. What is relatively new here is the attack on all disciplinary boundaries on the philosophical grounds of semiotics and the theory of discourse. Academic meanings and the liberal humanist model of the disciplines and education are under question on other grounds in Britain with universities and polytechnics channelled by central government into resourcing less the pure abstract disciplines, and more technological and vocational courses and projects. 'Britain' needs engineers and managers, not philosophers and ethnomusicologists. The coincidence of these questionings – post-structuralist questioning of disciplinary identity and the 'new vocationalism' – poses questions of political strategy to which I will come soon.

WHAT SHOULD ARCHAEOLOGISTS DO? POLITICS?

If we say that archaeology is what archaeologists do, an ethics is implied – what *should* archaeologists do? And in particular – what should academics in archaeology do?

The ideology critiques of archaeology ('critical' archaeology) which have been produced particularly since the late 1970s have located archaeological theories and practices firmly in the contemporary world and have drawn attention to the political nature of this location. Archaeological knowledges are involved. This book represents another current: argument is presented concerning textuality and discourse. 'Writing' is not at all innocent, textuality constitutes reality, and discourse (thoroughly material) is to be examined in terms of strategies for producing meaning: power–truth–knowledge. Maley puts it succinctly as discussion around the textuality of history and the historicity of texts.

Following this body of work are calls for archaeologists to be more reflective of their place in contemporary post-modernity, for a politics of the discipline. So one answer to the question of what archaeologists should be doing is that they should be doing politics. For most, if not all, of the writers in this book this is to be a radical politics of criticising and opposing authorities – the system of the discipline or publishing industry, the professorial system of patronage, or public archaeology.

What does this critical position mean and involve?

Bagnal's elucidation of the work of the three French feminists Cixous, Irigaray and Kristeva, shows the contrast between working within institutionalised structures of power and meaning (in this case of masculinity), and outside, attempting to forge new modes of power and expressions, opposing the institution. Moran and Hides present an extreme oppositional strategy – opposition to anything labelled archaeology. But they are hardly working outside the discipline here in this book. There is the problem of devising, setting up and practising alternative ways of doing, feeling and writing. Archaeology the institution is dammed in theory – what comes next? Moran and Hides don't apply themselves much to this question, nor do they seem very interested in what might come after the fall of institutional archaeology – there are more important things.

There are suggestions elsewhere in the book as to what archaeologists might do in being critical. The main focus is on new ways of writing the past. Burr writes of the aesthetic, the centrality of metaphor and irrationality (p. 57). Yates is for writing the liberation of 'becoming from

CONCLUSION

ontology' (p. 195). Bapty too relates aesthetic consciousness and calls for a regaining of innocence: the archaeological project as a regaining of myth. Maley re-emphasises a critical approach. Walsh is alone in standing for the *archaeological* expert. Tilley is most explicit on strategy, on what to do: writing to involve the reader, critical reading, self-reflection, and looking out for the careerist colleague in the micropolitics of the academy. Archaeology is to be embraced as an 'intervention in the present, part of living' (p. 130).

But are these internal or oppositional strategies – working within or outside the discipline? Are they meant to change anything? Are they to break down disciplinary distinctions? Will anyone else necessarily follow these suggestions? Are they ends in themselves? I am not clear about these matters.

Moran and Hides warn of the danger of being contained within the academic structures you are opposing. These ways of working or recommended attitudes or philosophies are perfectly compatible with an elite academy. Ian Hodder has also pointed out in an article in *Norwegian Archaeological Review* (1989) that the writing of the critique this book represents has and does depend on the very structures criticised (see this article for many of the points I am raising). We might write cross-disciplinary works (this book is an example) or avoid the main academic publishers, or produce alternative texts. This may be acceptable to some; but it is not challenging or changing the system, if that is the aim. So this book addresses the question of what academics in archaeology should be doing. It gestures towards the political, an involvement in the present, but severely limits the scope of this involvement.

There is a marked shift in many of the chapters away from questions of history (in the sense of what and how particular things emerge in history) and people's experience, towards language. That is, of course, the post-structuralist moment (in spite of Foucault's historical works). The exhortation is to write, express differently, to experience and express textuality. Here I would like to bring in an old distinction between the aestheticisation of politics and a politicisation of writing. I think that this book is encouraging an aestheticisation of politics because there is no real politics in the book. Its absence is translated into new ways of writing, a stylistics. This is not immediately 'political' or 'rational', but it does have an ethical component (for example, it is good to involve the reader). In opposition to totalising (political) theory – another 'system' – much of the book's politics is gestural or of the individual writer – a personal stand, an aesthetic exploration. In the background are grand abstracts: philosophical shifts – post-modernity, the end of epistemology. In opposition to totalising theory is a liberating pluralism; although not just anything goes.

Here I see another coincidence. Heritage, the packaged post-modern past, also depends upon an aesthetics of style: neither rational nor political, it is a history of affect, but without a critical edge – anything goes. Involving pastiche and humour it feeds on the entertaining or libidinal gesture, is diffused and engages local sentiment, but in the service of an abstraction – the *national* heritage. Walsh deals with some of the aspects of this coincidence and the question of heritage.

A politicisation of writing would involve bringing 'political' questions into academic writing. These include the simple issues I am addressing now and those I have mentioned – changes in state and university education, academic disciplines and funding, and the public past as it is becoming. For me these questions are central to theory; they are what theory would most profitably be about.

Power: *contra* Foucault, power is not only dispersed and capillary, but also located, in university authorities, committees, government departments. These agencies do act and change things. So why not find some way of using these mechanisms of power?

Theory: I am firmly in support of a political archaeology rooted in the present, but involving a theory constructed from the ground up, a bottom-up theory, beginning with our practice now and what it means. Top-down theory finds traces of those practices and meanings in high abstract discussions. I do not think we can afford this indulgence any more.

READING AND WRITING: WHY, HOW AND WHO DO WE READ?

I am not now in sympathy with the mode of reading to be found in much of this book. Belonging to top-down theory it synthesises, problematises, abstracts and packages for the academy. Here are potted introductions and excursions into many of the newly fashionable great thinkers, made palatable for student consumption and for those without the time for a slow and symptomatic reading. It is ironic, given the much proclaimed death of the author, that the bodies of writings headed by a name such as Foucault or Derrida should be treated as a unity and thoroughly worked over for theoretical consistencies, inconsistencies, trends and ideas. These are great authors; look within their pages for the answers to the questions you should be asking. And a whole publishing industry of secondary literature helps you do this. Such reading (for it is not really writing) aids the assimilation of fascinating writers into the academy; and so assimilated, what they might say to us is neutralised.

But many of the writers referenced in these pages do address vital issues. This book shows this. This is why it should be read.

How should we read? Tilley has some good pointers. Here are some ideas taken from how I would like to think of these writers and others.

Power and a will to truth may well secrete texts, but their medium is people. We read people: and we are reading as persons. I am not thinking of a return to the ideology of the creative mind or personality. What I mean is that Derrida for example has his own projects, his own historical existence as a French intellectual in the political and academic life before and after the failure of radical left-wing activism in 1968. He is not only to be read as a textual presence wrecking the logocentric metaphysics of post-Socratic western thought. Apart from any ideology critique which may apply to an author (relating their work to political processes and cultural codes), this means situating a writer relative to the purpose we have in reading, in our political and cultural project. I feel it is better to read to inform my own projects, reading for what a writer says to me now, in this particular region of my experience, reading books for myself, ourselves.

We might want to read Foucault 'for himself' or for what the texts represent in themselves. But we might also recognise that acting on that reading and writing in a particular way might further his simplification and assimilation into the academy. I do not think I can presume to say what Foucault really meant (and there is a tone in this book of such an expert knowledge of authors). There is always a surplus; that is why these writers are worth reading; they are always much more than their readings. And it does not matter whether we get *them* right. I *can* say: here is something or some question which means to me, to us; and look, Foucault has a great deal to say which might inform us how we might think and act. Relating what I read to self, experience, politics; this is a particularist and I might even say inductive approach. I think of it as involving something of a rescue of meaning. In the gap between the work of writing and myself lies the possibility of a redemption of meaning, a particular meaning born in my creative reading, a meaning which overshoots the text I have read. This 'redemption' of meaning is, I believe, an active strategy of avoiding the neat assimilation of writers who can inform, because every true reading is a new one, located in the moment of reading, saturated with prospect, project, questioning.

There are signs of this particular or particularist way of reading in this book and, of course, there are many ways of reading. But I am thinking here of the question of what archaeologists should be doing; and for the purpose of establishing an archaeological readership of post-structuralist writers, establishing a forum for the enlightened discussion of the key issues found in this book, it is important that we get our reading right and do not read ourselves into an elitist and esoteric ghetto, talking to ourselves and producing the odd introductory text for 'beginners'. The way to convince other *archaeologists* that Foucault is worth reading is to show how he relates to what we think about and do as archaeologists. I have stressed us as archaeologists (with all the implications that has for the 'discipline') because we risk the danger of denying ourselves as archaeologists when other archaeologists are not interested in Foucault, so we avoid archaeology and write about post-structuralism perhaps hoping to find another academic department (devoted to interdisciplinary studies?) which might indulge the fascination for such philosophy.

'Particularist' reading might also help overcome archaeology's parasitic reliance on the theory and philosophy of other disciplines. Not that we should not read and use such work, but I think particularist readings will foreground the relation of 'external' theory to archaeological practices and problems.

HOW ARE WE TO WRITE? HOW IS THE PAST TO BE WRITTEN?

This book has a fair amount in it about writing and style; some authors even try out some ways of presenting themselves which are not normally found in archaeological texts. The question of writing and style is an important one for me, but not because writing is an academic addendum to the political which is what the aestheticisation of politics involves. I will mention rhetoric. Rhetoric is a practical theory of discourse established long before post-structuralism. I think this is something fertile to look into because rhetoric is about purpose (political or other), power and persuasion, relating medium and message. And persuasion seems to me to be a vital element in what we should be doing.

Considering rhetoric and stylistics would not only be an aid to political criticism. Above all it involves an engagement with a much neglected technical aspect of what archaeologists do – writing. It would be to push the question of what it is to write the archaeological past. With others I am increasingly wanting to tackle the affective side of archaeology, the subjective experience at the heart of archaeology. An archaeological poetics, in the sense of a science of the production of archaeological writings, will help understand, explore and experiment with the expression of archaeological pasts and presents. I will return to the subjective and affective later.

WHAT IS THE ARCHAEOLOGICAL PAST?

This book brings me to think again of the nature of archaeology as a subject and about some of the things I am doing as an academic archaeologist. These arguments about the materiality of archaeological practices – that archaeology is done today – imply the question of the object of archaeology. What is the archaeological past? Archaeologists deal for most of the time with artefacts and their context in the past. But of course it is not as simple as that. There is a dialectic of past and present and this book deals with themes within and around this crucial relation. The serious questioning of the idea of presence and identity (the existence and self-identity of the past), the perpetual deferring of meaning (the concept *différance* and the slippery signifier), and the abandonment of a search for the origin (there is no past as origin for our interpretation of the meaning of the past) are the main elements in a post-structuralist account of the dialectic of past–present.

Yates presents a critique of the idea of the past context of an artefact giving it meaning (contextual archaeology). There is never any such stability to allow definite assignation of meaning, to pin down the signifier. There is no origin of meaning to dig down to; the past has no relative autonomy, argues Yates. Instead, the past 'is active in the present only as a trace, and is effective through the processes and powers of the unconscious' (p. 160). So the past becomes another element in a horizontal chain of signifiers. Mirrors everywhere, past and present are not alternatives. There was and is only *différance*. After this collapsing of the dialectic into an idealist sameness of *différance*, Yates backs off to reassert archaeology as a discourse on borders and margins (past–present being one). Bapty's dealing with polarities and opposites in terms of dialectics and Nietzsche leads him to suggest archaeology's particular suitability for going beyond polarities such as past and present and data and theory, beyond truth to myth rather than history.

These are very stimulating ways of dealing with the relation past–present. One thing I particularly like is the shift from 'Being' to 'becoming', from static categorisation and identity to relationality and a process of becoming (true processual thinking?). I think this is an excellent, and true, way of conceiving of oppositions such as past and present (past and present becoming other than what they 'are') and it applies to the objects of our work generally. Yates, and Nordbladh and Yates give fine examples of this 'processual' thinking.

As indicated, Bapty raises the question of truth. I ask the question: *To what extent are our accounts of the past true?*

Relativism and pluralism are two elements in this question touched on in this book. In that the past is produced in the present and the present context is vital in understanding the past produced, and in that the fluid non-system of difference encompassing past and present involves different (mis)readings, a pluralism of approaches and pasts is to be sanctioned. But how are good and bad archaeologies to be distinguished? Is some sort of relativism to be accepted?

Tilley's pragmatism relates truth to political strategy: truth is not absolute, but local. The will to truth is associated with power-knowledge. 'It is important to abandon a simplistic focus on an absolute distinction between truth and falsity in analysing texts. . . . Rather we ask: why *these* statements rather than others and what interests do they serve?' (p. 151). A good truth would be one which related to good interests, and for Tilley those interests are basically those of an iconoclasm, an irreverent opposition to authority and the academy, and a liberation from prohibition on what may be said.

Waterman discusses the question of truth in relation to the concept of ideology. Is ideology false consciousness in opposition to true scientific discourse? Are some archaeologies ideological and false, and others true and non-ideological? These are thorny questions. I think Waterman rightly argues that 'the authority which derives from truth claims in discourse is an essential armature for the formulation of political programmes' (p. 98). Ideology as a concept which relates what is written (discourse) to social context in a way that allows truth to be distinguished from falsity is a vital way of avoiding relativism or a political paralysis, a negative struggle of opposition and no hope of change.

These are all questions of knowledge and the subject (subject in every sense: subjectivity–objectivity, self, subjection–power, the discipline). Epistemology haunts us, however much post-structuralism may have destroyed it. I think these questions need bringing to the front, and this is something the book does not do. Again it is a task of persuasion. To show and convince that post-structuralist *archaeologies* are better, more faithful, truthful or whatever, and to make sure that these terms, these measures are adequately conceived.

I will stay with the relation past–present but move away from the academy and ask: *Why is archaeology popular?*

This might seem a strange question to ask in this book. I could say that the question is present in its conspicuous absence, though Walsh has something to say. But archaeology is much more than an academic subject. Also I have already asked the question of an audience or readership for this book. I now want to consider archaeology's 'public'. It will help to first ask: *What has popular archaeology become?*

Heritage, the media and leisure industries, sentiments of local and national identity, are all partly involved and I'll consider these. Heritage is not a rational history or portrayal of a past that may have existed (in the sense of discursive history). It is more emblematic, iconic, an agglomeration of discrete places, objects, themes saturated with associations and meanings. It is above all a sense experience: sights, sounds, smells, evocations edited together in a cultural video.

How is heritage to be understood? Walsh gives one answer. It is to be seen as part of post-modern culture, commodification, and an unfettered capitalist free market. There is undoubtedly some truth in this, but I do not think that it is enough. That heritage supplies evocative sense experience is a clue; heritage affects people. And to understand how and why it affects people, to understand the subjective response, we can

CONCLUSION

relate heritage to ideas of how things come to mean and be significant in people's everyday lives. This is to do with identity (individual, cultural and national), making sense of the world around us, being-in-the-world (even in a theme park on a Sunday afternoon), to do with sense of history, historicity: becoming a person. The aura of the spectacular archaeological find or site, the sense of uniqueness, its enchantment, we might relate to a lack of such sentiment in everyday life, a consequence of its rationalisation, the draining of commodities of significance and meaning, human associations.

The reasons why archaeology is popular concerns for a large part subjectivity. Archaeology deals with sentiments which resonate in people's lives. It can be made to involve mystery, romance, nostalgia and suspense – key elements in a re-enchantment of everyday life.

The chapters by Bagnal, Yates, and Nordbladh and Yates have much of great value about subjectivity and identity. In particular sexual identity. Waterman writes of people's subjectivity and the concept of ideology. But how are such ideas to be used?

What is our response to popular archaeology?

Walsh criticises the ideology of post-modernity. He sees archaeology the discipline under threat from heritage and consumerism: 'archaeology reduced to an image of capitalism' (p. 287). His response is to reassert the discipline and emphasise the role of the expert who might educate the masses and reveal the error of their ways. There is much to be said for the enlightening power of education, but I am disturbed by Walsh's fear of ordinary people, his patronising reference to them as 'punters', and his opinion of them as less than intelligent and discriminating: 'the public's ability to differentiate between truth and falsity . . . must be questioned as the role of the "expert" or the intellectual is marginalised' (p. 288).

Critique may be offered from academic or professional security. We may bemoan cultural decadence and the fallacies of heritage and fringe popular archaeologies, while getting on with 'real' archaeology – digging another site or reading post-structuralism. But will this security last and is it right?

The feelings evoked by heritage, feelings of nationality and identity, are real. They cannot be dismissed as false consciousness or ideology. They do not go away when demolished with theory. And do these things mean nothing to us, our families? Have we forgotten them? I think of school trips up the Northumberland coast in the sixties, visiting medieval border castles with my mam and dad, finding the 'past' on my first dig on Hadrian's Wall – senses of local feeling and identity which inform my archaeology even now. Are these sentiments incidental, irrelevant in the pursuit of a scientific and distanced past? Or are we to write of replacing heritage with a floating signifier and plays of difference?

Fringe archaeologies are another aspect of the question of response.

Are they too, and the people who believe in them, to be dismissed by the knowledgeable expert? And what of the British or American archaeologist digging in Greece? How are we to think of their personal experience of foreign summer excavation of a classical 'civilisation' when contrasted with popular Greek feelings of nationalism and a great Greek past?

Feminism has taught me that any thought or politics which doesn't take such personal experience into account is fatally flawed. And is this not where theory comes in? This is why we might read on subjectivity, identity, on the limits of objectivity, on the sociology of knowledge. The new 'problematic' of which this book is a part, entails asking such basic questions. Not asking what Cixous writes, but what she says to us on the questions we value. Reading not some smart new French philosophical text, but reading the signs around us, in our experience and projects.

I may have argued that theory may be used to work on popular pasts and archaeologies in terms of our understanding of subjectivity and identity and everyday life in the 1990s, but the question of how to respond to popular archaeologies has not been fully answered.

Walsh vilifies 'Catherine Cookson Country' in South Tyneside, England. This tourist trail based on characters from the popular novelist Catherine Cookson is pure fantasy for Walsh, an amalgam of disparate nothings creating something, and founded on a nostalgia for a past that never happened. Now Catherine Cookson is a real writer, a very popular historical novelist. She may not belong to the canon of English literature, but her writing appeals to a lot of people through her effective and sympathetic rendering of locality, character and a past not too distant which finds echoes in people's memories now. Nor, to be fair, should her work be dismissed as soft nostalgia. She has tapped resonances which do not simply belong to the dream world of post-modern kitsch. Her narratives meet a fundamental way of making sense of everyday life – telling stories.

Can we not learn from this achievement? I am not proposing a vulgarisation of what we do or write, only stressing the point that ordinary people are not cultural dupes fooled by ideology into a fantasy of false consciousness. Academics conspicuously do not have all the answers, however expert they may feel. Heritage works with a fragmented collage, a 'cut and mix' bricolage born of a video culture. Can we not learn from this and get in on what is happening? If we have nothing positive to do or say to people, if we cannot stimulate them with our ideas, we should stop what we are doing.

If the choice is made to challenge disciplinary boundaries, perhaps this might be done not only on the ground of abstract theory, but also on the basis of a political reading of what is happening – conservative vocationalism. Here we might enter the arguments about changes in higher education, about the technological component of courses, about

CONCLUSION

access to education for more adults, devise new uses for science funding, new courses.

I am now talking around another question: *How do we talk to people about archaeology?*

There is an essential place for an academic argument, careful working out of specialist matters. For a lot of people that may be enough. But I see it as a beginning. This book represents a new philosophically informed critical questioning approach in the social sciences. I hope that a basic attitude will be to take the public and those uninformed about post-structuralism seriously, and not just try to pass on a message suitably watered down. The great things about the archaeology which this book promises is that it will get down to basics, not afraid to ask awkward questions, to break down old assumptions and experiment with new, better and for me exciting ways of thinking, writing and presenting the archaeological past. I remember the great disappointment of reading my first 'real' archaeological textbook – the mass of unrelieved listing of sites, cultures, artefact types.

The sort of things talked about in this book hold out a promise, a way forward, a way of tackling what are my final questions: *What has feeling for the past to do with archaeology? What is the place of experience and the subjective in archaeology? What of creativity and imagination?*

The simplicity of archaeology as objective science was never seriously tenable, and at last we seem to be in a position to think the question of subjectivity: thinking of what the archaeological past means to me and others (beyond raw objectivity), and of dealing with this in archaeological work. I have talked of capturing popular imagination, of moving beyond the academy into questions of everyday life. How might we work on experience, subjectivity and identity in archaeology? Here are some ideas, echoes of many in this book.

Give up the posture of masculine mastery and individualism. Why not accept our vulnerability and move away from the idea of a hard science to 'soft' thinking? As Tilley writes of humour, our writing must be multivocal, to be taken in many ways, some not so serious. We might aim to find the first person plural, ourselves, our common interests and identities.

Experiment and creativity. Why not try out different writings, different presentations? Working on the 'technical' aspects of our archaeology – they hold the key to political progress. Learn of bricolage, montage and pastiche and turn them to our purpose. Find a way between science and narrative.

Show and write our book in process, in progress, rather than definitive final versions. We can write the becoming of a past now rather than a chapter in a history for all time. This is so much the case for archaeology: seen to be based on practical workings with material culture, broken pasts, almost lost, brought to presence.

Flexibility and a fluidity of categories. Rather than fixed categories determining a concept-world in advance, we might use constellations of concepts, each finding its meanings in the others.

Particularity – refusing to totalise. Engaging directly with ordinary issues, being sensitive to local matters, to the cultural fragment.

Re-enchanting the past; mobilising the affective. We can capture the imagination to re-embody the past in bringing it into the present.

A positive reading of possibility. Processes of hegemonic power can be exposed so we can use them. This is finding the positive, the other side of negative and deconstructive critique. (We never live a total, all-encompassing ideology, totally fooled; there are always gaps and inconsistencies, and people use and consume ideological products to their own ends.) Reading the signs around us for possibility. Playing the seer. Prescience rather than science.

I have ended with what I hope will not be taken as prescription but exhortation. We can avoid critical isolation, putting other archaeologies down and doing something different. The questions I have worked through touch all who work in archaeology and deal, I think, with many things of archaeology and the past which fascinate so many of us.

REFERENCES

Althusser, L. and Balibar, E. (1979) *Reading Capital*, trans. B. Brewster, London: Verso.

Hodder, I. (1989) 'Comments on archaeology in the 1990s', *Norwegian Archaeological Review*, 22(1).

Index

Ablett, L. 206
Adorno, T. 144, 212
Almgren, B. 180
Almgren, O. 199
Althusser, L. 3, 91, 92, 93, 148, 298
Andalusia 192
Anna O. 162
Annales School 12
apartheid 72–4
Artaud, A. 44–6
Ashley, L. 280
Aspeberget 184
Auntie Greta 205

Bakhtin, M. 41
Bakunin, M. 86
Balibar, E. 298
Baltzer, L. 199
Barker, M. 81, 87
Barrett, J. 156, 157, 159, 167, 223, 266
Barthes, R. 3, 8–10, 19, 29, 41, 43, 146, 167; death of the author 9–10, 41, 146; *Mythologies* 8–9; *S/Z* 9
Bateson, G. 3, 18, 39
Baudrillard, J. 4, 42, 277, 279, 280, 281–3
Beamish Museum 286
Beaumont, V. 205
Beauvoir, S. de 113, 123 n.3
Beckett, S. 189, 191
Belsey, C. 22
Benjamin, W. 144, 145
Bennett, A. 173
Bentham, J. 267
Berkeley, G. 38, 41
Berman, M. 128
Binford, L. 2, 127, 138–41, 145, 167, 263, 264

Bloch, M. 217
Bogue, R. 29, 188
Bohuslän (Sweden) 175ff.
Borges, J.L. 3, 46
Bourdieu, P. 2, 3, 35, 41, 42, 48, 266
Bourke, E. 287
Boy George 179
Brandes, S. 192
Breuer, F. 162
Burenhult, G. 183
Byrne, D. 279

Carroll, L. 36, 44–6, 52
Carter, A. 3, 46–7
Childe, V.G. 263
Chippindale, C. 217, 261
Chomsky, N. 212
Clarke, D. 168, 263, 264, 271
Clement, C. 113, 123 n.3
Clifford, J. 42, 50
Cixous, H. 23, 27, 29, 103, 104, 105–11, 122, 294, 300, 308; 'The laugh of the medusa' 107
Collingwood, R.G. 2, 12, 215, 218, 219 n.3, 263
contextual archaeology 155–60, 168–70, 207–8, 210–11, 214–15, 218, 267–8; *see also* Hodder
Cookson, C. 285, 289, 309
Cooper, D. 55
Coward, R. 22, 29, 231
critical theory 86
Culler, J. 29
Cunliffe, B. 270

Daniel G. 260
Darwin, C. 260, 278
Deleuze, G. 3, 17–19, 44, 53, 191, 198,

222, 235, 252
Derrida, J. 1, 3, 6–8, 10–12, 14, 15, 19, 24, 26, 29, 41, 42, 51, 52, 61, 62–5, 71, 72–4, 75, 155, 156, 164, 165–7, 168, 169–70, 171–2, 173, 182, 191, 212, 233, 234, 242, 253–4, 279, 281, 294, 295, 296, 297, 302, 303; on apartheid 72–4; on différance 7–8; and Nietzsche 253–4; on Rousseau 10–11; relation to Saussure 6–7; on subjectivity 19–21; on the unconscious 165–7, 171–2
Descartes, R. 11, 19, 37–8, 41–2, 52, 56, 57 n.5, 191
Dews, P. 11, 29, 86, 90, 98
différance 7–8, 10–11, 14, 234, 254, 295
discourse 51, 136–8; fields of 175; and political critique 50–5; and 'science' 138–41
Dora 163
Dreyfus, H.L. 29
Dumont, L. 56
dungeons and dragons 288
Dupin 165
Durkheim, E. 188
Dyflin (Dublin) 287

Eagleton, A. 11, 30, 289
écriture 41
Eco, U. 173
ego 65, 189–90, 191, 193, 227, 231
Ellis, J. 22, 29, 231
Elverheim, I. 180, 183
English Heritage 217
ergon 7, 173
ethnoarchaeology 214–15, 216–17

Face, The 281
Fannon, F. 47
Feuerbach, L.A. 38
Flannery, K. 264
Frank, E. 206
Frazer, N. 279
Fredsjö, Å. 199
Freeman, D. 39
Frere, S.S. 270
Freud, S. 3, 26, 27, 56, 114, 153, 159, 161–3, 166–7, 173–4, 190, 207, 224, 226–7, 229, 234, 294, 295, 297; basic model of psyche 161–3; and homosexuality 173–4; and sexuality 226–7; *see also* gender
Frosh, S. 29, 174, 228

Foster, H. 281
Foucault, M. 3, 10, 12–17, 18, 19, 21–2, 26, 27, 28, 29, 43, 47, 50–4, 55, 56, 61, 62–4, 79, 149, 189, 239, 256–60, 279, 294, 296, 297, 301, 302, 303, 304; archaeology 12–13, 65–72, 256–7; concept of *episteme* 257; genealogy 13–17, 258–9; and ideology 79–101; and madness 50–3, 256–7; and Nietzsche 15–17, 63–4; and power 14–15
Fuentes, C. 46

Geertz, C. 40, 97
genealogy and archaeology 260–8; *see also* Foucault
gender and biology 224–5; Deleuze and Guattari on 235; Freud on 226–7, 228–9; Lacan on 229–32, 234; Marcuse on 227–8; and rock art 175–87; *see also* homosexuality, subjective identity, woman
Gero, J. 150
Gibbs, L. 266
Giddens, A. 2, 3, 191, 218, 223
Gilroy, P. 86–7
Glob, P.V. 183, 185, 186, 199
Gordon, C. 98
Gramsci, A. 98
Guattari, F. 3, 17–19, 44, 53, 179–80, 187, 191, 222, 235

Habermas, J. 49, 88, 96, 97, 129, 218
Hall, S. 81, 84, 87–8, 90, 91
Harland, R. 241, 280
Hebidge, D. 279, 281, 285, 287, 288
Hegel, G.W.F. 38, 191, 212, 241, 251
Heidegger, M. 191, 212
heritage industry 4, 28, 302, 306
Heraclitus 38
Hewison, R. 280, 286
Hirst, P.Q. 87, 96
Hitler, A. 56
Hodder, I.R. 2, 154–60, 167, 185, 207–10, 213, 214, 215, 216, 219, 222, 266, 267, 271, 273, 301
homosexuality 173–5, 180
Hoy, D.C. 84, 90, 97–8
Husserl, E. 8, 19, 20, 212
hymen 24

id 227, 231
ideology and archaeological writing

INDEX

208–11; ideology critique in archaeology 300; Foucault's problems with 79–101
Irigaray, L. 23–4, 27, 29, 103, 104, 105, 117–22, 177, 179, 186, 294, 300

Jakobson, R. 164
Jameson, F. 11, 30, 43, 44, 47, 49, 154, 175, 277, 279, 281, 283, 284, 289, 290
Jessop, R. 81
Jorvik (York) 287

Kafka, F. 3, 27, 188–9, 191
Kant, I. 8, 38, 173, 212, 241
Kohl, P. 29
Kristeva, J. 3, 7, 23, 24–5, 27, 29, 103, 104, 105, 111–17, 122, 123 n.4, 171, 222, 294, 300

Lacan, J. 3, 6, 17, 21, 22–3, 24, 26, 29, 43, 61, 114, 123 n.4, 154, 155, 163–5, 167, 168, 171, 229–32, 234, 283, 294, 295
Laing, R. 55, 190
Lamarck, J.L. de Monet 260
Laplanche, J. 29
Leach, E. 2
Leclaire, M. 29
Leitch, V. 29, 30
Lenin, V.I. 71
Lentricchia, F. 10, 29, 30
Leone, M. 266
Leroi-Gourhan, A. 2
Lévi-Strauss, C. 3, 5, 57 n.6
Levine, S. 280
Little Hans 162–3, 226, 229
Lodziak, C. 80
Lomas, H. 288
Lubbock, J. 262
Lyotard, J-F. 29, 277

MacCannel, J.F. 29
McClintock, A. 72
McQuail, D. 290
Macherey, P. 3, 127, 148–9, 160, 172
Mallarmé, S. 11
Malmer, M. 176
Maltegård Stone (Denmark) 186–7
Man, P. de 30
Mandt, G. 177, 183
Marcus, G. 50
Marcuse, H. 3, 227–8, 235, 236 n.1

Marstrander, S. 199
Martin, R. 211
Marquez, G.G. 46
Marx, K. 38, 68, 70, 71, 72, 82, 85, 128, 241, 278, 281, 282, 283, 284
Marxism 62, 71, 81, 84, 90, 91, 95, 129, 281
Mao Tse-Tung 89
Mauss, M. 48, 188
Mead, M. 39
Medvedev 41
Melanesia 141
Merquior, J.G. 29
Miller, D. 2, 46
modernity 128–9; and archaeology 129–30
modernism 129
Moi, T. 29
Montelius, O. 262
Montesquieu, C-L. 261
Morgan, L.H. 261
Munch, E. 190
Munn, N. 48

Narcissus 159
Nerval, G. de 52
new archaeology 1–2; and science 138–41
Nicholson, L. 279
Nietzsche, F. 3, 12, 14, 15–16, 18, 43, 52–4, 56, 57 n.5, 63–4, 198, 239, 240–53, 263, 295, 296, 299, 305
Nixon, R. 72
Nordbladh, J. 2, 199
Norris, C. 29

Pangloss 42
parergon 8, 173
Parmenides 212
Pêcheux, M. 127
Petrie, F. 262
Picasso, P. 190
Pitt-Rivers, General 261, 262
Plato 8, 11, 41, 42, 212
Poe, E.A. 164, 167
post-modernism 278–93; and architecture 280; and ethnography 39–40, 42–3, 47–50; and heritage industry 284ff.; and Marxism 289–90
post-structuralism and feminism 103–123; foundations in Saussurian linguistics 4–8; and post-modernism 289–90; unity of 3–4, 295

313

INDEX

Presley, E. 288
processual archaeology *see* new archaeology
Pryor, F. 218
psychoanalysis *see* Freud, Lacan, gender, subjective identity, woman

Rabinow, P. 29, 83, 89
Rat-Man 190
Raunds Heritage Park 286
reading *see* writing
Reich, W. 56
Renfrew, A.C. 2, 264
Ricoeur, P. 89
Rished 185
Rochefort, C. 114
rock art 175–87, 193–7; marriage ceremonies in 180–7, 192–3
Rosvall, J. 199
Rousseau, J-J. 8
Rowlands, M.J. 261
Russian Formalists 41
Ryan, M. 11, 30, 289

Sabloff, J. 264
Sacks, O. 188–9
Sade, D.A.F. de 52
Sahlins, M. 141
Said, E. 39
Salmond, A. 47–8
Samoa 192
Samsa, Gregor 188–9, 190
Samuel, R. 180–1
Saussure, F. de 4ff., 155, 168, 234
Schiffer, M. 2, 127, 139–40, 146, 264, 270
schizophrenia 189, 283–4
Schreber, D.P. 190
science 138–41
sex *see* gender, homosexuality, woman
Shakespeare, W. 44
Shanks, M. 2, 140, 218, 263, 266, 268, 271, 291
Sheridan, A. 29
Shore, B. 192
Smart, B. 84
Sollers, P. 171
Souvaraine 86
Sørensen, M-L. 159
Spencer, H. 260
Stephen, D. 189, 190
Stonehenge 217, 268

structuralism *see* Saussure, Derrida, Lévi-Strauss
Sturrock, J. 29
subjective identity 19–25, 26–7, 187–97; of women 22–5; *see also* gender, woman
Sumner, C. 95
super-ego 56, 227, 234
superman 15, 198
supplement 8
Swift, J. 49

Tarkovsky, A. 56
text archaeological record as 154–60; and meaning 142–3
textuality 28
Thatcher, M. 49
Thatcherism 88
Thompson, E.P. 82, 83, 88, 89, 90, 96, 97, 262
Thomsen, C. 262
Tilley, C. 2, 141, 216, 218, 263, 266, 268, 271, 291
Tyler, S. 48, 50

unconscious 160–7; Derrida on 165–7, 172; Freud on 161–3; Lacan on 163–5; and archaeological writing 172–87

Vico 261
Victoria and Albert Museum 288
Vitlycke 180–1
Voltaire 42

Wiener, A. 49
Wigan Pier Heritage Centre 286, 289
Wolf-Man 162, 190
woman body of 106–7; diversity of 109–10, 116; identity of – Cixous on 105–11; Kristeva on 111–17; Irigaray on 117–22; and psychoanalysis 114–16, 119–22, 123 n.4
Worsaae, J.J.A. 262
writing in archaeology 205–20; death of author 9–10, 27–8; and ideology 143–7; and reading 147–51; and unconscious 172–87; and women 107–8, 111

Zola, E. 86